Locational Analysis:

Locational Analysis

An Interregional Econometric
Model of Agriculture, Mining,
Manufacturing, and Services

Curtis C. Harris, Jr.
University of Maryland

Frank E. Hopkins
*State University of New York
at Binghamton*

Lexington Books
D.C. Heath and Company
Lexington, Massachusetts
Toronto   London

Library of Congress Cataloging-in-Publication Information

Harris, Curtis C.
  Location analysis.
  Includes bibliographical references.
    1. Industries, Location of—Mathematical models.
  I. Hopkins, Frank E., joint author. II. Title.
HC79.D5H36   338'.09   72-5853
ISBN 0-669-84731-3

Published simultaneously in Canada.

Printed in the United States of America.

International Standard Book Number: 0-669-84731-3

Library of Congress Catalog Card Number: 72-5853

Contents

v

List of Figures

List of Tables

Preface

Presented in the book is an interregional, multi-industry model designed to explain industrial location. Empirical research on industrial location has not kept pace with theory; much of it has been in the partial equilibrium framework either of one industry or of one particular location factor, such as transport cost, wages, or taxes.

The model considers two groups of stimuli to industry location—regional factor prices and regional agglomeration effects. Multivariable regression analysis is used to examine the importance of various explanatory variables on location as measured by the change in output. The model accounts for interregional and interindustry relationships. In addition to the objective of explaining industry location, the model has been designed to be the cornerstone of a larger multiregional, multi-industry forecasting model.

In developing the model it was necessary to reject the traditional tools for determining the effect of transportation costs on industrial location. Instead, the model uses marginal transportation costs produced by a linear programming transportation algorithm.

The theory of the location model is presented in the second chapter. This chapter is divided into four sections. The first discusses the general influence of location upon profits; the second develops the structure of our location model; the third reviews traditional location theory and its relationship to the location model; and the fourth discusses some of the limitations of the model.

The transportation variable is discussed in Chapter 3. First, the transportation variable is defined; then the mathematical properties of the linear programming transportation algorithm relevant to the construction of the transportation variable are presented. This chapter also contains a discussion on the computional and statistical problems encountered in solving the linear programs and their resolution.

The data used in this study are discussed in Chapter 4. The regional delineation of the location model is discussed in the first section. The county supply and demand estimates that are used as constraints in the linear transportation problem are reported in the next two sections and discussed in greater detail in Appendixes A and B. The procedures used to construct the coefficients of the objective function of the transportation problem are presented in the last section and discussed in greater detail in Appendix C.

Chapter 5 presents the regression equations, explaining the variables and examining the results in summary form. Chapter 6 examines the results in detail by industry sector.

This book is designed for the advanced student and the practitioner in the fields of regional economics, economic geography, regional science, industrial organization, management science, and social accounting. The book is not an introduction to the field of industrial location, but we assume the reader has some knowledge of statistics, linear programming, location theory, and social income accounting.

The study benefited from the advice and council of Professors Clopper Almon, Jr., and John H. Cumberland. Professor Almon also permitted us to utilize the resources of the Maryland Interindustry Forecasting Project. Mrs. Marianne Russek was responsible for writing many of the computer programs required to analyze and compile the social statistics used in the study. Kenneth McConnell, William Donnelly, III, Stanley Wolfson, and Stephen Merchant were employed as research assistants during a large part of the project's history and also provided intellectual advice. William Krause, Pyung Han, and Kurt Bayer also served briefly as research assistants. The typing was provided by the secretarial staffs of the Bureau of Business and Economic Research of the University of Maryland, and the School of Management of the State University of New York at Binghamton.

Financial assistance for the project was provided first by the Economic Development Administration of the Department of Commerce, then by the National Science Foundation. The computer time was supported in part through the facilities of the Computer Science Centers of the University of Maryland and the State University of New York at Binghamton.

1 Introduction

A small municipality hoping to attract industry exempts new firms from property taxes for 10 years. The Governor of New York reduces public expenditures, which he proposed and initially considered vital, because he fears the tax increases necessary to pay for them will drive industry from his state. A Midwestern riverfront city pressures their congressman to secure an Army Corps of Engineers' dredging project to improve transportation facilities in the hope that its construction will result in a permanent increase in regional income. A manufacturer claims labor costs are too high in the Northeast and decides to open his new factory in the South. The president of an aerospace firm believes his company's most important need is a highly skilled labor force and decides the best location for his firm is in an area rich in amenities such as the Southwest.

Will the municipality acquire new industry? Can the Governor retain industry for New York by sacrificing public services? Will improved water transportation help the economic development of a Midwestern city? Can a manufacturer really lower his labor cost and increase his profits by moving South? Will the aerospace firm actually attract scientists to warmer and dryer climates?

A 10-year grace period on property taxation may be accompanied by a demand for a public capital expenditure program for schools, sewers, and streets which, for lack of taxes, cannot be met. The resulting congestion may discourage more industry than the tax concession attracted. Corporate offices could be leaving New York City and moving to Connecticut because of the high crime rate, stagnating pollution, and the low level of public services, not the rate of taxation. The Midwestern town may not improve its economic position by building new waterways, because motor carrier and rail may be more efficient transport modes for the agricultural commodities of the region. The northern manufacturer may have a high antiunion bias and, while lowering man-hour labor cost by the move South, he may have to pay a high cost of training unskilled workers. Thus his total labor cost may increase. The aerospace firm could find that physicists and engineers prefer skiing to sunbathing.

To answer any one of the questions posed above, it is necessary to have a broad understanding of the factors that affect a region's economic activity. It is convenient to divide those economic factors that generate primary income from others. Clearly, we must concentrate on the primary factors. Within them there are three broad categories, only one of which we shall study. The first stems from the large, footloose population which receives income through social

1

security transfer payments, property income, and private pension plans. This population is becoming increasingly important in our country. The elder generation, after a lifetime at hard labor, naturally seeks to maximize the utility of their leisure years. The rapid development of Florida, Arizona, and California can partially be credited to this age group's affinity for the amenities of these states.

The second major primary income generator is the public sector. The national defense budget of $80 billion, the state and local governments' cash deposits in commercial banks, the billions Congress authorizes in Public Works programs, the $40-billion-plus price-tag of the Interstate Highway System, the development of capital plants for higher education by state governments, etc., all have had a large effect on regional development. The governmental role in regional development is not particularly new. The cities of Constantinople, Madrid, St. Petersburg, Washington, D.C., Ankara, and most recently Brazilia owe their existence to a governmental directive.

The third, and we believe the most important primary income generating factor in our economy, is industrial activity. The subject of this book is, therefore, the theoretical and empirical analysis of industrial location. We shall not attempt to answer all the questions raised at the beginning of this chapter; however, we believe such specific questions should be answered against the background of a more general understanding of regional development, such as this study offers.

Location Theory

Location theory can be studied at the level of the firm or the industry. Plant location studies involve a very detailed analysis that is not possible or appropriate at the industry level. Since we are interested in the broad question of regional economic growth, this location study will be at the industry level. It is true that industries are composed of firms and plants and that it is difficult to draw a line between the two in a discussion of location, yet some such distinction is required.

The theory of the location of industrial activity is a well-developed field of study beginning with the work of Von Thunen.[1] The work of Weber, while constrained by a number of limiting assumptions including a competitive output market, fixed coefficient production functions, stability of market and input sites, can still serve to explain the locational patterns of industries in our present era.[2] The classic example is the iron and steel industry. Isard analyzed the development of the industry from the early 1900s to 1950 using Weberian analysis.[3] The same basic techniques were used by Cumberland and Isard in analyzing the potential of New England as a site for an integrated iron and steel plant.[4] Isard and Kuenne, using industrial impact analysis, an empirical tool developed from input-output analysis and Weberian theory, attempted to explain the long-range effect of an iron and steel complex in the New York-Philadelphia region.[5] While these empirical studies constituted a sophisticated form of analysis, they, as their authors do not hesitate to state, are limited by many of Weber's restrictive assumptions.

The development of location theory since Weber's time has a foundation in Weber's initial work, but this development has continuously attempted to breathe realism into his theory by examining and modifying the basic assumptions. Chronologically, the first major modification was made by Hoover, who introduced the theory of production, characterized by economies of scale, input substitution and a realistic transportation rate structure.[6] Losch improved Weber's theory by introducing the demand factor.[7] The quantity demanded was seen to be influenced by the distance of the consumer from the production site, since transportation cost had to be added to the factory price. The fusion of Losch's theory with that of Weber and Hoover demonstrated that the location decision was profit motivated. Isard completed this synthesis by reducing location theory and its specialized vocabulary to a generalized profit-maximizing theory of the firm.[8] The generalized theory defined the transport input "as the movement of a unit of weight over a unit distance" that could be substituted for other inputs such as labor, taxes, land, and capital, in the profit-maximizing decision process of the firm.[9] The development of location theory in the 1960s has become highly mathematical. Linear and nonlinear programming has been introduced as a method of theoretical analysis. A prime example of this trend is the work of Cooper, who has generalized Weber's problem of finding the minimum transport cost site for one firm to that of n factories given m demand sites.[10]

The Model

While the theoretical aspects of the study of industrial location are well developed, there is a great need for further empirical research. Indeed, much of the empirical analysis is in the partial equilibrium framework either of one industry or of one particular location factor, such as transport cost, wages, or taxes.[11] It has been shown, however, that the optimal profit-maximizing location site will only rarely coincide with the transport cost-minimizing site.[12] Indeed, today's optimal location depends on yesterday's actual location and upon tomorrow's demand and prices. Economies of scale, the relocation of other industries and of population enter any decision on location. A model of *the* optimal location of a single industry is therefore likely to be of little relevance.

To explain industrial location, we need, rather, a model of interregional, multi-industry disequilibrium adjustment. This book presents such a model. In its construction, we have considered two general groups of stimuli, inertiorial and anti-inertioral. To the second group belong knowledge that wages, transportation cost, land cost, etc., are lower and revenues higher in other regions. The inertioral stimuli include agglomeration economies, such as a well-developed infrastructure of a region, and a highly skilled labor force, which tend to keep a firm in a region perhaps longer than the input prices would indicate. The model is fully explained in Chapter 2.

Regression analysis is used to examine the importance of the determinates of location as measured by the change in output. For example, the results as reported in Chapters 5 and 6 show that the change in output in the Grain Mill Products industry between 1965 and 1966 is inversely related to the transport cost of shipping the final product, the transport cost of obtaining crops and the price of land; and it is directly related to the level of output in the Grain Mill Products industry.

In developing the model, it was necessary to go beyond the traditional tools of location theory for determining the effect of transportation cost upon industrial location. We have constructed a transportation variable with a strong theoretical foundation—shadow prices from a linear programming transportation algorithm—to explain the effect of transport cost upon locational behavior. Because of the historical importance of transportation cost in location theory, we have devoted Chapter 3 to the discussion of this variable.

There are 99 industry sectors in this study; they are listed with their SIC codes in Table 1-1. The sectors correspond closely to the Office of Business Economics' (OBE) input-output sectors. After the publication of the 1958 input-output table, OBE published additional industry details in Food and Kindred Products, Primary Nonferrous Metals Manufacturing and Electric, Gas, Water and Sanitary Services. We include this additional detail in our set of industries. In addition we have the Wholesale and Retail Trade sector divided into separate sectors with Retail Trade further broken down into 11 types of retail outlets. OBEs industry set contains two government enterprises and three dummy industries—Business Travel, Entertainment and Gifts, Office Supplies, and Scrap, Used and Second-hand Goods. Because of the lack of regional data on these industries, we handle them differently. The government enterprises are combined with the general government sectors which is a part of final demand; Business Travel and Office Supplies are assumed to be a part of the Business Services sector; and the Scrap sector is dropped.

Location equations were developed for 84 of the 99 industries listed in Table 1-1. There are no equations for the construction, transportation, and trade industries. By definition, the output in transportation and trade industries is the difference between the value of the goods when received by the industries and the value when sold (the mark-up margin); therefore the output of these industries depends on the demand of the purchasing sectors and the mark-up rates. In other words, we have no independent county output estimates in these industries and thus do not have location equations. Also, we do not have

Table 1-1
Input-Output Sectors and Their SIC Numbers

Output Sectors	SIC Numbers					
1 Livestock	PT 01	PT 02				
2 Crops	PT 01	PT 02				
3 Forestry and Fishery Products	08	09				
4 Agricultural Services	071	072	073	074		
5 Iron Ore Mining	101	106				
6 Nonferrous Ore Mining	102	103	104	105	108	109
7 Coal Mining	11	12				
8 Petroleum Mining	131	132				
9 Minerals Mining	141	142	144	145	148	149
10 Chemical Mining	147					
11 New Construction	138	PT 15	PT 16	PT 17		
12 Maintenance Construction	PT 15	PT 16	PT 17			
13 Ordnance	19					
14 Meat Packing	201					
15 Dairy Products	202					
16 Canned and Frozen Foods	203					
17 Grain Mill Products	204					
18 Bakery Products	205					
19 Sugar	206					
20 Candy	207					
21 Beverages	208					
22 Misc. Food Products	209					
23 Tobacco	21					
24 Fabrics and Yarn	221	222	223	224	226	228
25 Rugs, Tire Cord, Misc. Textiles	227	229				
26 Apparel	225	23	3992	−239		
27 Household Textiles and Upholstery	239					
28 Lumber and Products Excluding Containers	24	−244				
29 Wooden Containers	244					
30 Household Furniture	251					
31 Office Furniture	25	−251				
32 Paper and Products, Excluding Containers	26	−265				
33 Paper Containers	265					
34 Printing and Publishing	27					
35 Basic Chemicals	281	286	287	289		
36 Plastics and Synthetics	282					

Table 1-1 (cont.)

Output Sectors	SIC Numbers						
37 Drugs, Cleaning and Toilet Items	283	284					
38 Paint and Allied Products	285						
39 Petroleum Refining	29						
40 Rubber and Plastic Products	30						
41 Leather Tanning	311	312					
42 Shoes and Other Leather Products	31	−311	−312				
43 Glass and Glass Products	321	322	323				
44 Stone and Clay Products	324	325	326	327	328	329	
45 Iron and Steel	331	332	3391	3399			
46 Copper	3331	3351	3362				
47 Aluminum	3334	3352	3361				
48 Other Nonferrous Metals	3332	3333	3339	334	3356	3357	3369	3392
49 Metal Containers	341	3491					
50 Heating, Plumbing, Structural Metal Products	343	344					
51 Stampings, Screw Machine Products	345	346					
52 Hardware, Plating, Wire Products	342	347	348	349	−3491		
53 Engines and Turbines	351						
54 Farm Machinery and Equipment	352						
55 Construction and Mining Machines	3531	3532	3533				
56 Material Handling Equipment	534	3535	3536				
57 Metalworking Machinery and Equipment	354						
58 Special Industrial Machinery	355						
59 General Industrial Machinery	356						
60 Machine Shops and Misc. Machinery	359						
61 Office and Computing Machines	357						
62 Service Industry Machines	358						
63 Electric Apparatus and Motors	361	362					
64 Household Appliances	363						
65 Electric Light and Wiring Equipment	364						
66 Communication Equipment	365	366					

Table 1-1 (cont.)

Output Sectors	SIC Numbers								
67 Electronic Components	367								
68 Batteries and Engine Electrical Equipment	369								
69 Motor Vehicles	371								
70 Aircraft and Parts	372								
71 Ships, Trains, Trailers, Cycles	373	374	375	379					
72 Instruments and Clocks	381	382	384	387					
73 Optical and Photographic Equipment	383	385	386						
74 Misc. Manufactured Products	39	−3992							
75 Transportation	40	41	42	44	45	46	47		
76 Communication	481	482	489						
77 Radio, TV Broadcasting	483								
78 Electric Utility	491	4931							
79 Gas Utility	492	4932							
80 Water Utility	494	495	496	497					
81 Wholesale Trade	50								
82 Finance and Insurance	60	61	62	63	64	66	67		
83 Real Estate and Rental	65	−654							
84 Hotels, Personal and Repair Services	70	72	76	−7694	−7699				
85 Business Services	654	73	7694	7699	81	89	−736	−892	
86 Automobile Repair Services	75								
87 Amusements and Recreation	78	79							
88 Medical and Educational Institutions	736	80	82	84	86	892			
89 Lumber, Hardware, Farm Equipment Stores	52								
90 General Merchandise Stores	53	−532							
91 Food Stores	54								
92 Automotive Dealers	55	2554							
93 Gasoline Service Stations	554								
94 Apparel, Accessory Stores	56								
95 Furniture Stores	57								
96 Eating, Drinking Places	58								
97 Drug and Proprietary Stores	591								
98 Other Retail Stores	59	−591							
99 Nonstore Retailers	532								

independent output estimates for maintenance construction. There is no equation for new construction because new construction is not just one industry but includes many different types of construction. A separate study would be required to thoroughly handle construction. Moreover, one of the purposes of this study is to test the importance of the transport variables, and new construction would not be influenced by transport cost since by definition the output is located at the demand site.

Even though location equations are developed only for 84 industries, it was necessary to estimate regional output for each of the 99 industries in order to compute demand by industry. The computation of the transportation variables requires regional estimates of supply and demand for each of the 71 industries producing transportable commodities. The computation also requires estimates of the cost of shipping a unit of each of the commodities between each pair of supplying and demanding regions.

The data sources and data estimating procedures are reported in Chapter 4 and Appendixes A to C. The regional units used in the study are the 3112 county-type areas reported by the Bureau of Census. The county output estimates for each industry for the years 1965 and 1966 have been made consistent with the national output estimates by Professor Almon's Maryland Interindustry Forecasting Project.[13]

2

The Location Model

This chapter presents the theoretical structure of the location model and relates the model to accepted theories of industrial location. The chapter is divided into four sections: The first discusses profits of firms at given locations; the second discusses changes in location and presents the structure of the model; the third discusses other location theories; and the fourth discusses the limitations of the model.

The Firm at a Given Location

It is assumed that business firms locate in order to maximize profits. Given the location, a firm will produce at the quantity that maximizes profits, but since a firm has a choice in location, it will select the location that yields the highest of the maxima. The maximum profits vary by location because revenue and cost functions vary by location.

Let us assume that a firm sets a delivered price and pays the transport cost of shipping the goods to its buyers. The firm's net price (delivered price less transport cost per unit) will fall as quantities increase, since in order to reach more customers, the transport cost must increase. Given the revenue function and the firm's cost function, the quantity produced and the market area of the firm is established. This relationship is illustrated in Figure 2-1. Curve TR represents total revenues with output priced at the set delivered price; NTR is the total revenue curve net of transport cost; and TC is the total cost curve excluding transport costs. The maximum profit quantity would be Q_m. Note that the maximum profits point would be the same if the transport costs had been added to the total cost curve instead of being subtracted from the total revenue curve.

It does not make any difference who pays the transport cost. If the buyer pays, the total revenue curve would be the same as NTR since in order to sell the same amount at each location the factory price would have to be set lower. Each buyer has a downward-sloping demand curve; and since he has to pay the transport cost, he would not demand as much for a given factory price as he would if the producer paid the transport cost. Therefore, in order for the producer to sell as much as before, he must lower the factory price to compensate for the transport cost.

The height and shape of the net total revenue curve for any firm would

9

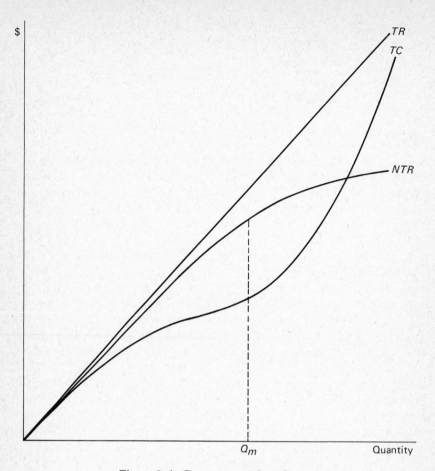

Figure 2-1. Revenue and Cost Curves.

depend on the density and distance of the buyers and the number and location of competing firms. The closer and the more densely located the buyers, the higher the total revenue curve since the transport cost of selling a given quantity is lower. The closer the competitors and the greater their numbers, the lower the total revenue curve. A producer with competitors located at the same place has to share the market with these competitors. He also has to share a portion of the market with competitors located elsewhere but close enough to offer some competition.

Thus the position of the total revenue curve varies by location, but because distance has to be overcome to sell the output, the curve will retain its concave shape regardless of the number of competitors. If there are a large number of competitors, a monopolistic competition situation may develop but not a situation of pure competition. A firm cannot sell unlimited quantities at a given

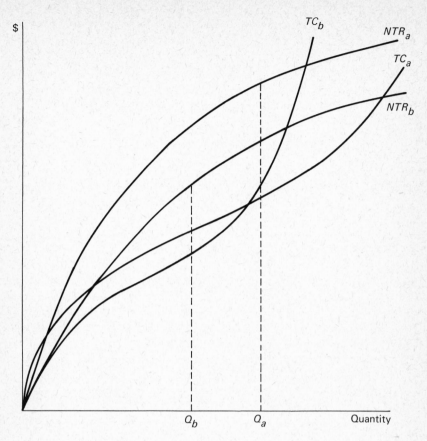

Figure 2-2. Maximum Profits at Locations A and B.

price; i.e., the price is a function of output. Net total revenue curves for two locations—A and B, are illustrated in Figure 2-2.

The firm's cost function also varies by location. The cost of obtaining materials depends directly on the proximity of suppliers and the number of other firms competing for the supplies. The greater the demand for materials, the greater the economic distance that has to be overcome; therefore, the price of the materials would be a function of the quantity demanded and would vary by location.

The prices of other inputs also depend on the quantity demanded. The labor supply curve, for example, would be upward-sloping because it would take higher wages to attract additional persons into the labor force or to entice them to commute or move from other places. If a firm is in a favorable location with regard to its market, its demand schedule for labor will be higher than at other locations; therefore, *ceteris paribus*, it is likely to pay higher wages.

Total cost curves for the two locations, A and B, are also illustrated in Figure 2-2. Note that total costs are higher at A than at B for small quantities but lower at large quantities. The maximum profit points are illustrated at quantities Q_A and Q_B; and the profits are higher at location A. In order for a firm to produce a given output, the quantity of transport services required varies by location, affecting both revenue and cost curves and consequently profits.

A Mathematical Structure

The implicit production function of a firm at a given location is defined as

$$(2.1) \qquad F(q_1, \ldots, q_n) = 0,$$

where q_i denotes the quantity of the ith output and input. Inputs are distinguished by a negative sign.

If the firm were in a purely competitive situation, prices of the outputs and inputs would be exogenous to the firm; but as we just saw in the previous section, prices of outputs and inputs faced by a firm are influenced both by the firm's location vis-à-vis its markets and by its volume of shipments vis-à-vis the shipments of competing firms.

Therefore, rather than assume that prices are exogenous as in a purely competitive model, we assume that output prices are a function of output and that input prices are a function of the quantity of inputs used in the production process; thus

$$(2.2) \qquad P_i = p_i(q_i) \qquad (i = 1, \ldots, n),$$

where P_i denotes prices of the ith output or input. Revenue or cost of the ith input or output is

$$(2.3) \qquad C_i = p_i(q_i)q_i \qquad (i = 1, \ldots, n).$$

We assume that over the relevant range of the firm's current activity an inverse function exists for (2.3) allowing us to represent q_i as a function of cost as

$$(2.4) \qquad q_i = H_i(C_i) \qquad (i = 1, \ldots, n).$$

Substituting (2.4) into (2.1), we have

$$(2.5) \qquad F[H_1(C_1), \ldots, H_n(C_n)] = 0.$$

The behavior of the profit-maximizing firm can be described by maximization of the Lagrangian expression,[1]

$$(2.6) \qquad L = \sum_{i=1}^{n} C_i + \lambda F[H_1(C_1), \ldots, H_n(C_n)],$$

where the first term on the right is a definition of profits, costs have a negative sign, and revenues a positive sign. Maximization of (2.6) will give us optimum values of the firm's output and input mix as a function of all the $H_1(C_i)$ and the C_i. If firms operate by the dictate of (2.6), it would be possible to construct an implicit function that will record optimum behavior for all relevant combinations of C_i as

$$(2.7) \qquad G(C_1, C_2, \ldots, C_n) = 0.$$

Total differentiation of (2.7) will show how the change in the cost of one of the inputs or outputs is related to the changes in the others as

$$(2.8) \qquad G_1 dC_1 + G_2 dC_2 + \ldots + G_n dC_n = 0,$$

where G_i is the partial derivative of (2.7) with respect to C_i.

Now assume that the firm is a one-product firm where the nth C represents revenue (output) and the remaining $(n - 1 = m)$ C's represent costs of the various types of inputs. Let

$$Q = C_n$$

and

$$B_i = -\frac{G_i}{G_n} \qquad (i = 1, \ldots, m).$$

Now (2.8) can be rewritten as

$$(2.9) \qquad dQ = \sum_{i=1}^{m} B_i dC_i,$$

which relates the marginal revenue of the firm at a given location to the changes in total costs associated with each of the inputs.

Changes in Location

Figure 2-2 shows that the firm at location A has higher profits than the firm at location B; it also shows that each firm produces an output that maximizes profits, given the prices and market conditions at each location. But these firms are not necessarily in locational equilibrium. Firm B would have an incentive to move since it knows profits are higher elsewhere. In the long run, unless there is a problem of discreteness in plant size, B would relocate, probably in the direction of A. Even A's location may not be optimum since profits could be higher at locations other than the two illustrated. Shifts in the location of the firms do not at any time guarantee equilibrium conditions. The shift of one firm would influence the profits of the other, and locational equilibrium may never be achieved.

In a more realistic situation there would be many locations from which to choose, and in most industries locational decisions would be made for many plants. At any given time firms attempt to maximize profits, given the uncertainties of decision-making, but also at any given time there are incentives to move. Looking at the situation at the industry level with individual locational sites aggregated into regions, shifts in location can be observed by the regional changes in the industry's output. A change in output may reflect the installation of new capacity, the abandonment of old plants, or changes in the utilization of capacity.

In their locational decisions firms would examine differences in regional product prices, input prices, and externalities; therefore, regional changes in an industry's output should be responsive to these factors. If, for example, marginal transport cost for shipping the products of a particular industry are low for locations in region X, *ceteris paribus*, then the change in the industry's output should be positive in region X and negative somewhere else (assuming no change in national output). Any input can be made available in any region for a price; therefore, the regional input prices should be a good indication of the regional accessibility to the inputs. Even land prices should reflect the availability of land sites. Generally the lower the price of an input, the more accessible it is for use in the region. The cost of obtaining material inputs, for example, would depend on how far they have to be shipped.

The Estimating Equations

The model that we hypothesize assumes that the regional change in an industry's value of output is a function of the marginal cost of obtaining each input and of agglomeration variables; it is

(2.10) $\Delta Q_{kj} = f(MC_{1j}, \ldots, MC_{mj}; AG_{1j}, \ldots, AG_{gj})$

$\qquad\qquad (j = 1, \ldots, NR; k = 1, \ldots, NI)$

where ΔQ_{kj} = change in value of output of industry k in region j,

$\qquad MC_{ij}$ = marginal cost of obtaining the ith input in region j,

$\qquad AG_{ij}$ = a variable measuring the agglomeration effects i in region j,

$\qquad m$ = number of inputs,

$\qquad g$ = number of agglomeration variables,

$\qquad NR$ = number of regions,

$\qquad NI$ = number of industries.

Parameters in the equations are to be estimated using ordinary least squares procedures with regional data as observations.

Since physical measures of output are not available, the change in value of output is used as the dependent variable. Because of this the model cannot account for the regional variation in factory prices. Marginal costs of inputs are used, whenever possible, instead of average costs (prices) since it is assumed, as stated above, that input prices are a function of output. The use of marginal costs is very important in transportation cost variables. The marginal costs are defined by differentiating equation (2.3) with respect to q_i.

The agglomeration variables are included in the equations (2.10) for the purpose of capturing the effects of externalities on changes in output. An example of an external economy to a firm would be a reduction in the cost of training labor brought about by a locational association with other firms that require labor with similar skills. The agglomeration of firms in this example would create a ready supply of well-trained workers. It is necessary to include these agglomeration variables because of the lack of information on the marginal costs associated with these externalities. Industry wage rates by region, for example, would not adequately reflect regional variation in cost of training workers.

The changes in production and the marginal costs are measured using annual data for the years 1965 and 1966. Many, if not all, producing regions will have some output change during the year since we are referring to all output changes and not just those associated with changes in capacity. Thus, the estimating equations are not designed to predict the optimum location of an additional unit of output, but to explain the location of many additional units. However, we can think of the locational decisions as being made for one unit (or a small number of units) at a time, while the changes noted during the year are the cumulative results of such decisions. At the beginning of a period there is a set of marginal costs for each region. Then, given the location of the marginal unit demanded, the production of this unit will take place in the location where marginal profits are maximized. Once this production decision has been made, the values of the marginal costs associated with each region will change. Thus, the maximum profit location of the next units might be somewhere else. This may be true even when the additional demand is located in the same place, as well as when the additional demand is at another location. If the location of demand changes, the maximum profit-producing location will be different, even if the marginal costs do not change.

The change in the locational patterns of most industries in this country has occurred by the slow process of expanding plants in one area, while the process of physical depreciation reduces an industry's size in another area.[2] The high cost of relocating existing capital justifies this evolutionary locational process. Thus, marginal costs from several previous time periods may influence the change in production observed during the current time period. Some of these changes are a result of changes in capacity, and locating capacity is part of the overall investment decision. The planning-construction period associated with added capacity may involve several years. Production coming from new investment in the current period may be a result of a decision made several years ago, and this decision would have been made in accordance with the marginal costs that existed at that time. In essence, we have a distributed lag situation in which investment decisions are made on expected costs and these expected costs are a function of existing costs. The equations that are used for prediction in this book would be improved by including marginal costs from several previous time periods, but we lack the data necessary to try this approach.

Estimates of the Marginal Costs

A convenient method of classifying inputs is the traditional grouping of materials, land, labor, and capital plus the spatial transportation inputs. Since output cannot be expressed in physical terms, the cost of materials is expressed in producers' prices at the point of shipment and does not include transportation cost. Because output is valued in producers' prices, the marginal cost of an additional dollar's worth of material is, of course, equal to one.

The costs having the most regional variation are the transportation costs of shipping both the outputs and the inputs. The procedure used for estimating the marginal transportation costs is to compute shadow prices from a linear programming transportation algorithm. There are two sets of shadow prices:

1. The cost of shipping a marginal dollar's worth of goods produced by industry i from region j
2. The cost of receiving a marginal dollar's worth of goods produced by industry i into region k

The shadow prices are used as independent variables in equation (2.10). For example, when trying to explain the location of the furniture industry, we note that one of the principal inputs is lumber. The transportation problem, solved for the lumber industry, would give us the marginal cost of getting an additional dollar's worth of lumber to each of the regions producing furniture. These marginal costs then would be used as one variable in explaining the location of the furniture industry. In addition, the cost of shipping furniture to its markets may also influence the location of the furniture industry. From the shadow prices produced with the transportation problem solved on the furniture industry, we can get the marginal costs of shipping an additional dollar's worth of furniture from each county.

The importance of empirically quantifying a transportation variable justifies a detailed discussion of the methodology; therefore this discussion is presented in the next chapter.

There seems to be little regional variation in interest rates, since markets, particularly those for industrial loans, are national in scope. Capital, however, may influence industrial location in other ways. Investment cost per square foot or per unit of output may vary by region, because of different construction costs. It may be that the cost of adding additional capacity to an existing plant is lower than building a new, smaller plant. Moreover, investment costs may vary because of climate, such as the need for heating equipment. Unfortunately, we do not have a variable measuring the marginal cost of constructing new capacity.

Another way that capital influences industrial location, and perhaps the most important way, is by the existence of capital stock. Suppose a firm is operating a plant that was located to maximize profits, given the marginal costs at the time it was built. Now let the marginal costs change to the degree that if the firm were making its original location decision, it would locate in a different region. But, given that the plant is already located, the regional changes in marginal costs may not be sufficient to make it profitable to abandon the old plant and build a new one elsewhere. The firm would still have to pay the fixed costs of the old plant, including the opportunity rate of interest on the investment (original value less depreciation) in the old plant. The profit from the new plant minus the fixed costs of the old plant would have to be greater than the profits from the old plant; it is the same as the decision to replace a plant on the same cite, only regional differences in the marginal costs are taken into account.

In order to incorporate the influence of capital stock on the change in output and because of the lack of measures of the marginal cost of capital, two additional explanatory variables are entered in equation (2.10)—the capital equipment purchased by the industry and the prior level of output. These variables were derived using the following reasoning.

The production function of an industry states that output is a function of employment and capital stock; therefore the change in output can be expressed as a function of the change in employment and the change in capital stock. The change in capital stock is defined as net investment, which in turn is defined as gross investment minus depreciation; and economic depreciation is directly related to use of capital, which can be expressed as a function of output. In the locational decision, employment is considered mobile, and the decision on the amount of employment is made simultaneously with the amount of output, given the level of capital stock. Thus, gross investment and the level of output variables are used to help explain the change in output. In the application of the model we use equipment purchases to represent gross investment since we do not have construction data by industry detail.

The cost of land also may influence the location decision. A firm located in an urban area may find the cost of additional land to facilitate expansion prohibitive. As an urban area develops, the value of land increases and activities occupying a site in an earlier period may be forced to relocate. Firms seeking to build new plants or expand old ones will, *ceteris paribus*, be attracted to areas with low land values. Land values, however, may be a more significant determinant of intracounty locational decisions than intercounty decisions. We will use the average value of agricultural land per acre as the marginal cost of land since most new plants are constructed on land that is previously free of structures.

Prevailing regional wage rates (annual earnings per worker in the industry being located) will be used as the cost of obtaining an additional unit of labor. Wage rates by themselves, however, do not always reflect all the labor costs; not included are externalities such as job training and labor migration costs. Let us explain with an example. Suppose a firm has a choice of locating in Washington, D.C., or Clay County, Kentucky. Assume that all factors influencing location, except labor costs, are equal at both sites. We know that wage rates are lower in Clay County, but this does not mean the firm will locate there. Washington may have an abundant supply of the type of skilled labor that the firm requires; therefore, the training and moving cost of labor would be zero. If the firm located in Clay County, it would have to bear the expense of training local workers or moving trained workers from other areas.

Agglomeration Variables

Since the marginal cost variables do not necessarily account for external economies or diseconomies, agglomeration variables are entered in the model.

The variables that are used to represent the agglomeration effects of a particular industry include population density, the output of the major supplying industries, and measures of the major buyers. The measures of major buyers of the output of a particular industry are:

Buyer	Measure
Other industries	Output by industry
Consumers	Personal consumption expenditures by industry
Government	Government expenditures by type
Construction contractors	Value of construction by type
Equipment manufacturers	Value of equipment purchases by sector
Foreigners	Exports by industry

In addition, the influence of an industry's prior output level on the change in its output accounts for agglomeration effects, as well as the level of capital stock.

These agglomeration variables not only serve to reflect the locational association of related activities but also serve as proxy variables for regional labor markets and the quality of a region's infrastructure. A strong association of industries in a region, for example, should reflect a well-developed labor market and infrastructure. Regions with these characteristics have a locational advantage over other regions.[3]

The Location Model and Traditional Theory

The first industry location theory was developed by Von Thunen in a study of agricultural land use around an urban center.[4] The theory has been improved upon by Losch[5] and Dunn[6] and extended to urban land use by Wingo[7] and Alonso.[8] Briefly stated, the theory says that each parcel of land will be used by the activity that bids the highest price and that the price that a potential user can bid at a given location depends largely on the distance, as expressed by transport or commuting cost, from the central city. At each location each individual user bids the difference between his revenue and costs, excluding land rent but including transport costs, for the quantity of land that maximizes his profits or utility. Since transport costs increase as the distance from the central city increases, the rent bid function of the individual will decrease with distance from the central city. Other costs also may change with location, but the theory places the dominant role on transportation costs. The rent bid functions of all participants establish the land market prices.

Land use theory is concerned with industry (and residential) location within a metropolitan region, whereas we are concerned here with interregional locations. In our application, however, our regions are counties, and many metropolitan regions consist of more than one county. Land prices would be expected to vary by county because of the amount of urbanization of the county, i.e., the amount of competition for land. Thus we include land prices as a variable in our model.

Our location model is completely consistent with land use theory. In fact, it may be argued that land use models would be a special case of the location model. The generalized form of our model is as applicable to intraregional industrial location as it is to interregional industrial location, although the empirical derivation of the explanatory variables would probably be different.

The study of the geographic location of industries as a business decision was originally developed by Weber[9] and improved upon by many, notably Hoover,[10] Losch,[11] Isard,[12] Greenhut,[13] and Cooper.[14] Weber's model was formulated under the assumptions of a fixed coefficient production function and a competitive output market. With output prices determined by the market, the firm would choose the location that minimized cost at the profit-maximizing production site. Hoover's contribution consisted of introducing the modern theory of the firm, economies of scale and variable factor proportions, into the location decision. One of the many contributions of Isard was to synthesize the location theory of Weber, Hoover, and others with the traditional theory of the firm and equilibrium of the industry using the language of marginal analysis familiar to all economists, rather than the specialized vocabulary developed by location theorists. Greenhut emphasized the often neglected effects of location on revenue, and Cooper extended the mathematics of Weber's locational equilibrium model.

We view our study as an application of Isard's analysis, treating transportation services as another input in the productive process, the utilization of which is determined by the profit maximization decision process of the firm. Utilizing the marginal cost of acquiring labor, land, and capital as well as variables representing agglomeration factors in the estimating, equations, we incorporate the cost minimization approach of Weber and Hoover; and by including the transport cost of shipping the final product, we account for the effect of location on revenue.

While we stress the consistency of our model with traditional location theory, we should remember that the major application of traditional theory is in optimizing the location of the individual firm, not the industry. This distinction is particularly important with reference to transportation cost and is the rationalization for using a marginal cost variable calculated from transportation linear programming algorithms, which are industry equilibrium flow models.

The classical procedure begins with the determination of the least cost transportation site of the locating firm given the locations of its suppliers and its product markets. Isodapanes—loci of points of equal transportation cost—are then constructed around the minimum transportation cost location. The optimum site would deviate from the minimum transportation cost site, if relative labor or agglomeration cost differentials at other sites were lower than the transportation cost differentials as specified by the location's isodapane.

Isodapanes, while reflecting transportation cost differentials between regions, are not suitable for use as transportation variables in our estimating equation. They are specified by the optimal site for *one* plant of a specified size, while the location model must determine the change in output of all plants in all regions of the United States. The value of an isodapane is dependent upon the number of input supply or demand points in a region. Consider the case of a small firm of 100 employees located within its main market 1,000 miles away from the minimum transportation cost county of the nation. The firm would not move from its traditional market to the low transportation cost site when the plant must be rebuilt, since profits would not be maximized. In particular, with factories of limited capacity, and spatially segregated markets, the use of a single minimum cost solution becomes inapplicable in calculating a transportation variable that will serve as a proxy for the transportation cost of a firm of any size class in every region. Thus, while the traditional Weberian analysis is satisfactory for locating one plant, it cannot be used for explaining the location of plants in many regions.

Indeed, even the generalized model of locating m firms of a given capacity so as to minimize total transportation cost cannot be used to construct a transportation variable. The model that Cooper presents, entitled "The Multiple Source Location–Allocation Problem III (Unequal Requirements-Limited Capacities)" in Section 5 of his paper, analyzes conditions closely parallel to those in many industries.[15] The model is designed to determine m points on a two-dimension plane to locate factories of fixed capacity given n fixed destination locations (which could be input sources as well as output markets by proper weighting of the materials transported), such that the location of these m points will minimize total transport costs.

Cooper's objective function is written as

$$(2.13) \qquad \min \phi = \sum_{i=1}^{m} \sum_{j=1}^{n} w_{ij} [(x_{Dj} - x_i)^2 + (y_{Dj} - y_i)^2]^{1/2}$$

where x and y are coordinates in two-dimensional space and w_{ij} is the amount supplied by the ith source to the jth destination. The constraints are

$$(2.14) \qquad C_i \geqslant \sum_{j=1}^{n} w_{ij} \qquad (i = 1, \ldots, m)$$

and

$$(2.15) \qquad \sum_{i=1}^{m} w_{ij} \geqslant R_j \qquad (j = 1, \ldots, n),$$

where C denotes capacity and R denotes requirements. This formulation of the problem, as Cooper goes into great detail to explain, is a nonconvex nonlinear programming problem. Assuming that it is possible to obtain reliable estimates of the sources of input supply and the markets for a single industry and that the existing m locations of the industry with their present capacity are perfectly mobile locationally, then a solution of Cooper's Problem III would yield a rearrangement of existing capacity in such a way as to minimize transport costs. The principle conclusion of the theory of pure competition stipulates, given the assumption that firms face perfectly elastic marginal revenue curves, that in the long run the industry through interaction between its constituent firms will minimize cost of production. Thus, if cost of production, excluding transportation cost, is identical over space, the competitive model in the long run would distribute industry over a nation, as dictated by a solution to Cooper's model.

The optimum solution could only be achieved by competition between firms in a relatively short period of time, e.g., annually, if the firms of the industry were extremely footloose, which is not the normal case in the United States.[16] Statistics derived from such an optimal solution could not be applied to a large number of different industries because the solution does not describe the locational behavior of U.S. industry. An additional reason for not utilizing the Cooper model is that labor, materials, and agglomeration inputs cannot be substituted for transportation inputs, as Isard's work has shown is a necessary condition for applying the theory of production to location theory.

Cooper's extension of Weber's theory illustrates the major deficiencies of traditional theory for a short-run industry adjustment model. Weber and Cooper assume that all inputs supply and demand centers are known before a firm's locational decision is made, implying that these centers will remain stationary for a period long enough so that the firm could recoup its capital cost. The transport-oriented optimizing solution would only be achieved by the profit-maximizing firm if the savings in transportation cost were greater than the cost of moving. Since the cost of moving includes construction of new capital facilities and the moving of old machines, it can be very high for most manufacturing industries. When the conditions of continuously adjusting input supply and market demand centers are combined with the high cost of relocation and the fact that firms do not operate in purely competitive industries, the industry's locational adjustment to a mathematical equilibrium calculated by Cooper's methods becomes highly doubtful.

The adjustment of an industry toward spatial equilibrium by the process described by Cooper also neglects the interdependency between industries competing for the same input supplies. The output of the lumber industry is utilized by the construction, furniture, and paper industries. In the short run, with the spatial distribution of the lumber industry fixed, firms in the furniture industry located near other industries requiring lumber, *ceteris paribus*, must either pay higher prices for the lumber or obtain it at a distant supply center, thus incurring higher transportation costs than a firm that is the only local demand source. The transportation cost of securing inputs thus will be a function not only of the furniture industry's proximity to supply centers but also of the spatial distribution of other industries competing for inputs used by the furniture industry. The Weber-Cooper model, which is essentially a long-run equilibrium location model of the single or multiplant firm, neglects the short-run interdependencies between industries, which a short-run adjustment location model cannot ignore. Our method of calculating marginal transportation cost (the shadow prices of a transportation linear programming algorithm) combines the optimizing behavior of the individual firm, national supply and demand constraints, and competition between industries for input supplies. The details of this technique will be discussed in the next chapter.

Critique

We have pointed out some of the shortcomings of existing locational theories and models in explaining the actual locational adjustments of industries; but we do not want to leave the impression that our model is free of limitations. In this section we discuss three aspects of the model: (1) the disequilibrium nature of the model, (2) the derivation of transportation variables from linear programming, and (3) the data used in the application of the model.

Disequilibrium. The model states that industries will adjust their regional outputs in response to regional differences in marginal costs and agglomeration effects. But what if the industry is already near a locational equilibrium? There would still be regional differences in the explanatory variables; yet there would be no response by the industry. Suppose that the location of demand for an industry's product remains stable over a long period of time and that producing firms make locational decisions each year based on transportation cost. As time passes and firms relocate, the changes in output would lose regional variance, and the importance of transportation costs on the locational decision would diminish. In other words, the location of the industry would approach an equilibrium situation in which locational decisions were not being made.

It is not likely that an industry would be in equilibrium at any given time, since both regional input prices and demand would have to be stable for long periods. However, some industries would be closer to equilibrium than others because the stability of demand and regional input prices varies by industry. Thus the model would be more applicable to some industries than to others. Moreover, some input prices (or other explanatory variables) would be more significant than others in explaining changes in output. If the regional variation of a particular input price remains relatively stable, its importance on locational decisions would diminish as time passes.

Transportation Variables. The transportation variables were computed using a linear program that determines optimum flow of goods from one region to another. Therefore, the shadow prices (transportation variables) produced by the linear programming algorithm reflect marginal transportation costs only under optimum conditions. We do not make the argument that the optimum trade flows are representative of the actual trade flows, but we do hypothesize that the marginal costs under optimal conditions reflect actual marginal transportation costs. Regions that show high marginal costs when trade flows are optimal are also apt to show high transportation costs when shipments are not optimal. Moreover, if shipments are not optimal, there will be a tendency for firms to minimize their transportation costs even though at any one point in time optimum conditions do not exist.

When trade flows are optimal, there are no cross-hauls; if region A ships to region B, region B will not ship to region A. There are two principal reasons why cross-hauls will always exist. One has to do with the aggregation of products into industry classifications. For example, basic chemicals include both industrial chemicals and fertilizers, and usually manufacturing plants specialize in a particular type of chemical. Thus we would observe trade going both ways between regions A and B in the chemical industry, but the product trade may actually be nearly optimal. These cross-hauls exist even in industries which we normally think of as having one product. For example, cars are normally considered one product, but because we have Ford cars and Chevrolet cars, we will observe cross-hauls. If the industry sectors were disaggregated into more detail, the optimum trade flows would be more in line with the actual trade flows. The second principal reason for observing cross-hauls is the geographic unit. If the geographic units are large areas, region A may be shipping to region B in the northern part of the regions and B to A in the southern part of the regions. By making the geographic unit as small as possible, we reduce one of the sources of cross-hauls.

In order to apply the linear programming algorithm, it is necessary to estimate the cost of shipping a unit of goods between each of the regions; and both rail and truck transport rates depend on the number of miles between the regions. Thus, with large geographic units such as states, it would be difficult to determine one single shipping point from which to compute distances. Each state would have many points of origin and destination, and in some of the large states the transfer costs of shipping from one point in a state to another are quite significant. The county geographic unit is more appropriate for computing transportation rates. The transport cost formulas that are actually used are based on distances between cities and not on the actual miles that a truck or a train travels from terminal to terminal. Thus, the county geographic unit would seem much more appropriate for estimating shadow prices than another geographic unit for which data can be obtained.

Data. The data period used in this study is 1965 and 1966, since these were the most recent years for which data were available when the project began. Unfortunately, it was a period in which the Viet Nam war had a large impact on industry output. The changes in output, for example, between 1965 and 1966 are very large in some cases, reflecting abnormal economic conditions. Marginal costs of the various inputs would not explain locational changes when much of the output change was being produced for the war effort. We attempted to minimize the influence of the war on output by assuming that the demand for defense expenditures is located at the source of supply and then subtracting the defense expenditures from output. The change in output as used in the equations has defense expenditures subtracted, but nevertheless, this effort would not eliminate the entire effect of the war.

Even if war were not a factor, year-to-year changes in output would be more difficult to explain than changes over a longer period of time. Changes that take place over a 5- or 10-year period would probably reflect changes in economic factors affecting the industries, and large year-to-year fluctuations would be averaged out. During a one-year period a strike or major reorganization of a manufacturing plant could cause output changes that cannot be explained in a general model. Moreover, large regional changes occur because of the building of new plants and the abandonment of old plants, and the resulting regional change in output is not a reflection of economic conditions of just that year. Large changes in one year can be a result of the accumulation of economic conditions for many years. These unexplainable large annual changes would also be more prevalent in small geographic areas than they would be in larger geographic areas, since smaller areas have fewer plants in a given industry and changes in one plant would result in large changes in the county data. If the geographic area were larger, say a state, then the changes in one plant would not be as noticeable, and decreases in one part of the state might be offset by increases in another part of the state.

The fact that we only have two years of data limits the specification of the model. An investment decision, for example, is influenced by economic conditions covering the years of the planning stage and the construction state if the investment involves a structure. And, depending on the industry, these stages may be 5 to 10 years long. Thus some of the regional changes of output in the 1965-1966 period would be better explained with cost data for years prior to 1965.

The equations include a series of agglomeration variables to help explain changes in output. Since we were restricted to two years' data, it was necessary to use the levels of output of major buyers and suppliers to explain the changes in output, although changes in output in these major buyers and suppliers may have been more appropriate. If data for one more year had been available, we could have used changes instead of levels to account for the influence of some firms locating near other firms. With more than three years of data we could have determined the appropriate lags.

3

The Transportation Variables

The purpose of this chapter is to explain the transportation variables that will be used in the location equations. A transportation variable is defined as the cost of transporting a marginal unit of output of an industry, given its existing market and production areas in the economy. The linear programming transportation algorithm provides a means of determining the marginal transportation cost in all counties currently supplying or demanding a commodity.

This chapter is divided into four sections. The first section presents an intercounty trade model. The second section discusses the economic interpretation of the transportation variable. The mathematical properties of transportation problems relevant to this study are examined in the third section. The last section discusses the computational and statistical problems encountered in solving the transportation problems and how they were resolved.

An Intercounty Trade Model

The hypothetical flow of a commodity between each pair of counties is recorded in the upper left-hand corner of each cell in Table 3-1. The jth column lists the amount of the commodity used in the jth county obtained from the sources of supply in the ith county, given by the rows of the table. The total demand D_j of the jth county equals the summation of the x_{ij} flows of the jth column:

$$(3.1) \qquad D_j = \sum_{i=1}^{3} x_{ij}$$

The utilized supply UTS_i is

$$(3.2) \qquad UTS_i = \sum_{j=1}^{4} x_{ij},$$

which can be less than the total supply, resulting in inventories I_i of a commodity. The lower right-hand of each cell t_{ij} records the transportation rate between the ith and jth counties. A detailed description of the method used to derive the transportation rate estimates, by commodity and region, and the procedure for calculating county supply and demand data can be found in

27

Table 3-1
Schematic Intercounty Flows for One Commodity

		Demanding Counties				Total County Supply	Utilized Supply	Inventories
		1	2	3	4			
Supplying Counties	1	x_{11} t_{11}	x_{12} t_{12}	x_{13} t_{13}	x_{14} t_{14}	S_1	UTS_1	I_1
	2	x_{21} t_{21}	x_{22} t_{22}	x_{23} t_{23}	x_{24} t_{24}	S_2	UTS_2	I_2
	3	x_{31} t_{31}	x_{32} t_{32}	x_{33} t_{33}	x_{34} t_{34}	S_3	UTS_3	I_3
Total County Demand		D_1	D_2	D_3	D_4			

Chapter 4 and Appendixes A to C. Since intercounty trade flow data by input-output (IO) industry are not available, estimates of these statistics must be made. The estimates are used for calculating the transportation variable since they establish the relevant transportation region of each county. A supply county's transportation region is given by the rows in the table, while a demand county's transportation region is given by the columns. The transportation variable of each county is obtained by determining the transportation cost on the marginal unit shipped into or out of a county.

In estimating these flows, it will be useful to assume that all economic units in their current locations attempt to minimize transportation cost in a competitive market in obtaining their supplies. Firms would more generally attempt to minimize the total cost, factory price plus transportation cost, of obtaining inputs, but since county price statistics are not available, we assume that factory prices are constant over the nation.

An Economic Interpretation of the Transportation Variables

In order to explain the transportation variables produced by a linear program, we will derive transportation variables *without reference* to linear programming and then show that the two sets of prices are *equivalent.*

Suppose there is one market being supplied by a number of producers located at various distances away from the market. Assume that each firm produces at the same constant cost, but that the output of any one firm is fixed. This

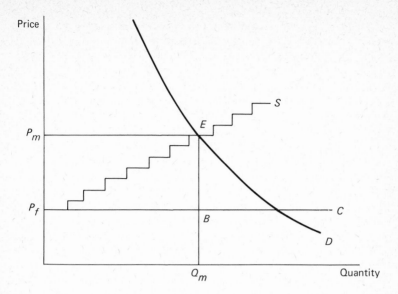

Figure 3-1. Market Equilibrium with One Market.

situation is illustrated in Figure 3-1. Curve D is the market demand curve, and C is the constant cost curve that includes normal profits. The unit cost is the factory price P_f. Each firm offers its supply to the market at a price equal to the factory price plus the transportation cost per unit. The supply curve is a stepped function as illustrated with line S. In order to derive curve S, the firms are ranked by their distance to the market. The vertical difference between the S and C curves is the unit transport cost, and the area bounded by P_fEB is the total transport cost. Market equilibrium is achieved where supply is equal to demand at price P_m and quantity Q_m. The remainder of the rectangle represents location rents, bounded by P_mEP_f. The vertical difference between S and the line P_mE is the per unit locational rents. The closer the firm is to the market, the greater its per unit rent. The marginal firm supplying the Q_m unit does not receive location rent.

The location rent that we referred to is similar to Ricardian rent. Ricardo presented his theory using agricultural land with different fertilities. As poorer quality land is used, the better quality land receives rent, and the rent of the marginal unit of land is zero. His supply curve increased because of poor quality land, whereas ours increases because of transport costs.[a]

In a more realistic situation there are many markets, and suppliers have a choice of sending their products to more than one market. In this situation each producer seeks the market or markets that return the highest rent; when all

---

[a]For an excellent presentation of location rents, see Edgar S. Dunn, Jr., *The Location of Agricultural Production*, University of Florida Press, Gainesville, Fla., 1954.

markets are in equilibrium, each supplier will receive the same rent from sales to all markets. That is, on the margin the firm is indifferent as to which market it supplies since the return would be the same from each market.

The difference between the factory price and the market price is equal to the transport costs and the location rent. Thus, for any market j and any supplier i the price difference is

$$(3.3) \qquad P_j - P_i = t_{ij} + \alpha_{i.} = \pi_{.j},$$

where $\alpha_{i.}$ is the location rent received by supplier i when the market is in equilibrium; $\alpha_{i.}$ is the same in all markets. The equation also defines the price difference as $\pi_{.j}$, the cost that market j pays above the factory price of obtaining the marginal unit of the product. Since $\alpha_{i.}$ is usually zero for the marginal supplier, the marginal cost is usually equal to the transport costs of shipping the marginal unit to market j. The rent of the marginal suppliers may not equal zero because of the lumpiness of the shipments.

The location rent $\alpha_{i.}$ is also a marginal value since the supplier can obtain the same rent by shifting its marginal unit to alternative markets. In equilibrium the supplier receives the rent from all sales to markets, but in a nonequilibrium situation the rent would differ from market to market. Since $\alpha_{i.}$ is the marginal revenue above the factory price of supplier i, it can be defined as a marginal cost simply by changing its sign. Thus, the marginal cost $\pi_{i.}$ of shipping goods by supplier i is

$$(3.4) \qquad \pi_{i.} = -\alpha_{i.}$$

We will refer to this equation later.

We will illustrate the determination of $\alpha_{i.}$, $\pi_{i.}$, and $\pi_{.j}$ with a small example with three suppliers and three demanders (markets) in an equilibrium situation. Since we work with county units in the application of the model, we will refer to these six entities as supplying counties and demanding counties. We assume that firms in a county act as a unit and that all units act as competitors.

The statistics of this example are presented in Table 3-2 in the same format as Table 3-1. The i to j transportation cost coefficients are in the lower right corner of the cells of Table 3-2. Supply and demand by county are also presented. Counties 1 through 3 are supply counties, while counties 4 through 6 are demand counties. The equilibrium flows are the numbers in the upper left corner of the cells. The equilibrium values of $\alpha_{i.}$, $\pi_{i.}$, and $\pi_{.j}$ are also presented.

Graphic representation of the three markets are shown in Figure 3-2. The supply curves S_j show the equilibrium flow of goods from the supplying counties to the jth market. In market d_4, county s_2 supplies four units of the product with a transport cost of \$1, and s_3 supplies three units with transport cost of \$3. County d_4 also could have acquired units from s_1 at a transport cost of \$3;

Table 3-2
Equilibrium Commodity Flow

	d_4	d_5	d_6	Supply	$\alpha_{i.}$	$\pi_{i.}$
s_1	0 3	2 4	1 3	3	1	−1
s_2	4 1	0 5	0 6	4	2	−2
s_3	3 3	2 5	0 8	5	0	0
Demand	7	4	1			
$\pi_{.j}$	3	5	4			

therefore the supply curve is extended horizontally beyond the equilibrium point. County s_2 receives rent of \$2 and supplies only to market d_4. County s_3 does not receive rent but supplies to markets d_4 and d_5.

The supply curve in market d_6 intersects the demand curve from below instead of from the left as in the other two markets. The next best alternative for d_6 would be to pay \$6 transport cost from s_2. It now buys its unit from s_1 at a transport cost of \$3 and a rent of \$1. It has to pay the rent to s_1 since s_1 can obtain a rent of \$1 in market d_5.

In order to prove that our example is in general equilibrium, we will show that demanding counties cannot lower their cost by altering their shipment patterns and that supply counties cannot increase their rents by modifying shipments patterns. If there is no motive for either demanders or suppliers to change their behavioral patterns, then by ·definition we will have shown the existence of general equilibrium.

Table 3-3 records the value of the $t_{ij} + \alpha_{i.}$ for all possible counties given the shipment pattern described in Table 3-2. The coefficients with an asterisk denote ij pairs where positive shipments occur. An examination of Table 3-3 shows that the individual demanding counties, given the values of $\alpha_{i.}$, cannot reduce their transportation cost by obtaining supplies from another county. Firms in county d_4 would not demand shipments from s_1, since they would have to pay a transportation cost of \$3 and a rent of \$1 for a total cost of \$4, which is greater than the totals ($t_{ij} + \alpha_{i.}$) of \$3 from the other supply counties. County d_5 would not attempt to obtain shipments from s_2 because it would have a transportation cost of \$7 which is greater than the current unit transportation cost of \$5 for shipments from s_1 or s_3. Demand county d_6 pays unit transportation cost of \$4 including the inducement in obtaining its shipment

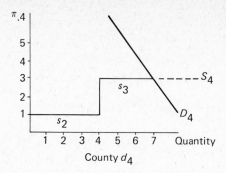

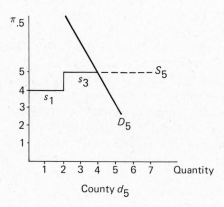

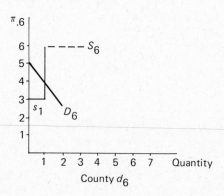

Figure 3–2. Market Equilibrium in Three Markets.

Table 3-3

$$t_{ij} + \alpha_i.$$

	d_4	d_5	d_6
s_1	4	5*	4*
s_2	3*	7	8
s_3	3*	5*	8

from s_1, whereas the transportation cost from the other counties even excluding the rents is greater than \$4. Thus there is not a motive for any of the demand counties to alter their shipment patterns given the set of marginal transportation costs listed in Table 3-2.

The supply counties are also in a state of equilibrium. Table 3-4 lists the rent that the ith supplying county would have to accept to create a state of indifference for the buyer in the jth county as to whether he should purchase from the ith supplier or from another county. The coefficients with an asterisk denote ij pairs where positive shipment occurs, and the rents for these pairs is simply $\alpha_{j.}$. The other cells in Table 3-4 were constructed by determining the total procurement cost ($t_{ij} + \alpha_{i.}$) that the jth demand county was currently paying from Table 3-3 and subtracting the value of t_{kj}, where k is the supply county not shipping to j. This difference is the rent that the kth supply county could receive from the jth demand county leaving the jth demand county still in a state of indifference between buying from k or i. County s_1 could attempt to sell output to county d_4, but it would have to lower its rent to zero to entice county d_4 to purchase a shipment. A zero rent from county d_4 would also imply zero rents from counties d_5 and d_6. Since this would result in a reduction in income to s_1, the attempt to ship to d_4 would not rationally be undertaken. An examination of shipments from counties s_2 and s_3 and their potential profit structure would also show that both counties are presently maximizing their rents.

Table 3-4
Indifferent Rent Levels

	d_4	d_5	d_6
s_1	0	1*	1*
s_2	2*	0	-2
s_3	0*	0*	-4

In equilibrium each demanding county pays the same for all units of the product, $\pi_{\cdot j}$, and each supplying county receives the same, $\alpha_{i \cdot}$, from all markets. These are characteristics of general equilibrium flows in a competitive trade model. They reflect the ability of some suppliers to extract locational rents and the ability of demanders to change their source of supply if a supplier attempts exploitation. If monopoly powers existed on the supply side, greater rents could be extracted and they could differ by market area. If monopsony powers existed, the rents could be lower.

Locational rents can only be obtained by suppliers that sell all of their product. If a supplier had excess supply (inventories), then his rent would be zero, since he cannot extract rent of products he doesn't sell, and in equilibrium the per unit rent must be the same for all units.

The reader may note that while we have determined values of x_{ij} and $\pi_{\cdot j}$ given equilibrium in our small hypothetical model, we have not discussed the determination of equilibrium itself. The reader is referred to other books for a theoretical discussion of the generation of equilibrium prices in a general equilibrium model.[1] We believe the existence of fluctuating prices in real markets, caused by the efforts of purchasers and sellers in their goal to maximize profits, is adequate evidence to support the realism of the model we have presented.

Some Properties of the Linear Programming Solution[b]

The costs paid by the demanding counties, $\pi_{\cdot j}$, and the negative of the locational rents received by the suppliers as described in the above model are identical to the shadow prices that would be outputs from a linear programming transportation algorithm. Substitution of equation (3.4) into (3.3) yields

$$(3.5) \qquad \pi_{\cdot j} = t_{ij} - \pi_{i \cdot}$$

The conditions for an optimal basis in a linear programming solution are:

$$(3.6) \qquad v_{ij} = t_{ij} - (\pi_{i \cdot} + \pi_{\cdot j}) = 0, \qquad \text{for all } x_{ij} > 0,$$

and

$$v_{ij} = t_{ij} - (\pi_{i \cdot} + \pi_{\cdot j}) \geqslant 0, \qquad \text{for all } x_{ij} = 0,$$

---

[b]We do not offer proofs of the properties. The reader is referred to one of the many good books on the subject. For example, see Clopper Almon, Jr., *Matrix Methods in Economics*, Addison-Wesley Publishing Co., Reading, Mass., 1967.

where v_{ij} are the opportunity costs or simplex criteria of an activity in the linear programming problem. These conditions also hold for all county pairs in Table 3-2.[c]

The equations for the linear programming problem are illustrated in Table 3-5. Equation (3.7) of Table 3-5 is the objective function of the linear program; it represents the minimization of transportation cost. This equation can be expressed in matrix form as

Table 3-5
Algebraic Representation of Linear Programming Problem

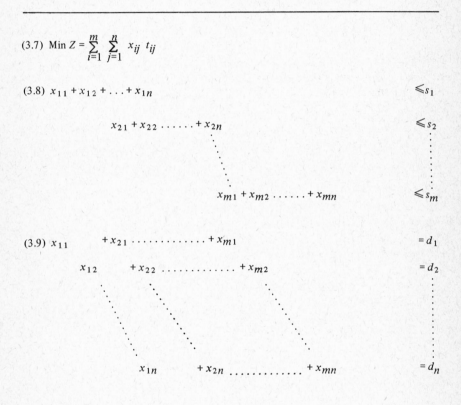

(3.7) $\text{Min } Z = \sum_{i=1}^{m} \sum_{j=1}^{n} x_{ij} \, t_{ij}$

(3.8) $x_{11} + x_{12} + \ldots + x_{1n}$ $\leqslant s_1$

$\quad\quad x_{21} + x_{22} \ldots\ldots + x_{2n}$ $\leqslant s_2$

$\quad\quad\quad\quad x_{m1} + x_{m2} \ldots\ldots + x_{mn}$ $\leqslant s_m$

(3.9) $x_{11} \quad\quad + x_{21} \cdots\cdots\cdots\cdots + x_{m1}$ $= d_1$

$\quad\quad x_{12} \quad\quad + x_{22} \cdots\cdots\cdots\cdots + x_{m2}$ $= d_2$

$\quad\quad\quad\quad x_{1n} \quad\quad + x_{2n} \cdots\cdots\cdots\cdots + x_{mn}$ $= d_n$

(3.10) $x_{ij} \geqslant 0$

---

[c]In most computational procedures any one of the $\pi_{i\bullet}$'s and $\pi_{\bullet j}$'s could be arbitrarily set to zero. They can be always adjusted so that rents are zero or positive by adding a constant K to $\pi_{\bullet j}$ and subtracting it from $\pi_{i\bullet}$, where $K = \max \pi_{i\bullet}$.

(3.11) $$\min Z = TX$$

where T is the matrix of transportation costs (t_{ij}'s) expressed as a row vector and X is the matrix of shipments (x_{ij}'s) expressed as a column vector. The matrix notation will be used to illustrate some of the properties of the transportation variable.[d] Equations (3.8) and (3.9) show the relationship of the shipment levels to the county supply (s_i) and demand (d_j) constraints. Both equations can be presented in matrix form as

(3.12) $$AX \leqslant B.$$

In this equation $B = \begin{bmatrix} S \\ D \end{bmatrix}$ is the column constraint vector and A is the activity matrix. The elements of A are either zero or 1. An entry of 1 corresponds to a position of x_{ij} in (3.8) and (3.9), while an entry of zero is placed in positions where x_{ij} does not occur. Thus each column of A will have a 1 in two positions, and all other elements will be zero. Equation (3.10) states that a shipment cannot occur at a negative level.

The establishment of the linear programming nature of the problem will allow us to utilize an established theorem of linear programming to illustrate the interpretation of π, the vector of marginal transportation costs, often referred to as shadow prices. They are defined as

(3.13) $$\Pi = T'C^{-1}.$$

The C matrix contains the activities in the basic feasible solution of the transportation problem; it is a square matrix formed from the columns of matrix A that are in the basic solution. The row vector T' contains the transportation cost coefficients of the activities in the basis ordered the same as the C matrix.

(3.14) $$Z = TX = T'X' = T'C^{-1}B = \Pi B$$

is a matrix reformulation and extension of equation (3.7) showing the formula for calculating the value of the objective function. The column vector X' denotes the use levels in the same order as T'. Differentiating (3.14) with respect to B yields the vector of partial derivatives

(3.15) $$\frac{\partial Z}{\partial b_i} = \pi_i$$

---

[d]Matrices and vectors are denoted by capital letters and single elements by small letters.

that gives a definition of the effect of a marginal change in any of the elements of B on the total cost of the system. The marginal cost of b_i is, of course, the resource's shadow price.

Thus, by solving the linear programming problem, we have an estimate of the marginal transportation cost of shipping a unit of production into or out of each county. The reliability of these estimates will, of course, vary by commodity depending upon the reliability of the data and how close the transportation cost minimization solution is to reality. In an attempt to align the transportation problem toward a realistic economic environment, a substantial effort was devoted toward defining the unit shipment and the construction of the transportation cost coefficients. The unit shipment has been designed to reflect the national distribution of shipments by weight for each commodity. The transportation cost coefficients have been constructed to incorporate economies of distance in transportation and competition between carriers by using Interstate Commerce Commission data rather than straight airline distance. These concepts are described more fully in Chapter 4 and Appendix C.

The Form of the Transportation Problem

While the flow pattern for most commodities is more accurately described by a surplus or shortage model, presented in Table 3-1, where supply is not equal to demand during the time period of the flow estimation, the transportation variables used in the regression equations will be obtained from a regular transportation problem where supply equals demand. The desirable numerical properties of the regular model far outweigh the disadvantages incurred by its departure from reality.

The transportation variable is calculated for each commodity, rather than aggregating over all the inputs and the output of an industry and creating a single transportation variable. This will allow the testing of the transportation variable of each input used by an industry, as well as testing for groups of inputs by aggregating the individual transportation variables.

The solution of a surplus transportation problem will generate $m + n$ flows, the same as the number of constraints in the system. The number $m + n$ is small compared to the $m \times n$ possible flows that could occur between m exporting counties and n importing counties. The actual number of intercounty flows would lie between both extremes.

A regular transportation problem has the characteristic that the total value of the activities, demand and supply, is known since total demand equals total supply. Thus in a problem with m supply and n demand centers there are $m + n$ − 1 independent activities in a basic feasible solution.

Triangularity of the Basis and Calculation
of the Shadow Prices

The theory of linear programming is relatively simple and straightforward compared to the computational problems that must be overcome in solving a linear program. Inversion of the basic activity matrix presents the greatest difficulty in terms of both the cost of computer time and the accuracy of the inverse matrix. With a typical computer with limited digital capacity, the inverse of a large matrix using standard inverse procedures would not be completely accurate. Fortunately, the C matrix of the linear program for transportation problems can be arranged in triangular form,[e] and since the opportunity cost of using the activities (simplex criteria) in the basis equals zero, we can use

$$(3.16) \qquad v_{ij} = t_{ij} - (\pi_{i.} + \pi_{.j}) = 0$$

to solve for the shadow prices equation by equation.

After the C matrix is in triangular form, it is assumed that either the supply or demand in the last activity is the redundant constraint and either $\pi_{.j}$ or $\pi_{i.}$ is set equal to zero. Once this is done, the shadow prices for the next-to-last activity can be computed and so on.

The tiangularization of C will not only drastically reduce the computer time utilized in solving the transportation problem, but it will also eliminate the problem of retaining significant digits in C^{-1} and in the shadow prices. Solving (3.13) for each $\pi_{i.}$ and $\pi_{.j}$ requires only addition and subtraction. Thus if t_{ij} is placed in integer form, the shadow prices themselves will always be in integer form, and since division is not utilized, rounding errors will be absent.

Computational Procedures

This section describes a number of problems we encountered in solving the transportation problems and in entering the transportation variables in the regression equations for explaining an industry's change in output. We will discuss some modifications necessitated by computer limitations and the numerical properties of the shadow prices.

Computer Limitations

The data estimation procedures (described in Chapter 4) yielded estimates of supply and demand for the industries for all counties reporting any employment

---

[e]All elements in a matrix in triangular form are zero above the main diagonal.

in the County Business Pattern data series. The data were estimated in $1,000 units, resulting in the large number of supply and demand constraints listed in the first two columns of Table 3-6. The original aim of the study was to solve a transportation problem for 71 commodity industries for all counties having an industry supply or demand greater than $1,000. Problems of this size could not be handled within the memory storage of the computer but could be solved, theoretically, with use of the auxiliary drum storage. After experimenting, this approach was abandoned because it was too time-consuming and the computer failure rate was too high. A sample run for IO 38 (Paint and Allied Products), lasting 10 minutes, resulted in only 26 iterations. Since this problem may contain thousands of feasible bases, the expense and time of obtaining a solution of the problem was too high. The number of constraints had to be reduced to provide a more efficient method of solving the transportation problem.

There were two procedures used to reduce the number of the constraints. The first consisted of restricting the general transportation problem by eliminating intracounty shipments by subtracting the smaller of the demand and supply constraints from the larger, if both exist in a county, and setting the smaller one to zero. Table 3-6 shows the number of supply and demand constraints remaining after this adjustment was made.

Before the constraint reductions, the average industry had 1,212 supply and 2,929 demand constraints. IO 2 (Agricultural Crops) had the largest number of constraints, 6,195, while IO 41 (Leather Tanning and Industrial Leather Products) had the smallest number, 2,471. Since the number of elements in the transportation cost coefficient matrix is $m \times n$, the number of elements for the industry with the average, largest, and smallest number of constraints would be 3,549,948, 9,894,324, and 820,020, respectively. After eliminating intracounty shipments, the average industry had 399 supply and 2,533 demand constraints. The coefficient matrices were reduced to 1,010,677, 2,326,860, and 278,275 elements for the industries with the average, largest, and smallest number of constraints, respectively.

The elimination of intracounty shipments, while reducing the computer time needed to solve the transportation problems, cannot directly generate shadow prices for the eliminated counties. Shadow prices were computed for the eliminated constraints using equation (3.16). Each is equal to the intracounty transportation cost of the commodity t_{ii} (the terminal cost), minus the shadow price of the county's constraint which remains in the program.

The shadow prices of the intracounty shipments fulfill the definition for marginal transportation cost presented in pages 28 to 34 since it can be shown that they come from a solution to a general transportation problem that includes both the intercounty and intracounty shipments. The shadow prices of the intercounty shipments of the general transportation problem will be the same as those in the regular transportation problem. All that is necessary to prove this is to show that addition of the intrashipments with T_n' costs, C_n activities, and B_n

Table 3-6
Possible Number of Supplying and Demanding Counties in Linear-Programming Problem

IND[a]	$1,000 Base		After Intracounty Adjustment		After Threshold Adjustment		Value of Threshold (000)	Percent of Value in Problem	
	Supply	Demand	Supply	Demand	Supply	Demand		Supply	Demand
1.	3083	3111	2455	656	270	190	$12250	46.9	69.7
2.	3084	3111	1860	1251	275	187	11870	51.3	58.6
3.	1230	3042	512	2541	115	432	550	89.3	79.8
5.	460	2139	308	1848	95	341	260	98.2	96.2
6.	822	2810	518	2252	166	309	390	95.3	93.9
7.	936	3104	337	2770	149	343	730	95.3	83.1
8.	1193	2498	690	1949	266	193	3860	91.1	93.7
9.	1860	3107	998	2112	241	214	2030	68.7	63.0
10.	521	3081	254	2831	80	389	260	93.8	87.6
13.	1472	3073	930	2143	217	236	500	96.9	89.5
14.	1966	3105	522	2583	222	231	7890	85.6	76.3
15.	2230	3108	754	2356	312	163	2960	78.9	72.5
16.	1388	3105	350	2755	207	248	2840	87.6	77.2
17.	2031	3111	455	2656	184	279	3120	83.7	63.1
18.	1588	3099	334	2767	197	261	1430	90.1	78.4
19.	430	3101	162	2940	91	543	320	95.8	90.7
20.	890	3093	174	2919	107	472	480	95.7	84.6
21.	2135	3108	599	2504	171	301	2160	86.4	80.5
22.	1846	3110	410	2701	155	330	1760	89.5	79.7
23.	322	3098	76	3022	54	868	650	98.3	92.6
24.	1061	3093	388	2704	195	264	3760	94.4	88.7
25.	891	3102	331	2776	137	368	920	95.5	85.4
26.	2156	3108	836	2273	213	242	7140	83.5	81.5
27.	948	3108	242	2867	128	396	880	93.9	83.7
28.	2505	3111	909	2202	232	221	3590	73.1	70.4
29.	1262	3079	589	2499	125	178	260	76.2	63.3
30.	1516	3103	384	2721	215	238	1880	90.7	79.7
31.	1517	3112	316	2796	190	270	820	90.2	75.9
32.	1392	3108	385	2724	209	246	3240	87.4	80.8
33.	935	3101	230	2871	167	305	1460	82.2	72.6
34.	2552	3106	693	2419	226	227	1600	90.6	88.7
35.	1669	3110	427	2684	202	255	3730	88.6	77.2
36.	980	2920	356	2562	151	338	1770	92.0	88.9
37.	1022	3112	136	2976	110	459	2020	94.2	83.9
38.	798	3109	120	2992	80	616	360	97.6	88.4
39.	1062	3112	197	2915	114	442	4970	95.2	78.1

Table 3-6 (cont.)

INDª	$1,000 Base Supply	Demand	After Intracounty Adjustment Supply	Demand	After Threshold Adjustment Supply	Demand	Value of Threshold (000)	Percent of Value in Problem Supply	Demand
40.	1711	3111	309	2803	180	286	3180	91.7	79.4
41.	395	2076	145	1919	79	276	260	97.4	94.6
42.	1122	3077	377	2699	219	235	1640	91.4	80.2
43.	1102	3103	324	2781	146	349	1060	95.8	86.3
44.	2393	3110	592	2520	257	199	2690	78.0	69.0
45.	1629	3105	385	2724	136	376	3410	93.8	86.2
46.	610	3097	161	2938	89	561	830	97.4	89.0
47.	946	2930	464	2459	145	349	920	91.4	89.7
48.	842	3109	231	2879	147	348	1340	96.6	89.7
49.	466	2905	114	2766	71	688	380	83.8	87.7
50.	1659	3112	356	2756	203	253	2700	89.2	75.5
51.	862	3109	190	2919	151	340	1040	93.9	86.2
52.	1268	3112	286	2836	181	285	2140	91.1	88.0
53.	558	3087	202	2885	132	386	490	97.2	88.2
54.	1329	3104	299	2806	118	430	1410	88.8	61.5
55.	998	3099	308	2794	179	287	1680	94.6	73.9
56.	662	3105	163	2942	102	494	550	89.4	82.3
57.	1131	3090	188	2905	120	422	880	95.1	88.3
58.	1024	3100	285	2818	165	309	1350	91.4	79.2
59.	1076	3094	207	2887	144	356	1600	88.8	79.9
60.	1665	3088	574	2530	203	248	370	91.0	86.6
61.	904	3111	314	2798	144	354	680	95.7	88.6
62.	799	3101	213	2889	142	361	830	94.3	84.0
63.	817	3105	235	2870	168	305	1760	95.4	85.1
64.	649	3101	253	2848	131	390	1290	95.7	83.4
65.	512	3104	156	2949	125	405	860	97.1	83.3
66.	1347	3109	485	2627	152	338	1860	95.0	85.3
67.	1001	3091	312	2780	180	286	1120	96.9	91.1
68.	673	3110	235	2875	160	315	490	94.2	83.3
69.	1579	3112	300	2812	112	449	7050	79.9	77.8
70.	1445	3104	676	2433	216	239	1200	92.0	87.8
71.	1354	3110	376	2735	184	274	1500	91.6	80.6
72.	761	3112	202	2910	119	425	970	95.7	86.3
73.	656	3102	98	3004	76	641	310	97.7	90.5
74.	2017	3112	268	2844	159	322	1710	91.1	80.5

See Chapter 1 for a definition of the input-output industries.

constraints to the optimum solution of the regular program does not make any of the simplex criteria of the general program negative, thus implying an optimal solution.[f] The addition of n intracounty shipment constraints B_n to B_r constraints of the regular problem, and the addition of n activities C_n to C_r, the basic feasible matrix of the regular problem, is illustrated in

$$(3.17) \quad \begin{bmatrix} C_{1,n} & 0 \\ \hline C_{2,n} & C_r \end{bmatrix} \cdot \begin{bmatrix} X'_n \\ \hline X'_r \end{bmatrix} = \begin{bmatrix} B_{1,n} \\ \hline B_r + B_{2,n} \end{bmatrix}$$

The value of the shadow prices of the general problem can be calculated using

$$(3.18) \quad \begin{bmatrix} \Pi_n & \Pi_r \end{bmatrix} \cdot \begin{bmatrix} C_{1,n} & 0 \\ \hline C_{2,n} & C_r \end{bmatrix} = \begin{bmatrix} T'_n & T'_r \end{bmatrix}$$

The C matrix of (3.17) and (3.18) is in triangular form, and C_n is divided into two parts. The $C_{1,n}$ sector is a diagonal matrix listing the activity of the constraint that was eliminated when the intracounty shipments were subtracted from the original constraints. The $C_{2,n}$ section contains the entries of the intracounty shipments for the constraints entered in the regular problem in their appropriate rows. This formulation has not altered the value of Π_r, since they are calculated by the method of equation (3.16). Thus the simplex criteria V_r remain nonnegative, and the simplex criteria of the newly introduced activities V_n equal zero, showing that the solution is optimal. Furthermore, (3.16) can therefore be used to calculate the shadow prices of the intracounty shipments.

Table 3-6 shows that, while eliminating intracounty shipments significantly reduced the size of the transportation cost coefficient matrix for each industry, the number of elements was still too large to fit in the memory of the computer. The last procedure for reducing the memory requirements consisted of raising the threshold level of the net supply and demand data from \$1,000 to a level, different for each industry, that would reduce the number of constraints until the transportation cost data could be handled internally in the computer. If N_S is the number of supply constraints and N_D the number of demand constraints, any combination satisfying

$$(3.19) \quad N_S * N_D + 10N_S + 12N_D = 56,610$$

would yield satisfactory results given our computer program and computer size. Table 3-6 lists the threshold levels and the number of constraints remaining after

----

[f]A proof that a situation where all the simplex criteria are zero or positive implies an optimal solution for a cost-minimizing problem may be found in Almon, op. cit., pp. 65-70.

this operation was performed. The last two columns show the supply and demand by industry, used both as constraints in the transportation problem and as the intracounty values for which shadow prices could be calculated, as a percent of the nation's supply and demand.

A major disadvantage of reducing the size of the transportation problem is that we could have eliminated a large proportion of the supply or demand of any commodity. This would greatly reduce the usefulness of the shadow prices in explaining industrial location at the national level. Fortunately, the data in Table 3-6 show that while a large number of counties were eliminated, the remaining average values of supply and demand was 88.8 and 82.1 percent, respectively. The IO industries disaggregated into groupings of agricultural, mining, and manufacturing as presented in Table 3-7 show that the coverage of the agricultural sector is poor, while that for mining and manufacturing is relatively complete.

An additional adjustment of the constraints was necessary before the transportation problems could be solved on the computer. Since we required a regular transportation problem, aggregate supply or demand had to be adjusted so that they would be equal. We chose to keep supply fixed and proportionately adjust demand, since it was thought that the supply estimates were more reliable than the demand estimates.

Numerical Properties of the Shadow Prices

The major reason for choosing the regular transportation problem instead of the surplus or shortage model was the numerical characteristics of the shadow prices from each model. The shadow prices of slack variables in the optimum basis of the surplus problem have a value of zero. In sample runs the number of slack variables entering the solution was a high percentage of the total variables. The larger the number of zeros in a shadow price data series, the smaller the variation in the series and the lower its ability as an independent variable to explain the variance in the change of shipment by county. A large number of zeros would also increase the potential for multicollinearity. Thus to improve the potential explanatory power of the transportation variable and reduce multicollinearity, it was decided to abandon the surplus model for the regular transportation problem.

Table 3-7
Average Percent of National Supply and Demand by Major Industrial Group

Sector	Supply	Demand
Agriculture (IO 1-4)	62.5	69.4
Mining (IO 5-10)	90.4	86.3
Manufacturing (IO 13-74)	89.9	82.3

4 Data Requirements

In order to derive the transportation variables as described in Chapter 3, it is necessary to estimate for each region: (1) supply by industry sector, (2) demand by industry sector, and (3) the cost of shipping a unit of the goods produced by each industry between each pair of regions. This chapter explains how these estimates are made. First, however, it is useful to discuss the regions used in this study.

The Regions

The set of regions used in this study is the 3,112 county-type areas reported in the *1966 County Business Patterns* (CBP). As will be described later, the CBP data are the foundation for many of the other data series that were estimated.

Because of the lack of data on any other basis, it was necessary to work with political subdivisions as our geographic regions. Counties are used instead of larger areas, such as states, because small geographic units seem to be more appropriate than large ones in calculating the transportation variables. As was seen in the last chapter, the transportation variables depend on solutions of a linear programming transportation model that assumes optimum flows among the regions. Optimum flows are those that minimize total transportation cost; thus shipments for any one commodity between any two regions would be in only one direction. In the real world we observe shipments in both directions between two regions; but as a general rule, the smaller the regions, the fewer the cross-hauls. Thus we would expect fewer cross-hauls at the county level than at the state level, meaning that we would expect the optimum flows to be closer to the actual flows at the county level than at the state level.[a]

Supply

Total supply by industry is the sum of domestic output and imports. Our method of estimating county domestic output requires county employment and payroll data; therefore the methods of obtaining the employment and payroll

---

[a]It should be pointed out that cross-hauls would be expected at our industry level of aggregation regardless of the size of the region, since an industry sector may include more than one product.

estimates will also be described. The imports that are added to supply by input-output industry sector are those defined as "competitive" or "transferred" imports. Other imports are not classified by input-output sector.

Domestic Output

County output figures are not directly available for any of the industries for the years 1965 and 1966. In order to make the estimates, it was necessary to apply either output-payroll ratios or output-employment ratios to county payroll or employment figures, respectively. In the manufacturing industries state output-payrolls for 1965 and 1966 were available and were applied to county payroll figures. In some service sectors, county output-employment ratios were obtained for 1963 and used in the estimates for 1965 and 1966. Whenever possible, output-payroll ratios were used instead of output-employment ratios because payrolls are more closely related to output, reflecting changes in the number of hours worked.

A summary of the county output estimating procedures is given in Table 4-1. A more detailed description is given in Appendix A. Since the output estimates depend on either county payroll or employment estimates, we will briefly describe the procedures for obtaining the payroll and employment estimates.

The major source of the county employment and payroll data is the Census publication *County Business Patterns* (CBP) for 1965 and 1966. This series is compiled using Social Security data and hence is a census rather than a survey, although some survey data is used in preparing the final results. A sample of the data presented by county and SIC industry detail is illustrated in Table 4-2. While the census is extensively detailed, it does have major weaknesses: lack of coverage and disclosure problems. The lack of coverage occurs for two reasons. The first is the Census Bureau's policy of only publishing county data for an industry with at least 100 employees or 10 reporting units in a county. A sample of this problem can be shown in Table 4-2. Note that the sum of the three-digit industries is less than the number given for the two-digit industry. The difference belongs to other three-digit industries with groups which are not reported because of their small size. The second reason for lack of coverage is illustrated in Table 4-3. While the Social Security System covered 88.6 percent of the total paid civilian employment in 1966, the CBP series covered only 66.7 percent of total employment. Estimates for these missing data are made from other sources of data. Note however that, except for self-employed persons, the manufacturing industries are fully covered by CBP data.

While the Census Bureau does not report the employment and payroll data when they reveal the operations of a firm, it does publish data on the number of reporting units by size group. A sample in Table 4-2 is industry SIC 204. The undisclosed employment data are estimated by multiplying the average employ-

Table 4-1

Summary of 1965 and 1966 County Output Estimating Procedures and Data Sources by Input-Output Sectors[a]

Input-Output Industry Sectors	Description of Estimating Procedures and Data Sources
Agriculture IO 1, 2	State "value of products sold" from *Farm Income Situation* distributed to counties using 1964 county "value of products sold" from *1964 Census of Agriculture*.
Forestry and Fisheries IO 3	State output/employment ratios for fishing from *Fishing Statistics* times county employment from *County Business Patterns*, and national fisheries output distributed to counties using county payrolls from *County Business Patterns*.
Construction IO 11, 12	Set equal to demand.
Manufacturing IO 13-74	State output/payroll ratios from *Annual Survey of Manufactures* times county payrolls from *County Business Patterns*.
Telephone and Telegraph IO 76	State output estimated from number of telephone calls given in *Statistics of Communications Common Carriers* distributed to counties using employment from *County Business Patterns*.
Electric Utilities IO 79	State output estimates from *Statistics of Electric Utilities* distributed to counties using employment in *County Business Patterns*.
Gas Utilities IO 80	State output estimates from *Statistical Abstract of the U.S.* distributed to counties using employment in *County Business Patterns*.
Trade and Selected Services IO 81, 84, 86, 87, 89-99	County output/employment ratios from *1963 Census of Business* times 1965 and 1966 employment from *County Business Patterns*.
Other Sectors IO 4, 5-10, 75, 77, 78, 82, 83, 85, 88	National output distributed to counties using paryolls from *County Business Patterns*.

[a]All output estimates are adjusted to sum to national totals supplied by Almon's Interindustry Forecasting Project. A detailed explanation of the estimating procedures is given in Appendix A.

Table 4-2
Sample of Data from County Business Patterns

SIC Code	Industry	Number of Employees, Mid-March Pay Period	Taxable Payrolls, January-March	Total Reporting Units	Number of Reporting Units, by Employment-size Class							
					1 to 3	4 to 7	8 to 19	20 to 49	50 to 99	100 to 249	250 to 499	500 or More
200	Canned and Frozen Foods	304	342	17	2	3	5	5	2	—	—	—
2033	Canned Fruits, Vegetables & Jellies	260	232	7	1	—	1	3	2	—	—	—
204	Grain Mill Products	(D)	(D)	7	1	1	2	1	2	—	—	—
2042	Prepared Feed for Animals and Fowls	(D)	(D)	3	—	—	1	—	2	—	—	—
205	Bakery Products	3050	3999	34	4	3	7	6	3	7	3	—
2051	Bread and Related Products	(D)	(D)	30	3	3	6	6	2	6	3	1
2052	Biscuit, Crackers, and Pretzels	(D)	(D)	4	1	—	1	—	1	1	—	1
206	Sugar	(D)	(D)	1	—	—	—	—	—	—	—	1
2062	Cane Sugar Refining	(D)	(D)	1	—	—	—	—	—	—	—	1
207	Confectionery and Related Products	480	392	18	3	2	4	6	2	1	—	—
2071	Candy and Other Confectionery	480	392	18	3	2	4	6	2	1	—	—
208	Beverage Industries	3717	5208	28	4	1	4	5	4	4	5	—
2082	Malt Liquors	1390	2273	4	—	—	—	1	—	1	1	1
2064	Wines, Brandy, and Brandy Spirits	(D)	(D)	2	—	—	—	—	2	—	—	—
2085	Distilled Liquor except Brady	(D)	(D)	3	—	—	1	1	1	—	—	—
2086	Bottled and Canned Soft Drinks	1096	1406	9	—	1	2	2	—	2	2	—
2087	Flavorings	597	773	10	4	—	2	1	1	1	1	—
209	Miscellaneous Food Preparations	1750	2552	34	5	11	4	8	2	3	1	1
2096	Shortening and Cooking Oils	(D)	(D)	2	—	—	—	1	—	1	—	—
2099	Food Preparations, N.E.C.	1372	1961	19	3	6	3	2	2	2	—	1
22	Textile Mill Products	1003	1217	14	2	1	3	3	3	1	1	—

Code	Industry											
221	Weaving Mills, Cotton	(D)	(D)	1	—	—	—	—	—	1	—	—
225	Knitting Mills	(D)	(D)	2	—	—	—	1	1	—	5	—
228	Yarn and Thread Mills	(D)	(D)	3	1	—	1	1	1	—	1	1
2281	Yarn Mills, except Wool	(D)	(D)	1	—	—	—	—	—	—	1	1
23	Apparel and Related Products	14650	14248	214	31	26	48	37	35	22	11	—
231	Men's and Boys' Suits and Coats	6067	6415	61	12	7	9	7	10	9	5	—
232	Men's and Boys' Furnishings	1832	1669	46	4	7	13	8	10	3	1	—
2321	Men's Dress Shirts and Nightwear	419	392	7	—	—	3	1	2	1	—	—
2323	Men's, Youths', and Boys' Neckwear	264	242	5	—	—	—	3	1	1	1	—
2327	Men's and Boys' Separate Trousers	781	737	21	3	6	5	2	3	1	1	—
2328	Work Clothing	127	100	4	—	1	—	2	1	—	—	—
2329	Men's and Boys' Clothing, N.E.C.	241	197	9	1	—	5	2	3	—	3	—
233	Women's and Misses' Outerwear	2251	2113	34	1	1	5	11	9	5	2	—
2331	Blouses, Waists, and Shirts	523	456	5	—	—	2	1	—	1	1	—
2335	Dresses	389	352	6	—	—	—	2	3	1	1	—
2337	Women's Suits, Coats and Skirts	609	609	10	—	—	2	3	3	—	1	—
2339	Women's Outwear, N.E.C.	730	695	13	1	—	1	5	3	3	—	—
234	Women's Undergarments	(D)	(D)	2	—	—	1	—	—	1	—	—
2341	Women's and Children's Underwear	(D)	(D)	2	—	—	1	—	—	1	—	—
235	Hats, Caps, and Millinery	262	211	6	1	—	1	3	—	1	—	—
2352	Men's and Boys' Hats and Caps	(D)	(D)	4	—	—	—	3	—	—	—	—
236	Children's Outerwear	(D)	(D)	5	1	1	—	3	3	—	—	—
2369	Children's Outerwear, N.E.C.	230	212	4	1	—	—	3	—	—	—	—
238	Miscellaneous Apparel and Accessories	1879	1521	8	—	—	1	2	1	1	2	1
2385	Waterproof Outer Garments	1633	1388	4	—	—	—	1	1	1	2	1
2389	Apparel, N.E.C.	(D)	(D)	1	—	—	—	—	1	1	—	1
239	Fabricated Textiles, N.E.C.	1887	1852	51	12	10	17	6	2	2	1	1

Table 4-2 (cont.)

SIC Code	Industry	Number of Employees, Mid-March Pay Period	Taxable Payrolls, January-March	Total Reporting Units	Number of Reporting Units, by Employment-size Class							
					1 to 3	4 to 7	8 to 19	20 to 49	50 to 99	100 to 249	250 to 499	500 or More
2391	Curtains and Draperies	81	54	10	1	4	5	–	–	–	–	–
2392	Housefurnishings, N.E.C.	918	975	12	2	2	5	–	1	1	–	–
2394	Canvas Products	142	144	10	2	2	3	3	–	–	–	–
2396	Apparel Findings	348	325	7	–	–	3	2	1	1	–	–
2397	Schiffli Machine Embroideries	(D)	(D)	1	–	–	–	–	–	–	1	–
24	Lumber and Wood Products	773	754	39	9	6	13	6	4	1	–	–
243	Millwork and Related Products	248	271	14	3	1	5	4	1	–	–	–
2431	Millwork Plants	(D)	(D)	12	3	–	4	4	1	–	–	–
244	Wooden Containers	349	321	9	1	2	2	–	3	1	–	–
2441	Nailed Wooden Boxes and Shook	(D)	(D)	6	1	1	2	–	2	–	–	–
2445	Cooperage	(D)	(D)	3	–	1	–	1	–	–	–	–
249	Miscellaneous Wood Products	115	102	10	3	2	4	1	–	1	–	–
25	Furniture and Fixtures	3470	3770	67	10	5	19	19	10	3	–	1
251	Household Furniture	1574	1766	46	5	1	17	12	9	2	–	–
2511	Wood Furniture, not Upholstered	175	189	9	2	1	2	3	1	–	–	–
2512	Wood Furniture, Upholstered	713	759	16	1	–	8	3	2	2	–	–
2514	Metal Household Furniture	287	356	8	1	–	3	1	3	–	–	–
2515	Mattresses and Bedsprings	399	462	13	1	–	4	5	3	–	–	–
254	Partitions and Fixtures	(D)	(D)	13	4	4	–	4	1	–	–	–
2541	Wood Partitions and Fixtures	147	222	8	2	2	–	3	1	–	–	–
259	Miscellaneous Furniture and Fixtures	(D)	(D)	5	–	–	1	2	–	1	–	–
2591	Venetian Blinds and Shades	(D)	(D)	4	–	–	1	1	–	1	–	1

ment size by the number of reporting units in each size group and aggregating the results. A figure of 1,000 employees was used as the average size for the "500 or more" group since it appeared to be a representative figure based on the national breakdown of the number of reporting units in size groupings greater than 500 employees as presented in Table 4-4.

Table 4-3

Estimated Percent Distribution of Paid Civilian Employment in United States, by Coverage Status under the Social Security Program: March 1966

Employment Group	Percent
Total, paid civilian employment	100.0
Covered by Social Security	88.6
In County Business Patterns scope	66.7
Not in County Business Patterns scope	21.9
Wage and salary workers	12.5
Agriculture	1.5
Domestic service	1.9
Government	8.1
Railroad employment[a]	1.0
Self-employed persons	9.4
Not covered by Social Security	11.4
Wage and salary workers	9.0
Agriculture	.2
Domestic service	1.3
Government	6.4
Other	1.1
Self-employed persons	2.4

Source: U.S. Department of Commerce, Bureau of Census, *1966 County Business Patterns, U.S. Summary*, p. 5.

[a]Includes railroad employment jointly covered by Social Security and Railroad Retirement Programs.

Table 4-4
U.S. Firms Classified by Employment Size

Total Reporting Units with 500 or More Employees	Number of Reporting Units by Employment-size Class				
	500-999	1,000-1,499	1,500-2,499	2,500-4,900	5,000 or more
8,803	5,589	1,467	910	594	243

Source: U.S. Department of Commerce, Bureau of Census, *1964 County Business Patterns, U.S. Summary*, pp. 5-21.

Figures were also estimated for data missing because of a reporting unit's small size. If the sum of the disclosed employment and the estimates of undisclosed employment of three-digit industries was less than the appropriate two-digit number, the residual was assigned to those three-digit industries which report no employment within that two-digit group according to the distribution of those three-digit industries at the state level.

Before estimates of undisclosed numbers and missing ones are accepted as data, they are adjusted in a matrix-balancing routine that adjusts all data in the matrix so that the sum of each row and column is equal to its respective row and column control total. The matrix is a region by industry matrix with actual data subtracted from the matrix and the region and industry control totals. Then the actual data are reentered into the matrix and the matrix is balanced again. This last balance is necessary because even when actual data are given for all cells in a particular row or column, there is no guarantee that the sum of the row or column is equal to its control total.

The adjustment procedures described above are performed separately for each SIC industry level and separately for state and county data. The first data matrix to be adjusted is the group of industry divisions at the state level where the column controls are the national totals for the industry divisions and the row controls are the state totals. Next, groups of two-digit industries within each industry division are adjusted, then the three-digit industries within each two-digit industry, and finally the four-digit industries within each three-digit industry are adjusted as necessary for aggregation into the input-output sectors. After the state data are adjusted, they in turn are used as controls for adjustment of the county data.

The payroll data were also adjusted at each SIC level and separately for state and county data. If the state (or county) payroll data were missing either because of the disclosure rules or because of small size, they were estimated by applying a national (or state) payroll-employment ratio to the state (or county) employment figure. These estimates of the missing data were adjusted by balancing matrices containing only these estimates, using the same procedure as was used for the employment adjustments.

Foreign Imports

National data by SIC groups were obtained for the value of imports by four methods of entry into the United States: (1) vessel, (2) overland from Canada, (3) overland from Mexico, and (4) air. The vessel control totals were allocated to counties using data in the quantity of imports by product class by port of entry published by the Corps of Engineers in *Waterborne Commerce*. The overland imports from Canada and Mexico were allocated to customs districts along the borders using data from *Highlights of U.S. Export and Import Trade*. The customs district data were allocated to counties along the border using employment in the land transportation industry as reported by *County Business Patterns.* The air imports by industry sector were allocated to counties containing major international airports based on the airport's share of imported manufactured goods using data from *Highlights.*

The imports come into the United States through 209 counties. Each SIC import total for each county was divided into competitive imports and others, and the competitive imports were aggregated into the input-output sectors. Competitive imports are those used as intermediate goods and are similar to or compete directly with goods produced in the United States.

Demand

As was described in the previous chapter, total demand as well as total supply is needed for each industry sector within each county. The total demand for each industry was derived as the sum of the various components of demand as illustrated in Table 4-5, where total demand is the sum of each row. The sections of the table filled in with cross lines are the sectors for which direct county estimates were made; estimates of row entries for the other sectors were made by applying national coefficients to county totals.

The intermediate (or interindustry) demand represents demand by the industrial sectors for goods and services from other industrial sectors that are used as inputs for the production of the outputs. For example, in order to produce steel, the primary metal industry demands iron ore from the metal mining industry. The intermediate demand for each industry's output is obtained by applying national input-output coefficients to the county outputs of all the industry sectors and summing the results.

By using the national coefficients, we are assuming that the input requirements per dollar of output at the county level is the same as at the national level. There are three interrelated principal reasons why this assumption may not be valid. One is that firms in different locations may use different technical production processes, thus requiring different inputs. Another reason is that prices of the inputs may vary by county, resulting in different combinations of inputs as the firms try to minimize costs. The third reason is that since we are working with industrial sectors, the mix of products within an industry may vary by location. Of the three reasons, the third is probably the most important; therefore, some attempt was made to correct for the situation. The national input-output table, as received from Almon's project, is an estimate of a product-to-product table so that an industry classification represents a product classification. Secondary products have been taken out of the industry in which they are produced and reassigned to the primary industry. For example, apparel produced in plants in the textile industry as a secondary product is reassigned to the apparel industry.

Table 4-5

Components of Total Demand by Industry[a]

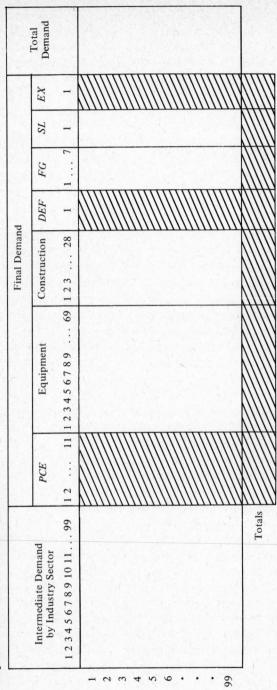

Intermediate Demand by Industry Sector	Final Demand							Total Demand
1 2 3 4 5 6 7 8 9 10 11 . . . 99	PCE	Equipment	Construction	DEF	FG	SL	EX	
	1 2 . . . 11	1 2 3 4 5 6 7 8 9 . . . 69	1 2 3 . . . 28	1	1 . . . 7	1	1	
1								
2								
3								
4								
5								
6								
·								
·								
·								
99								
Totals								

[a]Direct county estimates are available for sections filled in with cross lines. Other estimates are made using national coefficients.

Explanation of final demand sections

PCE: Personal Consumption Expenditures by 11 types of retail outlets

Equipment: Gross private equipment by 69 purchasing sectors

Construction: Private and public construction by 28 types

FG: Federal government purchases by 7 functional groupings excluding construction

SL: State and local government purchases excluding construction

EX: Gross Foreign Exports

DEF: Federal Defense Expenditures

In order to apply the national coefficients to regional data, it is necessary to assume that regional ratios of primary products to secondary products for each industry are the same as the national ratios, since the regional output data is reported on an establishment basis. The county data are adjusted proportionally to sum to the national output controls which are on a product basis.

Personal Consumption Expenditures

Total county merchandise sales by 11 types of retail outlets are reported in the *1963 Census of Business.* In addition, sales classified by 186 merchandise lines for each of the 11 outlets are available for SMSA's and rest-of-the-state areas.

The first step in the estimating procedures was to adjust the 1963 census data to allow for data not reported primarily because of the disclosure rules. Next, the sales by merchandise line were converted into sales by input-output sector. All the estimating procedures are reported in detail in Appendix B. In order to obtain merchandise line detail for each county, it was assumed that each county's merchandise line distribution was the same as either the appropriate SMSA distribution or the appropriate rest-of-the-state area.

Not all input-output sectors sell directly to consumers, and some sell services that are not reported as merchandise. Sales not going through retail outlets, e.g., medical services, were estimated by assuming that the county ratio of consumption to output for each sector was the same as the national ratio.

The last step was to update the 1963 data to 1965 and 1966. A large matrix of the 1963 data was set up with the national input-output totals as column controls and with county sales by retail outlet as row controls. Since there are 3,112 counties and 11 outlets, there were 34,322 rows in the matrix. The 1963 matrix was balanced; then the controls for 1965 and 1966 controls were substituted for the 1963 controls and the matrix rebalanced. The new control totals for 1965 and 1966 were estimated by applying a sales-payroll ratio for each outlet to the county payrolls as reported in *County Business Patterns.* The sales-payroll ratios were by state, derived from 1963 data.

Investment Expenditures

Construction by 28 different types was estimated for 1965 and 1966 for each county. Seventeen of the types were private construction and the other 11 were public construction. Data for 20 of these types were estimated using county data by type of construction from the F.W. Dodge Division, McGraw-Hill Information Systems Company. Two of our 28 sectors were not covered in the Dodge data, and in six other sectors the regional coverage of Dodge data was too incomplete. The 28 sectors and detail on the estimating procedures are given in

Appendix B. The 28 types of construction were converted into construction by the input-output producing sectors using national coefficients.

County equipment purchases were estimated for 69 different sectors for 1965 and 1966. Farm equipment purchases were estimated from farm equipment sales reported in the *1963 Census of Business* and updated to 1965 and 1966 using the same procedures described for updating personal consumption expenditures. National construction equipment was allocated to counties using the total construction data series.

Estimates of equipment purchases by the manufacturing sectors were first made at the state level, then at the county level. State estimates were made by distributing the national figures according to total investment as reported in the *Annual Survey of Manufactures, 1965 and 1966.* The state figures were distributed to counties using Dodge construction data, which were aggregated into manufacturing sectors corresponding to equipment purchasing sectors. National equipment purchases in other sectors were allocated to counties using output that had been aggregated to the appropriate equipment sectors.

Detail on the equipment sectors is given in Appendix B. The county equipment by purchasing sector was converted to input-output producing sector using national coefficients.

Government Expenditures

County data on federal government expenditures by functional category were obtained from the Office of Management and Budget (OMB) for fiscal year 1968. These were used to distribute both 1965 and 1966 national totals to counties for seven types of expenditures. The national totals are for purchases of goods and services and do not include government payrolls and construction expenditures.

Total defense expenditures were distributed to counties using county data on prime defense contracts. In order to obtain the industry sales to defense, a large county by industry matrix was set up with the county defense expenditures as row control totals and the national industry totals as column control totals. The initial distribution of the county defense totals to industry producing sector was made using county output of the producing sectors; then the matrix was balanced to its control totals. This procedure was used instead of using national coefficients because the various contracts, such as for aircraft and ordinance, require different inputs. Moreover, the location of the demand for defense expenditures is being defined as the location of the prime contractor; therefore the county defense demand for each industry must be equal to or less than the industry's output.

County estimates for NASA and general government expenditures were made using the OMB data and then converted to input-output producing sectors using the national coefficients. There were four exceptions to this rule, however, since the federal government "sells" some items to the private sectors and these transactions are recorded as negative entries in the sale of industry output to the government sectors. The government sells inventories and performs services such as meat inspection. The four industry sectors affected are Livestock, Crops, Forestry and Fisheries, and Lumber. The national entries for these four sectors were allocated directly to counties using OMB data instead of national coefficients.

Exports

Exports were allocated in a manner similar to the method described for allocating imports. Data on quantities of exports by SIC industry sector and by port obtained from *Waterborne Commerce* were used to allocate national exports by vessel to counties. Overland exports to Canada and Mexico were allocated to customs districts using data from *Highlights of U.S. Export and Import Trade* and then to counties using employment in the land transportation industry. Exports by air for all manufacturing goods were used to allocate commodity exports by air. The SIC industry data were aggregated to the input-output sectors for each of the 209 exporting counties involved.

Transportation Cost

This section briefly describes the procedures used to calculate the coefficients of the objective function of the linear programming transportation problem—transportation rates between counties for each commodity. The section is subdivided into four parts. In the first part, the definition of a transportation rate is analyzed in terms of the cost incurred by the carriers and the process by which the Interstate Commerce Commission (ICC) approves the rates that carriers charge users. The first part also contains a discussion of the modes of transportation utilized by industry. The next two parts illustrate the procedure utilized in calculating transportation rates for rail and trucking. The last part presents our method of incorporating shipments of different weights by both rail and truck into the coefficients. Appendix C reports these procedures in detail.

Rate-Making Procedures

As is well known, the price level of transportation services is not determined by the competitive market but is regulated by the ICC. The ICC does not set prices, but it approves or disapproves rates proposed by the carriers under criteria outlined by Congress.[1] The rate-setting procedure for each carrier is a function of intermode competition, national aims outlined in the National Transportation Acts, and provision for an adequate rate of return for the carrier. For our purposes, we can ignore the political aspects of the nation's transportation policy and concentrate upon the cost incurred by the carrier in transporting a commodity between counties and the markup that the carrier can apply to this cost. This procedure will determine the rates carriers can charge their customers. Fortunately, both the costs and the markup ratios can be obtained through publications of the Bureau of Accounts of the ICC.

The cost incurred by the carrier can be expressed in algebraic form as

$$(4.1) \qquad C_{ij} = Ter_i + Lh_{ij} + Ter_j,$$

where $\quad C_{ij}$ = total cost of shipment between the i and j region,

$\qquad Ter$ = terminal cost,

$\qquad Lh$ = line-haul cost.

Terminal cost includes the expenses of pickup or delivery, platform handling, and billing and collecting, whereas line-haul cost consists of the expense of the carrier while the shipment is actually in transit. Terminal cost is a function of shipment size, mode of transit, type of container (e.g., railroad car), and region, whereas line-haul cost is a function of shipment size, mode of transit, type of container, and distance.

The distance measurements used were obtained from the Bureau of Public Roads.[2] These measurements are particularly useful for the location model, since they approximate actual land transportation routes, rather than the unsophisticated use of straight airline distances between counties.

The *1963 Census of Transportation* lists shipments by commodity, weight bracket, and mode of transportation. The industrial classification scheme used in the Census of Transportation differs from the SIC codes; therefore we established a relationship between both systems, as reported in Appendix C.

There are five principal modes of transportation—rail, highway (common carrier and private truck), water, air, and pipeline; but transportation rates are calculated only for rail and highway traffic. Table 4-6 shows the percent of the total U.S. output by IO industry that is transported by each mode of transportation.

Pipelines have been eliminated from consideration since they are highly specialized carriers, transporting petroleum products. Air transport is normally utilized when time, rather than cost, is the major constraint affecting the shipper. The time constraint usually occurs because of spoilage possibilities (flowers and fresh food) or emergency shipments (spare parts).[3] Thus, only in abnormal circumstances would most industries ship their inputs or outputs by

Table 4-6

Percent of Input-Output Sector Output Shipped by Mode of Transport, 1963

Industry Sector	Mode of Transport						
	Rail	Motor Carrier	Private Truck	Air	Water	Others	Unknown
14	31.8	32.3	35.2	–	.1	.5	.1
15	17.0	25.4	57.5	–	–	.1	–
16	39.3	36.4	21.8	–	1.9	.1	.5
17	68.6	10.9	20.2	–	.1	.1	.1
18	–	–	–	–	–	–	–
19	57.5	20.7	19.8	–	1.8	.1	.01
20	23.5	68.8	5.7	–	.7	1.3	–
21	19.8	24.7	52.9	–	2.4	.1	.1
22	63.0	21.9	13.9	–	.7	.1	.4
23	50.8	47.0	.3	–	–	1.7	.2
24	11.3	64.0	23.7	.0	.0	1.0	.0
25	16.3	61.3	21.0	.0	.0	1.0	.3
26	2.5	60.0	12.2	1.1	–	22.7	.5
27	16.7	71.0	8.4	–	–	3.8	.1
28	55.7	14.0	28.3	–	2.2	–	–
29	23.3	42.3	34.4	–	–	–	–
30	22.3	33.4	43.1	–	–	1.0	.2
31	28.1	54.7	15.7	–	–	1.4	.2
32	60.7	27.6	8.1	–	2.6	1.0	.2
33	15.4	52.6	30.8	–	.1	1.0	.1
34	–	–	–	–	–	–	–
35	59.0	22.1	17.0	.0	1.3	.3	.3
36	40.4	47.0	9.5	.1	1.7	.6	.7
37	21.2	72.3	2.2	–	2.1	1.7	.6
38	9.7	65.7	19.3	–	4.4	.8	.1
39	7.5	11.0	8.1	–	73.0	.4	–
40	21.3	68.6	7.8	.2	.3	1.5	.3
41	3.0	56.8	36.1	.6	–	3.0	.6
42	.9	5.2	93.3	.0	.0	.6	.0
43	24.0	60.7	14.7	–	.2	.2	.2
44	30.9	35.5	26.5	–	6.9	.0	.1
45	51.0	38.9	4.2	–	5.5	.3	.1
46	48.8	36.7	13.5	.0	.1	.2	.6
47	41.3	42.0	15.8	.0	.7	.2	.0
48	53.1	35.3	9.9	.1	.7	.4	.6
49	33.6	38.7	27.1	–	.2	.2	.2
50	37.3	35.5	23.9	.1	1.8	.8	.4
51	25.4	63.8	8.2	.2	.3	1.7	.3

Table 4-6 (cont.)

Industry Sector	Rail	Motor Carrier	Private Truck	Air	Water	Others	Unknown
52	19.3	59.5	15.3	.3	1.1	4.2	.3
53	25.3	59.6	12.9	.3	.2	1.2	.4
54	38.4	44.4	15.2	.2	–	1.4	.4
55	55.3	39.9	3.7	.1	.2	.7	.0
56	5.3	71.0	19.1	.2	2.6	1.0	1.0
57	58.2	35.7	3.9	.2	.2	1.6	.2
58	21.6	66.4	8.9	.2	.1	2.6	.2
59	11.4	73.6	9.4	.5	.2	3.2	1.7
60	22.9	60.8	9.2	.9	2.3	3.6	.3
61	15.0	69.5	.7	4.7	2.0	7.9	.1
62	22.4	64.7	9.8	.1	.6	2.0	.4
63	15.0	62.2	17.4	1.7	.4	3.0	.3
64	61.8	28.5	7.1	.1	.1	2.1	.3
65	14.1	68.0	13.8	.3	1.4	2.3	.1
66	18.8	61.8	5.0	1.2	.5	12.6	.2
67	23.2	44.3	22.8	2.3	.5	5.3	1.7
68	9.1	66.4	21.9	.4	.4	1.7	.1
69	50.7	43.0	5.4	.1	.3	.3	.2
70	14.6	62.2	7.4	6.8	–	8.9	–
71	47.1	26.3	23.6	.1	.2	2.6	.3
72	10.5	69.9	9.6	.7	.4	8.6	.2

Source: U.S. Department of Commerce, Bureau of Census, *1963 Census of Transportation.* Vol. III, Commodity Transportation Survey, Table 1.

air. We are not concerned with these cases, but only with the normal transportation cost that must be overcome when a firm enters or expands production in a county. Water transportation achieves cost advantages over rail and highway only at very long distances or for large bulk items,[4] but as revealed by the percentages in Table 4-6 these conditions are not normally fulfilled. Therefore, water transport was not included in the model. Although it would have been possible to include transportation costs for these three modes in the model, the time and effort involved would be too great considering the relative unimportance of these modes compared with the rail and highway modes.

Rail Rate Calculation

The method used to calculate rail transportation rates was derived from a paper entitled, "Transport Cost, Pricing, and Regulation," by Merrill J. Roberts,[5] who applies a markup ratio classified by commodity type to out-of-pocket costs. Out-of-pocket costs are the expenses incurred by the carrier, both terminal and line-haul, to transport a commodity from origin to destination, averaged over an extended time period, excluding allocation of capital equipment depreciation rates and other overhead expenses. They are similar to total variable cost where the variation refers to many, not just one shipment. The markup ratios used by Roberts are ratios of revenue to out-of-pocket costs by commodity found in the ICC, Bureau of Accounts, *Distribution of Rail Revenue Contribution by Commodity Groups–1960.*

The latest publication of this series is for the year 1961; however, a substitute publication, *Procedures for Developing Rail Revenue Contribution by Commodity and Territory*, is issued yearly. While not providing the ratios, it does provide the necessary statistics and outlines the method used to calculate these ratios for 1965. The data were listed by shipments within and between three major regions: Official (New England, Middle Atlantic, Eastern, and Mid-West), South (east of the Mississippi River), and West.

Out-of-pocket costs rather than fully distributed costs were used as the base to obtain estimates of the transportation rates, because of the *de facto* policy of the ICC in settling rate controversies. Roberts[6] reports that in a survey of 350 ICC decisions on rate reduction controversies between March 14, 1960, and May 25, 1962, only eight of 252 that presented cost data used fully distributed cost information; the remainder used out-of-pocket cost information. Thus, by not requiring full-distributed cost in its hearings, the ICC has allowed out-of-pocket costs to be the base upon which rates are formulated. Additional support for using out-of-pocket cost as a basis for approximating rail rates has been supplied in a statement by the Bureau of Accounts of the ICC,[7]

... Rates based solely on the fully distributed costs ... would not have the benefit of being guided by that prominent principle of ratemaking which involves the recognition of derived demand ... also ... known as differential charging, product discrimination .... Regardless of terminology, rates made without adherence to this principle will result in reductions on high-grade traffic and concomitant increases on low-grade volume traffic. Historically, rates reflect continuous interplay of economic forces. ... Therefore, the ratios of revenue to out-of-pocket costs ... have a ratemaking significance which is not possessed by the ratios of revenue to fully distributed costs. ...

Highway Cost Calculation

The procedure used for calculating common carrier trucking costs was derived from *Cost of Transporting Freight by Class I and Class II Motor Carriers of General Commodities for 1965*, compiled by the Interstate Commerce Commission. The out-of-pocket costs of the motor carriers plus a markup adequate to ensure sufficient revenue, including a reasonable return on invested capital, are used as the rate the common carrier would charge its customers. We assume that these charges apply to all trucking, including intrastate common carriers, and private trucking not under ICC jurisdiction.

The Motor Carrier cost information is divided into 13 regions, identified in Table 4-7. The regional delineation is not a simple disaggregation of the country into 13 contiguous regions, but a hierarchy of regions, beginning with the nation (Transcontinental) and ending on an elementary level (within New England). The markup ratios listed in the table are those that the ICC recommends be applied to out-of-pocket cost. They differ regionally because of regional differentials in interest rates. The rates derived in this fashion apply to all commodities assuming average operating conditions. Actual variations in operating conditions that affect rates include circuity of routes, density of shipment, partial pickup and delivery service, jointness of round-trips, and running speed.

The Unit Shipment Bundle

The coefficients of the transportation problem are designed to reflect the fact that transportation rates vary by size of shipment as well as distance and

Table 4-7
Motor Carrier Regions and Markup Ratios

Region Number	Region or Territory	Markup Ratios
1	Central	1.1796
2	Eastern-Central	1.1818
3	Middle Atlantic	1.1790
4	Middlewest	1.1772
	New England:	
5	Within New England–Group I	1.1801
6	Between New England and New York City area and beyond–Group II	1.1833
7	Pacific	1.1778
8	Rocky Mountain	1.1758
	Southern:	
9	Southern (Intra)	1.1749
10	East-South	1.1753
11	South-Central	1.1743
12	Southwest	1.1774
13	Transcontinental	1.1776

Source: Interstate Commerce Commission, *Cost of Transporting Freight by Class I, Class II Motor Carriers of General Commodities for 1965*, pp. 2 and 6.

transport mode. Trucking rates are usually lower for small shipments transported short distances, while rail shipments because of their high terminal cost and relatively lower line-haul cost have a cost advantage on large shipments transported great distances. Thus the choice of the amount shipped drastically affects the mode of transportation used. To overcome this problem, each shipment unit consisted of a distribution of shipments varying by number and weight which were derived with national data from the *1963 Census of Transportation*, instead of a single shipment. The lower figure between rail and trucking for each weight bracket was chosen and their summation used as the coefficient of the objective function. This procedure assumes that each industry attempts to minimize transportation costs and that except for rate differentials it is indifferent to the mode of transportation it uses.

5

The Location Equations

Location theory, as presented in Chapter 2, indicates that the regional change in an industry's output is a function of the marginal costs of obtaining the necessary inputs, including the transportation input needed for shipping the final products and the agglomeration effects not reflected in the marginal costs we computed. Therefore, each industry's regression equation, given below, includes both the marginal costs and the agglomeration variables as explanatory variables, although the marginal costs are given preference.

The results of the regression equations are discussed in summary form in this chapter. In the next chapter the results of the general model are presented by industry group.

The Equations

The form of the regression equations used to explain the regional change in output is

$$(5.1) \quad \Delta QD_{ij} = b_{0i} + b_{1i}TQ_{ij} + b_{2i}TI_{1j} + b_{3i}TI_{2j} + b_{4i}TI_{3j}$$

$$+ b_{5i}TI_{4j} + b_{6i}WR_{ij} + b_{7i}VL_j + b_{8i}Q_{ij} + b_{9i}EQ_{ij}$$

$$+ b_{10i}DEN_j + b_{11i}MB_{i1j} + b_{12j}MB_{i2j} + b_{13i}MB_{i3j}$$

$$+ b_{14i}MB_{i4j} + b_{15i}MS_{i1j} + b_{16i}MS_{i2j} + b_{17i}MS_{i3j}$$

$$+ b_{18i}MS_{i4j} + e_{ij}, \quad (i = 1, \ldots, N; j = 1, \ldots, M)$$

ΔQD_{ij} = change in output, with sales to the federal government for defense removed, of industry i in county j between 1965 and 1966 measured in thousands of dollars at 1966 factory prices,

TQ_{ij} = transport cost of shipping the marginal unit of output from industry i out of county j in 1965, measured in cents per dollar of output,

TI_{kj} = transport cost of obtaining the marginal unit of input from major supplying industry k into county j in 1965, $k \leq 4$, measured in cents per dollar of output,

WR_{ij} = annual wage rate in industry i in county j in 1965, measured in thousands of 1966 dollars per unit of employment,

65

VL_j = value of land (dollars per acre) in county j in 1964,[1]

Q_{ij} = output of industry i in county j in 1965, measured in thousands of 1966 dollars,

EQ_{ij} = equipment investment in 1965 by the equipment purchasing sector for which industry i is a part, in county j, measured in thousands of 1966 dollars,

DEN_j = number of people per square mile in 1965 in region j,

MB_{ikj} = a representation of major buying sector k in county j that bought goods from industry i in 1965, $k \leqslant 4$, measured in thousands of 1966 dollars,

MS_{ikj} = output of major supplying sector k in county j that sold goods to industry i in 1965, $k \leqslant 4$,

b_{ki} = parameters estimated in equation for industry i, $k = 1, 18$,

e_{ij} = error term for industry i county j,

N = number of industries,

M = number of regions.

The major supplying and buying sectors for each industry are identified in Chapter 6. County output of the supplying industries is used as the measure of available supply. Buying sectors, however, can be consumers, government, construction contractors, equipment purchasers and foreigners, as well as other industries. The notation and measures used for these other buying sectors is:

PCE_{ij} = personal consumption expenditures of goods produced by industry i sold in county j in 1965, measured in thousands of 1966 dollars,

PI_j = personal income of residents in county j in 1965 measured in thousands of 1966 dollars (used as a substitute for PCE_i when independent data estimates of PCE_i were not available),

GOV_{kj} = government expenditures by type k spent in county j in 1965, measured in thousands of 1966 dollars (see Table 5-1 for the identification of type k),

CN_{kj} = value of construction by type k in county j in 1965, measured in thousands of 1966 dollars (see Table 5-1 for the identification of type k),

EQ_{kj} = value of equipment by purchasing sector k in county j in 1965, measured in thousands of 1966 dollars (see Table 5-1 for the identification of type k),

EX_{ij} = value of foreign exports produced by industry i shipped through ports in county j in 1965, measured in thousands of 1966 dollars.

It is hypothesized that the county variation in the change in the output of an industry can be explained by the county variation in the independent variables, and that meaningful coefficients can be obtained using ordinary least squares. The results are presented in Table 5-2.

Table 5-1
Definitions of Equipment, Construction, and Government Sectors

	Equipment Purchasing Sectors
1	Farm
2	Mining
3	Oil and Gas Wells
4	Construction
5	Ordnance
6	Meat Products
7	Tobacco
8	Fabrics and Yarn
9	Rugs, Tire Cord
10	Apparel
11	Household Textiles and Upholstery
12	Lumber and Products Excluding Containers
13	Wooden Containers
14	Household Furniture
15	Office Furniture
16	Paper, Excluding Containers
17	Paper Containers
18	Printing and Publishing
19	Basic Chemicals
20	Plastic and Synthetics
21	Drugs, Cleaning, and Toilet Items
22	Paint
23	Petroleum Refining
24	Rubber and Plastic
25	Leather Tanning
26	Shoes and Other Leather Products
27	Glass and Products
28	Stone and Clay Products
29	Iron and Steel
30	Nonferrous Metals
31	Metal Containers
32	Heating, Plumbing, Structural Metal
33	Stampings, Screw Machine Products
34	Hardware, Plating, Wire Products and Valves
35	Engines and Turbines
36	Farm Machinery and Equipment
37	Construction and Material Handling Equipment
38	Metal-working Machinery
39	Special Industrial Machinery
40	General Industrial Machinery

Table 5-1 (cont.)

	Equipment Purchasing Sectors (Cont.)
41	Machine Shops and Misc.
42	Office and Computing Machines
43	Service Industry Machinery
44	Electric Apparatus and Motors
45	Household Appliances
46	Electric Lighting and Wirings
47	Communication Equipment
48	Electronic Components
49	Batteries, X-Ray, and Engine Electrical Equipment
50	Motor Vehicles
51	Aircraft and Parts
52	Ships, Trains, and Cycles
53	Instruments and Clocks
54	Optical and Photographic Equipment
55	Misc. Manufacturing
56	Transportation
57	Communication
58	Utility
59	Trade
60	Finance and Insurance
61	Service
62	Dairy Products
63	Canned and Frozen Foods
64	Grain Mill Products
65	Bakery Products
66	Sugar
67	Confectionery
68	Beverages
69	Misc. Foods

	Construction Sectors
1	Residential
2	Additions and Alterations to Residences
3	Nonhousekeeping Residential Construction
4	Industrial
5	Offices
6	Stores, Restaurants, and Garages
7	Religious
8	Educational
9	Hospital and Institutional

Table 5-1 (cont.)

	Construction Sectors (Cont.)
10	Misc. Nonresidential Buildings
11	Farm Construction
12	Oil and Gas Well Drilling and Exploration
13	Railroad
14	Telephone
15	Electric Utility
16	Gas and Petroleum Pipelines
17	All Other Private Construction
18	Highway
19	Military
20	Conservation
21	Sewer Systems
22	Water Systems
23	Public Residential Construction
24	Public Industrial Construction
25	Public Educational
26	Public Hospital
27	Other Public Structures
28	Misc. Public

	Government Sectors
1	Defense
2	National Aeronautics and Space Administration
3	Federal Government Not Listed Elsewhere
4	Federal Government Enterprises
5	Expenditures From or Sales To the Livestock Sector
6	Expenditures From or Sales To the Crop Sector
7	Expenditures From or Sales To the Forestry and Fisheries Sector
8	Expenditures From or Sales To the Lumber Sector
9	State and Local Government

Defense expenditures were removed from output when used in the dependent variable because defense contracts awards are usually not influenced by transport costs and other input prices, and because it was assumed that the demand for defense goods is located at the production site. Equations were run with changes in output that included defense expenditures and were inferior to those in Table 5-2. When output was used as an independent variable, defense expenditures were not netted out.

Table 5-2

Equations Explaining Change in Output by Industry Sector, 1965-1966 (Constraints on the Entry of Hypothesized Variables)

1 Livestock

No. Obsv. = 1986   R-Square = .9530   R-Square (Level of Output) = .9990

$$\Delta GD(1,T) = 686.0029 - 3.1572\ TI(2,T-1) - 45.5465\ TI(17,T-1) - 15.0971\ WR(1,T-1) - .1642\ VL(T-1) + .1606\ Q(1,T-1)$$
$$(53.1178)\quad(.3156)\qquad\qquad(12.9313)\qquad\qquad(2.7407)\qquad\qquad(.0207)\qquad\quad(.0009)$$
$$+ .0081\ EQ(1,T-1) + .0046\ Q(15,T-1)$$
$$(.0054)\qquad\qquad(.0008)$$

2 Crops

No. Obsv. = 1850   R-Square = .5066   R-Square (Level of Output) = .9956

$$\Delta QD(2,T) = 845.6774 - .0643\ Q(2,T-1) - 24.2427\ TI(35,T-1) + .0337\ EQ(1,T-1)$$
$$(71.7014)\quad(.0018)\qquad\quad(7.4963)\qquad\qquad(.0157)$$

3 Forestry & Fishery Products

No. Obsv. = 147   R-Square = .1977   R-Square (Level of Output) = .9867

$$\Delta QD(3,T) = -217.7721 - .0444\ VL(T-1) + .0348\ Q(3,T-1) + .1261\ EQ(1,T-1) + .0435\ Q(25,T-1)$$
$$(132.9830)\quad(.0183)\qquad\quad(.0122)\qquad\qquad(.0578)\qquad\qquad(.0211)$$

4 Agricultural Services

No. Obsv. = 2070   R-Square = .0717   R-Square (Level of Ouput) = .9786

$$\Delta QD(4,T) = 138.9870 - 13.1345\ TI(52,T-1) - 6.0136\ WR(4,T-1) - .0455\ Q(4,T-1) + .0061\ EQ(1,T-1) + .0174\ DEN(T-1)$$
$$(97.7236)\quad(12.0538)\qquad\qquad(1.8341)\qquad\qquad(.0042)\qquad\quad(.0043)\qquad\qquad(.0038)$$
$$+ .0010\ Q(1,T-1) + .0028\ Q(3,T-1) + .0024\ Q(17,T-1)$$
$$(.0004)\qquad\qquad(.0020)\qquad\qquad(.0005)$$

5 Iron Ore Mining

No. Obsv. = 56   R-Square = .5365   R-Square (Level of Output) = .9707

$$\Delta QD(5,T) = 3233.5542 - 1395.7708\ TI(55,T-1) - .1676\ Q(5,T-1) + .3966\ EQ(2,T-1) + 1.2140\ Q(55,T-1)$$
$$(2450.8592)\quad(823.9421)\qquad\qquad(.0305)\qquad\quad(.2023)\qquad\qquad(.3110)$$

6 Non-ferrous Ore Mining

No. Obsv. = 75   R-Square = .1897   R-Square (Level of Output) = .9872

$$\Delta QD(6,T) = -390.0107 + .0559\ Q(6,T-1)$$
$$(516.9745)\quad(.0135)$$

7 Coal Mining   No. Obsv. = 198   R-Square = .2568   R-Square (Level of Output) = .9340

$\Delta QD(7,T) = -424.1714 - 66.9190\ WR(7,T-1) - .1750\ VL(T-1) + .0452\ Q(7,T-1) + .1810\ EQ(2,T-1) + .0239\ A(78,T-1)$
$\quad\quad (680.4455)\quad (66.4235)\quad\quad\quad\quad (.0909)\quad\quad\quad\quad (.0270)\quad\quad\quad (.1412)\quad\quad\quad (.0146)$
$\quad\quad + .0767\ Q(55,T-1)$
$\quad\quad\quad (.0253)$

8 Petroleum Mining   No. Obsv. = 214   R-Square = .5650   R-Square (Level of Output) = .9914

$\Delta QD(8,T) = -2056.1253 - 38.4500\ TQ(8,T-1) - 313.7358\ TI(35,T-1) + .1156\ Q(8,T-1) + .1655\ DEN(T-1)$
$\quad\quad (3021.6564)\quad (35.5675)\quad\quad\quad\quad (100.1881)\quad\quad\quad\quad (.0075)\quad\quad\quad (.0715)$

9 Minerals Mining   No. Obsv. = 439   R-Square = .3105   R-Square (Level of Output) = .9916

$\Delta QD(9,T) = 76.0503 - 42.7184\ TI(55,T-1) + .0324\ Q(9,T-1) + .0031\ A(12,T-1)$
$\quad\quad (95.3193)\quad (41.9791)\quad\quad\quad\quad (.0059)\quad\quad\quad (.0004)$

10 Chemical Mining   No. Obsv. = 52   R-Square = .1688   R-Square (Level of Output) = .9350

$\Delta QD(10,T) = 5734.8723 - 607.7148\ TI(35,T-1) + .0637\ Q(10,T-1) + .1311\ Q(55,T-1)$
$\quad\quad (3175.3654)\quad (284.6094)\quad\quad\quad\quad (.0412)\quad\quad\quad (.0990)$

13 Ordnance   No. Obsv. - 391   R-Square = .1638   R-Square (Level of Output) = .9637

$\Delta QD(13,T) = 27977.0759 - 5072.9437\ TI(67,T-1) - 218.5744\ WR(13,T-1) - .3463\ VL(T-1) - .0853\ Q(13,T-1) + .1270\ GOV(3,T-1)$
$\quad\quad (10873.3290)\ (2012.8259)\quad\quad\quad (161.7231)\quad\quad\quad\quad (.2597)\quad\quad\quad (.0104)\quad\quad\quad (.0720)$
$\quad\quad + .0303\ Q(70,T-1)$
$\quad\quad\quad (.0057)$

14 Meat Packing   No. Obsv. = 535   R-Square = .2440   R-Square (Level of Output) = .9934

$\Delta QD(14,T) = 1157.2826 - .0548\ Q(14,T-1) - .3059\ VL(T-1) + 1.0460\ EQ(6,T-1) + .0041\ Q(85,T-1) + .0128\ Q(40,T-1)$
$\quad\quad (346.5728)\quad (.0048)\quad\quad\quad\quad (.1164)\quad\quad\quad (.9136)\quad\quad\quad (.0013)\quad\quad\quad (.0116)$

15 Dairy Products   No. Obsv. = 664   R-Square = .2419   R-Square (Level of Output) = .9972

$\Delta QD(15,T) = -120.6544 - 72.3531\ TQ(15,T-1) - .0362\ Q(15,T-1) - 40.0473\ WR(15,T-1) + 1.3212\ EQ(62,T-1) + .0034\ Q(1,T-1)$
$\quad\quad (256.7774)\quad (44.2405)\quad\quad\quad\quad (.0027)\quad\quad\quad (28.8861)\quad\quad\quad (.2216)\quad\quad\quad (.0019)$

Table 5-2 (cont.)

16 Canned & Frozen Foods

No. Obsv. = 280   R-Square = .2974   R-Square (Level of Output) = .9890

ΔQD(16,T) = 1505.4159 − 204.5869 TI(43,T−1) − .0649 Q(16,T−1) + .0366 Q(2,T−1)
(837.2888) (166.6717)   (.0062)   (.0083)

17 Grain Mill Products

No. Obsv. = 369   R-Square = .0587   R-Square (Level of Output) = .9875

ΔQD(17,T) = 1666.9910 − 455.1991 TQ(17,T−1) − 13.7547 TI(2.T−1) − .2501 VL(T−1) + .0274 Q(17,T−1)
(1533.3486) (415.7343)   (9.8099)   (.1871)   (.0062)

18 Bakery Products

No. Obsv. = 421   R-Square = .1084   R-Square (Level of Output) = .9970

ΔQD(18,T) = 75.4860 − 144.2342 TI(17,T−1) + .0127 Q(18,T−1) + .0065 Q(32,T−1)
(297.2731) (120.6636)   (.0046)   (.0038)

19 Sugar

No. Obsv. = 32   R-Square = .6052   R-Square (Level of Output) = .9936

ΔQD(19,T) = −4858.8434 − 64.8125 TQ(19,T−1) + .0770 Q(19,T−1) + 1.5504 EQ(66,T−1) − .4715 VL(T−1)
(2003.2964) (28.9285)   (.0223)   (.5020)   (.2384)

20 Candy

No. Obsv. = 130   R-Square = .3302   R-Square (Level of Output) = .9988

ΔQD(20,T) = 3590.2016 − 41.8515 TI(19,T−1) + .0243 Q(20,T−1)
(2275.8690) (28.8952)   (.0031)

21 Beverages.

No. Obsv. = 414   R-Square = .4641   R-Square (Level of Output) = .9869

ΔQD(21,T) = −120.8707 − 660.6392 TQ(21,T−1) − 274.5663 WR(21,T−1) − .1048 VL(T−1) + .1226 Q(21,T−1)
(984.8571) (561.9801)   (71.9929)   (.0717)   (.0067)

22 Misc. Food Products

No. Obsv. = 406   R-Square = .0806   R-Square (Level of Output) = .9845

ΔQD(22,T) = 9827.4718 − 10.5879 TI(2,T−1) − 1306.4968 TI(49,T−1) − 1183.4287 TI(17,T−1) − 95.0466 WR(22,T−1)
(4866.1248) (9.5205)   (1089.9658)   (699.3926)   (37.6333)
− .0811 VL(T−1) − .0278 Q(22,T−1) + .1235 PCE(22,T−1) + .0273 EX(22,T−1)
(.0613)   (.0096)   (.0265)   (.0259)

23 Tobacco   No. Obsv. = 35   R-Square = .3227   R-Square (Level of Output) = .9871

$\Delta QD(23,T) = 30260.6411 - 94896.2393\ TQ(23,T-1) - 36577.8330\ TI(33,T-1) - 5.2237\ EMP(23,T-1) - 1.0816\ VLT(T-1)$
    (15375.7620) (76755.5820)   (21603.1450)   (2.0002)   (.9187)

24 Fabrics & Yarn   No. Obsv. = 184   R-Square = .4207   R-Square (Level of Output) = .9920

$\Delta QD(24,T) = 2350.2840 - 293.8593\ TI(35,T-1) - .4796\ VL(T-1) + .0812\ Q(24,T-1)$
    (2250.0072) (245.9383)   (.3881)   (.0072)

25 Rugs, Tire Cord, Misc. Textiles   No. Obsv. = 94   R-Square = .5617   R-Square (Level of Output) = .9934

$\Delta QD(25,T) = 1906.4508 + .0911\ Q(25,T-1) - 346.7943\ TI(36,T-1) - 213.9060\ TI(1,T-1) + .0872\ DEN(T-1) + .0027\ Q(24,T-1)$
    (1531.2002) (.0105)   (227.8562)   (188.8928)   (.0437)   (.0017)

26 Apparel   No. Obsv. = 691   R-Square = .1912   R-Square (Level of Output) = .9983

$\Delta QD(26,T) = 919.8396 - 2442.8751\ TI(74,T-1) + .0299\ PCE(26,T-1) + .0140\ Q(24,T-1) + .0134\ Q(36,T-1) + .0189\ Q(27,T-1)$
    (580.4342) (2091.8558)   (.0056)   (.0035)   (.0117)   (.0144)

27 Household Textiles & Upholst.   No. Obsv. = 174   R-Square = .7135   R-Square (Level of Output) = .9977

$\Delta QD(27,T) = 1737.6255 - 7998.9948\ TI(24,T-1) - .1011\ Q(27,T-1) - 319.9049\ WR(27,T-1) + .2845\ DEN(T-1) + .0963\ PCE(27,T-1)$
    (722.1130) (7022.6248)   (.0061)   (158.4757)   (.0325)   (.0203)
$+ .0032\ Q(24,T-1)$
    (.0026)

28 Lumber & Prod. Exc. Containers   No. Obsv. = 993   R-Square = .0547   R-Square (Level of Output) = .9965

$\Delta QD(28,T) = 205.9331 - .0141\ Q(28,T-1)$
    (45.0616) (.0019)

29 Wooden Containers   No. Obsv. = 176   R-Square = .5675   R-Square (Level of Output) = .9855

$\Delta QD(29,T) = -57.9409 + .1304\ Q(29,T-1) + .7985\ EQ(13,T-1)$
    (22.0942) (.0116)   (.2822)

30 Household Furniture   No. Obsv. = 358   R-Square = .2403   R-Square (Level of Output) = .9928

$\Delta QD(30,T) = 1489.7761 - 185.2298\ TI(52,T-1) - .0255\ Q(30,T-1) + 3.5865\ EQ(14,T-1)$
    (1183.2689) (148.7258)   (.0057)   (.3518)

Table 5-2 (cont.)

31 Office Furniture

No. Obsv. = 249   R-Square = .8967   R-Square (Level of Output) = .9973

$$\Delta QD(31,T) = 812.5435 - .1402\,Q(31,T-1) - 53.7152\,TI(45,T-1) - 62.1055\,TI(28,T-1) + 1.4012\,EQ(15,T-1) + .0235\,DEN(T-1)$$
$$(436.2204)\ (.0036) \qquad (21.4306) \qquad\qquad (47.3238) \qquad\qquad (.3021) \qquad\qquad (.0083)$$
$$+ .0002\,Q(45,T-1)$$
$$(.0002)$$

32 Paper & Prod. Exc. Containers

No. Obsv. = 443   R-Square = .5401   R-Square (Level of Output) = .9959

$$\Delta QD(32,T) = -567.1604 - 1149.0523\,TQ(32,T-1) - 1028.4136\,TI(33,T-1) + .0628\,Q(32,T-1) + .1085\,EQ(16,T-1)$$
$$(565.0441)\ (662.3673) \qquad\qquad (382.6180) \qquad\qquad (.0049) \qquad\qquad (.0357)$$
$$+ .0088\,Q(28,T-1) + .0055\,Q(35,T-1)$$
$$(.0065) \qquad\qquad (.0040)$$

33 Paper Containers

No. Obsv. = 182   R-Square = .7478   R-Square (Level of Ouput) = .9975

$$\Delta QD(33,T) = -401.1727 - 415.6233\,TQ(33,T-1) + .0938\,Q(33,T-1)$$
$$(265.6896)\ (318.1762) \qquad\qquad (.0041)$$

34 Printing & Publishing

No. Obsv. = 998   R-Square = .9913   R-Square (Level of Output) = .9996

$$\Delta QD(34,T) = 372.8599 - 422.3030\,TI(32,T-1) - .0346\,VL(T-1) + .2699\,Q(34,T-1) + .2166\,EQ(18,T-1)$$
$$(295.5404)\ (255.2096) \qquad\qquad (.0271) \qquad\qquad (.0013) \qquad\qquad (.0443)$$

35 Basic Chemicals

No. Obsv. = 344   R-Square = .2357   R-Square (Level of Output) = .9938

$$\Delta QD(35,T) = 2750.5103 - 757.5576\,TI(49,T-1) + .0432\,Q(35,T-1)$$
$$(2075.2710)\ (608.2271) \qquad\qquad (.0043)$$

36 Plastics & Synthetics

No. Obsv. = 222   R-Square = .2717   R-Square (Level of Output) = .9932

$$\Delta QD(36,T) = 323.6674 + .0441\,Q(36,T-1) - .1713\,DEN(T-1) + .0053\,Q(40,T-1) + .0051\,Q(26,T-1)$$
$$(254.5717)\ (.0062) \qquad\qquad (.0940) \qquad\qquad (.0027) \qquad\qquad (.0034)$$

37 Drugs, Cleaning & Toilet Items

No. Obsv. = 139   R-Square = .0570   R-Square (Level of Output) = .9966

$$\Delta QD(37,T) = 3599.3320 - 1852.9264\,TI(40,T-1) + .0116\,Q(37,T-1)$$
$$(1213.9284)\ (1114.7733) \qquad\qquad (.0050)$$

75

38 Paint & Allied Products No. Obsv. = 207 R-Square = .2102 R-Square (Level of Output) = .9740

$\Delta QD(38,T) = -2866.7228 - 302.0263\ TQ(38,T-1) - 216.4786\ WR(38,T-1) - .0683\ VL(T-1) - .0940\ Q(38,T-1) + .0261\ Q(50,T-1)$
$\quad(3424.0838)\quad(258.5034)\qquad\qquad(125.6303)\qquad\qquad(.0463)\qquad(.0190)\qquad(.0128)$

39 Petroleum Refining No. Obsv. = 358 R-Square = .2300 R-Square (Level of Output) = .9885

$\Delta QD(39,T) = 25064.2170 - 217.9090\ TI(8,T-1) - 432.0826\ TI(35,T-1) + .0390\ Q(39,T-1) + .0703\ Q(35,T-1)$
$\quad(9869.3228)\ (105.0181)\qquad(280.1590)\qquad\qquad(.0066)\qquad(.0176)$

40 Rubber & Plastic Products No. Obsv. = 308 R-Square = .3772 R-Square (Level of Output) = .9967

$\Delta QD(40,T) = -430.8063 - 1022.3132\ TQ(40,T-1) + .0209\ Q(40,T-1) + .7232\ EQ(24,T-1) + .0005\ Q(69,T-1) + .0460\ Q(36,T-1)$
$\quad(481.8378)\quad(582.9665)\qquad\qquad(.0044)\qquad(.1727)\qquad(.0005)\qquad(.0121)$

41 Leather Tanning No. Obsv. = 122 R-Square = .1044 R-Square (Level of Output) = .9898

$\Delta QD(41,T) = 523.7533 - 78501.5850\ TQ(41,T-1) - 1184.0440\ TI(37,T-1) - 89.6860\ WR(41,T-1) + .0448\ DEN(T-1)$
$\quad(662.1741)\ (56263.0381)\qquad(980.6467)\qquad\qquad(66.8080)\qquad(.0208)$
$\quad + .0031\ Q(35,T-1)$
$\quad\ \ (.0026)$

42 Shoes & Other Leather Products No. Obsv. = 227 R-Square = .3312 R-Square (Level of Output) = .9965

$\Delta QD(42,T) = -180.1544 + .0166\ Q(42,T-1) + .9464\ EQ(26,T-1) + .0961\ DEN(T-1)$
$\quad(118.9141)\ (.0052)\qquad(.6272)\qquad(.0218)$

43 Glass & Glass Products No. Obsv. = 182 R-Square = .7206 R-Square (Level of Output) = .9928

$\Delta QD(43,T) = 544.6578 - 90.1950\ TI(35,T-1) - .1225\ Q(43,T-1) + .0008\ Q(69,T-1)$
$\quad(488.2223)\ (51.1826)\qquad(.0059)\qquad(.0003)$

44 Stone & Clay Products No. Obsv. = 688 R-Square = .1685 R-Square (Level of Output) = .9932

$\Delta QD(44,T) = 281.7298 - 41.8674\ TQ(44,T-1) - 926.4359\ TI(32,T-1) + .0272\ Q(44,T-1) + .0600\ EQ(28,T-1) + .0461\ DEN(T-1)$
$\quad(336.4479)\ (17.6319)\qquad(263.9026)\qquad\qquad(.0054)\qquad(.0568)\qquad(.0305)$
$\quad + .0142\ CN(18,T-1)$
$\quad\ \ (.0101)$

Table 5-2 (cont.)

---

45 Iron & Steel

No. Obsv. = 317   R-Square = .6366   R-Square (Level of Output) = .9972

$$\Delta QD(45,T) = 7672.4152 - 997.7335\ TI(52,T-1) + .0557\ Q(45,T-1) + .0101\ Q(69,T-1) + .0326\ Q(50,T-1)$$
(7589.4398) (988.1346)   (.0039)   (.0015)   (.0187)

46 Copper

No. Obsv. = 64   R-Square = .4237   R-Square (Level of Output) = .9876

$$\Delta QD(46,T) = -7896.3217 - 8023.4596\ TQ(46,T-1) - 3060.8782\ TI(48,T-1) + .0962\ Q(46,T-1) + 1.0833\ EQ(30,T-1)$$
(6500.6314) (3430.2836)   (1511.8788)   (.0195)   (.6149)

$$+ .0882\ Q(6,T-1)$$
(.0878)

47 Aluminum

No. Obsv. = 90   R-Square = .0483   R-Square (Level of Output) = .9811

$$\Delta QD(47,T) = 1268.1538 - 995.0485\ TQ(47,T-1) - 4660.5592\ TI(6,T-1)$$
(2408.5334) (843.0475)   (2361.1995)

48 Other Non-ferrous Metals

No. Obsv. = 94   R-Square = .8709   R-Square (Level of Output) = .9924

$$\Delta QD(48,T) = 4743.7563 - 1109.6452\ WR(48,T-1) + .2917\ Q(48,T-1) + .0054\ Q(45,T-1)$$
(3217.8399) (473.6342)   (.0147)   (.0049)

49 Metal Containers

No. Obsv. = 50   R-Square = .5127   R-Square (Level of Output) = .9962

$$\Delta QD(49,T) = 23.1236 - .1485\ VL(T-1) + .0209\ Q(49,T-1) + .0137\ Q(21,T-1) + .0126\ Q(37,T-1)$$
(878.3475) (.1317)   (.0176)   (.0073)   (.0068)

50 Heating, Plumbing, Struc Metal

No. Obsv. = 370   R-Square = .6376   R-Square (Level of Output) = .9953

$$\Delta QD(50,T) = 634.7874 - 169.7304\ TI(47,T-1) - .0395\ VL(T-1) + .0917\ Q(50,T-1) + .0246\ CN(4,T-1)$$
(729.4376) (140.7784)   (.0257)   (.0059)   (.0154)

51 Stampings, Screw Machine Prod.

No. Obsv. = 181   R-Square = .8004   R-Square (Level of Output) = .9942

$$\Delta QD(51,T) = 1809.7593 - 353.7261\ TI(45,T-1) - .0938\ VL(T-1) + .1818\ Q(51,T-1)$$
(1251.0985) (156.0674)   (.0841)   (.0069)

52 Hardware, Plating, Wire Prod.   No. Obsv. = 286   R-Square = .5872   R-Square (Level of Output) = .9963

$$\Delta QD(52,T) = -2242.4133 - 303.8758\ TQ(52,T-1) + .0187\ Q(52,T-1) - .1896\ VL(T-1) + .0555\ Q(48,T-1) + .0026\ Q(85,T-1)$$
$$(2007.2585)\ (278.8805) \qquad (.0070) \qquad\qquad (.0437) \qquad\quad (.0082) \qquad\quad (.0005)$$
$$+ .0049\ Q(35,T-1)$$
$$(.0042)$$

53 Engines & Turbines   No. Obsv. = 75   R-Square = .4331   R-Square (Level of Output) = .9953

$$\Delta QD(53,T) = 1818.5500 - 286.6666\ TI(57,T-1) + .0151\ Q(53,T-1) + 2.4833\ EQ(35,T-1)$$
$$(1661.3664)\ (265.9711) \qquad (.0104) \qquad\qquad (.5264)$$

54 Farm Machinery & Equipment   No. Obsv. = 158   R-Square = .7670   R-Square (Level of Output) = .9886

$$\Delta QD(54,T) = 674.5134 - 134.1770\ TI(45,T-1) + 13.4614\ EQ(36,T-1) - .5790\ DEN(T-1) + .3795\ EQ(1,T-1) + .3777\ EX(54,T-1)$$
$$(1394.5349)\ (120.9232) \qquad (.6721) \qquad\qquad (.4403) \qquad\quad (.1276) \qquad\quad (.0840)$$

55 Construction & Mining Machines   No. Obsv. = 142   R-Square = .0514   R-Square (Level of Output) = .9918

$$\Delta QD(55,T) = -50.0673 + .0127\ Q(55,T-1) + .0112\ Q(59,T-1)$$
$$(370.1478)\ (.0100) \qquad\quad (.0103)$$

56 Material Handling Equipment   No. Obsv. = 83   R-Square = .7906   R-Square (Level of Output) = .9937

$$\Delta QD(56,T) = 789.1194 - 114.1305\ TI(45,T-1) - .0861\ VL(T-1) + .1275\ Q(56,T-1) + .6059\ EQ(37,T-1) + .0172\ Q(63,T-1)$$
$$(870.3374)\ (88.5964) \qquad (.0458) \qquad\qquad (.0208) \qquad\quad (.3408) \qquad\quad (.0076)$$

57 Metalworking Machinery & Equip   No. Obsv. = 221   R-Square = .4454   R-Square (Level of Output) = .9911

$$\Delta QD(57,T) = 3672.8464 - 345.7907\ TI(45,T-1) + .0675\ DEN(T-1) + .1276\ EQ(29,T-1) + .9716\ EQ(30,T-1) + .0054\ Q(69,T-1)$$
$$(1278.5424)\ (157.5030) \qquad (.0746) \qquad\qquad (.0603) \qquad\quad (.1544) \qquad\quad (.0007)$$
$$+ .0035\ Q(70,T-1)$$
$$(.0026)$$

58 Special Industrial Machinery   No. Obsv. = 173   R-Square = .3010   R-Square (Level of Output) = .9912

$$\Delta QD(58,T) = 1662.2357 - 56.8099\ TI(45,T-1) + .5139\ EQ(39,T-1) + .0939\ DEN(T-1) + .0643\ EQ(16,T-1) + .1817\ EQ(18,T-1)$$
$$(537.3128)\ (53.1684) \qquad (.3816) \qquad\qquad (.0312) \qquad\quad (.0411) \qquad\quad (.0630)$$
$$+ .0183\ Q(59,T-1)$$
$$(.0061)$$

Table 5-2 (cont.)

59 General Industrial Machinery

No. Obsv. = 192   R-Square = .4963   R-Square (Level of Output) = .9898

ΔQD(59,T) = 4898.3300 − 684.7245 TI(52,T−1) + .0941 Q(59,T−1) + .1052 EQ(19,T−1) + .0383 EX(59,T−1) + .0165 Q(54,T−1)
(3642.3389) (468.3477)   (.0095)   (.0679)   (.0353)   (.0095)

60 Machine Shops & Misc Machinery

No. Obsv. = 269   R-Square = .7153   R-Square (Level of Output) = .9930

ΔQD(60,T) = 28.8761 − .0169 VL(T−1) + .1472 Q(60,T−1) + .0003 Q(69,T−1)
(119.3743) (.0154)   (.0065)   (.0002)

61 Office & Computing Machines

No. Obsv. = 129   R-Square = .3928   R-Square (Level of Output) = .9619

ΔQD(61,T) = 52597.8218 − 9159.1746 TI(67,T−1) + .1522 EQ(42,T−1) + .1003 EX(61,T−1)
(16440.5349) (3112.1087)   (.0193)   (.0836)

62 Service Industry Machines

No. Obsv. = 138   R-Square = .6505   R-Square (Level of Output) = .9881

ΔQD(62,T) = 529.6402 − 1281.9450 TI(63,T−1) + .1447 Q(62,T−1) + 2.1655 EQ(43.T−1)
(680.1920) (1041.2890)   (.0142)   (.8504)

63 Electric Apparatus & Motors

No. Obsv. = 149   R-Square = .6322   R-Square (Level of Output) = .9934

ΔQD(63,T) = −1565.5771 − 2681.6180 TQ(63,T−1) + .1126 Q(63,T−1)
(696.4089) (1283.9747)   (.0072)

64 Household Appliances

No. Obsv. = 102   R-Square = .6063   R-Square (Level of Output) = .9957

ΔQD(64,T) = 3684.4582 − 4198.3674 TI(63,T−1) − 361.9689 WR(64,T−1) − .2482 VL(T−1) − .0278 Q(64,T−1) + .6347 EQ(45,T−1)
(1913.2429) (2421.8760)   (219.9935)   (.0445)   (.0101)   (.4552)
+ .3194 PCE(64,T−1)
(.0286)

65 Electric Light & Wiring Equip.

No. Obsv. = 119   R-Square = .4215   R-Square (Level of Output) = .9969

ΔQD(65,T) = 628.8881 − 223.4520 TI(48,T−1) − .0796 VL(T−1) + .0202 Q(65,T−1) + .6338 EQ(46,T−1) + .2501 PCE(65,T−1)
(488.0151) (155.4782)   (.0196)   (.0093)   (.2023)   (.1317)

66 Communication Equipment   No. Obsv. = 131   R-Square = .9037   R-Square (Level of Output) = .9920

$$\Delta QD(66,T) = 19696.8169 - 87870.2607\ TI(30,T-1) - 1497.1761\ WR(66,T-1) - .6295\ VL(T-1) + .2996\ Q(66,T-1)$$
$$(5214.2513)\ (20650.6260)\qquad\qquad (551.9078)\qquad\qquad (.1894)\qquad\ (.0120)$$
$$+ .4380\ EQ(57,T-1)$$
$$(.1344)$$

67 Electronic Components   No. Obsv. = 153   R-Square = .8881   R-Square (Level of Output) = .9932

$$\Delta QD(67,T) = -95.2123 + .2176\ Q(67,T-1) + 1.0581\ EQ(48,T-1) + .0134\ Q(84,T-1) + .0183\ Q(13,T-1)$$
$$(485.9931)\ (.0150)\qquad (.2648)\qquad\qquad (.0058)\qquad\qquad (.0044)$$

68 Batteries & Engine Elec Equip.   No. Obsv. = 102   R-Square = .7408   R-Square (Level of Output) = .9906

$$\Delta QD(68,T) = 126.2384 - 1614.8325\ TQ(68,T-1) - 107.5711\ WR(68,T-1) + .1495\ Q(68,T-1) + 1.1533\ EQ(49,T-1) + .0028\ Q(45,T-1)$$
$$(817.9053)\ (1143.7901)\qquad (91.5482)\qquad\qquad (.0130)\qquad\qquad (.3357)\qquad\qquad (.0011)$$

69 Motor Vehicles   No. Obsv. = 249   R-Square = .4065   R-Square (Level of Output) = .9986

$$\Delta QD(69,T) = 9448.1775 - 1153.8984\ TI(45,T-1) - .0298\ Q(69,T-1)$$
$$(3730.9404)\ (418.1631)\qquad\qquad (.0023)$$

70 Aircraft & Parts   No. Obsv. = 168   R-Square = .9888   R-Square (Level of Output) = .9990

$$\Delta QD(70,T) = 6228.8604 - 5080.5855\ TI(66,T-1) - .6804\ VL(T-1) + .3000\ Q(70,T-1)$$
$$(4315.3273)\ (3192.9851)\qquad\qquad (.2771)\qquad (.0025)$$

71 Ships, Trains, Trailers, Cycles   No. Obsv. = 171   R-Square = .2500   R-Square (Level of Output) = .9962

$$\Delta QD(71,T) = 594.1846 - 651.5906\ EQ(71,T-1) - 255.4289\ TI(28,T-1) + .0235\ Q(71,T-1) + .1038\ DEN(T-1) + .0028\ Q(45,T-1)$$
$$(1581.6642)\ (548.6429)\qquad\qquad (154.6653)\qquad\qquad (.0055)\qquad (.0711)\qquad\qquad (.0014)$$

72 Instruments & Clocks   No. Obsv. = 104   R-Square = .8788   R-Square (Level of Output) = .9921

$$\Delta QD(72,T) = -1248.9830 - 5339.4827\ TQ(72,T-1) - .1969\ Q(72,T-1) + .0196\ Q(40,T-1)$$
$$(1017.7879)\ (5105.9899)\qquad\qquad (.0103)\qquad (.0090)$$

Table 5-2 (cont.)

73 Optical & Photographic Equip. No. Obsv. = 81 R-Square = .9943 R-Square (Level of Output) = .9998

$$\Delta QD(73,T) = 1023.4077 - 1247.2034\ TI(32,T-1) + .2247\ Q(73,T-1) + .0081\ Q(35,T-1)$$
$$(1082.4064)\quad (844.3855)\qquad\qquad (.0020)\qquad\qquad (.0031)$$

74 Misc. Manufactured Products No. Obsv. = 361 R-Square = .5604 R-Square (Level of Output) = .9984

$$\Delta QD(74,T) = -112.0406 - 1595.0599\ TQ(74,T-1) - 102.4078\ WR(74,T-1) - .2106\ VL(T-1) + .0328\ Q(74,T-1) + 1.3055\ EQ(55,T-1)$$
$$(425.4683)\quad (881.2377)\qquad\qquad (78.3023)\qquad\qquad (.0301)\qquad (.0046)\qquad (.2834)$$
$$+ .0123\ Q(36,T-1) + .0074\ Q(40,T-1) + .0077\ Q(48,T-1)$$
$$(.0048)\qquad\qquad (.0019)\qquad\qquad (.0043)$$

76 Communication No. Obsv. = 1814 R-Square = .7308 R-Square (Level of Output) = .9962

$$\Delta QD(76,T) = 19.9277 + .1044\ Q(76,T-1) + .1906\ DEN(T-1) + .0029\ Q(66,T-1)$$
$$(42.3914)\ (.0025)\qquad\qquad (.0435)\qquad\qquad (.0013)$$

77 Radio, TV Broadcasting No. Obsv. = 1088 R-Square = .8103 R-Square (Level of Output) = .9077

$$\Delta QD(77,T) = -158.9734 - .9022\ Q(77,T-1) + .7199\ DEN(T-1) + .0411\ Q(85,T-1)$$
$$(171.3748)\ (.0209)\qquad\qquad (.0791)\qquad\qquad (.0007)$$

78 Electric Utility No. Obsv. = 1577 R-Square = .6199 R-Square (Level of Output) = .9943

$$\Delta QD(78,T) = -174.3373 - .1074\ VL(T-1) + .0729\ Q(78,T-1) + .0066\ Q(39,T-1) + .0452\ Q(79,T-1)$$
$$(63.8483)\ (.0238)\qquad\qquad (.0042)\qquad\qquad (.0009)\qquad\qquad (.0055)$$

79 Gas Utility No. Obsv. = 735 R-Square = .7785 R-Square (Level of Output) = .9949

$$\Delta QD(79,T) = -204.1123 + .1538\ Q(79,T-1)$$
$$(78.0138)\ (.0030)$$

80 Water Utility No. Obsv. = 189 R-Square = .5319 R-Square (Level of Output) = .9975

$$\Delta QD(80,T) = -19.7177 - .0698\ Q(80,T-1) - .0989\ VL(T-1) + .0005\ PI(T-1) + .0033\ Q(35,T-1)$$
$$(95.2003)\ (.0053)\qquad\qquad (.0150)\qquad\qquad (.0001)\qquad\qquad (.0025)$$

82 Finance & Insurance   No. Obsv. = 2493   R-Square = .8032   R-Square (Level of Output) = .9993

ΔQD(82,T) = 743.5662 − 712.3968 TI(34,T−1) − 586.4663 TI(32,T−1) + .0565 Q(82,T−1)
(305.2897) (474.8608)   (321.1663)   (.0006)

83 Real Estate & Rental   No. Obsv. = 1510   R-Square = .4097   R-Square (Level of Output) = .9992

ΔQD(83,T) = 2024.7130 − .9868 VL(T−1) + .0294 Q(83,T−1)
(349.6044) (.1547)   (.0011)

84 Hotels, Personal & Repair Svc.   No. Obsv. = 1836   R-Square = .3632   R-Square (Level of Output) = .9987

ΔQD(84,T) = 2637.1312 − 427.2949 TI(67,T−1) − 690.1571 TI(74,T−1) − .2650 VL(T−1) + .0179 Q(84,T−1) + .0180 Q(67,T−1)
(750.9287) (134.4186)   (304.6869)   (.0172)   (.0017)   (.0030)
+ .0111 Q(37,T−1)
(.0015)

85 Business Services   No. Obsv. = 1072   R-Square = .9721   R-Square (Level of Output) = .9995

ΔQD(85,T) = 459.7303 − 4433.1010 TI(34,T−1) + .1425 Q(85,T−1) + .2225 DEN(T−1)
(530.3898) (1262.2669)   (.0011)   (.1207)

86 Automobile Repair Services   No. Obsv. = 1164   R-Square = .5108   R-Square (Level of Output) = .9976

ΔQD(86,T) = 27.1743 − .2177 VL(T−1) + .0566 Q(86,T−1) + .0138 Q(68,T−1)
(61.1911) (.0173)   (.0019)   (.0108)

87 Amusements & Recreation   No. Obsv. = 963   R-Square = 4942   R-Square (Level of Output) = .9986

ΔQD(87,T) = −56.0622 − .4190 VL(T−1) + .0231 Q(87,T−1) + .0773 Q(77,T−1)
(55.1693) (.0165)   (.0020)   (.0073)

88 Medical & Educational Instit.   No. Obsv. = 1849   R-Square = .1594   R-Square (Level of Output) = .9994

ΔQD(88,T) = 223.9908 − 9.5490 WR(88,T−1) + .0084 Q(88,T−1) + .1399 DEN(T−1)
(100.1946) (9.4867)   (.0008)   (.0378)

Statistical Procedures

A well-developed body of literature on the correct specification of the location equations does not exist. This is in contrast to the highly developed research in estimating production functions of the CES type. The regression equations presented in Table 5-2 are therefore a first major step in a process aimed at developing well-specified location equations. This specification search procedure has been termed by Theil as "regression strategy."[2] There are three parts to this operation. The first involves using data to search for the specification of an equation. The next task consists of using a second set of independent data to estimate the parameters of the specified model. The third step generates and tests the accuracy of predictions made from the estimated parameters, using another independent set of observations. This study is solely concerned with the first part of Theil's regression strategy. Thus considerable control was exercised in developing the equations. Our objective was not to maximize the explanatory power (R^2) of the equations, but to have a meaningful model with coefficients that would have reasonable economic interpretation corresponding to the theoretical specifications of the model developed in Chapter 2.

Theil suggests two basic methods to procede in specifying a model. The first consists of beginning with a critical set of variables in the initial regression. This set of variables is increased by introducing additional independent variables in order of decreasing theoretical importance in a step-wise regression program until a coefficient becomes insignificant and the iterative procedure stops. Theil defines this as "extending the set of explanatory variables."[3] The second method is to order all variables according to their theoretical importance and run a regression including all variables. Subsequent regressions are run reducing the number of independent variables, ordered by their theoretical importance, until the last retained variable is significant. Theil defines this as "reducing the set of explanatory variables."[4]

The procedure utilized in this study is a modification of the extension method. Variables were ordered according to our hypothesized theoretical importance with the maximum number of variables in any equation restricted to 18. Transportation variables were entered first, primarily because of their treatment in the literature, but also because of interest in testing their significance. These were followed by the cost and agglomeration variables as ordered in equation (5.1).

The least-squares regression routine was set up to preserve the theoretical order of variables entering the equation but was not terminated when a variable became insignificant.

As with most if not all econometric models there is some degree of linear dependence among the independent variables. If this multicollinearity is severe, there can be drastic effects on the values of the coefficients in the model. It can increase the standard errors of the coefficients, it can be the cause of a wrong sign on a coefficient, and it can affect the value of individual coefficients. Any degree of multicollinearity can have some effect on the results. In a step-wise regression the coefficient on the fourth variable, for example, may be insignificant, but the fifth one may be significant even though the fifth variable has less theoretical importance.

Thus in order for a variable to be retained in our procedure, it had to pass two tests in addition to the standard t test of statistical significance. The sign on the coefficient had to have the postulated theoretical sign and the variable itself must not have severe multicollinearity with other variables in the equation.

The routine also reexamines variables that had been rejected. Suppose the first two variables have entered the equation and the third one is rejected either because the coefficient was not significant or had the wrong sign. Now suppose the fourth variable enters the program. Then before examining the fifth variable, the third one would be reexamined to see if it now passes all the tests. If the third variable had been rejected because of multicollinearity with preceding independent variables, then it would not be reexamined again since the multicollinearity cannot be reduced by the addition of another variable. If a new variable to be entered causes a previously entered variable to become insignificant or violate its sign restriction, then the new variable is dropped since the variable already in the equation is preferred.

The dropping of multicollinear variables from an equation has been called the historical rule-of-thumb approach by Ferrar and Glauber.[5] Our decision rule stated that variables were rejected if the coefficient of determination (R^2) of the independent variable to be entered with those independent variables already in the equation exceeds 0.70. This rule should eliminate drastic effects on the coefficients from severe multicollinearity, but it would not eliminate all effects. Remaining multicollinearity still would cause an entering variable to affect the significance and sign of its coefficient or other coefficients in the equation. The decision rule for the test of significance was that the t ratio had to be greater than 1; i.e., the standard error could not exceed the coefficient.

In addition to specifying the order of the entering variables, the theory developed in Chapter 2 provided us with *a priori* knowledge of the proper signs on most of the variables. The expected sign on b_1 through b_7, the cost variables, is negative, while the expected sign on b_9 and the agglomeration variables b_{11} through b_{18} is positive. Output and population density were unrestricted in sign. When a variable produced a coefficient with an incorrect sign, we followed one procedure suggested by Christ[6] and dropped the variable from the equation.

These decision rules were designed to ease our burden in estimating the equations. The order procedure, however, reduced the efficiency of the estimates in a few equations. This occurred when a variable was accepted with a low t ratio, and many of the subsequent variables were prevented from entering the equation because the initial variable became insignificant. Given an economic justification, the order rule was violated when this occurred in order to improve the explanatory power of the equation.

The number of observations in each equation is fewer than the number (3,112) of counties. In all equations, counties were eliminated as observations if the level of output less sales to defense were zero. For some industries characterized by large-sized plants, the number of counties with production was fewer than 100. In addition, observations were eliminated in some industries because of two data problems. Because of the computer limitations the transportation variables were computed directly only for those counties that had large excess of supply or demand, and counties not in this set were assigned values of the transportation variables of the closest counties that had direct estimates. In industries where this was a severe problem, the set of observations was limited to the set that had direct estimates of the output transportation variables (TQ). The other data problem had to do with estimating missing data not reported by the Bureau of Census because of disclosure rules. After our data had been estimated, errors in the County Business Patterns data were found; and because of these errors, our matrix-balancing procedure to estimate undisclosed data (described in Appendix A) created some unrealistic extreme estimates of employment (and thus output) in small counties. Therefore counties with these extreme estimates for particular industries were eliminated as observations.

Although the dependent variable in the equation is the change in output, the objective in many applications of the model would be to explain the location of output levels; therefore, we computed the coefficients of determination, measuring how well the regional variation in output is explained by the independent variables in the regression equation. The results also presented in Table 5-2 are computed as follows:

$$(5.2) \qquad R^2(QD) = 1 - \frac{\sum_{i=1}^{n} (QD_i^t - \hat{QD}_i^t)^2 \cdot (n-1)}{\sum_{i=1}^{n} (QD_i^t - \overline{QD}^t)^2 \cdot (n-k)}$$

where $\hat{QD}_i^t = QD_i^{t-1} + \Delta\hat{QD}_i$

$\Delta\hat{QD}_i$ = predicted change in output using Equation (5.1),

$\overline{QD}^t$ = mean level of output less sales to defense in year t,

n = number of observations,

k = number of variables in (5.1).

Results by Variable

The results as given in Table 5-2 are presented in summary form in Table 5-3. The symbols + or − in the table indicate the signs on the coefficients. The signs

Table 5-3
Summary of Results by Industry

Industry	TQ	TI	WR	VL	Q[a]	EQ	DEN	MB	MS
1 Livestock	2,17		−	−	+	+		Q_{15}	
2 Crops		35		−	+				
3 Forestry and Fishery Products			−	+	+				Q_{25}
4 Agricultural Services		52	−	−	+	+		Q_1,Q_3	Q_{17}
5 Iron Ore Mining		55		−	+				Q_{55}
6 Nonferrous Ore Mining					+				
7 Coal Mining			−	−	+	+		Q_{78}	Q_{55}
8 Petroleum Mining	−	35			+	+			
9 Minerals Mining		55			+			Q_{12}	
10 Chemical Mining		35			+				Q_{55}
13 Ordnance		67	−	−	−			GOV_3	Q_{70}
14 Meat Packing			−	−	+			Q_{85}	Q_{40}
15 Dairy Products	−		−	−	−	+			Q_1
16 Canned and Frozen Foods		43			−				Q_2
17 Grain Mill Products	−	2	−	+					
18 Bakery Products		17		+					Q_{32}
19 Sugar	−		−	+	+				
20 Candy		19		+					
21 Beverages	−		−	−	+				
22 Misc. Food Products	2,49, 17		−	−	−			PCE_{22}, EX_{22}	
23 Tobacco	−	33	−	−					
24 Fabrics and Yarn		35	−	+					
25 Rugs, Tire Cord, Misc. Textiles		36,1		+		+		Q_{24}	
26 Apparel		74						PCE_{26}	Q_{24},Q_{36},Q_{27}
27 Household Textiles and Upholstery		24	−	−		+		PCE_{27}	Q_{24}
28 Lumber and Products, Excluding Containers				−					
29 Wooden Containers				+	+				
30 Household Furniture		52	−	+					
31 Office Furniture		45,28	−	+	+				Q_{45}
32 Paper and Products, Excluding Containers	−	33		+	+				Q_{28},Q_{35}
33 Paper Containers	−			+					
34 Printing and Publishing		32	−	+	+				
35 Basic Chemicals		49		+					
36 Plastics and Synthetics				+			−	Q_{40},Q_{26}	
37 Drugs, Cleaning, and Toilet Items		40		+					
38 Paint and Allied Products	−		−	−	−			Q_{50}	

Table 5-3 (cont.)

Industry	TQ	TI	WR	VL	Q^a	EQ	DEN	MB	MS
39 Petroleum Refining		8,35			+				Q_{35}
40 Rubber and Plastic Products	–			+	+			Q_{69}	Q_{36}
41 Leather Tanning	–	37	–			+			Q_{35}
42 Shoes and Other Leather Products				+	+	+			
43 Glass and Glass Products		35		–				Q_{69}	
44 Stone and Clay Products	–	32		+	+	+		CN_{18}	
45 Iron and Steel		52		+				Q_{69},Q_{50}	
46 Copper	–	48		+	+				Q_6
47 Aluminum	–	6							
48 Other Nonferrous Metals				+				Q_{45}	
49 Metal Containers			–	+				Q_{21},Q_{37}	
50 Heating, Plumbing, Structural Metal		47	–	+				CN_4	
51 Stampings, Screw Machinery Products		45	–	+					
52 Hardware, Plating, Wire Products	–		–	+					Q_{48},Q_{85}
53 Engines and Turbines		57		+	+				
54 Farm Machinery and Equipment		45			+	–		EQ_1,EX_{54}	
55 Construction and Mining Machinery					+				Q_{59}
56 Material Handling Equipment		45	–	+	+				Q_{63}
57 Metal-working Machinery and Equipment		45				+		$EQ_{29},$ $EQ_{30},$ Q_{69}	
58 Special Industrial Machinery		45			+	+		$EQ_{16},$ EQ_{18}	Q_{59}
59 General Industrial Machinery		52		+				$EQ_{19},$ $EX_{59},$ Q_{54}	
60 Machine Shops and Misc. Machinery			–	+				Q_{69}	
61 Office and Computing Machines		67			+			EX_{61}	
62 Service Industry Machines		63		+	+				
63 Electric Apparatus and Motors	–			+					
64 Household Appliances		63	–	–	–	+		PCE_{64}	
65 Electric Light and Wiring Equipment		48	–	+	+			PCE_{65}	
66 Communication Equipment		30	–	–	+	+			
67 Electronic Components				+	+			Q_{84},Q_{13}	
68 Batteries and Engine Electrical Equipment	–		–	+	+				Q_{45}

Table 5-3 (cont.)

Industry	TQ	TI	WR	VL	Q^a	EQ	DEN	MB	MS
69 Motor Vehicles		45	−						
70 Aircraft and Parts		66	−	+					
71 Ships, Trains, Trailers, Cycles	−	28	+	+					Q_{45}
72 Instruments and Clocks	−			−					Q_{40}
73 Optical and Photographic Equipment		32	+						Q_{35}
74 Misc. Manufactured Products	−		−	−	+	+		Q_{36}	
76 Communication			+			+			Q_{66}
77 Radio, TV Broadcasting			−			+		Q_{85}	
78 Electric Utility			−	+					Q_{39},Q_{79}
79 Gas Utility			+						
80 Water Utility			−	−			PI		Q_{35}
82 Finance and Insurance		34,32	+						
83 Real Estate and Rental			−	+					
84 Hotels, Personal and Repair Services		67,74	−	+					Q_{67},Q_{37}
85 Business Services		34	+			+			
86 Automobile Repair Services			−	+					Q_{68}
87 Amusements and Recreation			−	+					
88 Medical and Educational Instit.	−		+	+					

[a]Employment was substituted for output in industry 23 (see Chapter 6).

on Q and DEN could be either + or −, whereas the signs on TI, TQ, WR, and VL were restricted to −, and the signs on EQ, MB, and MS were restricted to +. The numbers in the TI columns refer to the industry numbers of the input transportation costs. The major buyers and suppliers are identified by symbols with industry subscripts in the MB and MS columns.

The Transportation Variables. The transportation variables were given top preference in the equation because of their prominence in location theory and our concern in testing the importance of transport costs in location decisions. The transportation variables are the marginal cost of transporting an additional dollar's worth of output either into or out of a county. The coefficients, as given in Table 5-2, show the change in output (in thousands) for each one-cent change in the transportation rate. For example, if the transport rate of shipping the marginal dollar's worth of Paper and Products, excluding containers (IO 32) out of a county were to increase 1 cent, then the change in industry's output of that county would decrease by $1,149,000. Continuing with the paper industry example, if the transport cost of shipping the marginal dollar's worth of paper containers (IO 33) into a county were to increase by 1 cent, then the change in output of IO 32 would decrease by $1,028,000 in the county. The coefficients for the other industries are similarly interpreted. The coefficients may appear large, but this is because a 1-cent increase in the transport cost is a large percentage increase. When evaluated at the means, a 1 percent increase in TQ_{32} is related to a .71 percent decrease in $\triangle QD_{32}$. A 1 percent increase in TI_{33} is related to a .70 decrease in $\triangle QD_{32}$. The elasticities may be higher in other industries; for example, there is a 3.8 percent decrease in $\triangle QD_{46}$ for each 1 percent increase in TQ_{46} when evaluated at the means.

It was hypothesized that the change in location of each industry producing transportable products would be inversely related both to the marginal cost of transporting these products (output shadow price) to their markets and to the marginal cost of transporting the inputs (input shadow price) from their points of production.

The output shadow price entered the equations in 20 of the 71 commodity industries. The transport shadow prices for acquiring inputs entered more industry equations than did the output shadow price. From one to four input shadow prices were entered in the attempt to explain change in output in each of 83 industries. At least one supply shadow price entered in 51 industry equations, and two prices were significant in five equations and three in one equation. The shadow prices from Basic Chemical industry (IO 35) and the Iron and Steel industry (IO 45) had the greatest influence in explaining the location of other industries; the iron and steel prices were significant in the equations for seven industries, and the chemical prices were significant in six equations.

The Wage Rate. Annual earnings per worker was significant in explaining change in output in 16 of the 84 industries. Wages are usually credited for the mass movement of the textiles to the South in the post-war period; however, in the 1965-1966 period, changes in output responded to wages only in the Household Textile industry (IO 27). In the equations of the other three textile industries (IO 24-26), the wage rate was not significant. Evidently by this time the movement of the textile industries to low wage areas had already largely been completed.

The wage rate variable is entered as thousands of dollars per employee; therefore the coefficient shows the dollar change in the change of output for every one dollar change in the wage rate. For example, for every one dollar increase in annual earnings per worker, the decrease in the change in output in the Household Appliance industry (IO 64) is $363.

The Value of Land. Land value per acre was significant in explaining output change in 30 industries. Other costs may be more important to most industries since land often is viewed as investment that is likely to appreciate in value. It is interesting to note, however, that many industries usually classified as performing central city functions responded to lower land values. Examples are Hotels and Personal Services (IO 84), Automotive Repair Services (IO 86), and

Amusements (IO 87). The land value variable was significant in 21 of the 62 manufacturing industries. The land value variable is entered as dollars per acre; therefore the coefficient expresses thousands of dollars. For example, in the Metal Containers industry (IO 49), a dollar increase in land value per acre is associated with a $148.50 decrease in the change in output.

Capital Costs. Another important cost to consider in explaining industry location is capital costs. With everything else held constant, a firm may seek locations where the cost of additional units of capacity are the lowest, taking into account both construction and financial charges. But perhaps more important for our purposes, the regional change in output may be largely influenced by the location of existing capital.

We would expect a positive sign on the coefficient of the gross investment variable, and a negative sign on the coefficient of the level of output variable if output were just a proxy for depreciation. However, the level of output may also be an indication of agglomeration economies; and if so, a positive sign would be expected. If there are agglomeration diseconomies in the industry, or there is substantial competition among firms in the industry, a negative sign would be expected. Thus, the sign associated with the level of output was allowed to be either positive or negative in the regression equation. The sign on the investment coefficient was controlled to be positive.

Output was significant in 76 of the 83 equations.[a] Its coefficient has a positive sign in 57 cases and a negative sign in 19 cases.

Gross equipment investment entered into 30 of the 84 industry equations and as to be expected, these 30 equations were concentrated in capital intensive industries. The equipment variable is recorded in thousands of dollars, the same as change in output; therefore the coefficient shows the change in the change in output for every dollar change in investment. For example, for every increase of one dollar of equipment investment by equipment purchasing sector No. 36 (Farm Machinery and Equipment), the increase in the change in output of the Farm Machinery and Equipment industry (IO 54) is $13.46.

Agglomeration Variables. The remaining variables in the equation are agglomeration variables. The first agglomeration variable, population density, is a proxy for congestion. Some industries are attracted to densely populated areas [such as Business Services (IO 85) and Medical and Educational Institutions] ; others are repulsed. The sign on this variable was unrestricted, since some industries can have an affinity for sparsely populated areas. Negative signs could also occur because zoning officials in populated areas could have a distaste for particular industries. The only two industries with negative signs were Plastics and Synthetics (IO 36) and Farm Machinery and Equipment (IO 54). There were 15

---

[a]Employment was used in place of output in Tobacco (IO 23) for reasons explained in Chapter 6.

positive coefficients. The reason the negative sign did not appear more frequently is that population density is very highly correlated with the value of land; therfore if the value of land is in an equation, population density is rejected because of multicollinearity.

The remaining agglomeration variables try to measure the advantages (external economies) of firms from being located in proximity to their major buyers and suppliers.

The possible external economies (or diseconomies) of being located near other firms in the same industry is already measured in the equation with the level of output variable. Firms can often achieve economies, by locating near their major buyers and suppliers, that are not reflected in the transport costs or prices of the principle inputs. In addition to direct reduction in costs proximity often reduces personal travel time and other communication inconveniences and allows more frequent face-to-face contact with buyers and suppliers. It reduces the uncertainty that is often associated with distance.

For each industry's equation, variables representing up to four major buyers and four major suppliers were entered. The buyers were given preference over the suppliers since the transport costs of obtaining the supplies from each individual supplier have already been entered in the equation.

The location of 32 of the industries was influenced by at least one major buying sector. Eight of these industries were influenced by two buying sectors, and two were related to three buying sectors. Personal consumption expenditures directly influenced the location of five industries. Foreign exports influenced four industries, and six equipment purchasing sectors influenced four industries.

The location of 32 industries was also influenced by at least one major supplying sector. Five of these industries were influenced by two supplying sectors, and one was influenced by three supplying sectors. For any given equation the individual major buying and supplying sectors may be highly correlated with each other and with the level of output of the industry in question; therefore once one of these variables enters an equation, the others are likely to be multicollinear or insignificant.

Interindustry Locational Relationships

Table 5-4 summarizes the interindustry location relationships that are revealed by the equations. The industries named at the left of the table influenced the location of the industries number in the columns. The influence of an industry is classified three ways: (1) through the transportation costs of supplying goods to be used as inputs, (2) as a major buyer of intermediate or capital goods, and (3) as a major supplier of goods. The following examples will help in reading the table: (1) The Petroleum Mining industry (IO 8) influenced the changes in

Table 5-4
Summary of Interindustry Relationships[a]

Industry	Through Input Transport Costs	As Major Buyers	As Major Suppliers
1 Livestock	25	4,54[b]	15
2 Crops	1,17,22		16
3 Forestry and Fishery Products		4	
6 Nonferrous Ore Mining	47		46
8 Petroleum Mining	39		
13 Ordnance		67	
15 Dairy Products		1	
17 Grain Mill Products	1,18,22		4
19 Sugar	20		
21 Beverages		49	
24 Fabrics and Yarn	27	25	26,27
25 Rugs, Tire Cord, Misc. Textiles			3
26 Apparel		36	
27 Household Textiles and Upholstery			26
28 Lumber and Products, Excluding Containers	31,71		32
30 Household Furniture	66		
32 Paper and Products, Excluding Containers	34,44,73,82	58[b]	18
33 Paper Containers	23,32		
34 Printing and Publishing	82,85	58[b]	
35 Basic Chemicals	2,8,10,24,39,43	59[b]	32,39,41,73,80
36 Plastics and Synthetics	25	74	26,40
37 Drugs, Cleaning, and Toilet Items	41	49	84
39 Petroleum Refining			78
40 Rubber and Plastic Products	37	36	14,72,74
43 Glass and Glass Products	16		
45 Iron and Steel	31,51,54,56,57,48,57[b] 58,59		31,68,71
47 Aluminum	50		
48 Other Nonferrous Metals	46,65	57[b]	52,74
49 Metal Containers	22,35		
50 Heating, Plumbing, Structural Metal Products		38,45	
52 Hardware, Plating, Wire Products	4,30,45,59		
54 Farm Machinery and Equipment		59	
55 Construction and Mining Machinery	5,9		5,7,10
57 Metal-working Machinery and Equipment	53		

Table 5-4 (cont.)

Industry	Through Input Transport Costs	As Major Buyers	As Major Suppliers
59 General Industrial Machinery			55,58
63 Electric Apparatus and Motors	62,64		56
66 Communication Equipment	70		76
67 Electronic Components	13,61,84		84
68 Batteries and Engine Electrical Equipment			86
69 Motor Vehicles		40,43,45,57,60	
70 Aircraft and Parts			13
74 Misc. Manufactured Products	26,84		
77 Radio, TV Broadcasting		87	
78 Electric Utility		7	
79 Gas Utility			78
84 Hotels, Personal and Repair Services		67	
85 Business Services		14,77	52

[a]The industries named on the left influenced the changes in location of the industries numbered in the columns.

[b]Indicates influence through the purchase of capital equipment.

location of the Petroleum Refining (IO 39) because of the high transport cost of shipping petroleum from the mine to the refinery; (2) the Metal Containers industry (IO 49) finds it advantageous to locate its changes in output near the Beverages industry (IO 21) since the Beverages industry is a major buyer of metal cans; (3) the Special Industrial Machinery industry, (IO 58) locates its changes in output near the Printing and Publishing industry (IO 34) because IO 34 is a major buyer of capital equipment produced by IO 58; and (4) the Copper industry (IO 46) finds it advantageous to locate its changes in output near the Nonferrous Ore Mining industry (IO 6) because IO 6 is a major supplier of its inputs.

The two industries having the most influences on change in output in other industries are the Basic Chemical industry (IO 35) and the Iron and Steel industry (IO 45). IO 35 influenced the location of 11 other industries, six through transport costs, one as major buyer and five because of the agglomeration effects of being a major supplier. IO 45 influenced the location of 10 other industries. Note that the Iron and Steel industry influenced the Metalworking Machinery and Equipment industry (IO 57) both because of shipping the steel used to produce the machines and because the Iron and Steel industry is a major buyer of the machines. Other important influencing industries are Agriculture, Paper, Rubber and Plastics, and Other Nonferrous Metals.

Future Research

The results of this study are very encouraging. The model explains a sizeable proportion of the regional variance in the change in output for most industries, and all the explanatory variables play some part, although not in all industries. The importance of the transportation variables was particularly encouraging. Of the 84 industries for which equations were estimated at least one transportation variable was significant in 61 of them.

Primary emphasis on future work should be one obtaining more and better data. We used data for two years whereas data over many years would be more appropriate in explaining location. Having data for additional years would allow the unusual year-to-year fluctuations to be averaged out and would enable a proper lag structure among the variables to be specified. The planning and construction period associated with relocation is long in some industries; therefore decisions on regional output levels in the current year could have been used on data of several years ago. Preparing the data for use in this study was a costly endeavor; yet with more resources better estimates could have been made.

Additional measures of input costs would be helpful, especially for capital. Construction costs per unit of capacity probably has some effect on location. Direct measures of capital stock along with characteristics of the capital stock such as age or vintage would be useful. Location in some industries may also be influenced by governmental action other than direct purchases, such as the tax structure and quality of public services.

The industrial location model has been designed to be the cornerstone of larger regional forecasting model.[b] Industrial activity is the most important primary income generator in regional economies; therefore before adequate regional projections can be made, a basic understanding of industrial location is essential. The regional forecasting model has the following recursive procedure:

1. Forecast regional output by industry using the industry location model.
2. Forecast regional employment and earnings by industry by relating them to the output forecasts and adjust totals for commuting in order to convert the regional figures from an establishment basis to a residential basis.
3. Forecast regional population using population migration equations, which are related to employment changes, and birth and death rates.
4. Forecast regional labor force based on the population estimates.
5. Forecast regional personal income by adding to earnings estimates of property income and transfer payments, which are related to population and unemployment.

[b]Such a model has been described by the senior author. See "A Multi-regional, Multi-industry Forecasting Model," *Papers of the Regional Science Association*, vol. 25 (1970). An application of the model will be reported in a forthcoming book.

6. Forecast regional personal consumption expenditures by industry sector by relating consumption to income.
7. Forecast or update other components of demand—capital expenditures, exports, governmental expenditures, and intermediate demand.
8. Recompute variables needed in location equations and repeat the steps.

6 Locational Analysis by Industry

This chapter examines each individual industry in detail. The input-output classified industries are grouped into 14 major categories that reflect interindustry dependences or common production or marketing characteristics within the group. These major groupings are discussed in the first section of the chapter. The 14 sections of the chapter that follow discuss the individual industries organized by major groups.

Major Industrial Groups

This section is divided into two parts. The first part presents the industry classification by major group. The second part presents the format that will be used in the other sections to analyze the location equations of the industries organized by major groups.

Group Definition

The goal of classifying industries by major groups was to identify basic industrial processes starting with raw material production and continuing through primary processing and fabrication. However, because of the aggregation in the basic input-output (IO) classification scheme, we were not able to proceed completely in this fashion. In particular, the agricultural industries, which produce raw materials for textiles, meat packing, bakery, canned and frozen foods, leather goods, etc., have a highly aggregative definition. Agriculture is composed of two industries: Livestock (IO-1) and Crops (IO-2). IO-3 also is combination of heterogeneous production processes: Forestry and Fishery Products. The first three IO sectors, however, do share the common characteristics of producing Biotic Raw Materials which is the name given to the first major industry group. Agricultural Services (IO-4) are also included in the first group. The industries associated with each group are given in Table 6-1.

The second group, Food Processing, contains those industries that convert or modify Biotic Raw Materials to produts marketed in retail food stores. The Tobacco Processing industry was placed in a separate group because of the regional specialization of the industry and its uncertain future because of the harmful effects of cigarette smoking. The fourth major group, Textiles and

95

Table 6-1
Major Industry Groups

Group Number	Group Title	IO Sectors[a]
1	Biotic Raw Materials	1, 2, 3, 4
2	Food Processing	14, 15, 16, 17, 18, 19, 20, 21, 22
3	Tobacco	23
4	Textiles and Textile Products	24, 25, 26, 27
5	Lumber and Lumber Products	28, 29, 30, 31, 32, 33, 34
6	Chemicals and Petroleum	8, 10, 35, 36, 37, 38, 39, 40
7	Leather and Footwear	41, 42
8	Minerals Mining and Processing	9, 43, 44
9	Metal Mining, Smelting, and Basic Products	5, 6, 45, 46, 47, 48, 49, 50, 51, 52
10	Heavy Machinery, Including Transportation Equipment	13, 53, 54, 55, 56, 57, 58, 59, 60, 69, 70, 71
11	Electric and Electronic Products	61, 62, 63, 64, 65, 66, 67, 68
12	Precision Manufacturing	72, 73, 74
13	Regulated Utilities	7, 76, 77, 78, 79, 80
14	Services	82, 83, 84, 85, 86, 87, 88

[a]See Table 1-1 for a definition of the industries.

Textile Products, consists of the industrial processes of transforming raw materials, either chemical or biotic, into yarn or tire cord and further conversion into cloth, apparel, etc. Lumber and Lumber Products, the fifth group, encompasses the process of converting raw forest products into finished lumber and lumber products including furniture, ·containers, wood pulp, paper, and books. The Chemical and Petroleum group consists of the petroleum and chemical mining industries and the industries that process the raw materials into finished products. The petroleum industry through the development of its petrochemical industrial complexes is continually increasing its chemical potential.

Leather and Footwear are classified together in the seventh since leather is the primary raw material for footwear. The Minerals Mining and Processing group includes sand, clay, and gravel mining and the glass, stone, and clay processing industries. The Basic Metal Mining, Smelting, and Basic Products group includes the mining and processing activities of the Iron and Steel, Copper, Aluminum and other Nonferrous metal industries. The major purchasers of the basic metals have been classified into three groups: Heavy Machinery, including Transportation Equipment, Electric and Electronic Products, and Precision Manufacturing.

The last two groups are Regulated Utilities and Services. The Regulated Utility group includes industries diverse in nature, but with the common characteristic of operation under public regulation: Communication, Radio and TV Broadcasting, Electric Utility, Gas Utility, and Water Utility. Coal Mining was also included in this group since its major market is the Electric Utility industry. The last major group Services consists of the service industries orientated to both consumer and industry. While the services that this group of industries provides are diverse in nature, they have the common characteristics of a highly labor-intensive productive process.

The Industrial groupings listed in Table 6-1 do not exhaust the 99 industries that are listed in Table 1-1. The missing industries include: New Construction (IO 11), Maintenance Construction (IO 12), Transportation (IO 75), Wholesale Trade (IO 81), and the 11 retail trade sectors (IO 89-99). Construction is located by building site and should be explained by investigating the determinates of construction expenditures, rather than using the location equations of the nature developed in this book. The location equations also did not seem appropriate for explaining the output in the transportation and trade sectors. The location of these sectors should be calculated by apportioning the respective markup margins of these services to the local levels.

Format of the Remaining Sections

The format of the remaining sections of this chapter has been designed to accomplish two goals. Its most basic aim is to provide a structure in which the location equations can be efficiently analyzed at the industry level. The second goal is to provide a qualitative analysis of the national and regional characteristics of each industry. It is hoped that this descriptive discussion will enable other investigators to build and improve upon what we have developed in this study.

Part of the analysis of each group will be devoted to examining the national characteristics of each industry. National information is useful in understanding factors motivating the spatial readjustment of industry. Major buyers and suppliers of each industry are identified utilizing a 1966 input-output table. The lists are given as each industry is discussed. The major buyers list shows the sectors used to represent the agglomeration effects of locating near markets. The major suppliers list serves two purposes. The commodity producing sectors in the list are those for which input transportation variables were computed and used in the equations. There are no more than four such sectors. The sectors used to measure agglomeration effects could be either the commodity producing sectors or the service sectors. There are some major supplying sectors that were not used in the equations because it was hypothesized that they would not have any effect on location. These are Maintenance Construction (IO 12), Transportation (IO 75), Wholesale Trade (IO 81), Retail Trade (IO 88-99), Finance and Insurance (IO 82), and Real Estate and Rental (IO 83). The number of major supplying sectors used as variables in the equations was limited to four. Those are the top four in the list not counting those just named.

Another part of the analysis examines the regional properties of each industry. An important empirical question is the determination of the degree of the locational mobility of an industry. What is the dividing line between a mobile and a stationary industry? The measure that will be used to measure mobility is the shift ratio.[1] This statistic is calculated by (1) summing the negative or positive differences in a region's actual growth from the growth that would have occurred if the output in the region grew at the national rate and (2) dividing the positive or negative number by the total output of the industry. A shift ratio of zero indicates that output in all regions grew by the same amount. The extent to which an industry is being spatially redistributed can be measured by the absolute value of the shift ratio. Thus a value of one indicates that output in the current period is being produced in regions that in the initial period had zero output and that all regions with output in the initial period have ceased production. Thus, a stationary industry has a low shift ratio, while a mobile industry has a high shift ratio.

The coefficient of localization will be computed in order to determine the extent of the regional concentration of an industry. This coefficient is calculated by (1) subtracting for each county its share of national industry output from its share of some selected basic statistic and (2) adding all positive or negative differences.[2] If this ratio approaches one, its maximum value, then the industry is highly concentrated in one or more counties out of the total of 3,112, relative to the spatial distribution of the basic statistic at the county level. Similarly, as the coefficient approaches zero, the county distribution of the output of the industry becomes identical with the county distribution of the basic statistic. Thus if the basic statistic is spatially diffuse, the coefficient of localization is an excellent measure of the relative spatial concentration of an industry. Coefficients were calculated with industry output relative to two basic statistics: personal income and the industry's total demand.[a] Personal income is used to represent the location of people, and the coefficients of localization relative to personal income measured the degree of an industry's orientation to consumer markets. The coefficients computed using an industry's total demand measure the industry's orientation to all its markets.

These measures do not reveal causal relationships. A coefficient of localization may show that Industry A, for example, is located near its major buyer Industry B, but the reason may be that B is supply oriented rather than A being market oriented. The coefficients of localization do not indicate the areas of regional concentration; therefore the important geographic concentrations of each industry at the state level will be listed.

[a]Both output and demand have been adjusted by subtracting out sales to the defense expenditures sector.

The location equations will be interpreted following the discussion of the regional characteristics of the industry. The analysis will discuss not only variables that had high significance levels in the equations but also those variables that failed the significance tests.

Two coefficients of determination (R^2) are given for each industry. The first measures how well the equation explains the regional variation in the change in output, and the second measures how well the regional variation in the level of output is explained with the change-in-output equation. The R^2's are *not* from two different equations.

The remaining sections of this chapter are extensive. The reader is advised to turn to the industries of greatest interest rather than attempt to sequentially wade through every page of the chapter.

Group 1: Biotic Raw Materials

These industries are natural resource industries, directly involved with the land, forest, and ocean. They are basic to human existence and are found in some form even among the most primitive peoples. Food travels great distances in the world economy, and the United States is one of the most important producers of food in the world. Because this industry is basic, old and important, it has been the focus of a long accumulation of public policy whose effects on the industry are extremely difficult to assess. In recent decades, employment in agriculture has declined steadily. Employment in fisheries has also declined rapidly, leveling off in recent years. Forestry, a small industry indeed when government employees are not counted, has grown somewhat, mainly in the area of timber management to be used for nonfood manufacture. Tremendous technological advances, reorganization of the industries from a managerial standpoint, and a reduction of underemployment have played important roles in the declines in agriculture and fisheries. Output in agriculture, although not growing at the national average, has increased despite the declines in employment. It is to be expected that output in both agriculture and fisheries will increase in the future as well.

Livestock and crops dominate this group, accounting for over 94 percent of output in 1965, as Table 6-2 listing the national statistics for the group illustrates. While forestry and fishing products and agricultural services are small in relation to livestock and crops, Table 6-2 shows that their growth in employment in 1966 was positive, while the two larger industries rates were negative. Except for fishing and forest products, the industries of the group are heavily dependent upon each other locationally. The output of crops is used as an input (feed) in the livestock industry, and agricultural services often take place near the site of agricultural activity.

The coefficients of localization show that all the industries in the group are

Table 6-2
Summary Statistics, Group 1: Biotic Raw Materials

Industry	Output 1966 Prices (000,000) 1965	1966	Employment (000) 1965	1966	Coefficient of Localization 1966 Output with Personal Income	Industry Demand	Output Shift Ratio 1965-1966
1 Livestock	29,869	30,375	2088	2009	.663	.506	.1614
2 Crops	23,388	24,608	1902	1771	.679	.539	.1385
3 Forestry and Fishery Products	1,106	1,112	29	31	.782	.754	.2041
4 Agricultural Services	1,807	1,816	229	245	.367	.517	.1086

only partially oriented locationally toward their markets, with little association in forestry and fishing products. Except for agricultural services, the industries are located closer to areas of total demand than to access of personal income. The shift ratios indicated that the industries are locationally stable from year to year.

Change in the overall product mix of the group is of particular interest in view of the striking reduction in human consumption of grain and other field crops since 1940. This is offset to the advantage of the group as a whole by the substitution of meat for grain in the human diet. Changes in dietary habits of Americans have also affected the output of the fisheries industry. It is difficult to predict whether other changes in diet can be expected in coming decades since this is a matter of the consumer's choices in response to variations in income, a problem of taste rather than economics. It would seem that the shift to greater meat consumption must level off, although there are still many groups within the economy who have yet to "catch up" in this regard. Perhaps the next area of shift will be toward greater diversification of diet, involving growth in the now less popular meats, and in fruits and nuts, vegetables, and horticultural specialties.

IO 1 Livestock

The livestock industry with an output of over $30 billion in 1966, is one of the largest industries in the study. While the industry is large and output is growing, employment fell approximately 79 thousand between 1965 and 1966. A major reason for the decline in employment over many years has been the movement of grazing from the range and farm to automated feedlots and poultry factories.

The industry is dominated by meat products as the following table shows.[3]

Product	Percent of Output
Meat	64.4
Dairy Farm Products	21.7
Poultry and Eggs	13.9

Changes in consumer tastes and rising incomes have drastically altered the product mix of meat consumption. The following table shows the percent of output by weight of meat accounted by beef, veal, lamb, and pork.[4]

Product	Percent of Total Meat	
	1950	1965
Pork	48.5	35.3
Beef	43.2	59.4
Veal	5.6	3.2
Lamb	2.7	2.1

Production of pork was slightly greater than beef in 1950, but by 1965 beef production was almost twice pork production. Lamb and veal production also declined slightly during this period. Locationally, counties specializing in beef production will grow more rapidly than counties specializing in pork production. While substitution of beef for pork production on a farm is possible, beef production appears to have an advantage in the mountainous sectors of the West and the Appalachian area.

Much of the dairy activity is located near urban areas and in the Midwest. Future changes in the distribution of population can be expected to affect the location of dairy farms. Growth of urban areas increases the competition for land, making it difficult to maintain types of agricultural activity that produce relatively small returns per acre. Changes in the production techniques of processing fluid milk[b] may allow substitution of increased transport cost for high rent and stimulate diary farming in the Midwest at the expense of other sections in the country.

The poultry and egg industry has become highly mechanized, and its production process resembles a factory rather than a farming operation. The relatively low price of poultry products achieved by large scale operations seems to ensure the growth of their sector.

The livestock industry is heavily dependent upon inputs from crops as the following summary from the 1966 interindustry table illustrates.

---

[b]See Group 2: Dairy Products, for a discussion of changing technology in this industry.

	Suppliers	Percent		Buyers	Percent
IO 2	Crops	30.3	IO 14	Meat Packing	49.3
IO 17	Grain Mill Products	12.5	IO 15	Dairy Products	16.6
IO 22	Misc. Food	1.7	IO 2	Crops	6.3
IO 4	Agricultural Services	1.6	PCE	5.9	5.9

Comparatively little of the output is sold directly to consumers. The products of the industry are processed by Meat Packing (IO 14) and Dairy Products (IO 15) before they reach the supermarket and restaurant.

The livestock industry requires vast tracts of land—approximately 25 percent of the continental U.S. in 1965.[5] California (17.7 percent) and Iowa (9.1 percent) were the leading livestock states. Other states producing high levels were Illinois (4.9 percent), Minnesota (4.5 percent), Texas (4.4 percent), Wisconsin (4.2 percent), and Nebraska (3.8 percent).

The regression equation (6.1) for livestock yielded very encouraging results. The coefficient of determination (R^2) for explaining the regional variance in the change in output was .9530, and the R^2 for explaining the variance in the level of output was .9990.

$$(6.1) \quad \Delta QD_1 = 686.0029 - 3.1572TI_2 - 45.5465TI_{17}$$
$$(53.1178) \quad (.3156) \quad (12.9313)$$

$$-15.097WR_1 - .1042VL + .1606Q_1$$
$$(2.7407) \quad (.0207) \quad (.0009)$$

$$+ .0081EQ_1 + .0046Q_{15}$$
$$(.0054) \quad (.0008)$$

Two of the three transportation variables (TQ_1, TI_2, and TI_{17}) were significant. They indicate the importance of low transportation cost in procuring feed from Crops (IO 2) and Grain Mill Products (IO 16). These variables, as well as wages, value of land, and equipment, show the importance of production costs in the livestock industry. Output, however, with a positive sign reflecting agglomeration factors, was the most important variable. The significance of Q_{15}, dairy products, confirmed the close association between dairy farms and dairy processing.

Three variables were not retained because of multicollinearity: TQ, DEN, and PCE. Q_{17} and Q_{22} both major supplying industries, had incorrect signs, while the other variables were either insignificant or would have forced previously entered variables to become insignificant.

IO 2 Crops

The crops industry shares many of the characteristics of the livestock industry. The output of crops is large, $23.4 billion in 1965. Production takes place on vast tracts of land, 33 percent of the continental U.S. total in 1965,[6] removed from urban centers and concentrations of personal income. The states with extensive areas tend to be the largest producers. California leads the nation with 14.7 percent of total output in 1965, followed by Texas (7.5 percent), Illinois (6.5 percent), North Carolina (4.4 percent), Florida (4.2 percent), and Iowa (3.9 percent).

Mechanization and lower acreage allotments has reduced the need for farm labor and also reduced the underemployment in rural areas, and therefore hastened migration to the cities. The migration has been particularly prevalent among blacks in the cotton belt of the South, whose labor has been replaced by mechanical cotton pickers.[7] Many of today's urban and racial problems stem from the displacement of farm labor and a lack of economic opportunity in rural areas. The decline in employment of over 130,000 workers or 6.8 percent of the labor force in crops in 1965 illustrates the magnitude of worker displacement.

Crops are an intermediate rather than a consumer good as the 1966 summary interindustry table below indicates.

Suppliers		Percent	Buyers		Percent
IO 1	Livestock	7.3	IO 1	Livestock	35.2
IO 35	Basic Chemicals	6.6	PCE		13.5
IO 39	Petroleum Refining	4.0	Exports		13.0
IO 4	Agricultural Services	3.5	IO 17	Grain Mills	10.6

PCE accounts for only 13.5 percent of sales, while livestock and grain mills together purchased 45.7 percent. The size of the export market (13.0 percent) does not truly reflect the superiority of U.S. farming techniques over the rest of the world. If trade barriers in the Common Market were removed and the political rivalries with Communist nations reduced, this percentage would be much higher. The major inputs are fertilizers and petroleum. Livestock is the major market of crops either by direct purchases or by indirect purchases from grain mill products. Thirty-five percent of grain mill products in 1966 were sold to livestock.

The regression equation (6.2) for crops yielded good results. The R^2 for the change in output was .5066, and the R^2 for the level of output was .9956.

$$(6.2) \quad \Delta QD_2 = 845.6774 - .0643Q_2 - 24.2427TI_{35} + .0337EQ_1$$
$$ (71.7014) \quad (.0018) \quad\quad (7.4963) \quad\quad (.0157)$$

The order of introducing variables was modified in this equation. In the initial regression output did not enter because it made previously entered variables insignificant. Since the change in output is partially a function of federal acreage allotment based on past output, it was decided to enter this variable before the transportation variables. Only one of the three transportation variables (TQ_2, TI_1, and TI_{35}) was significant. The retention of TI_{35} reflects the importance of fertilizer and insecticides in this industry. The importance of mechanized farming is confirmed by the significance of EQ_1.

Five variables were rejected because of incorrect signs: TI_1, WR_2, Q_1, Q_{35}, and Q_4. The other variables were insignificant.

IO 3 Forestry and Fisheries Products

The forestry and fisheries products industry is a combination of two diverse subproducts and one of the smallest industries in the study. In terms of employment fisheries dominated the industry in 1965 with 75.89 percent of total employment.[8] Forestry products are small in relation to fishing, primarily because lumbering is included in IO 28 Lumber and Lumber Products.

The forestry industry includes the gathering of forest products, the maintenance of timber tracts, the operation of forest nurseries, and other forestry services. Many of these activities are carried out principally by employees of the federal government and therefore are not included in the industry. However, with a greater demand for timber more companies are employing personnel of their own to perform forestry services on private tracts.[9]

In fisheries, the decade from 1950 to 1960 was affected by a marked change in consumer buying habits, culminated by a relaxation of the "fish on Friday" doctrine of the Roman Catholic Church, by rapid advances in technology, by foreign competition, and by a complex web of government regulation. Many fishery products may be classified economically as "inferior goods" products that consumers purchase in decreasing quantities as their incomes rise. This seems to be bringing about a change in product mix for the fisheries industry, favoring certain types of shellfish and crustaceans as well as the more delicate types of ocean and lake fish, to the detriment of the old standbys. The locational effect of these shifts is reinforced by the fact that foreign competition in deep-sea fisheries is particulary keen. Many of the "luxury"-type fisheries, particularly the lobster, shellfish, and shrimp fisheries, do not involve fishing on the high seas and are not seriously subject to foreign competition, except insofar as seafoods are substitutes for one another. Pollution and the sea lamprey have all but eliminated the fishing industry in the Great Lakes during the 1960s. Efforts to control the lamprey appear successful, and stocking of the lakes with Pacific salmon could bring about a revival of commercial fishing in the 1970s.

The sales of the forestry and fisheries industry as presented in the 1966 summary interindustry table reveal the dual composition of the industry.

Suppliers		Percent	Buyers		Percent
IO 4	Agricultural	6.1	IO 28	Lumber	55.0
IO 25	Rugs, Textiles	3.9	PCE		34.6
IO 39	Petroleum Refining	3.3	IO 16	Canned and Frozen Foods	18.8
IO 22	Misc. Food Products	2.3	IO 26	Apparel	6.8

The sales total more than 100 percent of domestic production, because of the large volume of foreign imports. The lumber industry is the major purchaser of forest products, while PCE and canned and frozen food are the major markets for fish.

Over 80 percent of the industry's output in 1965 was concentrated in five states. Massachusetts was the largest producer (24.1 percent), followed by California (21.5 percent), Texas (10.2 percent), Florida (8.4 percent), and Louisiana (5.0 percent).

The regression equation (6.3) yielded moderate results given the diverse structure of the industry. The R^2 for the change in output was .1977 and .9867 for the level of output.

$$(6.3) \qquad \Delta QD_3 = -217.7721 - .0444VL + .0348Q_3$$
$$(132.9830) \quad (.0183) \quad\quad (.0122)$$

$$+ .1261EQ_1 + .0435Q_{25}$$
$$(.0578) \quad\quad (.0211)$$

A major problem in analyzing the equation is whether to attribute the retention or rejection of variables to the influence of forestry or fisheries. Both of the transportation variables (TQ_3 and TI_{25}) were insignificant. The forestry sector of the industry is presumably responsible for the significance of VL, while Q_{25}, rugs, tire cord, and miscellaneous textiles has been retained because of the importance of fish line and nets to fisheries. Output and equipment were also significant.

DEN and Q_{26} were not retained because of multicollinearity. The other variables were rejected because of insignificance.

IO 4 Agricultural Services

Agricultural services encompasses a number of activities that are contracted out by livestock and crops industries, such as cotton ginning, milling, corn shelling, hay baling, sorting, grading, and packing of fruits and vegetables, crops dusting, veterinarian services and animal breeding. The industry also includes horticultural services such as cemetery upkeep, landscape gardening, and tree planting. The summary 1966 interindustry table presented below shows that the industry's major markets are the other industries of the biotic raw materials group.

	Suppliers	Percent		Buyers	Percent
IO 1	Livestock	12.5	IO 2	Crops	51.6
IO 52	Hardware	8.9	IO 1	Livestock	26.8
IO 33	Paper Containers	4.8	IO 81	Wholesale Trade	12.6
IO 17	Grain Mills	2.1	IO 3	Forestry and Fishery	7.5

The distribution of agricultural services by state closely parallels that of livestock and crops. California (16.8 percent) and Michigan (16.3 percent) were the largest providers of these services in 1965. Other states with important contributions are Florida (7.6 percent), New York (6.3 percent), Texas (5.0 percent), Pennsylvania (4.8 percent), and Illinois (3.8 percent). The industry shares the high stability characteristics of most services industries. Its shift ratio was .1086.

The regression equation (6.4) for this industry yielded poor results. The R^2 for the change in output was only .0717. However, the R^2 for the level of output was .9786.

(6.4)
$$\Delta QD_4 = 138.9870 - 13.1345 TI_{52} - 6.0136 WR_4 - .0455 Q_4$$
$$(97.7236) \quad (12.0538) \quad (1.8341) \quad (.0042)$$

$$+ .0061 EQ_1 + .0174 DEN + .0010 Q_1$$
$$(.0043) \quad (.0038) \quad (.0004)$$

$$+ .0028 Q_3 + .0024 Q_{17}$$
$$(.0020) \quad (.0005)$$

A transportation variable for shipping the industry's output to market was not included in the equation since the industry produces nontransportable services. Transportation variables were extended for the four transportable input commodities listed in the summary interindustry table. The variable TI_{52} was significant, while the first TI_1 and third TI_{33} were multicollinear, and the fourth TI_{17} has an incorrect sign. Wages, output, and equipment expenditures were significant, but land value was not retained because of multicollinearity. The positive sign of the population (DEN) is an indication of the influence of urban regions on the industry. The other variables in the equation reflect agglomeration factors.

Q_{81} was not retained because of multicollinearity. The other variables were either insignificant or forced previously entered variables to insignificance.

Group 2: Food Processing

The nine industries in the food processing group are distributed over a wide range of product groups. Any operations performed on edible agricultural or fishery output are classified in this group. Slaughtering of animals, pasteurizing of milk, packaging of fresh fish, and similar operations are included, as well as those of a more clearly manufacturing nature such as flour milling, sugar refining, and oil pressing. Each of the nine industries is affected somewhat differently by technology, location of demand, and location of inputs. Their processes and transportation requirements vary considerably. Table 6-3 presents some national statistics and other summary measures.

In food processing, the relation of bulk of input to bulk of output is often an important consideration. Spoilage of product and damage to input and output goods in transportation is a prime factor as well. Transportation technology and improvements in transportation networks are important to the location of growth in the food industry. Over the past two decades, frozen food technology has had a striking influence on the location of fruit, vegetable, and poultry processing. In addition, the practice of freezing foods has had an effect on the agriculture related to these products. To prevent inputs from spoiling, some processing plants locate close to the source of supply.

The growth rate in value of output of the Group 2 industries over the last two decades has been relatively low compared with other industries in the study. This should be expected, since aggregate expenditures on food usually are income inelastic. However, there has been considerable substitu-

Table 6-3
Summary Statistics, Group 2: Food Processing

Industry	Output 1966 Prices (000,000) 1965	1966	Employment (000) 1965	1966	Coefficient of Localization 1966 Output with Personal Income	1966 Output with Industry Demand	Output Shift Ratio 1965-1966
14 Meat Packing	23,624	23,725	312	317	.542	.491	.1030
15 Dairy Products	12,542	12,139	259	252	.345	.296	.0876
16 Canned and Frozen Foods	8,069	8,301	208	225	.590	.532	.1459
17 Grain Mill	9,028	9,328	114	113	.595	.511	.1602
18 Bakery Products	6,301	6,350	281	281	.380	.347	.0752
19 Sugar	1,957	2,011	31	32	.850	.619	.2347
20 Candy	2,364	2,500	81	85	.616	.543	.1031
21 Beverages	11,759	12,659	218	228	.427	.374	.0864
22 Misc. Food Products	8,724	9,206	140	142	.466	.376	.1130

tion between products in the food processing group, as evidenced by high-income elasticities of some products, noticeably meat and beverages.

The coefficients of localization for the group show that bakery products and dairy products are relatively oriented locationally toward consumers, although not perfectly since there are some nonurban geographic concentrations in these industries. The locations of the sugar and candy industries have the least orientation toward consumers. Most of the output in this group of industries is sold as final products to consumers. The shift ratios show that the industries in this group are fairly stable locationally.

IO 14 Meat Packing

Improvements in both transportation and processing technology have affected the location of meat packing, as well as poultry processing. Because fresh meat spoils easily, it has been the practice to ship live animals to the market area for slaughtering. This has its disadvantages, since the animals tend to lose weight and become ill during transit. With refrigerated transportation and increased speed for many truck hauls over the past decade, it has become possible to locate packing plants in the rural areas where beef is finished, rather than in large cities.

The industry is divided into three major products. Meat packing plants, particularly in terms of value added, are the most important sector of the industry.[10]

| | | | Percent of | |
SIC	Product	Employment	Output	Value Added
2011 Meat Packing Plants		55.0	62.5	72.4
2013 Sausages and Other Prepared Meats		17.5	20.9	14.0
2015 Poultry Dressing Plants		27.5	16.6	13.6

The high value added per employee in meatpacking can be explained by the high level of automation found in the industry since the mid-1950s.[11] The animals are suspended along rails, while mechanical hide pullers, power knives and conveyor systems process the animal.

The input-output structure of the industry is extremely simple as the following summary table indicates:

	Suppliers	Percent		Buyers	Percent
IO 1	Livestock	61.3	PCE		74.6
IO 33	Paper Containers	.8	IO 85	Business Services	3.8
IO 40	Rubber and Plastic	.8	Export		1.2

The livestock industry is the major supplier, while personal consumption is the major market.

The livestock industry is moderately concentrated with eight states producing over 53 percent of total output in 1965. The state with the largest production was Iowa (12.3 percent), followed by California (8.3 percent), Illinois (7.1 percent), Minnesota (6.1 percent), Nebraska (6.0 percent), Texas (4.6 percent), Ohio (4.6 percent), and Pennsylvania (4.2 percent).

Regression equation (6.14) for meatpacking yielded moderate results. The R^2 for the change in output was .2440 but was .9934 for the level of output.

$$(6.14) \quad \Delta QD_{14} = 1157.2826 - .0548Q_{14} - .3059VL + 1.0460EQ_6$$
$$(346.5728) \quad (.0048) \quad (.1164) \quad (.9136)$$

$$+ .0041Q_{85} + .0128Q_{40}$$
$$(.0013) \quad (.0116)$$

The transportation variables (TQ_{14} and TI_1) were both insignificant. Output was entered before wages and land value because output was not accepted in the original equation. The current movement of the industry from urban to rural areas provided a strong argument for violating the variable order specifications. The significance of value of land and equipment expenditures also reflect this rural movement. The significance of Q_{85} and Q_{40} reveals the importance of advertising and packaging in the industry.

DEN, PCE, EX_{14}, and Q_{33} were not retained because of multicollinearity. The other variables failed to pass significance tests.

IO 15 Dairy Products

The dairy industry is dominated by the processing of fluid milk as the following table listing the major products of the dairy industry indicates.[12]

SIC	Product	Percent of Output
2021	Creamery Butter	3.3
2022	Cheese, Natural and Processed	6.5
2023	Condensed and Evaporated Milk	10.8
2024	Ice Cream and Frozen Desserts	11.6
2026	Fluid Milk	67.8

The technology of all sectors of the dairy industry is highly automated.[c]

[c]*Technological Trends in Major American Industries*, Bulletin No. 1474, U.S. Department of Labor, Feb. 1968, pp. 120-125 is the source of the technological discussion of the dairy industry.

Raw milk is channeled through central control systems for the processing of homogenized milk and through continuous processes for the manufacturing of milk products such as cheese and ice cream. The development of automated processes has occurred simultaneously with a change in the distribution system of the dairy industry. Store purchased milk products are rapidly eliminating home delivery service. Both of these developments will tend to increase the geographic concentration of the industry, since large-scale processing plants have become both technically and economically feasible.

The interindustry structure of the industry is dominated by sales to consumers and purchases from livestock as the following summary table indicates.

	Suppliers	Percent		Buyers	Percent
IO 1	Livestock	38.0		PCE	70.7
IO 33	Paper Containers	3.5		Federal Government	3.6
IO 32	Paper and Prod.	1.4			
IO 49	Metal Containers	1.0			

Five Midwestern states accounted for 33.5 percent of the output in 1965. The largest producer in the Midwestern group was Wisconsin (11.6 percent), followed by Illinois (6.3 percent), Ohio (6.0 percent), Minnesota (5.5 percent), and Michigan (4.3 percent). Other states with appreciable output levels were California (9.6 percent), Pennsylvania (6.5 percent), Texas (3.9 percent), and New York (3.7 percent).

The results obtained in the regression equation (6.15) were moderately acceptable. The R^2 for change in output was .2419, and for the level of output it was .9972.

$$(6.15) \quad \Delta QD_{15} = -120.6544 - 72.3531TQ_{15} - .0362Q_{15}$$
$$\phantom{(6.15) \quad \Delta QD_{15} = } (256.7774) \quad (44.2405) \quad\quad (.0027)$$

$$- 40.0473WR_{15} + 1.3212EQ_{62} + .0034Q_1$$
$$ (28.8861) \quad\quad (.2216) \quad\quad\quad (.0019)$$

Only one of the five transportation variables (TQ_{15}, TI_1, TI_{23}, TI_{32}, and TI_{49}) was significant. The equation, while not completely satisfactory, does reflect the locational pressures discussed earlier. Transport cost of shipping the product to market TQ_{15}, wages, and capital investment all have significantly influenced the change in supply patterns. The other significant variable reflects the agglomeration factor between livestock and dairy products.

PCE was not retained because of multicollinearity, while Q_{32} had an incorrect sign. The other variables were not retained either because of statistical insignificance or because they forced previously entered variables to insignificance.

IO 16 Canned and Frozen Foods

The spatial readjustment of the canned and frozen foods industry has been dominated, since World War II, by innovations in frozen foods. Canned foods, however, still accounted for a larger share of output (51.2 percent) in 1967 than either dehydrated, pickled, or frozen food. Vegetables and fruits, whether frozen or canned, predominate over fish and seafood as the raw material of the industry as the following table indicates.[13]

SIC	Product	Percent of Output
2031	Canned and Cured Seafood	5.04
2032	Canned Specialties	16.78
2033	Canned Fruits and Vegetables	39.38
2034	Dehydrated Food Products	4.67
2035	Pickles, Sauces, and Salad Dressings	8.23
2036	Fresh or Frozen Packaged Fish	4.59
2037	Frozen Fruits and Vegetables	21.28

The growth of the frozen foods sector of the industry has occurred in areas closest to biotic raw materials sites, farms, and ports. The importance of biotic raw materials as well as glass and metal containers as inputs, is illustrated in the following summary of the industry's input-output table.

	Suppliers	Percent	Buyers	Percent
IO 2	Crops	12.7	PCE	83.8
IO 49	Metal Containers	8.3	Export	2.7
IO 3	Forestry and Fishing	4.4		
IO 43	Glass and Glass Products	3.4		

The consumer orientation of the industry is also apparent from the table. The partial resource orientation of the industry has resulted in a moderate degree of spatial concentration. California produced the largest proportion of the nation's output in 1965 (21.8 percent), followed by Florida (8.3 percent), Illinois (8.3 percent), New York (7.3 percent), Pennsylvania (6.1 percent), and New Jersey (7.3 percent).

The regression equation (6.16) yielded moderate results with an R^2 of .2974 for change in output and .9890 for the level of output.

$$(6.16) \quad \Delta QD_{16} = 1505.4159 - 204.5869 TI_{43} - .0649 Q_{16} + .0366 Q_2$$
$$(837.2888) \quad (166.6717) \quad (.0062) \quad (.0083)$$

Only one of the five transportation variables (TQ_{16}, TI_2, TI_{49}, TI_3, and TI_{43}) was retained. TQ_{16} and TI_2 were multicollinear, while the others were insignificant. The negative sign on output Q_{16} may suggest that the industry is more mobile in the long run than the shift ratio of .1459 for 1965 indicates. The agglomeration variable Q_2 shows the close relationship of the canned and frozen foods industry to crops.

EQ_{63}, PCE, Q_{49}, and Q_{43} were not retained in the equation because of incorrect signs. The other variables were rejected because they were insignificant or forced previously entered variables to insignificance.

IO 17 Grain Mill Products

The sales of the grain mill products industry, unlike the others in the food processing group, except for sugar, are not concentrated in the personal consumption sector as the following table summarizing the 1966 interindustry relations of grain mill products illustrates.

	Suppliers	Percent		Buyers	Percent
IO 2	Crops	26.0	IO 1	Livestock	35.4
IO 22	Misc. Food	8.8	PCE		24.5
IO 32	Paper and Prod. Exc.	2.4	Exports		5.0

More of the output is sold for animal consumption than for direct sales to humans. Crops, as would be expected, is the major input of the industry.

The following table showing the output, proportions of the products of the industry further illustrates the importance of sales to the livestock industry.[14]

SIC	Product	Percent of Output
20 41	Flour and Other Grain Mill Products	17.04
20 42	Prepared Feeds for Animals and Fowls	42.56
20 43	Cereal Preparations	16.42
20 44	Rice Milling	3.60
20 45	Blended and Prepared Flour	8.08
20 46	Wet Corn Milling	12.26

The production process of this industry is weight losing. This factor is partially responsible for the high spatial concentration of the industry in the Midwest, the major site of the crop industries. The location of the major market, livestock, in the same areas as crops intensifies the pressure for concentration of the industry.

Six states in the Midwest accounted for more than 48 percent of the output in 1965: Illinois (16.8 percent), Iowa (9.9 percent), Missouri (7.3 percent), Michigan (6.1 percent), Indiana (4.8 percent), and Minnesota (3.7 percent). The only two other states with appreciable output levels were Texas (6.1 percent) and California (5.9 percent).

The regression equation (6.17) produced extremely poor results with an R^2 of .0587 for the change in output. The R^2 for predicted levels was considerably higher at .9875.

$$(6.17) \quad \Delta QD_{17} = 1666.9910 - 455.1991 TQ_{17} - 13.7457 TI_2$$
$$(1533.3486) \quad (415.7343) \quad\quad (9.8099)$$

$$- .2501 VL + .0274 Q_{17}$$
$$(.1871) \quad\quad (.0062)$$

The t ratios for all the variables in (6.17), except Q_{17}, just exceed the critical ratio of one. Two of the four transportation variables (TQ_{17}, TI_2, TI_{22}, and TI_{32}) were retained. The others were multicollinear. The significance of TQ_{17} reveals the importance of the market to the industry, while the retention of TI_2 is caused by the weight losing nature of the production process of the industry.

DEN was not retained because of multicollinearity. The other variables either were insignificant or had an incorrect sign or they were not entered because they forced previously entered variables to become insignificant.

IO 18 Bakery Products

Bakery products are manufactured by bulk-adding processes; for this reason, plus the perishability of the output and increased difficulty of transport, they tend to locate in market regions. However, some products, such as cookies and crackers, are distributed nationally from central plants. Here, the economies of scale outweigh the economies of transportation by diffused location.

Market orientation in bakery products implies locations dependent upon population since as the summary 1966 interindustry table below indicates, personal consumption expenditures accounted for 94.7 percent of the sales of the industry.

	Suppliers	Percent	Buyers	Percent
IO 17	Grain Mills	17.0	PCE	94.7
IO 22	Misc. Food	4.9		
IO 19	Sugar	3.3		
IO 32	Paper and Products Excluding Containers	3.0		

The major material inputs, excluding paper, are purchased from the other sectors of the food processing group.

The production of SIC 2051 bread, cake, and other products dominates the industry with 78.8 percent of output. The remaining output is SIC 2052 cookies and crackers.[15]

Since the industry is consumer oriented, the heavily populated states produce the greatest proportion of the industry's output. California had the largest percentage (12.7) in 1965. Other states producing more than five percent were Illinois (9.2 percent), Pennsylvania (8.3 percent), Ohio (6.2 percent), New Jersey (5.3 percent), New York (5.3 percent), and Texas (5 percent).

The regression equation (6.18) explained very little of the variance of the change in output; the R^2 was .1084. However, since the industry is extremely stable with a shift ratio of .0752, the R^2 for output levels was .9970.

$$(6.18) \qquad \Delta QD_{18} = 75.4860 - 144.2342 TI_{17} + .0127 Q_{18} + .0065 Q_{32}$$
$$(297.2731) \quad (120.6636) \qquad (.0046) \qquad (.0038)$$

Only one of the four transportation variables (TQ_{18}, TI_{17}, TI_{22}, and TI_{19}) was significant. The significance of TI_{19} and the positive sign on the agglomeration variables (Q_{18}, Q_{32}) reflect production cost and thus cannot account for a large proportion of the unexplained variance of a market orientated industry. Unfortunately, a major market oriented variable PCE was multicollinear with previously entered variables. EQ_{65} and Q_{22} were also rejected because of multicollinearity. The other variables were not retained in the equation because they either were statistically insignificant or forced previously entered variables to insignificance.

IO 19 Sugar

While sugar's largest market, excluding itself, is personal consumption expenditures, its primary usefulness is as an intermediate good purchased by the other food processing industries as the following table summarizing the 1966 interindustry relations of the industry indicates.

Suppliers	Percent	Buyers		Percent
IO 2 Crops	23.2	PCE		28.1
IO 34 Printing and Publishing	1.0	IO 21	Beverages	13.8
IO 33 Paper Containers	.7	IO 18	Bakery	8.5
		IO 20	Candy	7.0

The industry purchases a high percentage of its own output (32.2 percent) which can easily be explained by the product structure of the industry. The following table shows the proportion of output of the subsectors of the industry.[16]

SIC	Product	Percent of Output
2061	Raw Cane Sugar	20.5
2062	Cane Sugar Refining	47.3
2063	Beet Sugar	32.2

The location of the industry is heavily influenced by the federal government's agricultural policies on sugar cane and beet planting, since the production process of the industry is weight losing and hence tied to areas where sugar cane or beets are cultivated.

In 1965 over 65 percent of its output was concentrated in six states. Louisiana had the largest production (14.1 percent). Other states in this group included California (12.0 percent), Hawaii (12.3 percent), New York (10.0 percent), Florida (8.7 percent), and Colorado (7.9 percent).

The results of the regression equation (6.19) were excellent considering the influence of governmental intervention. The R^2 was .6052 for the change in output and .9936 in the level of output.

$$(6.19) \qquad \Delta QD_{19} = -4858.8434 - 64.8125 TQ_{19} + .0770 Q_{19}$$
$$(2003.2964) \quad (28.9285) \qquad (.0223)$$

$$+ 1.5504 EQ_{66} - .4715 VL$$
$$(.5020) \qquad (.2384)$$

Only one transportation variable of those entered (TQ_{19}, TI_2, TI_{34}, TI_{33}) was significant. The positive sign on output reflects agglomeration factors, while the significance of VL and EQ_{66} reflect cost factors.

DEN was not included because of multicollinearity. The other variables were not retained because of insignificance.

IO 20 Candy

The candy industry is somewhat similar to the sugar industry in size of output and spatial concentration. Compared with other industries in the food processing group both are small and locationally the most concentrated. However, the industries differ in their spatial mobility. Whereas sugar had the highest locational changes during 1965, the candy industry was very stable.

Over three-fourths of the industry's output in 1965 was concentrated in seven states. The two states having the largest output levels were Illinois (29.8 percent) and Pennsylvania (15.7 percent). Other states with significant production levels were New York (9.0 percent), California (7.0 percent), New Jersey (6.3 percent), Massachusetts (5.7 percent), and Georgia (3.6 percent).

The input-output structure of the industry is uncomplicated as the following table illustrates.

	Suppliers	Percent	Buyers	Percent
IO 19	Sugar	6.4	*PCE*	82.9
IO 33	Paper Containers	5.4	IO 85 Business Services	4.3
IO 2	Crops	3.1		

Crops and sugar constitute its major raw materials, while the magnitude of the paper containers input shows the importance of packaging to the industry. Personal consumption is the largest market for candy. The industry purchases 9.3 percent of its own input, presumably in the form of chocolate and cocoa products as the following table delineating the products of the industry indicates.[17]

SIC	Product	Percent of Output
2071	Confectionary Products	69.0
2072	Chocolate and Cocoa Products	15.7
2073	Chewing Gum	15.2

The regression equation (6.20) yielded moderate results. The R^2 for the change in output was .3302, and .9988 for the level of output.

$$(6.20) \quad \Delta QD_{20} = \underset{(2275.8690)}{3590.2016} - \underset{(28.8952)}{41.8515 TI_{19}} + \underset{(.0031)}{.0243 Q_{20}}$$

Only one of the four transportation variables entered (TQ_{20}, TI_{19}, TI_{33}, TI_2) was significant. Two were significant, TQ_{20} and TI_{33} were rejected because of multicollinearity, and TI_2 had an incorrect sign. The positive sign on output reflects the locational concentration and stability in the industry. EQ_{67} and Q_{33} were not retained because of multicollinearity, while WR_{20} and Q_{19} had incorrect signs. The other variables were rejected either because of insignificance or because they forced previously entered variables to insignificance.

IO 21 Beverages

The beverage industry is composed of a varied array of products from soft drinks and beer to wines and hard liquor as the following table illustrates.[18]

SIC	Product	Percent of Output
2082	Malt Liquors	32.3
2083	Malt	1.0

SIC	Product	Percent of Output
2084	Wines, Brandy, and Brandy Spirits	4.0
2085	Distilled Liquors, excluding Brandy	15.4
2086	Bottled and Canned Soft Drinks	35.1
2087	Flavoring Extracts and Syrups, NEC	12.2

Soft drinks and beer, relatively good consumer substitutes, however, dominate the market accounting for over 67 percent of output in 1967. Since both of these products involve high weight gain, in the form of water in production, the industry tends to be market oriented. Since consumers are the major market for beverages, as the following table summarizing the 1966 interindustry relations of the industry indicates, beverage production is oriented toward population centers.

	Suppliers	Percent		Buyers	Percent
IO 85	Business Services	6.8	PCE		79.1
IO 49	Metal Containers	6.1	IO 85	Business Services 8.6	
IO 43	Glass and Glass Products	5.1			
IO 19	Sugar	2.7			
IO 2	Crops	2.6			

The inputs from sugar and crops combined total was less than either glass or metal containers or business services illustrating the relative unimportance of the raw material inputs in the beverage productive process.

No state produced more than 9 percent and only seven states produced more than 5 percent of the industry's output in 1965. California had the largest output (8.6 percent), followed by Wisconsin (7.9 percent), Illinois (7.9 percent), New York (7.5 percent), New Jersey (6.0 percent), Kentucky (5.2 percent), and Texas (5.1 percent).

The regression equation (6.21) yielded good results. The R^2 for the change in output was .4641, and for the level of output .9869.

$$(6.21) \quad \Delta QD_{21} = -120.8707 - 660.6392 TQ_{21} - 274.5663 WR_{21}$$
$$(984.8571) \quad (561.9801) \qquad (71.9929)$$

$$- .1048 V_1 + .1226 Q_{21}$$
$$(.0717) \qquad (.0067)$$

Only one of the five transportation variables entered (TQ_{21}, TI_{49}, TI_{43}, TI_{19}, TI_2) was retained. The significance of TQ_{21} substantiates the market orientation hypothesis. Wages and the value of land were significant, but the major explanation of the variance in the change in output came from the industry's output level. The market orientation and capital intensity of the industry are reflected in the output variable.

Three variables were not retained because of incorrect signs: EQ_{68}, Q_{49} and Q_{43}. *DEN* was multicollinear, while the other variables were rejected because of their own insignificance or because of causing previously entered variables to lose significance.

IO 22 Misc. Food Products

The miscellaneous food products industry has a highly diversified subset of products ranging from vegetable and animal oils to roasted coffee, manufactured ice to macaroni and spaghetti as indicated by the following table.[19]

SIC	Product	Percent of Output
2091	Cottonseed Oil Mills	2.2
2092	Soybean Oil Mills	7.3
2093	Vegetable Oil Mills, NEC	1.4
2094	Animal and Marine Fats and Oils	7.0
2095	Roasted Coffee	24.6
2096	Shortening and Cooking Oils	13.2
2097	Manufactured Ice	2.6
2098	Macaroni and Spaghetti	4.1
2099	Food Preparations, NEC	37.6

This diversity may explain the poor statistical results obtained in the regression equation.

The major input for the industry is crops as the summary input-output table presented below indicates.

	Suppliers	Percent		Buyers	Percent
IO 2	Crops	23.2	PCE		52.6
IO 85	Business Services	4.1	IO 17	Grain Mills	9.4
IO 49	Metal Containers	1.9			
IO 43	Glass and Glass Products	1.6		Exports	6.5

California produced the largest percentage of the industry's output in 1965 with 13.0 percent. Other states with significant output levels were Illinois (12.4 percent), New Jersey (8.4 percent), Texas (7.9 percent), and Ohio (5.0 percent).

The regression equation (6.22) had a low R^2 of .0806 for the change in output, but a high one for the level of output of .9845.

$$(6.22) \quad \Delta QD_{22} = 9827.4718 - 10.5879TI_2 - 1306.4968TI_{49}$$
$$(4866.1248) \quad (9.5205) \quad (1089.9658)$$

$$- 1183.4287TI_{17} - 95.0466WR_{22} - .0811VL$$
$$(699.3926) \qquad (37.6333) \qquad (.0613)$$

$$- .0278Q_{22} + .1235PCE_{22} + .0273EX_{22}$$
$$(.0096) \qquad (.0265) \qquad (.0259)$$

The equation had eight significant variables, six of which were cost oriented. The lack of market and agglomeration variables can be explained by the diversity of the product of the industry. One market variable PCE_{22} that was highly significant with a positive sign presumably reflects the luxury items in SIC 2099 that accounted for 37 percent of the industry's output. This product group includes items such as: chocolate syrup and cocoa, cider, corn chips, honey, pancake syrup, potato chips, and vinegar.

Three of the five transportation variables entered (TQ_{22}, TI_2, TI_{49}, TI_{43}, and TI_{17}) were retained. The transportation variables that were retained reflect the cost of the transporting the high volume inputs of crops, grain mill products, and metal containers. TQ_{22} and TI_{43} were rejected because of multicollinearity. The wage and output variables were highly significant, while the value of land was only moderately significant.

Two other variables were not retained because of multicollinearity: DEN and Q_{85}. The other variables either were insignificant or forced previously entered variables to insignificance.

Group 3: Tobacco

The tobacco industry (IO 23) is the only industry in Group 3. Group 3 is the smallest group in terms of output and employment in the study, as illustrated in Table 6-4.

The input-output structure of the industry is relatively simple. Over 40 percent of the inputs are purchased from either crops or the tobacco industry itself. The following table illustrates the interindustry relationships:

	Suppliers	Percent	Buyers	Percent
IO 2	Crops	17.9	PCE	68.6
IO 85	Business Services	4.7	Exports	7.9
IO 33	Paper Containers	1.2		
IO 34	Printing and Publishing	1.0		

The industry purchases a high percentage of its own output (22.1 percent), mainly in the form of dried and stemmed tobacco and reconstituted tobacco sheet to be used in the manufacturing of cigarettes, cigars, pipe and chewing tobacco. Although consumers are the major buyers of tobacco products, the industry is highly concentrated geographically away from consumer centers and in the raw material producing areas.

Table 6-4
Summary Statistics, Group 3: Tobacco

	Output 1966 Prices (000,000)		Employment (000)		Coefficient of Localization 1966 Output with		Output Shift Ratio
Industry	1965	1966	1965	1966	Personal Income	Industry Demand	1965-1966
23 Tobacco	7440	7290	75	72	.911	.707	.1105

Since the United States is one of the few nations producing tobacco in exportable quantities large enough to satisfy the world's tobacco habit, it is not surprising that exports constitute a sizable portion of its sales.

In the manufacture of tobacco, the making of cigars and cigarettes are the only two easily identifiable activities as the following table illustrates.[20]

SIC	Product	Percent of Employment	Percent of Output
2111	Cigarettes	48.7	80.7
2121	Cigars	25.3	9.6
2131	Chewing and Smoking Tobacco	4.8	3.1
2141	Tobacco Stemming and Drying	21.2	6.6

The industry has been undergoing a rapid degree of automation since the mid-1950s, particularly in the manufacturing of the cigarettes.[d] Conveyor systems, computer controlled inventory, accounting and production systems, have all increased output per worker. Changes also occurred in the tobacco stemming and drying sector with the increased production of reconstituted tobacco sheet made from a mixture finely ground natural leaf materials and adhesives. This production process can be mechanized and has reduced labor cost by eliminating the labor intensive task of removing the leaf rib from the tobacco leaf. Material costs have also been reduced since previously unutilized tobacco can be incorporated in the tobacco sheet. The increase in labor productivity is expected to continue, and regardless of what occurs in output trends, employment in the industry is expected to decline.

In 1950, cigarette and cigar manufacturing accounted for slightly under 70 percent of total employment in the tobacco industry, with 40 percent in cigars and 28 percent in cigarettes. By 1960, the percentage had reversed. In 1967, cigar manufacture employed 25 percent of the total, and cigarettes 48 percent. There are locational implications in this shifting of employment, since of the five important tobacco manufacturing states, two, Pennsylvania and Florida, depend on cigar manufacturing, while the others, North Carolina,

---

[d]*Technological Trends in Major American Industries*, pp. 141-147, is the source for the discussion on the changing technology of the tobacco industry.

Virginia, and Kentucky, have most of their employment in cigarette making. As of 1965, the percentage shares of total output in the tobacco industry for these states were: Kentucky (31.4 percent), North Carolina (21.0 percent), Pennsylvania (9.2 percent), Virginia (29.4 percent), and Florida (2.8 percent). The actual shifts in the tobacco industry from 1950 to 1960 reflect the more definite preference for cigarettes. Florida and Pennsylvania showed departure in a negative direction from the average rate of employment growth, while Virginia, Kentucky, and particularly North Carolina showed better-than-average growth. It is impossible to predict the effects of the recent health reports on cigarettes on the growth, prosperity, and even existence of the tobacco industry over the next decades. The industry's past locational behavior depended on changes in taste, and future patterns may also.

The regression equation (6.23) yielded moderate results with an R^2 of .3227 for the change in output and .9971 for the level of output.

$$(6.23) \quad \Delta QD_{23} = 30260.6411 - 94896.2393 TQ_{23} - 36577.8330 TI_{33}$$
$$(15375.7620) \quad (76755.5820) \quad (21603.1450)$$

$$- 5.2237 EMP_{23} - 1.0816 VL$$
$$(2.0002) \quad (.9187)$$

Two of the four transportation variables (TQ_{23}, TI_2, TI_{33} and TI_{34}) entered were significant. The retention of TQ_{23} reflects the consumer products of the industry, while TI_{33} indicates the importance of paper containers. The past history of the industry suggested that employment should have a large negative effect on the dependent variable. The rapid consolidation of the industry into large automated factories from labor-intensive production techniques has increased labor productivity and resulted in declining employment levels at the most efficient production sites. Therefore employment EMP_{23} was substituted for output Q_{23} in the equation, and it was entered immediately after the transportation variables. Value of land was marginally significant.

DEN was not retained in the equation because of multicollinearity. The other variables were rejected either because of insignificance or because they forced previously entered variables to insignificance.

Group 4: Textile and Textile Products

The four industries in this group transform organic fibers obtained from the biotic raw materials group or synthetic fibers purchased from the chemicals and petroleum group into thread, cord, cloth, fabric, and apparel. This group is of moderate size, employing 2.3 million and producing output valued at $47.2 billion in 1965. The industries in the group traditionally require low skilled labor, and over the past 700 years the industry has migrated from high-wage and economically developed areas to low-wage and underdeveloped areas. Indeed, this group generally appears to be the vehicle for economic development of many underdeveloped areas, particularly New England in the nineteenth century, the American South, and Eastern Asia in the twentieth century. In the United States the development of the Southern textile industry, while raising living standards in that area, has created economic problems in New England because of its decline. The migration of textile production is continuing on an international rather than an intranational level. Foreign competition, particularly from Japan, has resulted in the establishment of "voluntary" import quotas. It is too early to determine if the current "voluntary" protectionist policy will become permanent and what will be its long-range locational effect.

Because of the large volume of cotton inputs, the governmental programs for cotton price stabilization is important to textile manufacture, and because of the involvement of large chemical companies in fiber manufacture, the government's antitrust policy can sometimes affect the input decisions of textile makers. Changes in other costs, however, have affected the location of the industry more in recent decades. Wool does lose a great deal of bulk in processing, but its location is an exception. Most wool manufactures are located either in a wool import center, e.g., Boston and its environs, or in areas of domestic supply. The industry as a whole is not particularly capital-using; thus when the successful shift to the South began, it took on the character of a migration. Textile manufacture has been associated with the industrialization of at least two regions that had substantial numbers of poor people. Now, with few untapped pools of unskilled labor remaining in the United States, the textile industry may proceed to increase worker productivity through mechanization and automatic control.

Large-scale enterprise is a prerequisite to the increase in capital stock associated with automating processes. Despite a long history of low levels of monopoly power, the firms in the textile industries have been growing in size for most of the postwar period. The increase in size of firms may be associated with increased predictability of plant location, as the managers of corporations of larger size are generally better able to afford expert advice, generally build larger plants requiring more careful locational planning, and they must consider a market of wider scope than is seen by the manager of a small firm. As the industry automates, there is indication that lower capital expenditures are required to automate existing plants than to build new ones.[21]

There are four industries in the group. Table 6.5 summarizes the national statistics of each industry in the group. Fabrics and yarn, and apparel, highly interrelated industries, dominate the group, accounting for over 84 percent of production in 1965. While production totals in these two industries differ by

Table 6-5
Summary Statistics, Group 4: Textiles and Textile Products

Industry	Output 1966 Prices (000,000) 1965	1966	Employment (000) 1965	1966	Coefficient of Localization 1966 Output with Personal Income	Industry Demand	Output Shift Ratio 1965-1966
24 Fabric and Yarn	18,572	19,714	568	598	.814	.457	.1605
25 Rugs, Tire Cord, Misc. Textiles	3,331	3,565	107	117	.693	.618	.3225
26 Apparel	21,387	22,676	1512	1556	.498	.416	.0741
27 Household Textiles and Upholstery	3,803	3,889	176	186	.528	.477	.1098

small amounts, lower labor productivity in apparel has resulted in employment levels in this industry almost three times as great as in fabrics and yarn. All the industries in the group are geographically concentrated, especially fabrics and yarn with coefficients of localization with respect to personal income ranging from between .498 and .814 and with respect to total demand ranging between .416 and .618.

The industries in the group show a high variation in their locational mobility. IO 25 is the most mobile industry in the study; its shift ratio is .3225. Apparel, however, is relatively stable; its shift ratio of .0741 is the sixth lowest of all agricultural, mining, and manufacturing industries.

IO 24 Fabrics and Yarn

The fabrics and yarn industry produces finished thread and yarn from raw wool and cotton and transforms both organic and synthetic thread to finished cloth. The industry is in a state of transition. Foreign competition, shifts between wool, cotton, and synthetics, as well as the production of an improved product, permanent press and stain resistant, are all modifying the industry's locational structure. If the industry is to grow and satisfy sophisticated consumer demands, it must apply the advanced technology available in other nations to U.S. factories. There have been progressive indications of change. A small number of mills, under construction in the mid-1960s, were being designed to use an advanced system of continuous manufacturing, which was originally developed in Japan.[22] How widespread technological improvements will become is an open question. Based upon past history, the prognosis for the future is poor. One author credits the lack of capital investments in the late nineteenth and early twentieth century in advance production processes in New England with a larger influence on the migration of the cotton textile industry to the South than the influence of regional wage differentials.[23]

The following table shows the relative size of the subsectors of the industry.[24]

SIC	Product	Percent of Output
221	Weaving Mills, Cotton	33.9
228	Yarn and Thread Mills	19.5
222	Weaving Mills, Synthetics	19.0
226	Textile Finishing, except Wool	14.7
223	Weaving and Finishing Mills, Wool	8.8
224	Narrow Fabric Mills	4.4

Cotton is still the largest product, while synthetics have surpassed wool in percentage terms.

The fabrics and yarn industry is an intermediate industry. The level of intraindustry transactions (33.8 percent) of output is high and consists of transfer of yarn to weaving mills and raw fabric to finishing mills. The major markets for fabrics and yarn are the other industries in the textile group, as the following table summarizing the interindustry relations of the industry indicates.

	Suppliers	Percent		Buyers	Percent
IO 36	Plastics and Synthetics	10.2	IO 26	Apparel	40.7
IO 2	Crops	7.0	IO 27	Household Textiles and Upholstery	8.6
IO 35	Basic Chemicals	2.8			
IO 25	Rugs, Tire Cord	2.5	IO 25	Rugs and Tire Cord	5.8

The major inputs are naturally crops, and plastics and synthetics.

The highest regional concentration of the industry occurs in the South. Five southern states accounted for over 73 percent of the nation's output in 1965: North Carolina (29.4 percent), South Carolina (23.3 percent), Georgia (11.6 percent), Virginia (4.9 percent), and Alabama (4.7 percent). Other states with significant output level were Pennsylvania (4.2 percent) and Massachusetts (3.7 percent).

The regression equation (6.24) produced good results with an R^2 of .4207 for the change in output and .9964 for the level of output

$$(6.24) \quad \Delta QD_{24} = \quad 2350.2840 - 293.8593TI_{35} - .4796VL + .0812Q_{24}$$
$$(2250.0072) \quad (245.9383) \quad (.3881) \quad (.0072)$$

Only one of the five transportation variables entered (TQ_{24}, TI_2, TI_{36}, TI_{35}, and TI_{25}) was retained. TI_{36} was multicollinear, while the others were insignificant. Wages were insignificant, hinting that wage differentials within the country are not as significant a determinate of locational change as had previously been believed. The positive sign Q_{24} is consistent with economies of scale found in the newly constructed plants.

EQ_{24} was rejected because of an incorrect sign, while *DEN* was multicollinear. The other variables either were insignificant or forced previously entered variables to insignificance.

IO 25 Rugs, Tire Cord, and Misc. Textiles

This industry is the smallest in the textile group, but it is extremely mobile. Its shift ratio of .3325 is the highest of all industries in the study. The industry is composed of two basic sectors: SIC 227 Floor Coverings and SIC 229 Misc. Textile Goods. SIC 229 is the larger of the two, accounting for 57 percent of output in 1967.[25]

The dual composition of the industry was reflected in its sales distribution in the 1966 summary interindustry table below.

	Suppliers	Percent		Buyers	Percent
IO 24	Fabric and Yarn	21.5	*PCE*		40.8
IO 36	Plastics and Synthetics	17.8	IO 27	Household Textiles	10.6
IO 1	Crops	4.2	IO 40	Rubber and Plastics	9.8
			IO 24	Fabric and Yarn	9.4

Rugs are sold primarily to *PCE*, while miscellaneous textiles are an intermediate product sold to fabrics and yarn, household textiles, and plastics. The two major inputs are fabrics and yarn and plastics and synthetics.

The industry, though closely associated with fabrics and yarn, has not migrated to the South to the extent occurring in the other textile industries. Indeed, four Northeastern states accounted for over 27 percent of the nation's output in 1965: Pennsylvania (9.6 percent), Massachusetts (7.4 percent), New York (5.9 percent), and New Jersey (4.1 percent). Ohio accounted for 4 percent, while California produced 4.3 percent. The state highest in output was Georgia (30.5 percent), which together with North Carolina (5.8 percent) and South Carolina (4.7 percent), accounted for over 40 percent of the industry's output.

The regression equation (6.25) yielded good results. The R^2 was .5617 for the change in output, and only .9934 for the level of output:

$$(6.25) \quad \Delta QD_{25} = 1906.4508 + .0911Q_{25} - 346.7943TI_{36}$$
$$(1531.2202) \quad (.0105) \quad (227.9562)$$

$$- 213.9060TI_1 + .0872DEN + .0027Q_{24}$$
$$(188.8928) \quad (.0437) \quad (.0017)$$

Two of the four transportation variables entered (TQ_{25}, TI_{24}, TI_{36}, and TI_1) were retained. Q_{27}, VL, and TI_{24} were multicollinear with other variables. The significance of Q_{24}, however, does affirm the industry's close ties with IO 24 Fabrics and Yarn. Output was interchanged with TI_{24} in the equation because of the importance of agglomeration factors in the industry. The other variables were rejected because of insignificance or because they forced previously entered variables to insignificance.

IO 26 Apparel

The processes of the apparel industry are reasonably simple; each factory requires only a few skilled workers—the cutters—and a large number of sewing machine operators. Equipment is light enough and slow enough in becoming obsolete that entry and exit of firms can be frequent. In spite of this the industry is locationally stable. Its shift ratio of .0741 was the fourth lowest of all nonservice industries. The location of the industry is dependent to some extent on the location of the wholesaling centers throughout the country. Regional markets such as Dallas serve a surrounding area of several states, for which it would be relatively easy for a plant located on one side of the market region to ship orders to the other side. The situation in New York, however, is rather more complicated, since this is a national market, and orders taken there may be shipped anywhere in the United States. The transportation network that links New York with the rest of the nation and the world gives it an almost unique advantage for the location of factories as well as wholesaling.

In its location, apparel appears to be subject to both market-access influences and resource features because apparel is a light manufacturing industry and because employees at low-skill levels are important in the processing, labor costs are among the most carefully controlled elements in the industry. Until recently, there have been pools of low-cost immigrant labor in the major market centers. More recently, the areas of important surplus labor have been agricultural regions of the South, the same regions that have attracted textile manufacture. Improvements in transportation and communications, especially the widespread use of trucks for long-haul shipping and the national roadbuilding program, have done a good deal to reduce the importance of being near New York in particular and markets in general. However, there are not unlimited supplies of inexpensive labor even in the South, and computers are already being applied to the design of clothing.

The most important material input is fabrics and yarn as the 1966 summary interindustry table presented below indicates.

	Suppliers	Percent		Buyers	Percent
IO 24	Fabrics and Yarn	26.9	PCE		75.6
IO 36	Plastics and Synthetics	2.4			

	Suppliers	Percent	Buyers	Percent
IO 74	Misc. Manufactur- ing Products	1.8		
IO 27	Household Textiles	1.6		

PCE is the major market. The industry purchases a large percent of its own output (18.58). These intraindustry transfers are primarily in the form of contract processing between manufacturers.[26]

The products of the industry are listed below.[27]

SIC	Product	Percent of Output
233	Women's and Misses' Outerwear	24.3
232	Men's and Boy's Furnishings	17.6
225	Knitting Mills	16.8
231	Men's and Boy's Suits and Coats	7.1
234	Women's, Children's Undergarments	6.6
235	Hats, Caps, and Millinery	4.2
238	Misc. Apparel and Accessories	4.1
237	Fur Goods	1.2

The major products are knit goods, men's and boy's furnishing, and women's and misses' outerwear. Knit products will increase their share of the market because technology and style changes have increased the use of knit fabrics in pants, jackets, suits, and dresses.[28]

The movement to the South from the Northeast has been small in comparison with other textile industries. North Carolina, Tennessee, and Texas with 9.7 percent, 4.4 percent, and 4.2 percent of the industry's output in 1965 were the only states in the South with significant output levels. The industry is still concentrated in the Northeast with four states accounting for over 45 percent of the industry's output. New York with 25.4 percent is the largest, followed by Pennsylvania (9.6 percent), New Jersey (6.2 percent), and Massachusetts (3.8 percent). Other states with appreciable output levels in 1965 were California (5.3 percent) and Illinois (5.2 percent).

The results of the regression equation (6.26) were moderate compared with the other industries in the textile group. The R^2 for the change in output was .1912, but for the level of output it was a very high .9966.

$$(6.26) \quad \Delta QD_{26} = 919.8396 - 2442.8751TI_{74} + .0299PCE_{26}$$
$$(580.4342) \quad (2091.8558) \quad (.0056)$$

$$+ .0140Q_{24} + .0134Q_{36} + .0189Q_{27}$$
$$(.0035) \quad (.0117) \quad (.0144)$$

Only one of the five transportation variables entered (TO_{26}, TI_{24}, TI_{36}, TI_{74}, and TI_{27}) was retained. TQ_{26} and TI_{27} were multicollinear, and TI_{24} and TI_{36} had incorrect signs. The significance of PCE confirms the market orientation hypothesis of the industry. The other significant agglomerative variables reflect cost factors.

Two other variables were rejected because of multicollinearity: Q_{26}, and Q_{74}. EQ_{10} was also rejected because of an incorrect sign, while the others were rejected because of insignificance or because they forced previously entered variables to insignificance.

IO 27 Household Textiles and Upholstery

This industry produces a widely diversified set of products as indicated in the table below.[29]

SIC	Product	Percent of Output
2792	Household Furnishings, NEC	27.5
2396	Automotive and Apparel Trimmings	22.2
2393	Textile Bags and Canvas	
2394	Products	16.2
2397	Schiffli Machine Embroideries and	
2399	Fabricated Textile Products, NEC	16.2
2391	Curtains and Draperies	12.0
2395	Pleating and Stitching	4.0

The largest product, household textiles, NEC, consist of kitchen textiles (towels, dust cloths, napkins, tableclothes, etc.), bed linens (pillowcases, sheets, etc.), wardrobe bags, etc., all not produced in weaving mills. The other products are sold to a wide variety of markets as the following 1966 summary interindustry table indicates.

	Suppliers	Percent	Buyers	Percent
IO 24	Fabrics and Yarn	29.5	PCE	49.0
IO 25	Rugs, Tire Cord	10.0	IO 69 Motor Vehicles	11.4
			IO 26 Apparel	8.2

Almost half of the output is sold to PCE, while the remainder is used as an input by the textile and auto industries. The major input is fabrics and yarn.

The industry is highly concentrated, even with the diversity of output. The state with the largest percent of output in 1965 was New York (19.2 percent). Michigan, the primary location of the automobile industry, produced 17.9 percent. Other states with appreciable output levels were New Jersey (7.8

percent), California (6.9 percent), North Carolina (5.7 percent), Massachusetts (4.6 percent), Pennsylvania (4.5 percent), and Georgia (4.1 percent).

The regression equation (6.27) yielded very good results. The R^2 for the change in output was .7135, and .9977 for the level of output.

(6.27) $\Delta QD_{27} = 1737.6255 - 7998.9948TI_{24} - .1011Q_{27}$
  (722.1130)   (7022.6248)   (.0061)

  $- 319.9049WR_{27} + .2845DEN + .0963PCE_{27}$
  (158.4757)   (.0325)   (.0203)

  $+ .0032Q_{24}$
  (.0026)

Two of the transportation variables entered (TQ_{27}, TI_{24}, and TI_{25}) were retained. TQ_{27} was multicollinear with other variables. The change in output is market orientated, as indicated by the significance levels of PCE and DEN. Three variables retained in the equation reflected cost considerations: Q_{27}, WR_{27}, and Q_{24}. The order of the variables was modified by interchanging Q_{27} with WR_{27} and VL, because of the importance of plant modernization. VL was multicollinear in (6.27).

Q_{26} was rejected because of multicollinearity. The remaining variables were insignificant or forced previously entered variables to insignificance.

Group 5: Lumber and Lumber Products

The industries of Group 5 are linked together by an interindustry chain, from lumber to furniture, modern containers, and paper, and finally from paper to publishing. The publishing industry is the largest of the group and has had the most rapidly growing employment as the statistics in Table 6-6 indicate.

The technology of the industries in Group 5 is highly diverse, ranging from the practices of unskilled workers in lumber camps to the techniques of skilled cabinet makers and automated factories in the furniture industries to the highly automated assembly-line procedures in the paper and publishing industries. The more automated industries tend to grow faster and are locationally more stable than the labor-intensive industries. The industries of the group, however, are locationally stable, with the exception of wooden container whose shift ratio is .2833. All other shift ratios are less than .13.

The lumber and furniture industries are not strongly oriented toward the location of their demand, nor to the location of consumers. The coefficients of localization for the paper containers and for publishing industries, however, show a definite demand orientation.

Table 6-6

Summary Statistics, Group 5: Lumber and Lumber Products

Industry	Output 1966 Prices (000,000) 1965	1966	Employment (000) 1965	1966	Coefficient of Localization 1966 Output with Personal Income	Industry Demand	Output Shift Ratio 1965-1966
28 Lumber and Products Excluding Containers	10,591	10,859	659	672	.642	.412	.0788
29 Wooden Containers	436	470	35	36	.674	.589	.2833
30 Household Furniture	4,518	4,745	325	342	.587	.568	.1048
31 Office Furniture	2,335	2,143	125	134	.511	.507	.1292
32 Paper and Products, Excluding Containers	13,268	14,166	411	428	.512	.369	.0687
33 Paper Containers	5,191	5,620	210	220	.471	.383	.1210
34 Printing and Publishing	15,579	19,772	1112	1142	.331	.214	.0421

IO 28 Lumber and Lumber Products, Excluding Containers

The lumber and lumber products industry consists of four SIC three-digit industries. Its product groups are given in the table below.[30]

SIC	Product	Percent of output
242	Sawmills and Planning Mills	37.5
243	Millwork, Plywood	34.2
249	Misc. Wood Products	14.5
241	Logging Camps and Contractors	13.8

The industry purchased a very large percentage (33.0) of its own output in 1966, as would be indicated by above listing of products. The major markets of the industry are housing construction, household furniture, and paper products, excluding containers, as the 1966 summary interindustry table presented below reveals. Construction other than housing accounted for 15.2 percent of the sales.

	Suppliers	Percent	Buyers	Percent
IO 3	Forestry and Fishing Products	9.5	Residential Construction	17.0
IO 52	Hardware, Plating Wire	1.7	IO 12 Maintenance Construction	8.2
			IO 32 Paper and Paper Excluding Containers	8.3
			IO 30 Household Furniture	5.8

The largest lumber-producing areas in the United States are in the Pacific Northwest and northern California. Oregon had the largest proportion of output of all states in 1965 with 17.6 percent, followed by California (10.9 percent) and Washington (10.2 percent). These areas produce softwood, which is important not only as solid building lumber but also as plywood and for pulp and chips used in the manufacture of paper and composition materials. Montana and Idaho have large untapped timber reserves, as do Alaska and Colorado, but it is mostly old timber that has not been systematically cared for and therefore includes a high percentage of unusable trees. Improved methods of using old trees and continued reduction in log size of cuts in other areas may entice more lumbering to the states.[31]

The most important hardwood region in the United States is the South, especially Arkansas and North Carolina (4.2 percent of 1965 output). The furniture industry depends on hardwoods. It should be added that the hardwood forests of the South face potential competition from those of Michigan and Wisconsin, whose present depleted condition from early development of furniture factories will probably be reversed. Southern timber crops are starting to suffer a similar malady, although government-sponsored sustained-yield cutting is beginning to help. In the South and Midwest, forests are replacing farms. Since early in this century, the federal government has had a program of buying submarginal farm land for return to the forests. Now medium-sized farms often have small commercial timber stands, especially in creek bottoms where other crops risk being washed away by flooding. An increase in this type of lumbering would mean a more dispersed locational pattern for the lumber and wood products industry as a whole.

The regression equation (6.28) yielded very poor results. The R^2 for the change in output was a disappointingly low .0547, while the R^2 for the level of output was a satisfactory .9965.

$$(6.28) \qquad \Delta QD_{28} = 205.9331 - .0141 Q_{28}$$
$$(45.0616) \quad (.0019)$$

None of the transportation variables (TQ_{28}, TI_3, and TI_{52}) were significant. Because of the importance of timber stands to the industry, output was entered after the transportation variables. This was the only significant variable.

Eleven variables were rejected because of incorrect signs: TQ_{28}, TI_3, TI_{52}, WR_{28}, EQ_{12}, CN_1, Q_{32}, Q_{12}, Q_{30}, and Q_{52}. The other variables were insignificant.

IO 29 Wooden Containers

The wooden container industry is a small industry producing only $36 million in output and employing 35,000 in 1965. The size of the industry is limited by the products it produces, because of their specialized uses as the table below indicates.[32]

SIC	Product	Percent of Output
2441	Nailed Wooded Boxes and Shook	51.7
2442	Wirebound Boxes and Crates	27.4
2443	Veneer and Plywood Containers	6.0
2445	Cooperage	14.9

The wooden container industry is faced with competition by containers made from more malleable materials such as paper, plastics, and metals and thus will remain very small. SIC 2441 and 2442 account for 80 percent of the industry's output. The products of these subsectors are sold principally to crops and beverages as the 1966 summary interindustry table reveals.

Suppliers		Percent	Buyers		Percent
IO 28	Lumber and Products, Excluding Wooden Containers	32.3	IO 2	Crops	20.7
			IO 21	Beverages	13.4
IO 45	Iron & Steel	9.5	IO 81	Wholesale Trade	10.9

California produced the largest percentage of output in 1965 (9.9 percent), followed by Georgia (6.2 percent) and Virginia (5.4 percent).

The results obtained in equation (6.29) were satisfactory. The R^2 for the change in output was .5675, and for the level of output .9855.

$$(6.29) \quad \Delta QD_{29} = -57.9409 + .1304Q_{29} + .7985EQ_{13}$$
$$(22.0942) \quad (.0116) \quad (.2822)$$

The three transportation variables (TQ_{29}, TI_{28}, and TI_{45}) were insignificant. Of the other variables entered only Q_{29} and EQ_{13} had t ratios greater than our critical value of one.

Q_{81} and Q_{45} were rejected because of incorrect signs. The other variables were not retained because of insignificance.

IO 30 Household Furniture

The household furniture industry is of moderate size. Sales were valued at $4.518 billion in 1965. The industry is dominated by the production of wood household furniture and upholstered household furniture as the following table indicates.[33]

SIC	Product	Percent of Output
2511	Wood Household Furniture	47.7
2512	Upholstered Household Furniture	24.8
2514	Metal Household Furniture	11.8
2515	Mattresses and Bedsprings	14.6
2519	Household Furniture, NEC	1.1

Personal consumption expenditures accounted for over three-fourths of industry sales in 1966 as the summary interindustry table indicates.

	Suppliers	Percent		Buyers	Percent
IO 28	Lumber and Products, Excluding Containers	13.9		*PCE*	78.2
				IO 66 Communication Equipment	5.8
IO 52	Hardware Plating Wire	6.6		Residential Construction	4.9
IO 40	Rubber and Plastics	6.4			
IO 24	Fabrics and Yarn	5.1			

The major input is naturally lumber, followed by fabrics and yarn, rubber and plastics and hardware.

The present location of the industry is scattered in a number of states, but moderately concentrated in the South. The major output of the industry occurred in North Carolina in 1965 with 20.7 percent of the industry's output. Seven other states produced more than 4 percent: California (8.8 percent), New York (6.7 percent), Virginia (6.5 percent), Indiana (6.4 percent), Illinois (4.6 percent), Pennsylvania (4.6 percent), and Tennessee (4.5 percent).

Changes in location and shifts in growth pattern for the furniture industry could come from the input side, either in changes in the location of lumber supplies or in the adoption of alternative types of inputs, such as metals or plastics. Changing conditions in the markets in which furnishings are sold may have an effect on the location of the industry, either through relocation of present buyers or through the changing product mix within the furniture industry. The changing location of population, and of personal consumption expenditures, is the most obvious case of the former type of change. The rapid growth through the 1950s of the furniture industry in California can be related to its influx of population.

The regression equation (6.30) explaining the change in output produced moderate results. The R^2 was .2403 for the change in output, and .9928 for the level of output.

$$(6.30) \quad \Delta QD_{30} = 1489.7761 - 185.2298 TI_{52} - .0255 Q_{30} + 3.5865 EQ_{14}$$
$$\quad\quad (1183.2689) \quad (148.7258) \quad (.0057) \quad (.3518)$$

Only one of the five variables of those entered (TQ_{30}, TI_{28}, TI_{52}, TI_{40}, and TI_{24}) was retained. The others were multicollinear. Output and equipment expenditures were the only other significant variables.

Q_{40} was rejected because of an incorrect sign. The other variables were either insignificant or forced previously entered variables to insignificance.

IO 31 Office Furniture

The office furniture industry is approximately half the size of the household furniture industry. Its products, however, differ considerably from the latter industry as the following table illustrates.[34]

SIC	Product	Percent of Output
252	Office Furniture	29.6
253	Public Building Furniture	16.0
254	Partitions and Fixtures	38.3
259	Misc. Furniture and Fixtures	16.1

The major product is partitions and fixtures and has no direct parallel in the household furniture industry. While the other products may be similar to the sectors of the household furniture industry, their input structure is substantially different (metals vs. lumber and plastics vs. fabrics) so as to constitute distinct commodities. A comparison of the household furniture industry's input structure with that of the 1966 summary interindustry table of the office furniture industry would verify the distinctions.

	Suppliers	Percent	Buyers	Percent
IO 45	Iron and Steel	10.6	Equipment Sectors	61.9
IO 28	Lumber and Products Excluding Containers	7.7	State and Local Governments	12.5
			Governments	6.5
IO 40	Rubber and Plastic Products	5.8		
IO 52	Hardware	3.9		

The switch from wood to metal after World War II has changed the production characteristics of the industry from a carpentry industry to a manufacturing process resembling fabricated metals. There are a number of basic reasons for the acceptance of metal office furniture and the rapid growth of the industry since World War II. Metal furniture is more durable than wood and thus a rational investment choice. The demand for office furniture has increased because of the substantial growth in the governmental sector of the economy and the transition of the private economy from manufacturing to service orientation requiring office rather than factory labor. As the interindustry table shows, office furniture is sold principally to state and local government and as equipment to private industry (mainly the trade and service industries). Sales to *PCE* are only 6.48 percent in contrast to the household furniture industry sales of *PCE* of 78.18 percent. A third reason for an expected continuation in the growth of the industry is the functional adaptability of the modular concept of office furniture. Office layouts can quickly be changed when required by rearranging partitions of modifying the basic desk units themselves. Modular office furniture is thus a substitute for maintenance construction.[e]

North Carolina had the highest proportion of the industry's output in 1965 (11.9 percent). Other states with similar output levels were California and New York with 10.3 percent. Over 28 percent of the industry's output was produced in five states producing iron and steel in significant quantities: Illinois (6.9 percent), Pennsylvania and Michigan (6.0 percent), Ohio (5.0 percent), and Indiana (4.7 percent).

The regression equation (6.31) yielded highly significant results. The R^2 for the change in output was .8967, while the R^2 for the level of output was .9973.

$$(6.31) \quad \Delta QD_{31} = 812.5435 - .1402Q_{31} - 53.7152TI_{45}$$
$$(436.2204) \quad (.0036) \quad (21.4306)$$

$$- 62.1055TI_{28} + 1.4012EQ_{15}$$
$$(47.3238) \quad (.3021)$$

$$+ .0235DEN + .0002Q_{45}$$
$$(.0083) \quad (.0002)$$

Two of the four transportation variables (TQ_{31}, TI_{45}, TI_{28}, and TI_{40}) were retained. The orientation of office furniture to the iron and steel industry was revealed by the significance of TI_{45} and Q_{45}. TQ_{31} and TI_{40} were dropped because of multicollinearity. The capital expenditure variable EQ_{15} and the level of output Q_{31} were both highly significant. The significance of *DEN* reveals that the industry is growing in urban areas.

Four additional variables were not retained because of multicollinearity: *VL*, GOV_9, PCE_{31}, and EQ_{61}. Three variables had incorrect signs: EQ_{59}, Q_{28}, and Q_{40}. The other variables were insignificant.

IO 32 Paper and Paper Products, Excluding Containers

The paper and paper products industry differs significantly from the others in the lumber group, except paper containers, in its type of manufacture and its

---

[e]*Growth Pace Setters in American Industry 1958-1968*, U.S. Department of Commerce, October 1968, pp. 80-82 discusses the market structure and product design of the industry as a determinate of its future growth.

type of markets. The manufacture of paper is growing rapidly, offering significant competition for available timber to the wood products and furniture industries. It has an advantage in this competition since it can take trees of considerably smaller size than are suitable for either lumber or furniture. The products of the industry and their relative sizes are listed below.[35]

SIC	Product	Percent of Output
261	Pulpmills	4.9
262	Papermills, Excluding Building Paper	32.2
262	Paperboard Mills	19.3
264	Misc. Converted Paper Products	41.3
266	Building Paper and Board Mills	2.3

The lines of intraindustry flows are clear from the product breakdown. Pulp mills provide the inputs to paper and paperboard mills; and thus output is fabricated into miscellaneous converted paper products and building paper board. The significance of the intraindustry flows is reflected in the industry purchasing 18.53 percent of its own output. Pulp provides cellulosic inputs to the manufacture of rayon, certain acetate plastics, and explosives. Chemicals derived from pulp are used as thickeners, dispersants, protective coatings, and tanning materials. The output of paper mills goes in rolls to thousands of daily newspaper establishments around the country and goes flat in varying sizes and shapes to the producers of magazines and books. Paper is used to manufacture boxes and bags. The summary of the 1966 interindustry relations follows.

	Suppliers	Percent		Buyers	Percent
IO 28	Lumber and Products, Exc. Containers	6.9	IO 34	Printing and Publishing	22.8
IO 35	Basic Chemicals	3.7	IO 33	Paper Containers	15.7
IO 33	Paper Containers	2.8	PCE		10.8

The channels of distribution necessary for the production of paper and paperboard make it necessary for any community that may want to attract a paper complex to have fairly direct access to acceptable pulping timber. The competition from Canada in the paper industry is enough to make cost considerations of this type crucial to the success of any new plant. From time to time, new technology makes a different type of timber acceptable for pulp purposes. The development of ways to utilize hardwoods and southern slash pine in the manufacture of paper has had the effect of opening up whole sections of the Southeast for the paper industry. Similar developments are having a like effect on the forests of the Northwest. The impetus to these developments is of course, the ever-expanding demand for paper, as printable surface, packaging, and office supplies.

No state produced more than 7.3 percent of the industry's output in 1965.

States that led in production were Wisconsin (7.3 percent), New York (7.3 percent), Pennsylvania (6.2 percent), Ohio (6.1 percent), California (5.6 percent), Illinois (5.5 percent), Michigan (5.2 percent), Massachusetts (4.7 percent), and Georgia (4.7 percent).

The regression equation (6.32) yielded successful results with an R^2 of .5401 for the change in output and .9959 for the level of output.

$$(6.32) \quad \Delta QD_{32} = -567.1504 - 1149.0523 TQ_{32} - 1028.4136 TI_{33}$$
$$(565.0441) \quad (662.3673) \quad (382.6180)$$

$$+ .0628 Q_{32} + .1085 EQ_{16} + .0088 Q_{28}$$
$$(.0049) \quad (.0357) \quad (.0065)$$

$$+ .0055 Q_{35}$$
$$(.0040)$$

Two of the four transportation variables (TQ_{32}, TI_{28}, TI_{35}, and TI_{33}) were significant. The retention of TQ_{32} indicates a degree of market orientation in the industry's output changes. Output and EQ_{16} were very significant. A number of agglomeration variables reflecting cost factors also retained significance.

Q_{33} was rejected because of multicollinearity. The other variables were either insignificant or forced previously entered variables to insignificance.

IO 33 Paper Containers

The paper container industry is a fabricating industry transforming purchased paper board, special food board and other materials into the products listed below in the table.[36]

SIC	Product	Percent of Output
2651	Folding Paperboard Boxes	20.5
2652	Setup Paperboard Boxes	4.8
2653	Corrugated and Solid Fiber Boxes	49.9
2654	Sanitary Food Containers	18.4
2655	Fiber Cans, Drums, Related Material	6.5

The rapid growth of this industry has been a function of technology and our rising standard of living. A major innovation in paper containers was the development of a waterproof fibre box. That product has put paper containers in a competitive position with respect to other waterproof containers. The use of aluminum in conjunction with paper has allowed the industry to successfully invade the province of metal containers in the food processing and petroleum industries.

The rising standard of living since World War II has been responsible for the great increase in convenience goods and prepared foods. These factors have stimulated the demand for paper containers. The market of the industry is highly diversified and does not depend upon a limited number of sectors for its continued expansion as the 1966 summary input-output table indicates.

	Suppliers	Percent		Buyers	Percent
IO 32	Paper and Products Excluding Containers	38.6	IO 15 Dairy Products		7.5
IO 35	Basic Chemicals	1.8	IO 32 Paper and Products, Excluding Containers		6.8
			IO 37 Drugs, Cleaning		5.2
			IO 40 Rubber and Plastic		4.1

The industry tends to locate in conjunction with other manufacturing industries in the large industrial states. Illinois had the largest share of the industry's output in 1965 with 10.4 percent. Other states with important output levels were: New York (9.3 percent), California (8.4 percent), Pennsylvania (8.0 percent), Ohio (7.3 percent), New Jersey (6.9 percent), Michigan (5.4 percent), and Massachusetts (4.4 percent).

The regression equation (6.33) yielded excellent results. The R^2 for the change in output was .7478 and .9975 for the level of output.

$$(6.33) \qquad \Delta QD_{33} = -\ 401.1727 - 415.6233 TQ_{33} + .0938 Q_{33}$$
$$(265.6896) \qquad (318.1762) \qquad (.0041)$$

The transportation variables were significant for only one of the three variables (TQ_{33}, TI_{32}, and TI_{35}) entered. The market orientation of changes in output is reflected by the significance of TQ_{33}, and the stability of the industry is indicated by the positive sign on Q_{33}.

Q_{32} and Q_{37} were not retained because of multicollinearity. The other variables were rejected because of insignificance or because they forced the previously entered variables to become insignificant.

IO 34 Printing and Publishing

This industry has the highest degree of locational stability in the study. Its shift ratio was only .0421. The newspaper sector is the primary cause of the stability. Newspapers dominate the industry as the following table indicates.[37]

SIC	Products	Percent of Output
2711	Newspapers	46.5
2721	Periodicals	25.0
273	Books	23.6
274	Book Printing	4.9

The industry has experienced rapid growth since World War II. This growth is expected to continue, because the major reading population between 18 and 64 will continue to grow until 1980. The technology of the industry is being revolutionized by the application of computers in typesetting, the switch from the letterpress to offset lithographic printing and the widespread use of color print.[38]

While *PCE* purchases a large share of the output of the industry, its major market is business services as the 1966 summary input-output table indicates.

	Suppliers	Percent		Buyers	Percent
IO 32	Papers and Products, Excluding Containers	18.2	IO 85	Business Services	43.9
IO 83	Real Estate and Rental	6.3	PCE		23.1
IO 85	Business Services	3.6			
IO 35	Basic Chemicals	2.7			
IO 73	Optical and Photograph	1.1			

While a number of inputs are important to the industry, paper dominates the input structure.

The industry tends to be located in urban areas and is spatially diffused throughout the nation. New York had the largest share of output in 1965 with 22.6 percent. Other states with significant output levels were: Illinois (10.1 percent), California (7.5 percent), Pennsylvania (6.2 percent), Ohio (5.7 percent), and Texas (5.5 percent).

The regression equation (6.34) produced excellent results, primarily because of the stability of the industry. The R^2 for the change in output was .9913 and .9996 for the level of output.

$$
(6.34) \quad \Delta QD_{34} = \underset{(295.5404)}{372.8599} - \underset{(255.2096)}{422.3030 TI_{32}} - \underset{(.0271)}{.0346 VL}
$$

$$
+ \underset{(.0013)}{.2699 Q_{34}} + \underset{(.0443)}{.2166 EQ_{18}}
$$

Only one of the four transportation variables (TQ_{34}, TI_{32}, TI_{35}, and TI_{73}) was significant. The retention of TI_{32} indicates the importance of paper to the industry. The value of land was barely significant. The output variable is highly significant which is not surprising, since in an extremely stable industry output will grow where it currently exists. The application of modern technology is reflected in the significance of EQ_{18}.

Three variables were not retained because of multicollinearity: *DEN*, Q_{85}, and *PCE*. The other variables were rejected because of insignificance or because they forced previously retained variables to insignificance.

Group 6: Chemicals and Petroleum

The industries in this group are closely related. The output of one is an important input of another. The products of the petroleum and chemical mining industries are sold to the basic chemical and petroleum refining industries. These products are purchased by the plastic and synthetics; drugs, cleaning and toilet items; paint and allied products; and rubber and plastics products industry. The latter industries also engage in appreciable transactions among themselves.

This group includes some of the largest (petroleum mining and refining, basic chemicals, and rubber and plastics) and the smallest (chemical mining and paint and allied products) industries in the study as Table 6-7 containing the national statistics of the group illustrates. The industries of the group share a number of common characteristics. They possess economies of scale and except for drugs, cleaning, and toilet items, the efficient plant is large in relation to the market.

Table 6-7

Summary Statistics, Group 6: Chemicals and Petroleum

Industry	Output 1966 Prices (000,000)	
	1965	1966
8 Petroleum Mining	10,400	10,923
10 Chemical Mining	929	949
35 Basic Chemicals	17,191	18,588
36 Plastics and Synthetics	6,813	7,557
37 Drugs, Cleaning, and Toilet Items	9,673	10,632
38 Paint and Allied Products	2,753	2,617
39 Petroleum Refining	20,622	21,412
40 Rubber and Plastic Products	10,876	11,872

	Employment (000)		Coefficient of Localization 1966 Output with		Output Shift Ratio
Industry	1965	1966	Personal Income	Total Demand	1965-1966
8	156	144	.849	.806	.1678
10	18	20	.944	.823	.2101
35	377	401	.562	.400	.1216
36	169	188	.707	.636	.1533
37	201	213	.574	.550	.1402
38	67	66	.558	.560	.1195
39	154	149	.690	.655	.1017
40	473	507	.523	.469	.1244

These technological factors have led to an oligopolistic industry structure with a high degree of locational concentration and stability. The coefficients of localization for personal income range from .523 to .944, while those for total demand fall between .400 and .823. Except for chemical mining, all the shift ratios are below .17.

The future locational development of all the industries in the group has become challenged in a number of regions because of their adverse ecological effects. Petroleum mining interferes with the environment through oil slicks caused by ship wrecks or blow-outs at sea-based wells. The traditional waste products of all mining occurs in chemical mining. Chemical plants pollute the air and water and are a party in environmental court suits in increasing numbers. Plastics and synthetics, paint and allied products, and rubber and elastic products face the same problems as basic chemicals. The petroleum refining industry affects the environment at the processing and consumption level. Gasoline exhaust is the primary determinate of air pollution in a number of our large cities. The long-run effects of consuming the products of the drugs, cleaning and toilet items industry are the subject of increasing scrutiny. This caution is probably justified as the thalidomide and hexachlorophene incident confirm. The productive processes of the industries are similar, involving highly complex transformations of simple inputs with a high level of waste. The industries differ primarily on the definition of their output, although this difference may be more apparent than real, since each industry usually produces secondary products of the other industries.

IO 8 Petroleum Mining

The location of the petroleum mining industry is primarily determined by nonmarket forces. The major effects of prorationing, depletion allowances, and import quotas have been used to encourage oil exploitation over a wider area than would be dictated by the competitive market. These three factors are a creation of the political system of the oil states and the federal government.[39] The location model is not designed, as the regression equations show, to incorporate political variables of this type.

Petroleum mining includes natural gas and natural gas liquids as well as crude petroleum. The following table shows that crude petroleum is the major product.[40]

	Product	Percent of Output
131	Crude Petroleum and Natural Gas	76.0
	Crude Petroleum	62.5
	Natural Gas	13.5
132	Natural Gas Liquids	24.0

The primary market of the industry is petroleum refining as the 1966 summary interindustry table reports.

Suppliers		Percent	Buyers		Percent
IO 83	Real Estate and Rental	21.5	IO 39	Petroleum Refining	91.1
IO 12	Maintenance Construction	3.5	IO 79	Gas Utility	18.5
IO 85	Bus Service	1.0			
IO 35	Basic Chemicals	.8			
IO 63	Service Industry Machines	.8			

The material inputs in this extractive industry are negligible. The major purchases are made from the real estate and with rental and maintenance construction sectors.

Since the industry must be located at the site of the mineral deposit, it is spatially concentrated. Four states accounted for over three-fourths of the output in 1965. Texas produced 39.7 percent, followed by Louisiana (15.6 percent), Oklahoma (9.4 percent), and California (9.1 percent).

The regression equation (6.8) yielded good results, considering the degree of governmental intervention in the industry. The R^2 for the change in output was .5650, and for the level of output .9914.

$$(6.8) \qquad \Delta QD_8 = 2056.1253 - 38.4500TQ_8 - 313.6358TI_{35}$$
$$(3021.6564) \quad (35.5675) \qquad (100.1881)$$

$$+ .1156Q_8 + .1655DEN$$
$$(.0075) \qquad (.0715)$$

Two of the three transportation variables (TQ_8, TI_{63}, and TI_{35}) were retained in the equation. The significance of TQ_8 and DEN indicates that the industry has some tendency to produce near markets whenever possible. The positive sign on output indicates the importance of past discoveries as opposed to new exploration in generating new supplies of oil.

Q_{39}, Q_{69}, Q_{63}, and Q_{35} were rejected because of incorrect signs. Three variables were multicollinear: VL, EQ_3, and Q_{85}. The other variables were not retained because of insignificance or their inclusion forced previously entered variables to insignificance.

IO 10 Chemical Mining

The chemical mining industry extracts and refines a number of dissimilar ores. The most important are potash, soda, and borate minerals; phosphate rock; and sulfur as the following table reveals.[41]

SIC	Product	Percent of Output
1472	Barite	2.1
1473	Fluorspar	1.5
1474	Potash, Soda, and Borate minerals	25.3
1475	Phosphate Rock	26.9
1476	Rock Salt	9.6
1477	Sulfur	34.2
1479	Chemical and Fertilizer Mining, NEC	.5

Over 96 percent of the domestic production of the industry is purchased by three sectors as the summary 1966 interindustry table reveals.

	Suppliers	Percent		Buyers	Percent
IO 55	Construction and Mining Machinery	5.3	IO 35	Basic Chemicals	68.0
IO 35	Basic Chemicals	3.8	Export		21.7
IO 45	Iron and Steel	3.2	IO 2	Crops	6.7
IO 75	Transportation	3.2			
IO 78	Electric Utility	3.0			
IO 79	Gas Utility	2.9			

Imports are a significant source of chemical minerals, amounting to 32.9 percent of national production in 1966. There is no commodity that dominates the input structure of the industry.

The industry is highly concentrated, as are most extractive industries, particularly at the product level. California's and New Mexico's production consists almost entirely of potash, soda, and borate minerals. Florida specializes almost exclusively in the mining of phosphate rock. Florida also had the greatest percentage (20.5) of the industry's output in 1965. Other states with significant output levels were New Mexico (16.2 percent), Louisiana (13.5 percent), California (11.4 percent), Texas (9.7 percent), and Utah (4.2 percent).

The regression equation (6.10) yielded poor results, presumably because of the diversity of the industry's output. The R^2 for the change in output was .1688, but for the level of output it was .9350.

$$(6.10) \quad \Delta QD_{10} = 5734.8723 - 607.7148 TI_{35} + .0637 Q_{10} + .1311 Q_{55}$$
$$(3175.3654) \quad (284.6094) \quad (.0412) \quad (.0990)$$

Only one of the four transportation variables (TQ_{10}, TI_{55}, TI_{35}, and TI_{45}) was significant. The retention of TI_{35} and Q_{55} indicate that the industry is cost oriented. The positive sign on Q_{10} reflects the fixed site nature of the mining process.

Q_{45} was not retained because of multicollinearity. The remaining variables were rejected because of insignificance.

IO 35 Basic Chemicals

The growth of the basic chemical industry is vital to the development of our national economy. The output of the industry is sold in widely diversified markets with all but a few industries making direct purchases. Thus the summary 1966 interindustry table presented below understates the importance of the industry.

	Suppliers	Percent		Buyers	Percent
IO 75	Transportation	2.8	IO 36	Plastics and Synthetics	13.1
IO 81	Wholesale Trade	2.7			
IO 85	Business Services	2.3	IO 2	Crops	8.1
IO 10	Chemical Mining	2.2		Exports	7.7
IO 79	Gas Utility	2.1		Defense	6.2
IO 78	Electric Utility	1.9			
IO 58	Material Handling Equipment	1.0			
IO 49	Metal Containers	1.0			

The table does reveal the extensive input structure, mainly in the form of services. The widely diversified markets of the industry create a problem in defining the products of the industry as the following table reveals.[42]

SIC	Product	Percent of Output
281	Industrial Chemicals	74.2
286	Gum and Wood Chemicals	1.0
287	Agricultural Chemicals	9.6
289	Misc. Chemicals	15.2

The main products are defined as industrial chemicals, which are sold to almost all the other industries in the study. Miscellaneous chemicals consist of adhesives and gelatin; explosives; printing industry; carbon black; and chemical preparations, NEC.

The oligopolistic structure of the industry reduces the influence of the competitive market on the industry. Companies combine to market new products, ". . . du Pont and National Distillers to manufacture ethyl alcohol; du Pont and Dow (Midland Ammonia) in synthetic ammonia; Ethyl and Dow (Ethyl-Dow) to manufacture ethylene dibromide; . . . ,"[43] etc., diminishing the ability of the competitive process to spatially allocate resources.

The economies that might be considered in locating a chemical plant—aside from those directly involved with transport costs of materials and product, or availability of labor—often involve matters of waste disposal and treatment. Communities oblivious to waste treatment problems or communities willing to share the costs of treatment facilities are the most attractive to chemical operations. In addition, adequate ways for processing—whether used directly in making chemicals or in cooling, heating, and similar needs—is essential for most chemical plants.

Relative rates of growth of consuming sectors provide a method for getting at shifts in output mix. Whether consumer and export demand for chemical products grows relatively more rapidly than demand generated through the other important buyers will surely have an effect on location. The existence of net exports in the output structure of this industry is a result of the extremely advanced technological developments available here, but not elsewhere. This type of technological advantage is likely to be lost through competition, especially over a long period.

The state with the largest percentage of output in 1965 was Texas with 11.3 percent. Other states producing significant values were: New Jersey (7.9 percent), Ohio (6.4 percent), Illinois (6.3 percent), Tennessee (5.7 percent), West Virginia (5.7 percent), California (5.4 percent), and Louisiana (5.2 percent).

The regression equation (6.35) yielded moderate results. The R^2 for the change in output was .2357, and it was .9938 for the level of output.

$$(6.35) \qquad \Delta QD_{35} = 2750.5103 - 757.5576 TI_{49} + .0432 Q_{35}$$
$$\qquad\qquad (2075.2710) \quad (608.2271) \qquad (.0043)$$

Only TI_{49} of the four transportation variables (TQ_{35}, TI_{10}, TI_{58}, and TI_{49}) was significant. Output is highly significant reflecting the economies of scale found in the industry.

WR_{35}, Q_2, EX_{35}, DEF_{35}, and Q_{10} were rejected because of incorrect signs. The other variables were rejected either because they were insignificant or their retention would have forced previously entered variables to insignificance.

IO 36 Plastics and Synthetics

This industry, except for cellulosic man-made fibers, has been developed in the last few decades. This development has been characterized by constant innovation, with new products constantly replacing older products. The industry is also one of the most rapidly growing in the nation, primarily because of the high quality of the output in relation to the natural products it is replacing. Indeed, prices are greater than or equal to those of their natural counterparts in synthetic rubber and organic fibers, noncellulosic.[f] The following table lists the major products of the industry.[44]

---

[f]*Growth Pacesetters in American Industry 1958-1968*, pp. 68-70, 111-114, 146-148, is the major source for the discussion of this industry.

SIC	Product	Percent of Output
2821	Plastic Materials and Resins	47.4
2822	Synthetic Rubber	12.6
2823	Cellulosic Man-made Fibers	12.3
2824	Organic Fibers, Noncellulosic	27.7

The products are diverse in terms of their primary markets. Plastic materials are sold as inputs to plastic fabricators to be made into containers or industrial products. Synthetic rubber is sold to the rubber industry to be fabricated into tires which are in turn sold to motor vehicles and *PCE*. Both fibers have the same markets: fabrics and yarn, and rugs and tire cord. The noncellulosic fibers have been replacing the cellulosic fibers in all three markets. These marketing relationships appear in the 1966 summary input-output table.

	Suppliers	Percent		Buyers	Percent
IO 35	Basic Chemical	35.2	IO 40	Rubber and Plastics	32.4
IO 32	Paper and Products, Excluding Containers	3.3	IO 24	Fabrics and Yarn	19.6
IO 85	Business Services	3.1	IO 25	Rugs and Tire Cord	9.3
			IO 26	Apparel	7.1

Its basic input is chemicals. The linkages of the industries in the chemical group are confirmed by this table via the transformation of basic chemicals by plastics and synthetics and then purchased by the rubber and plastic products industry.

The industry is regionally concentrated primarily because of the large scale of plant. Virginia produced the largest percentage (12.7) of any state in 1965. Other states with significant production levels were: Tennessee (9.9 percent), Pennsylvania (8.7 percent), West Virginia (5.3 percent), Florida (5.2 percent), Ohio (5.0 percent), and North Carolina (4.8 percent).

The regression equation (6.36) produced moderate results. The R^2 for the change in outputs was .2717, and it was .9046 for the level of output.

$$(6.36) \quad \Delta QD_{36} = 323.6674 + .0441 Q_{36} - .1713 DEN$$
$$(254.5717) \quad (.0062) \quad (.0940)$$

$$+ .0053 Q_{40} + .0051 Q_{26}$$
$$(.0027) \quad (.0034)$$

None of the three transportation variables (TQ_{36}, TI_{35}, and TI_{32}) were retained. The significance of Q_{40} and Q_{26} indicate a market orientation of the change in output. The negative sign on *DEN* could be related to the undesirability of plants located in urban areas.

VL was not retained because of multicollinearity, while TI_{32} and Q_{24} had incorrect signs. The others were rejected because they were insignificant or forced previously entered variables to insignificance.

IO 37 Drugs, Cleaning, and Toilet Items

This industry produces a number of highly dissimilar products ranging from antibiotics to floor cleaners. The major product groups appear in the table below.[45]

SIC	Product	Percent of Output
2831	Biological Drugs	1.4
2833	Medicinals and Botanicals	3.8
2834	Pharmaceutical Preparations	39.7
2841	Soap and Other Detergents	22.0
2842	Polishes and Sanitation Goods	9.4
2843	Surface Active Agents	2.4
2844	Toilet Preparations	21.3

Pharmaceutical preparations dominate the industry. This sector has grown rapidly as the demand for medical services fostered by medical insurance and Medicare has increased. The age distribution of population favors the growth of this sector since the over-65 age group, requiring more drugs than other age groups, will increase in coming years.[46]

The major markets are *PCE*, medical and educational institutions, state and local government and exports as the 1966 summary input-output table indicates.

	Suppliers	Percent		Buyers	Percent
IO 85	Business Services	16.5	*PCE*		63.5
IO 35	Basic Chemicals	7.6	IO 88	Medical and Educational Institutions	7.7
IO 40	Rubber and Plastic	4.1			
IO 33	Paper Containers	2.6	State and Local Government		5.6
IO 49	Metal Containers	2.0	Export		3.6

The industry purchases 6.36 percent of its own output. The input structure shows the importance of the products of the other industries in the group (basic chemicals and rubber and plastic products) to the industry. The most important input is advertising, which originates in business services.

Illinois had the largest share of production with 15.9 percent in 1965, followed by New Jersey with 12.2 percent. Other states with substantial output levels were New York (9.4 percent), Pennsylvania (8.2 percent), Indiana (8.1

percent), California (7.5 percent), Ohio (6.7 percent), and Michigan (6.5 percent).

The regression equation (6.37) produced extremely poor results. The R^2 for the change in output was only .0570, one of the lowest in the study, while the R^2 for the level of output was a respectable .9966.

$$(6.37) \qquad \Delta QD_{37} = 3599.3320 - 1852.9264TI_{40} + .0116Q_{37}$$
$$(1213.9284) \qquad (1114.7733) \qquad (.0050)$$

Of the five transportation variables (TQ_{37}, TI_{35}, TI_{40}, TI_{33}, and TI_{49}) only one was significant. Output level was the only other significant variable.

TQ_{37} and Q_{33} were not retained because of multicollinearity. The other variables were rejected because they were either insignificant or forced previously entered variables to insignificance.

IO 38 Paint and Allied Products

The paint and allied products industry is composed of a single four-digit industry SIC 2581. Its product is relatively homogeneous compared with other industries, although there is some diversification within the industry. Latex and acrylic paints are replacing ancient oil based paints in most uses.

The industry resembles the basic chemical industry in its productive process. A few inputs are modified by chemical and other processes to yield the final product. Regardless of the amount of "do-it-yourself" home painting, the major market for paint still resides in construction, as the 1966 summary interindustry table shows.

	Suppliers	Percent		Buyers	Percent
IO 35	Basic Chemicals	20.7	IO 12	Maintenance Construction	36.8
IO 36	Plastics and Synthetics	8.5			
IO 49	Metal Containers	6.4	IO 69	Motor Vehicles	6.5
IO 81	Wholesale Trade	5.2	IO 50	Heating, Plumbing	4.7
IO 39	Petroleum Refining	3.8			
				Residential Construction	3.6

The input structure reflects the interdependencies of the group. Basic chemicals are the major input, while plastics and synthetics and petroleum refining are utilized in significant quantities.

Illinois had the largest share of production in 1965 with 16.6 percent, followed by California with 14.6 percent. Other states with appreciable output levels were Ohio (9.6 percent), New Jersey and Michigan (7.2 percent), Pennsylvania (7.0 percent), Texas (4.4 percent), and Kentucky (4.1 percent).

The regression equation (6.38) produced moderate results. The R^2 for the change in output was .2102, and .9740 for the level of output.

$$(6.38) \quad \Delta QD_{38} = - \ 2866.7228 \ - \ 302.0263 TQ_{38} \ - \ 216.4786 WR_{38}$$
$$(3424.0838) \quad (258.5034) \qquad (125.6303)$$

$$- \ .0683 VL \ - \ .0940 Q_{38} \ + \ .0261 Q_{50}$$
$$(.0463) \qquad (.0190) \qquad (.0128)$$

There were five transportation variables entered in the equation: TQ_{38}, TI_{35}, TI_{36}, TI_{49}, and TI_{39}. The significance of TQ_{38} and Q_{50} indicates a degree of market orientation of the output changes. While EQ_{22} had an incorrect sign, all the other cost variables were retained in the equation.

Two variables were not retained because of multicollinearity: DEN and Q_{12}. The other variables were rejected either because of insignificance or their inclusion forced previously entered variables to become insignificant.

IO 39 Petroleum Refining

The petroleum refining industry is the largest in the chemical group and one of the largest in the study in terms of output. Sales were over $21 billion in 1966. The employment in the industry is relatively low; only 155,000 in 1965. The high level of productivity per worker reflects the capital intensity and economies of scale in the industry. Economies of scale have been substantial enough so that the number of refineries declined from 361 to 282 between 1947 and 1963, while output almost doubled during this time period.[47]

Large-sized plants are very expensive to obtain in terms of time and money. Planning and building a new refinery takes years and costs tens of millions of dollars. These factors account for the locational stability and concentration of the industry.[48]

The state with the largest share of output in 1965 was California with 17.7 percent, followed by Texas with 13.9 percent. Other states with large output levels were Louisiana (11.8 percent), Pennsylvania (9.8 percent), Illinois (9.3 percent), Indiana (7.3 percent), Ohio (6.7 percent), and Kansas (4.4 percent).

The industry's input-output structure is exceedingly simple as the 1966 summary table indicates.

Suppliers	Percent	Buyers	Percent
IO 8 Petroleum Mining	48.5	PCE	44.4
IO 85 Business Services	2.4	IO 81 Wholesale Trade	4.0
IO 83 Real Estate and Rental	2.0		
IO 35 Basic Chemicals	1.8		

The primary inputs are the products of the petroleum mining industry. The use of other commodities in the production process is exceedingly small. Its major market is *PCE* primarily in the form of gasoline and oil, which is indicated in the following product table.[49]

SIC	Product	Percent of Output
291	Petroleum Refining	92.1
295	Paving and Roofing Materials	5.4
299	Misc. Petroleum and Coal Products	2.6

The regression equations (6.39) produced moderate results. The R^2 for the change in output was .2300 and .9885 for the level of output.

$$(6.39) \quad \Delta QD_{39} = 25064.2170 - 217.9090TI_8 - 432.0826TI_{35}$$
$$(9869.3228) \quad (105.0181) \quad (280.1590)$$

$$- .0390Q_{39} + .0703Q_{35}$$
$$(.0066) \quad (.0176)$$

Raw material transportation costs are important to the petroleum industry, as the significance of two of the three transportation variables (TQ_{39}, TI_8, and TI_{35}) indicates. The most significant variable was output, reflecting the economies of scale in the industry. The retention of Q_{35} and TI_{35} show the interdependence between chemicals and petroleum refining.

Q_8 and Q_{85} were rejected because of incorrect signs. The other variables were rejected either because of statistical significance or because they forced previously entered variables to insignificance.

IO 40 Rubber and Plastics Products

The rubber and plastics products industry employed 473,000 workers in 1965, more than any other industry in the chemical group. However, output ranked fourth. Low labor productivity in one sector of the industry, miscellaneous plastics products, is the primary reason for these statistics as the table below illustrates.[50]

SIC	Product	Percent of Employment	Output
3011	Tires and Inner Tubes	17.9	29.3
3021	Rubber Footwear	5.6	3.4
3031	Reclaimed Rubber	.3	.2
3069	Fabricated Rubber Products, NFC	27.4	24.6
3079	Misc. Plastics Products	48.7	42.4

The miscellaneous plastic products industry consists of 74 subproducts ranging from aquarium accessories to ice chests or coolers to work gloves. This industry has grown rapidly since 1940. It is characterized by low capital requirements, and entrance into the industry is relatively easy.[51] The tires and inner tube sector differs considerably from miscellaneous plastic products. Its product is well defined, there are high capital cost and economies of scale in the industry, and productivity is high.[52] Both sectors purchase their major input from IO 36 plastics and synthetics as the 1966 summary IO table illustrates.

	Suppliers	Percent	Buyers	Percent
IO 36	Plastics and Synthetics	18.7	PCE	19.1
IO 25	Rugs and Tire Cord	3.0	IO 69 Motor Vehicles	8.7
IO 35	Basic Chemicals	3.0	IO 37 Drugs, Cleaning	3.7

While PCE and motor vehicles are the major markets, no market overwhelmingly dominates the industry.

Ohio accounted for 20.3 percent of production in 1965, more than three times the level of any other state. The location of the tire and inner tube industry in Akron, Ohio, is the primary reason for this large percentage. Other states with significant output levels were California (6.9 percent), New Jersey (6.8 percent), Massachusetts (6.7 percent), Illinois (6.3 percent), Pennsylvania (5.5 percent), New York (5.3 percent), and Indiana (5.2 percent). Michigan, the site of the automobile industry, produced only 4.6 percent.

The regression equation (6.40) produced good results. The R^2 for the change in output was .3772 and .9967 for the level of output.

$$(6.40) \quad \Delta QD_{40} = -\ 430.8063 - 1022.3132 TQ_{40} + .0209 Q_{40}$$
$$(481.8378) \quad (582.9665) \quad (.0044)$$

$$+\ .7232 EQ_{24} + .0005 Q_{69} + .0460 Q_{36}$$
$$(.1727) \quad (.0005) \quad (.0121)$$

Only one of the four transportation variables ($TQ_{40}, TI_{36}, TI_{35}$, and TI_{25}) was retained. TI_{25} was multicollinear, while TI_{36} and TI_{25} had incorrect signs. The significance of TQ_{40} and Q_{69} reveals market orientation in the changes in output. Output and EQ_{24} were the only other cost variables to be retained. The wage rate was insignificant. The importance of plastics and synthetics as inputs was confirmed by the significance of Q_{36}.

The other variables were rejected either because of insignificance or because they forced previously entered variables to insignificance.

Group 7: Leather and Footwear

The leather and footwear group is composed of two industries within the two-digit classification SIC 31. Future growth of these industries is uncertain. Foreign competition from Italian and Far Eastern merchants has undercut the ability of domestic shoe producers to compete, and the development of synthetic leathers has affected the use of natural leathers. The drive for clean rivers also has affected leather tanning in a negative manner. Tanning wastes, which historically had been dumped untreated into local streams, now have to be removed from the processing liquid before the liquid is returned to the environment. This requirement has raised production costs and will accelerate the abandonment of obsolete tanning plants.

The national statistics presented in Table 6-8 show the importance of IO 42 shoes and other leather products compared with IO 41 leather tanning. Both of the industries are geographically concentrated as their coefficients of localization illustrate. Shift ratios indicate that these industries are locationally stable.

Table 6-8
Summary Statistics, Group 7: Leather and Footwear

Industry	Output 1966 Prices (000,000) 1965	1966	Employment (000) 1965	1966	Coefficient of Localization 1966 Output with Personal Income	Industry Demand	Output Shift Ratio 1965-1966
41 Leather and Tanning	1014	988	38	40	.760	.534	.1306
42 Shoes and Other Leather Products	3923	3965	314	325	.646	.625	.1208

IO 41 Leather Tanning

Leather tanning is an extremely old industry extending back to ancient eras in Egypt and the Near East. The basic raw material of leather tanning is animal hides, which is a perishable by-product of the food processing industry.

There are two basic products in the industry: SIC 311 leather tanning and finishing and SIC 312 industrial leather belting. Leather tanning accounted for 91 percent of the industry's output in 1967.[53] The major use of finished leather is as an input to the shoe and other leather products industry (IO 42) as the following table summarizing the 1966 interindustry relations of the industry illustrates:

	Suppliers	Percent		Buyers	Percent
IO 35	Basic Chemicals	7.7		IO 42 Shoes and Other	65.2
IO 37	Drugs, Cleaning	3.6		IO 26 Apparel	6.3

The major competitive threat to the industry in recent years has been the development of synthetic leathers (Corfram) in the mid-1960s as a replacement for natural leather in shoe manufacturing. Corfram enjoyed initial success because of its durability and its potential for increasing the rate of automation of shoe manufacturing. Corfram, however, had one undesirable property: its inability to allow moisture and air to pass through it. This led to consumer discomfort particularly in the hot summer months and was eventually responsible for the demise of Corfram production in 1971.

While the industry is small in size with an output of $1,014 million and employment of 38,000 in 1965, its negative growth has adversely affected regional development in the Northeast, its highest area of concentration. Five states in the Northeast accounted for almost half the industry's output in 1965, the largest being Massachusetts (23.7 percent), followed by New York (7.9 percent), New Jersey (7.6 percent), Pennsylvania (6.8 percent) and New Hampshire (3.5 percent). Other states with large concentrations were Wisconsin (13.7 percent), Illinois (9.8 percent), and Michigan (3.5 percent).

The R^2 for equation (6.41) was only .1044, while the R^2 for the level of output was .9898.

$$(6.41) \quad \Delta QD_{41} = 523.7533 - 78501.5850 TQ_{41} - 1184.0440 TI_{37}$$
$$(662.1741) \quad (56263.0381) \quad (980.6467)$$

$$- 89.6860 WR_{41} + .0448 DEN + .0031 Q_{35}$$
$$(66.8080) \quad (.0208) \quad (.0026)$$

Of the three transportation variables entered in the equation (TQ_{41}, TI_{35}, TI_{37}) two were significant. Although TI_{35} was not significant, the influence of the chemical industry on leather tanning was revealed by the significance of Q_{35}.

VL, Q_{26}, and Q_{37} were not retained because of multicollinearity. EQ_{25} had an incorrect sign, while the others were rejected because of insignificance.

IO 42 Shoes and Other Leather Products

The effect of the failure of Corfram on the shoe industry as well as the influences of protectionist political pressure on future industry growth is too early to determine. The major reason for introducing man-made materials was that it facilitated automation in the shoe industry.[g] Its rejection by consumers, however, does not imply that automation will be frustrated. Indeed, the use of man-made materials was part of an innovative trend beginning in the 1950s.

[g]*Technological Trends in Major American Industries*, pp. 191-194 is the major source for the technical discussion of this industry.

Automated systems exist for molding bottoms to leather uppers, materials handling, and the manufacture of uppers.

Shoes constitute the major product of this industry, comprising 69.5 percent of output in 1967. The following table shows the other products of the industry.[54]

SIC	Product	Percent of Output
313	Footwear Cut Stock	6.2
314	Footwear, Rubber	69.5
315	Leather Gloves and Mittens	2.0
316	Luggage	7.9
317	Handbags, Personal Goods	12.1
3199	Leather Goods, NEC	2.3

All the other products, except handbags, contribute little to the total output of the industry.

The following table showing the 1966 input-output structure of the industry illustrates the importance of *PCE* to the industry:

	Suppliers	Percent		Buyers	Percent
IO 41	Leather Tanning	15.9	*PCE*		89.9
IO 40	Rubber and Plastic	10.3	IO 84	Hotel and Personal Services	5.0
IO 24	Fabric and Yarn	3.3			
IO 25	Rugs, Tire Cord	2.6			

The poor growth of this industry has affected the regional growth of the same areas in the same manner as its closely associated industry, IO 41 Leather Tanning. Six states in the Northeast accounted for more than 53 percent of the industry's output, with New York (14.7 percent) and Massachusetts (14.4 percent) the largest, followed by Pennsylvania (7.4 percent), Maine (6.1 percent), New Hampshire (4.8 percent), and New Jersey (4.4 percent). Other states with important concentrations of output were Missouri (9.9 percent), Illinois (5.6 percent), Wisconsin (5.3 percent), and Tennessee (5.1 percent).

The regression equation (6.42) yielded acceptable results. The R^2 for the change in output was .3312 and .9965 for the level of output.

$$(6.42) \quad \Delta QD_{42} = -180.1544 + .0166Q_{42} + .9464EQ_{26} + .0961DEN$$
$$(118.9141) \quad (.0052) \quad (.6272) \quad (.0218)$$

The five transportation variables (TQ_{42}, TI_{41}, TI_{40}, TI_{24}, and TI_{25}) were rejected because of insignificance. The positive sign on Q_{42} indicates that this industry is locationally stable. The retention of EQ_{26} confirms the importance of automation in the industry.

VL was rejected because of multicollinearity, while *PCE*, Q_{84}, Q_{40}, and Q_{25} had incorrect signs. The other variables were not retained because of insignificance or because they forced previously entered variables to insignificance.

Group 8: Minerals Mining and Processing

There are three industries in this group—mineral mining, glass and glass products, and stone and clay products. Minerals mining is unique among resource industries; it is mobile from year to year because its growth in a region depends on the demand for its output in a market area of subnational scope. There is no doubt that this is a necessary industry, but it is extremely small in size, especially compared with the main industry it serves—construction. In this respect, it is similar to the metal mining industry, which also embodies a process that is overshadowed by what the economy can do with the output once it is processed. The stone and clay products industry is principally an intermediary between stone and clay extraction and construction and because of the huge transport costs associated with the products, the industry is located near its markets. The glass and glass products industry is dependent upon sand in large quantities in its production process, and its location is determined by the availability of sand. Its major markets include sales of containers to the food industry and flat glass to the auto industry.

The national statistics presented in Table 6-9 show that the industries are relatively small in size measured by all criteria compared to other industries in the study.

Table 6-9
Summary Statistics, Group 8: Minerals Mining and Processing

Industry	Output 1966 Prices (000,000)		Employment (000)		Coefficient of Localization 1966 Output with		Output Shift Ratio 1965-1966
	1965	1966	1965	1966	Personal Income	Industry Demand	
9 Mineral Mining	3939	4158	108	107	.560	.543	.2703
43 Glass and Glass Products	3956	3416	165	175	.703	.659	.0887
44 Stone and Clay Products	8865	9268	455	471	.394	.357	.1064

IO 9 Minerals Mining

The minerals mining industry consists of a large array of SIC subsectors listed below.[55]

SIC	Product	Percent of Output
141	Dimension Stone	1.1
142	Crushed and Broken Stone	46.1
144	Sand and Gravel	34.2
145	Clay and Related Minerals	10.5
148	Nonmetallic Minerals Services	.7
149	Misc. Nonmetallic Minerals	7.3

The product distributions corroborate the observation from the input-output summary presented below that the major products of IO 9 are sold mainly as raw materials for the products of IO 44.

	Suppliers	Percent		Buyers	Percent
IO 40	Rubber and Plastic	4.1	IO 44	Stone and Clay	44.9
IO 55	Construction and Mining	3.0		Highway Construction	30.3
IO 83	Real Estate and Rental	2.6	IO 12	Maintenance Construction	19.5
IO 53	Engines and Turbines	2.4	IO 45	Iron and Steel	5.1

Capital inputs are important to the industry, because of the heavy work required and the low initial value of the materials processed in the industry.

Since the products of the industry are found throughout the United States, it is not surprising that the states with the largest populations also have the highest concentration of the output of the industry. California, the most populous state, had the largest percentage (13.1) in 1965 of all the states. Six other states produced more than 4 percent: Illinois (7.0 percent), Texas (5.8 percent), Georgia (4.9 percent), New York (4.8 percent), Ohio (4.7 percent), and Pennsylvania (4.5 percent).

The R^2 for the change in output was .3105, and .9916 for the level of output.

$$(6.9) \quad \Delta QD_9 = 76.0503 - 42.7184 TI_{55} + .0324 Q_9 + .0031 Q_{12}$$
$$(95.3193) \quad (41.9791) \qquad (.0059) \qquad (.0004)$$

Of the four transportation variables (TQ_9, TI_{40}, TI_{55}, TI_{53}), only one was retained. TI_{53} was multicollinear, while TQ_9 and TI_{40} had incorrect signs. The importance of capital equipment to the industry is revealed by the high significance of TI_{55}. The advantage of producing near markets is exemplified through the significance of Q_{12}, maintenance construction.

VL and DEN were not retained in the equation because of multicollinearity, while Q_{44} and Q_{45} had incorrect signs. The remaining variables were statistically insignificant or forced previously entered variables to insignificance.

IO 43 Glass and Glass Products

The glass industry is a small industry, in comparison to its major users, the food and motor vehicles industries, with an output of $3.9 billion and employment of 165,000 in 1965. Its input-output structure may be summarized as follows:

	Suppliers	Percent		Buyers	Percent
IO 35	Basic Chemicals	6.3	IO 21	Beverages	17.5
IO 33	Paper Containers	5.5	IO 69	Motor Vehicles	11.2
IO 85	Bus Services	2.4	IO 16	Canned and	
IO 40	Rubber and Plastic	2.2		Frozen Foods	8.3
			PCE		7.7

Containers dominate the output flows to the food, chemicals, and trade industries, while the major consumers of flat glass are motor vehicles and construction. Light bulb and other vacuum tube envelopes are sold to the electrical equipment industry, while individual consumers purchase glassware for the most part. The importance of the various types of glass manufacture is presented in the following table.[56]

SIC	Product	Percent of Output
321	Flat Glass	18.2
322	Glass, Glassware, Pressed or Blown	64.8
323	Products of Purchased Glass	17.0

Containers are included in SIC 322 and account for this sector's dominance of the industry.

Glass is far less interesting when examined by input rather than sales. The paper and allied products purchased by the glass industry are containers for the finished product. The process of glass making is based on sand, which is a rather inexpensive commodity even though particular types of sand are preferred. Glass is made by cooling molten materials in such a manner that they do not crystallize, but remain viscose enough to act like solids. Until recently, the fuel has been gas or oil, gas being somewhat preferable because of its clean burning. Lately, electric heat has been introduced. Fiberglass is made somewhat differently. It is a promising structural material as well as an interesting textile. The manufacture of bottles is a very automatic process because it is a high-volume operation and because it gets sharp competition from other materials.

Actual distribution of output by states in 1965 reflected the location of sand suitable for glassmaking and good market access. Ohio and Pennsylvania had high percentages of output, 15.0 and 11.0 percent, respectively. Other states having large percentages were Illinois (9.0 percent), New York (8.7 percent), New Jersey (8 percent), California (7.2 percent), West Virginia (7.0 percent), and Indiana (4.5 percent).

The regression equation (6.43) yields good results with an R^2 of .7206 for the change in output and .9928 for the level of output.

(6.43)　　$\Delta QD_{43} = 544.6578 - 90.1950 TI_{35} - .1225 Q_{43} + .0008 Q_{69}$
　　　　　　(488.2223)　(51.1826)　　　(.0059)　　　(.0003)

Only one of the four transportation variables (TQ_{43}, TI_{35}, TI_{33}, TI_{40}) was retained. The level of output Q_{43} was responsible for explaining most of the variance of the dependent variable. The industry is locationally stable with a shift ratio of .0887 and the decline in output between 1965 and 1966 was evenly spread throughout the industry. Changes in output had a degree of market orientation as indicated by the significance of Q_{69}.

Three variables were not retained because of incorrect signs: Q_{21}, Q_{35}, and Q_{33}. The other rejected variables were insignificant or caused previously entered variables to become insignificant.

IO 44 Stone and Clay Products

The major function of the industry is the processing of the output of IO 9 minerals mining which in turn is sold to the construction industry as illustrated in its input-output structure below:

	Suppliers	Percent		Buyers	Percent
IO 9	Minerals Mining	9.3		Housing Construction	17.2
IO 75	Transportation	5.4		Highway Construction	7.2
IO 85	Business Services	2.1		Industrial Construction	6.4
IO 35	Basic Chemicals	1.5	IO 12	Maintenance	
IO 32	Paper and Products, Excluding Containers	1.4		Construction	5.2

Concrete, gypsum, and plaster products dominate the industry as the following table illustrates:[57]

SIC	Product	Percent of Output
3241	Cement, Hydraulic	17.8
325	Structural Clay Products	12.7
326	Pottery and Related Products	6.3
327	Concrete, Gypsum, Plaster Products	37.5
3281	Cut Stone and Stone Products	2.2
329	Misc. Nonmetal Mineral Products	23.4

Cement of all types is obviously connected with construction, as are gypsum and plaster. The inputs to these sectors are crushed and broken stone, sand, and gravel. In addition to the structural group, some china and pottery, made from clay, ceramic, and refractory materials, find their way into the construction industry as plumbing fixtures and electrical insulation. Abrasives are used in construction too, although metal working abrasives account for most of the value of sales for this sector. Dimension and cut stone have no important uses outside the construction industry.

Location of the industry is rather dispersed. California, with 10.6 percent of output in 1965, followed by Ohio (8.8 percent), Texas (7.4 percent), Pennsylvania (6.5 percent), New York (6.2 percent), Illinois and New Jersey (5.3 percent), are the largest producers of stone and clay products.

The regression equation (6.44) yielded poor results. The R^2 factor for the change in output was only .1685, and .9932 for the level of output.

(6.44) $\quad \Delta QD_{44} = 281.7298 - 41.8674TQ_{44} - 926.4359TI_{32}$
$\qquad\qquad\qquad$ (336.4479) $\quad$ (17.6319) $\qquad$ (263.9026)

$\qquad\qquad\qquad + .0272Q_{44} + .0600EQ_{28} + .0461DEN$
$\qquad\qquad\qquad\quad$ (.0054) $\qquad$ (.0568) $\qquad$ (.0305)

The weight and bulk of the products of the industry explain the significance of TQ_{44} and IT_{32}. TI_{35} was not retained because of insignificance, while TI_9 had an incorrect sign. The importance of locating near growing urban areas is confirmed by the significance of Q_{44}, DEN and CN_{18}. CN_{18} is the value of highway construction.

Four additional variables were rejected because of multicollinearity: VL, CN_1, Q_{12} and Q_{85}. WR_{44} had an incorrect sign. The other variables were not retained because of insignificance or because they forced previously entered variables to insignificance.

Group 9: Metal Mining, Smelting, and Basic Products

The metals group produces the raw materials for most capital goods production as well as many of the most important consumer products. Machinery, farm equipment, motor vehicles and other transportation equipment all depend to some extent on the metals industries. The location of the market industries are factors in the location of some metals plants.

In terms of size, the most important of these industries is primary iron and steel as is seen in Table 6-10. While iron and steel is about three times larger than the next largest industry in the group, the other industries are still large

Table 6-10

Summary Statistics, Group 9: Metal Mining, Smelting, and Basic Products

Industry	Output 1966 Prices (000,000)		Employment (000)		Coefficient of Localization 1966 Output with		Output Shift Ratio
	1965	1966	1965	1966	Personal Income	Industry Demand	1965-1966
5 Iron Ore Mining	813	860	28	28	.938	.925	.2328
6 Nonferrous Ore Mining	2,108	2,204	55	58	.910	.703	.1948
45 Iron and Steel	22,633	25,161	973	971	.639	.456	.0956
46 Copper	5,903	6,553	74	77	.757	.430	.1828
47 Aluminum	4,647	5,161	121	136	.657	.383	.2723
48 Other Nonferrous Metals	6,163	7,414	144	158	.630	.564	.2040
49 Metal Containers	3,097	3,330	54	64	.666	.601	.1641
50 Heating, Plumbing, Structural Metal Products	8,830	9,683	434	462	.373	.413	.0921
51 Stampings, Screw Machine Products	5,576	6,331	264	287	.567	.451	.1038
52 Hardware, Plating, Wire Products	7,791	8,385	457	491	.463	.396	.0989

compared with others in the study. Output in each industry in the group, except the mining industries, exceeded $3 billion in 1965.

The industries of this group are generally characterized by rather large firms, well-organized channels of distribution from plant to plant, and heavy capital-using plants. All these have had their effects on location, as have the policies of the federal government and the political and economic situation in various foreign countries. The industries in this group are among the most geographically concentrated in the study primarily because of the large size of the plants in the group. The coefficients of localization with respect to personal income range from .373 to .938, and with respect to total demand they range from .396 to .925.

The types of markets in which output is sold and in which supplies are bought are important in determining the response of one of these industries to the location of these markets. The market for steel, for example, has undergone drastic changes. Where once it was the only possible input for any number of vital processes and thus enjoyed a certain monopolistic power regardless of the organizational structure of the industry, its influence has been undermined by competition from nonferrous metals, plastic, concrete and other materials, changing tastes, and product improvement. The mobility of the industries in this group varies considerably with shift ratios ranging between .0921 and .2323.

IO 5 Iron Ore Mining

The chief sources of iron ore for U.S. industry have been in the Great Lakes area and near Birmingham, Alabama. During the past two decades, both these sources of supply have been severely depleted. Works in Alabama now depend on imported ores, and until the discovery of methods to use the taconite ores present in Michigan and Wisconsin, it appeared that the same would be true of the steel centers of the Northeast and East North Central. During the 1950s, a perceptible shift of the iron and steel industry took place to sites that could use any of several sources of imported ores. Works in Baltimore and Philadelphia, as well as in Houston and Birmingham, have this feature of dependence on the world market. Most ore comes from Venezuela and Labrador, although some is also sent from Chile. Imports were almost 70 percent as large as domestic production in 1966.

The domestic industry is divided into two sectors: SIC 101 iron ores, and SIC 106 ferroalloy ores, except vanadiam. Iron ore accounted for 89.8 percent of output in 1967.[58]

The industry is highly concentrated, reflecting ore deposit locations. Over 82 percent of total output in 1965 was concentrated in seven states. The largest of these was Minnesota with 46.0 percent. Other states in this group were Colorado (9.1 percent), Pennsylvania (5.8 percent), Michigan (5.6 percent), California (5.4 percent), New York (5.3 percent), and Montana (4.3 percent).

The input-output structure of the industry is presented in the following table:

	Suppliers	Percent		Buyers	Percent
IO 83	Real Estate and Rental	12.6	IO 45	Iron and Steel	63.4
IO 85	Business Services	3.7	Export		11.0
IO 55	Construction and Mining Equipment	3.1	IO 35	Basic Chemicals	10.7
IO 45	Iron and Steel	2.3			
IO 35	Basic Chemicals	2.1			

As expected the major market is IO 45 basic iron and steel.

The regression Equation (6.5) produced good results with R^2's of .5365 for the change in output and .9707 for the level of output.

$$(6.5) \quad \Delta QD_5 = 3233.5542 - 1395.7708 TI_{55} - .1676 Q_5$$
$$(2450.8592) \quad (823.9421) \quad (.0305)$$

$$+ .3966 EQ_2 + 1.2140 Q_{55}$$
$$(.2023) \quad (.3110)$$

Four transportation variables were entered in the equation: TQ_5, TI_{55}, TI_{45}, and TI_{35}, but only TI_{55} was significant and retained in the equation. TI_{45} and

TI_{35} were multicollinear with other variables. The importance of equipment investment was substantiated by the high levels of significance on Q_5, EQ_2, and Q_{55}.

EX_5 was multicollinear, while WR_5, Q_{45}, and Q_{35} had incorrect signs. All the other variables not retained in the equation were insignificant.

IO 6 Nonferrous Ore Mining

The nonferrous ore mining industry is among the most difficult of the mining industries to analyze because of the heterogeneity of its output. Ores of copper, lead, zinc, aluminum, gold, silver, and metal mining services are included in the industry. It is for the most part controlled by multiunit, multi-industry firms operating on an international scale. Nonferrous ore mining is the initial step in a process of value addition that touches almost every industry in the manufacturing group.

Nonferrous ore mines are necessarily located with deposits of metal, which all too often turn out to be in rugged wilderness where no other economic activity could be carried on profitably. Growth in mining activities is generally associated with the opening of mines, that is, with the discovery of new deposits.

The relative importance of the major nonferrous ore mining groups is given in the table below.[59]

SIC	Product	Percent of Output
102	Copper Ores	54.8
103	Lead and Zinc Ores	12.2
104	Gold and Silver Ores	5.1
105	Bauxite and Other Aluminum Ores	2.3
108	Metal Mining Services	3.9
109	Miscellaneous Metal Ores	21.6

Copper, lead, and zinc ores dominate the industry. The miscellaneous metal ores classification includes the important metals of uranium, radium and vanadium.

The direct interindustry transactions are summarized as follows:

	Suppliers	Percent		Buyers	Percent
IO 35	Basic Chemicals	4.0	IO 46	Copper	34.1
IO 60	Machine Shop	3.8	IO 48	Nonferrous	16.1
IO 55	Construction and		IO 47	Aluminum	10.0
	Mining	2.9	IO 35	Basic Chemicals	6.0
IO 45	Iron and Steel	2.2			

The major purchasers of nonferrous ore are the primary nonferrous metal processing industries: copper, aluminum, and other nonferrous metals.

Two states accounted for 45 percent of output in 1965: Arizona (29.4 percent) and Utah (15.4 percent). Other states producing significant output levels were New Mexico (9.4 percent), Montana (7.8 percent), Colorado (4.5 percent), and Nevada (3.8 percent). These six states produce over 70 percent of the total, indicating the Mountain State orientation of the industry.

Gold is mined chiefly in South Dakota, but also in Colorado and Alaska. Silver comes mainly from Idaho. Lead and zinc are generally found in the same areas. Missouri holds first place among states in lead and zinc production, with Idaho, Utah, and Colorado also important. Iron is mined chiefly in Michigan and Wisconsin. Most copper is mined in Arizona, but substantial quantities are produced in Utah and Montana. Other copper-producing states are Michigan, Nevada, and New Mexico, with a small amount in New York and some in North Carolina and Colorado. The extraction of bauxite for the production of aluminum was of very little importance in the industry's domestic output.

All metal mining must compete with imports. Imported ore, mostly from Chile, is a significant competitor of the copper mining sector. Manganese, an essential ingredient in iron and steel, is entirely imported, coming mainly from India and South Africa. Nickel ores are also imported, largely from Canada. Bauxite comes from Jamaica.

In addition to competition from imports, metal mining is affected by competition in the form of government stockpiles and recirculation of scrap. In the case of uranium and other radioactive metals, the release of government supplies will probably hold down employment growth over the next decade. The reuse of obsolete scrap is already important in the case of lead, iron, and copper.

The regression equation (6.6) yielded poor results. The R^2 for the change in output was .1897; however it was .9872 for the level of output. The only significant variable was the level of output.

$$(6.6) \qquad \Delta QD_6 = -390.0107 + .0559Q_6$$
$$(516.9745) \quad (.0135)$$

All of the five transportation variables (TQ_6, TI_{35}, TI_{60}, TI_{55}, and TI_{45}) were rejected because of insignificance. The diversity of products and hence inputs of the industry could be the cause of this failure. EQ_2 was not retained in the equation because of multicollinearity.

Q_{46} was not retained because of an incorrect sign. The other variables were rejected because of insignificance.

IO 45 Primary Iron and Steel

Primary iron and steel includes coke oven and blast furnace products, steel ingot and semifinished shapes, hot rolled sheet and strip, bars and bar shapes, plates, structural shapes and piling, steel wire, pipe and tube, cold rolled sheet and strip, forgings, and foundries. Its location is fairly well defined at the state level, mainly because of the large plant size associated with most of the industry's production. In 1965, the states with the largest output percentages were Pennsylvania (24.7 percent), Ohio (17.3 percent), Indiana (10.8 percent), Michigan (8.8 percent), Illinois (7.8 percent), New York (4.0 percent), and Alabama (3.9 percent). These states account for more than three-quarters of the nation's output.

The input structure of this industry is straightforward; its outputs are distributed to a variety of industrial markets. Primary iron and steel are intermediate products, with few sales to final demand. The 1966 distribution of important inputs and outputs is:

	Suppliers	Percent		Buyers	Percent
IO 5	Iron Ore Mining	4.8	IO 69	Motor Vehicles	13.7
IO 7	Coal Mining	2.2	IO 50	Heating and Plumbing	9.7
IO 35	Basic Chemicals	2.2			
IO 52	Hardware, Plating	1.7	IO 52	Hardware and Plating	5.6
			IO 51	Stamping, Screw	4.6

Sales to fabricated metals (IO 50-52) generally represents another production link along the way to inclusion of steel in construction and motor vehicles. The primary iron and steel industry is an important consumer of capital equipment as well, with its most important purchases made from industrial machinery and construction. Food and kindred products and the federal government are the other important buyers of fabricated metals, representing markets for containers and ordnance, respectively. These are mentioned because the product composition of the sales of the buyers of primary iron and steel output is reflected in the product composition of orders for the iron and steel industry. The industry also purchases 20.6 percent of its own output. This high figure can be explained by examining the following table.[60]

SIC	Product	Percent of Output
331	Blast Furnace, Basic Steel	22.0
332	Iron and Steel Foundries	56.9
3391	Iron and Steel Forgings	13.1
3399	Primary Metal Products, NEC	8.0

Pig iron produced in blast furnaces is sold to steel producers, while basic steel is purchased by foundries and forges.

It is difficult to draw the product distribution of the industry on an establishment basis, because of the existence in the industry of integrated, semi-integrated, and nonintegrated works. Thus, establishments classified primarily as blast furnaces, steel works, and rolling mills also produce most of the steel pipe and tube, although there are some other establishments whose primary product classification is steel pipe and tube manufacture. Integrated works are the dominate type of establishment. The economies involved in this type of operation are associated with the cost of reheating metal shapes. However, the product mix of the steel industry includes an even more complex assortment of materials for the more sophisticated demands of modern engineering. Where demand is low or irregular, the use of nonintegrated works can prove more economical. Special steel products, whether forgings, castings, extrusions, or rolling mill products, are often made on a regional basis from ingots or semifinished shapes, rather than in the central integrated plants.

Iron is produced almost exclusively as an input to the manufacture of steel. The most economical method of making iron has for some time been the blast furnace process, in which a charge of alternating layers of iron ore and coke is burned from the bottom in a conical furnace. Dwindling supplies of coal have led to increased interest in using coke more efficiently in blast furnaces and in doing away with this method entirely. Developments in iron-making technology could have varying effects not only on the locational distribution but also on the location of the entire primary iron and steel industry.

Inputs into steel manufacture in addition to iron and coke are limestone, air, and water. The chief alloys are manganese, nickel, chromium, molybdenum, vanadium, columbine, titanium, and cobalt. The volumes of the alloys are relatively low, and so their ease of availability is not a prime consideration in locating steel works. If the supply of limestone were a problem, it is likely that substitute materials could be found. The location of iron, both from furnace and scrap sources, is the most important input factor in the location of steel works being built at present. On the input side, these developments appear to make the location of steel works more flexible than in the past, to loosen the grip of coal and iron ore transportation costs, and to make possible location in market areas. With high scrap usage rates prevalent in steel-making, the buyer of steel also becomes a source of input.

The regression equation (6.45) produced good results. The R^2 for the change in output was .6366, and for the level of output was .9972.

$$(6.45) \qquad \Delta QD_{45} = 7672.4152 - 997.7335TI_{52} + .0557Q_{45}$$
$$(7589.4398) \quad (988.1346) \qquad (.0039)$$

$$+ .0101Q_{69} + .0326Q_{50}$$
$$(.0015) \qquad (.0187)$$

Only one of the five transportation variables (TQ_{45}, TI_5, TI_{35}, TI_7, and TI_{52}) was retained in the equation. The significance of Q_{69} and Q_{50} shows a degree of market orientation in the industry. The high significance and position sign of Q_{45} show the importance of economies of scale in the industry.

TQ_{45} and Q_{52} were not retained in the equation because of multicollinearity. TI_{35} and TI_7 had incorrect signs. The other variables were rejected either because they were insignificant or because they forced previously entered variables to insignificance.

IO 46 Copper

The importance of copper is in its electrolytic properties. The enormous rise of electrical products over the past two decades has been reflected in the demand for copper. Recent developments in aluminum-handling technology and in integrated circuits may work against the continuation of the close relations between electrical equipment growth and copper growth.

On the basis of input considerations, copper and brass mills can be divided into two types. One smelts and refines new copper, and the other takes new copper and scrap as inputs for different processes. New copper is refined near its place of extraction. Much of this is done in Arizona, Utah, and Montana, the biggest copper mining states. Basic shapes of new copper go to other copper and brass mills for further processing. The usage of scrap is much higher in copper and brass than in aluminum or iron and steel, amounting to from 40 to 50 percent of the charge for a melt. Scrap suppliers are copper buyers, especially metal fabricators. Market orientation is reinforced by having the market and the source of materials identical.

The newest alloying and forming plants are almost entirely automated, a radical departure from traditional practice. To automate economically, firms have had to plan on larger plant output of individual products, e.g., bars, rods, sheet, and tube, than they produced at any one location by standard methods. This requires locations planned to serve markets several times as large as those served by old plants. As a result of the innovational nature of the installation of computers, employment has not been increasing as rapidly in relation to output as it might be expected to in the future. However, copper has recently been in short supply, and if this shortage persists, a tendency to design away from copper may develop. The following table summarizes the important interindustry relations for 1966.

Suppliers		Percent	Buyers		Percent
IO 6	Nonferrous Ore	12.2	IO 48	Other Non-ferrous metals	21.7
IO 81	Wholesale Trade	4.0	IO 52	Hardware, Plating	5.7
IO 75	Transportation	2.1	Exports		4.0
IO 48	Other Nonferrous metals	1.1	IO 62	Service Industry Machines	3.8
IO 9	Minerals Mining	.4	IO 51	Stamping and Screw Machine Products	3.5

The largest sales are to IO 48 nonferrous metals and consists of copper which is used in the manufacture of electrical wire. The industry also purchased 39.7 percent of its own output, mainly in the form of primary copper as the following table indicates.[61]

SIC	Product	Percent of Output
3331	Primary Copper	22.0
3351	Copper Rolling and Drawing	59.0
3362	Brass, Bronze and Copper Castings	19.0

The industry is centered in three areas of the country. Over 40 percent of the industry's output in 1965 was produced near the source of copper ore in the Mountain states of Colorado (17.2 percent), Arizona (15.3 percent), and Montana (7.5 percent). Three Midwestern states accounted for over 16 percent: Illinois (6.0 percent), Michigan (5.5 percent), and Ohio (5.0 percent). The Middle Atlantic States produced over 20 percent of the nation's total: New Jersey (8.2 percent), Pennsylvania (7.5 percent), and New York (4.5 percent).

The regression equation (6.46) yielded an R^2 of .4237 for the change in output and .9876 for the level of output.

$$(6.46) \quad \Delta QD_{46} = -\ 7896.3217\ -\ 8023.4596 TQ_{46}\ -\ 3060.8782 TI_{48}$$
$$(6500.6314) \quad (3430.2836) \quad (1511.8788)$$

$$+\ .0962 Q_{46}\ +\ 1.0833 EQ_{30}\ +\ .0882 Q_6$$
$$(.0195) \quad (.6149) \quad (.0878)$$

Two of the three transportation variables (TQ_{46}, TI_6, and TI_{48}) were significant. The retention of TQ_{46} shows that the changes in output are somewhat market oriented. TI_{48} shows the importance of the primary metals and fabricated metal industries. The important economies of scale in the industry are revealed by the positive sign on output. Plant modernization is also important as retention of the equipment expenditure variable EQ_{30} confirms.

Three variables were not retained because of multicollinearity: TI_6 Q_{52}, and Q_9. The other variables were not retained in the equation because of statistical insignificance.

IO 47 Aluminum

Aluminum is the most rapidly growing sector of the basic metals group. For all practical purposes, this metal has been in use for no more than 20 or 25 years, and only since 1950 has it begun to shift noticeably to mass production. Rather recently, the high volume production of military aircraft and the accumulation of supplies of missiles and rockets has slowed down, leading to the aggressive pursuit of new markets by aluminum makers.

Aluminum engine blocks are used on some American and foreign cars, especially those from countries where fuel cost makes weight a more important consideration than it is here. Even without the requirement of lightness, aluminum is now used instead of steel or copper in cylinder heads, crankcases, oil pans, pistons, and water jackets.[62]

This interesting metal is also commonly used as siding material for vans, truck trailers, and railway box cars. Aluminum is nearly as good a conductor as copper, but until recently it has been too hard to splice (requiring a non-oxygen-containing atmosphere) to be of use in most electrical applications. The crossing of this technological barrier has been especially welcome to long-distance power transmission, since the lighter weight of aluminum makes possible wider spacing of carrying towers. Aluminum cans, drums, kegs, bottle and can tops, trays, plates, as well as aluminum utensils, steam jackets, and fittings, are important to the food and kindred products industry. These reach final demand by way of the fabricating metals industries.

The major input and sales of the industry for 1966 are summarized in the table below:

Suppliers		Percent	Buyers		Percent
IO 6	Nonferrous Ore	2.8	IO 50	Heating, Plumbing	8.9
IO 60	Machine Shop	1.7			
IO 48	Other Nonferrous	1.6	IO 70	Aircraft and Parts	5.7
			IO 69	Motor Vehicles	5.5

The industry purchases are an extremely large percentage (40.5) of its own output. This large intradependency can be understood by examining the subsectors of the industry in the table below.[63]

SIC	Product	Percent of Output
3334	Primary Aluminum	35.8
3352	Aluminum Rolling and Drawing	41.4
3361	Aluminum Castings	22.8

Primary aluminum is sold to the remainder of the industry.

There is apparently a market factor in recent plant locations in the Tennessee Valley and nearby since they are well situated to serve not only aircraft manufacturers but also metal fabrication, machine works, and motor vehicles manufacture in the manufacturing belt to the north and east. The industry is diffuse at the state level with thirteen states each accounting for more than 3.5 percent of total output in 1965. Ohio, which accounted for only 9.6 percent of total output in 1965, led all states in production. Other states with appreciable output were Illinois (8.3 percent), Indiana (7.8 percent), Tennessee (7.0 percent), Alabama (6.0 percent), Washington (5.9 percent), California (5.4 percent), New York (4.9 percent), Pennsylvania (4.6 percent), Michigan (4.0 percent), Iowa (3.7 percent), and West Virginia (3.6 percent).

The regression equation (6.47) produced very poor results. The R^2 for the change in output was only .0483, but for the level of output it was .9811.

$$(6.47) \quad \Delta QD_{47} = 1268.1538 - 995.0485TQ_{47} - 4660.5592TI_6$$
$$(2408.5334) \quad (843.0475) \quad (2361.1995)$$

Only two of the four transportation variables (TQ_{47}, TI_6, TI_{60}, and TI_{48}) were significant. The others were multicollinear. The market orientation of the industry that is possible is reflected in the significance of TQ_{47}. The importance of cheap transport of ore is revealed by the retention of TI_6.

WR_{47} and Q_{48} were not retained because of incorrect signs. The other variables were rejected because of statistical insignificance or they forced previously entered variables to insignificance.

IO 48 Other Nonferrous Metals

The type of products manufactured in this industry are quite diverse, ranging from primary metals to wire to casting and forging as indicated in the following table.[64]

SIC	Product	Percent of Output
3332	Primary Lead	1.8
3333	Primary Zinc	4.4
3339	Primary Nonferrous Metals	5.1
334	Secondary Nonferrous Metals	9.9
3356	Nonferrous Rolling and Drawing	12.8
3357	Nonferrous Wiredrawing, Insulating	48.6
3369	Nonferrous Casting	12.9
3392	Nonferrous Forgings	5.6

The largest product SIC 3356 nonferrous wiredrawing, insulating accounted for almost half the industry's output in 1967. This subsector includes copper electrical wire which helps account for its large size.

Zinc is the most important of the other nonferrous metals. It is sold principally to primary iron and steel and fabricated metals. Zinc is separated as a by-product of iron ore processing, although it also occurs with lead and silver. Zinc coatings prevent iron parts from corroding. This is its major use, although it is still sometimes used for roofing, gutters, and similar construction applications.

Lead is of some importance among nonferrous metals. Its major use is in storage batteries, although it is also an additive to gasoline and a shielding material. Lead was once considered a by-product of silver production, but the reverse is now the case. The most important use of silver used to be in coinage, and its production will undoubtedly be affected by the introduction of "sandwich" coins in the 1960s. Because silver does not oxidize on heating, it can be bonded to ceramic parts needed for capacitors; this property makes it the best choice for certain types of high-duty bearings and engine parts. Silver sold to miscellaneous manufacture is used not only in instruments manufacture but also for tableware, jewelry, and musical instruments.

An interesting experimental metal is titanium, which is best described as a super-aluminum. It is some 40 percent lighter than an equal-strength steel and behaves well at rather high and low temperatures. Like aluminum, it forms a protective oxide on contact with moist air. Welding and metal-working techniques required for its use are similar to those used on aluminum. Development of commercially feasible processes for reduction, refining, and working of this metal are under way. The major projected use of titanium is in the supersonic transport planes, and some high-speed military aircraft already use this metal in their outer shells. Major ores containing titanium are ilmenite and rutile, often found in coastal regions, now mined chiefly in Florida. The fact that these ores are rather plentiful is further indication that this metal may be important in the future.

The major markets of this industry reflects its heterogeneous products as illustrated in a summary of the 1966 input-output table presented below:

	Suppliers	Percent	Buyers	Percent
IO 46	Copper	14.7	Telephone Construction	8.7
IO 6	Nonferrous	3.9	IO 70 Aircraft and Parts	8.1
IO 47	Aluminum	3.2	IO 45 Iron and Steel	6.0
IO 36	Plasters and Synthetics	2.2	Electrical Apparatus	5.5

The industry purchases 17.24 percent of its own output presumably in the form of primary metal.

Five highly industrialized states accounted for more than 48 percent of the output in 1965: Illinois (12.8 percent), Indiana (11.2 percent), Pennsylvania (9.8 percent), New York (7.2 percent), and Ohio (7.1 percent). Other states with high output levels were Texas (5.9 percent), New Jersey (5.7 percent), California (5.5 percent), Colorado (4.9 percent), and Massachusetts (4.3 percent).

The regression equation (6.48) produced surprisingly good results given the diversity of products in the industry. The R^2 was .8709 for the change in output, and it was .9924 for the level of output.

$$(6.48) \quad \Delta QD_{48} = 4743.7563 - 1109.6452WR_{48} + .2917Q_{48} + .0054Q_{45}$$
$$\quad (3217.8399) \quad (473.6342) \quad (.0147) \quad (.0049)$$

Change in output is influenced by both cost and market considerations. None of the five transportation variables (TQ_{48}, TI_{46}, TI_{6}, TI_{47}, TI_{36}) were retained. The output variable reflecting economies of scale appears to be more important than the others. A degree of market orientation of the industry is revealed in the significance of Q_{45}.

Q_{47} was not retained in the equation because of multicollinearity, while Q_{46} had an incorrect sign. The other variables were either insignificant or forced previously entered variables to insignificance.

IO 49 Metal Containers

The metal container industry traditionally consisted of two operations: fabrication and labeling of the plate by the can manufacturer at his plant; and closing of the can at the cannery. Until the 1950 anti-trust judgments against American Can Company, both operations were controlled by the metal container industry.[h] Closing machines owned by the industry were based to canneries with the provision that the canneries would purchase all their plate from the leasor. The 1950 decision directed the metal container industry to allow the consumer to purchase the closing machines at a court determined price. Ownership of closing machines allowed large consumers of metal cans to internalize their metal container operations. Campbell Soup, one of the major customers of Continental, began producing their own cans after 1950 and rapidly became the nation's third-largest can producer. Other canners who followed this path were Del Monte, Stokely-Van Camp, and Minnesota Valley Canning Company. The metal container industry also faces severe competition from plastic containers, glass, and aluminum. To combat these threats, the can companies have begun to diversify by purchasing other container firms.

The production process of the industry is highly automated. Continuous high-speed assembly lines characterize the industry. The operations require few inputs other than the metal plate, paint and paper labels as the 1966 summary interindustry table reveals.

Suppliers		Percent	Buyers		Percent
IO 45	Iron and Steel	40.1	IO 21	Beverages	25.7
IO 47	Aluminum	4.6	IO 16	Canned and Frozen Foods	24.4

[h]Charles H. Hessin, "The Metal Container Industry," in *The Structure of American Industry* ed. by Walter Admans, The MacMillan Company, New York, is the major source for the disruption of the metal container industry.

Suppliers		Percent	Buyers		Percent
IO 34	Printing and Publishing	4.1	IO 37	Drugs, Cleaning, etc.	7.6
IO 38	Paint and Allied	2.9	IO 35	Basic Chemicals	6.5

While steel is the major input, the size of alumunim is not negligible and it is growing. Aluminum, however, has the disadvantage that it is almost indestructible. Tin cans will rust and return to nature, but aluminum beer cans could grace our roadsides forever. This threat of land pollution has resulted in a number of states and communities passing laws requiring all beverages to be sold in returnable containers. The long-run impact of these laws could be drastic, since beverages account for over one-fourth of sales and are the largest market of the industry.

California, which is a major location for the food processing industries, had the largest share of metal container output in 1965 with 18.6 percent. Illinois, which ranked third in production of meat packing; canned and frozen foods; and beverages had the second largest output of metal containers with 17.6 percent. Other states with appreciable output levels were New Jersey (11.2 percent), Pennsylvania (7.5 percent), New York (6.6 percent), Maryland (5.6 percent), and Florida (5.3 percent).

The regression equation (6.49) yielded good results. The R^2 for the change in output was .5127, and the R^2 for output levels was .9962.

$$(6.49) \qquad \Delta QD_{49} = \underset{(878.3475)}{23.1236} - \underset{(.1317)}{.1485VL} + \underset{(.0176)}{.0209Q_{49}}$$

$$+ \underset{(.0073)}{.0137Q_{21}} + \underset{(.0068)}{.0126Q_{37}}$$

All the transportation variables (TQ_{49}, TI_{45}, TI_{47}, TI_{34}, and TI_{38}) were insignificant. The only cost variable retained in the equation was land value. The positive signs on Q_{49} reflects economies of scale. A degree of market orientation of the industry is revealed by the significance of Q_{21} and Q_{37}.

Six variables were rejected because of multicollinearity: EQ_{31}, DEN, Q_{35}, Q_{47}, Q_{34}, and Q_{38}. The remaining variables were either insignificant or forced previously entered variables to insignificance.

IO 50 Heating, Plumbing, and Structural Metal

This industry produces commodities primarily utilized in the construction industry as the 1966 summary interindustry table reveals.

	Suppliers	Percent		Buyers	Percent
IO 45	Iron and Steel	23.4		Housing Construction	10.8
IO 47	Other Nonferrous	4.6		Equipment Sectors	9.6
IO 52	Hardware, Plating	4.0		Industrial Construction	9.4
IO 85	Business Services	1.7		IO 12 Maintenance	
IO 51	Stamping, Screw	1.5		Construction	6.6

The principal equipment purchasing sector consists of the utility industries. The primary input is iron and steel. The industry produces a large array of products as indicated in the table below.[65]

SIC	Product	Percent of Output
3431	Metal Sanitary Ware	2.06
3432	Plumbing Fittings and Brass Goods	3.32
3433	Heating Equipment, etc., Electric	8.78
344	Fabricated Structural Metal Products	85.83

SIC 344 dominates the industry. It includes fabricated structural steel, metal doors, fabricated platework, sheet and architectural metal work.

The production process requires heavy use of machines, which show as important inputs both on current and capital accounts. The machining operations of this industry are very similar to those of the machinery industries, with the only possible conceptual difference being the usual feature that operations of this industry are aimed at production of rigid structures, while machinery implies the incorporation of moving parts. The labor input of fabricated metals is traditionally highly skilled and highly paid. The design and completion of many of the products of this industry is often on the basis of extremely small batches, so automatic processes have been slow in being introduced.

Pennsylvania produced the largest percent (10.8) of output of any state in 1965. Other states with appreciable output levels were Ohio (9.6 percent), California (9.4 percent), Illinois (7.1 percent), New York (6.8 percent), Texas (5.2 percent), and Michigan (5.2 percent).

The regression equation (6.50) produced good results. The R^2 for the change in output was .6376, while the R^2 for the level of output was .9953.

$$(6.50) \qquad \Delta QD_{50} = 634.7874 - 169.7304 TI_{47} - .0395 VL$$
$$(729.4376) \quad (140.7784) \quad\quad (.0257)$$

$$+ .0917 Q_{50} + .0246 CN_4$$
$$(.0059) \quad\quad (.0154)$$

Only one of the five transportation variables (TQ_{50}, TI_{45}, TI_{47}, TI_{52}, and TI_{51}) was retained. Value of land was marginally significant, but output had the highest level of significance primarily because of the stability of the industry. The retention of CN_4, industrial construction, reveals a degree of market orientation in the industry.

Four variables were not retained because of multicollinearity: DEN, Q_{12}, EQ_{58} (utilities), and Q_{52}. EQ_{32} and Q_{47} had incorrect signs. The other variables were rejected either because of insignificance or because they forced previously entered variable to insignificance.

IO 51 Stamping, Screw Machine Products

The production of this industry in 1967 was approximately two-thirds metal stampings and one-third screw machine products.[66] Screw machine products include bolts, nuts, screws, rivets, and washers, as well as basic metals and plastic materials transformed into unassembled products by screw machines. Metal stampings are manufactured from sheet metal and sold to varied industries, to be used as appliance casings or auto bodies. The primary markets for the industry are electronic and transportation equipment as the 1966 summary interindustry table reveals.

	Suppliers	Percent		Buyers	Percent
IO 45	Iron and Steel	21.4	IO 69	Motor Vehicles	23.2
IO 47	Aluminum	3.2	IO 70	Aircraft Parts	5.4
IO 46	Copper	2.7	IO 67	Electronic Companies	5.2
			IO 66	Communications Equipment	4.5

The major inputs are the basic metals industries of the group.

Michigan, the site of the auto industry, the major buyer of the industry, had the largest state output in 1965 with 15.6 percent of the total. Other states with large output levels were Illinois (14.6 percent), Ohio (14.2 percent), Pennsylvania (10.1 percent), New York (7.0 percent), Wisconsin (5.7 percent), and California (5.4 percent).

The regression equation (6.51) produced excellent results. The R^2 for change in output was .8004, and for the output level it was .9942.

$$(6.51) \quad \Delta QD_{51} = 1809.7593 - 353.7261 TI_{45} - .0938 VL + .1818 Q_{51}$$
$$(1251.0985) \quad (156.0674) \quad \quad (.0841) \quad \quad (.0069)$$

One of the five transportation variables (TQ_{51}, TI_{45}, TI_{47}, TI_{51}, and TI_{46}) entered was retained. The high cost of transporting steel is reflected in the significance of TI_{45}. The cost of plant expansion as reflected in VL is a determinant of locational mobility. The positive sign and high significance of Q_{51} reflect the economies of scale and locational stability in the industry.

TQ_{51}, EQ_{33}, and DEN were not retained because of multicollinearity. Q_{66} and Q_{47} had incorrect signs. The other variables were rejected either because they were insignificant or forced previously entered variables to insignificance.

IO 52 Hardware, Plating, and Wire Products

This industry produces a wide range of products, as the following table illustrates.[67]

SIC	Product	Percent of Output
342	Cutlery, Hand Tools, and Hardware	35.1
347	Metal Plating, Coating, and Polishing	11.9
348	Misc. Fabricated Wire Products	11.5
349	Safes and Vaults, Steel Springs, Pipes, Valves and Pipie Fittings, Metal Tubes, Foil and Leaf	41.4

This industry, along with the others in the group, is primarily an intermediate good, although 6.8 percent is sold to *PCE* as the 1966 summary interindustry table indicates.

	Suppliers	Percent		Buyers	Percent
IO 45	Iron and Steel	14.2	IO 69	Motor Vehicles	11.8
IO 46	Copper	2.4	PCE		6.8
IO 48	Other Nonferrous Metals	2.2	IO 45	Iron and Steel	4.2
IO 85	Business Services	2.0	IO 50	Heating, Plumbing	4.1
IO 35	Basic Chemicals	1.6			

IO 51 and IO 52 both had the same major buyer, motor vehicles. The basic metals are also the major inputs of the industry.

Michigan, as in IO 51, had the largest share of output of any state with 13.1 percent in 1965. Other states with appreciable output levels were Illinois (11.9 percent), Ohio (11.8 percent), California (8.2 percent), Pennsylvania (7.2 percent), and New York and New Jersey (6.3 percent).

The regression equation (6.52) produced good results. The R^2 for the change in output was .5872, while for the level of output it was .9963.

$$(6.52) \quad \Delta QD_{52} = - 2242.4133 - 303.8758 TQ_{52} + .0187 Q_{52}$$
$$(2007.2595) \quad (278.8805) \quad (.0070)$$

$$- .1896 VL + .0555 Q_{48} + .0026 Q_{85} + .0049 Q_{35}$$
$$(.0437) \quad (.0082) \quad (.0005) \quad (.0042)$$

Of the five transportation variables (TQ_{52}, TI_{45}, TI_{46}, TI_{48}, and TI_{35}) only TQ_{52} was retained. While TQ_{52} reveals a degree of market orientation, costs are also very important. Value of land is highly significant, while the agglomeration variables Q_{48}, Q_{85}, and Q_{35} reflect cost considerations. Indeed, the most significant variable was the agglomeration variable Q_{48}. The significance and positive sign of Q_{52} show the importance of economies of scale and locational stability in the industry.

Three variables were not retained because of multicollinearity: *DEN, PCE,* and Q_{50}. Q_{69} and Q_{45} had incorrect signs. The other variables were rejected because they were either insignificant or forced previously entered variables to insignificance.

Group 10: Heavy Machinery, Including Transportation Equipment

The 12 industries in this group are essential to a vigorous economy. They produce the majority of investment goods, counting motor vehicles as an investment for the average citizen. While motor vehicles dominate the group in terms of output, the other industries are also large in absolute terms. The products of this group are complex in relation to those of fabricated metals.[i] While fabricated metals are rigid structures, the commodities in this group are partially composed of moving parts powered by gasoline, diesel fuel, electricity, or steam. They do, however, share the fabricated metal industries' demand for iron and steel. Except for IO 70 aircraft and parts and IO 13 ordnance, iron and steel are the major input of all the industries in the group.

Table 6-11, which contains the national statistics of the group, reveals how large motor vehicles is compared with the rest of the group. It accounts for 47.5 percent of the group output. Regardless of the type of production, job-shop or assembly-line, all the industries in the group are capital-intensive. This accounts for their high level of spatial concentration. Coefficients of localization with respect to personal income range from .424 to .767 with four industry values exceeding .700. The coefficients with respect to total demand are somewhat lower, indicating that the buyers are other industries and not consumers.

The spatial stability of the industries range from extremely stable to fairly mobile. Metal working machinery and equipment, and motor vehicles have shift ratios below one, while four of the industries have shift ratios greater than two.

IO 13 Ordnance

The location and development of the ordnance is primarily a function of federal government expenditures as the 1966 summary interindustry table indicates.

---

[i]Fabricated metals in this context includes: IO49 metal containers; IO50 heating, plumbing, and structural metal products; IO51 stampings, screw machine products; and IO52 hardware, plating, and wire products.

Table 6-11
Summary Statistics, Group 10: Heavy Machinery, Including Transportation Equipment

Industry	Output 1966 Prices (000,000)		Employment (000)		Coefficient of Localization 1966 Output with		Output Shift Ratio 1965-1966
	1965	1966	1965	1966	Personal Income	Industry Demand	
13 Ordnance	6715	6773	225	251	.754	.598	.1995
53 Engines and Turbines	2600	2898	100	109	.763	.696	.2227
54 Farm Machinery and Equipment	3148	3840	135	143	.767	.717	.1960
55 Construction and Mining Machines	4191	4311	187	200	.679	.735	.1300
56 Material Handling Equipment	2275	2698	75	83	.625	.638	.2103
57 Metal-working Machinery and Equipment	6384	7333	319	348	.604	.443	.0606
58 Special Industrial Machinery	3945	4528	202	214	.534	.537	.1316
59 General Industrial Machinery	5828	6482	279	302	.554	.504	.0919
60 Machine Shops and Machinery	2423	2817	170	202	.424	.376	.1163
69 Motor Vehicles	49961	49356	870	922	.659	.371	.0805
70 Aircraft and Parts	14557	17578	648	761	.738	.708	.2116
71 Ships, Trains, Trailers and Cycles	6113	6698	288	329	.606	.555	.2296

	Suppliers	Percent		Buyers	Percent
IO 70	Aircraft and Parts	8.2		Defense 69.0	69.0
IO 67	Electronic Components	4.6		Federal Government	
IO 45	Iron and Steel	3.5		Nondefense	14.4
IO 66	Communications Equipment	2.8		PCE	4.5

The industry produces a wide variety of dissimilar commodities ranging from small arms to tanks and guided missiles as the table illustrates.[68]

SIC	Product	Percent of Output
1925	Complete Guided Missiles	50.1
1929	Ammunition, Excluding Small Arms, NEC	26.6
193	Tanks and Tank Components	4.3
194	Sighting and Fire Control Equipment	1.1
195	Small arms	4.1

SIC	Product	Percent of Output
196	Small arms ammunition	6.4
1911	Guns, Howitzers, and Mortars	7.4
1999	and Ordnance and Accessories, NEC	

Guided missiles dominate the industry as the table illustrates. The industry is spatially concentrated, with California producing 34.8 percent of the industry's output in 1965. Other states which had high output levels were Florida (8.6 percent), Missouri (5.9 percent), Kansas (4.5 percent), and Alabama (4.2 percent).

The regression equation (6.13) produced acceptable results given the diversity of the output of the industry and the unknown influence of politics upon the regional distribution of the industry. The R^2 for the change in output was .1639, and it was .9637 for the level of output.

$$(6.13) \quad \Delta QD_{13} = 27977.0759 - 5072.9437TI_{67} - 218.5744WR_{13}$$
$$(10873.3290) \quad (2012.8259) \quad (161.7231)$$

$$- .3463VL - .0853Q_{13} + .1270GOV_3 + .0303Q_{70}$$
$$(.2597) \quad (.0104) \quad (.0720) \quad (.0057)$$

Transportation cost has only a slight influence on the location of the industry. Only one of the five transportation variables (TQ_{13}, TI_{70}, TI_{67}, TI_{45}, and TI_{66}) was significant. Cost considerations appear important with significance for both value of land and output. While ΔQD_{13} measures change in output less federal government defense purchases, the volume of general government purchases of ordnance does exert an influence on the spatial distribution of the industry as the significance of GOV_3 reveals. The importance of aircraft and parts is confirmed by the significance of Q_{70}.

Three variables were not retained because of multicollinearity: DEN, DEF_3, and PCE. Five variables had incorrect signs: TQ_{13}, TI_{45}, TI_{66}, EQ_5, and Q_{45}. The other variables were rejected either because of insignificance or because of forcing previously entered variables to insignificance.

IO 53 Engines and Turbines

The engines and turbines industry consists of SIC 3511 steam engines and turbines and SIC 3519 internal combustion engines not elsewhere classified. SIC 3519, which excludes aircraft rocket and automotive (except diesel), accounted for two thirds of the industry's output in 1967.[69] The industry's major market is equipment, primarily utility, as the 1966 summary interindustry table indicates.

Suppliers		Percent	Buyers	Percent
IO 45	Iron and Steel	12.1	Equipment Sectors	20.0
IO 60	Machine Shop	3.6	Export	12.7
IO 57	Metal-Working		Defense	7.9
	Machinery	3.2	IO 54 Farm Machinery	7.8
IO 59	General Industrial	3.2		

Iron and steel is the major input, followed by purchases of other products in the heavy machinery group. Most of the equipment is bought by the utility industries.

The industry is concentrated primarily in the Midwest, with four states accounting for over half of the industries output in 1965: Wisconsin (20.1 percent), Michigan (19.7 percent), Illinois (10.8), and Indiana (7.3 percent). Other states with high output levels were New York (12.1 percent), Pennsylvania (11.6 percent), and Massachusetts (5.3 percent).

The regression equation (6.53) for the industry yielded good results. The R^2 for the change in output was .4331, while the R^2 for the output level was .9953.

$$(6.53) \quad \Delta QD_{53} = 1818.5500 - 286.666 TI_{57} + .0151 Q_{53} + 2.4833 EQ_{35}$$
$$(1661.3664) \quad (265.9711) \quad (.0104) \quad (.5264)$$

Only one of the five transportation variables (TQ_{53}, TI_{45}, TI_{60}, TI_{57}, and TI_{59}) was retained. All the others were rejected because of multicollinearity. The significance of output and equipment expenditures indicates the importance of economies of scale to the industry. All the remaining variables were rejected either because of their own insignificance or because they forced previously entered variables to insignificance.

IO 54 Farm Machinery and Equipment

This industry, while a four-digit industry (SIC 3522), produces a wide variety of products, including tractors, harvestors, dairy equipment, incubators. Its major market is agricultural equipment as the 1966 summary interindustry reveals.

Suppliers		Percent	Buyers	Percent
IO 45	Iron and Steel	15.5	Equipment sectors	76.1
IO 59	General Industrial	9.0	Exports	9.8
IO 53	Engines and Turbines	6.2	IO 2	5.4
IO 60	Machine Shop	3.9		

Iron and steel is the most important input. A large quantity of general industrial equipment is also purchased for current account.

This industry is expected to continue to grow rapidly because of the increased mechanization of the agricultural and livestock industries.[70] Exports are primarily to Canada, but should extend to other countries as modern agriculture is introduced into underdeveloped nations. The industry is heavily concentrated in the Midwest with seven states accounting for over three-quarters of the industry's output in 1965: Illinois (22.8 percent), Iowa (20.0 percent), Wisconsin (11.6 percent), Michigan (8.3 percent), Minnesota (4.4 percent), Indiana (4.1 percent), and Ohio (4.1 percent). Kentucky produced 4.2 percent.

The regression equation (6.54) produced good results. The R^2 for the change in output was .7670, while the R^2 for the level of output was .9886.

$$(6.54) \quad \Delta QD_{54} = \quad 674.5134 \ - \ 134.1770TI_{45} \ + \ 13.4614EQ_{36}$$
$$(1394.5349) \quad (120.9232) \quad \quad (.6721)$$

$$- \ .5790DEN \ + \ .3795EQ_1 \ + \ .3777EX_{54}$$
$$(.4403) \quad \quad (.1276) \quad \quad (.0840)$$

Only one of the five transportation variables (TQ_{54}, TI_{45}, TI_{59}, TI_{53}, and TI_{60}) was retained. The significance of TI_{45} shows the industry's relation to iron and steel. The other transportation variables were multicollinear. The industry appears to be dependent upon capital equipment as indicated by the significance of EQ_{36}. The retention of EQ_1 and EX_{54} shows that the industry is market-oriented. The negative sign on DEN shows that output is growing in nonurban areas. The growing importance of the export market is confirmed by the high significance of exports.

IO 55 Construction and Mining Machines

This industry is composed of three sectors: SIC 3531 construction machinery, SIC 3532 mining machinery, and SIC 3533 oilfield machinery. Construction machinery is the largest sector, accounting for 71.7 percent of total sales in 1967.[71] Mining machinery's share was 10.8 percent, while oilfield machinery's was 17.5 percent. The industry's output is also sold in large quantities to foreign nations as the 1966 summary interindustry table reveals.

	Suppliers	Percent		Buyers	Percent
IO 45	Iron and Steel	15.7		Equipment Sectors	51.1
IO 59	General Industrial Machinery	5.4		Export	24.5
IO 57	Metalworking Machinery	4.2			
IO 53	Engines and Turbines	4.1			

The primary inputs are iron and steel and the output of other industries in the heavy machinery group.

The industry is locationally concentrated in the Midwest, with five states accounting for over 61 percent of the industry's output in 1965: Illinois (33.6 percent), Ohio (10.0 percent), Wisconsin (9.6 percent), Iowa (4.4 percent), and Michigan (3.6 percent). Other states with high output levels were Texas (11.6 percent), California (4.6 percent), and Pennsylvania (4.4 percent).

The regression equation (6.55) produced poor results. The R^2 for the change in output was only .0514, although the R^2 for the level of output was a high .9918.

$$(6.55) \qquad \Delta QD_{55} = - \quad 50.0673 + .0127Q_{55} + .0112Q_{59}$$
$$(370.1478) \quad (.0100) \qquad (.0103)$$

None of the five transportation variables (TQ_{55}, TI_{45}, TI_{59}, TI_{57}, and TI_{53}) were significant. Output and Q_{59} were only marginally significant.

Six variables were not retained because of incorrect signs: EQ_{37}, EX_{55}, EQ_2, EQ_4, Q_{45}, and Q_{57}. The other variables were rejected because of statistical insignificance.

IO 56 Materials Handling Equipment

The products of this industry include SIC 3534 elevators and moving stairways, SIC 3535 conveyors and conveying equipment, and SIC 3536 hoists, cranes, and monorails. In 1967 the division of output among the three sectors was 23.0, 48.7, and 28.3 percent, respectively.[72]

The major markets of the industry are the equipment purchasing sectors, primarily mining and miscellaneous manufacturers, as the 1966 summary interindustry table reveals.

	Suppliers	Percent	Buyers	Percent
IO 45	Iron and Steel	10.1	Equipment Sectors	53.9
IO 59	General Industrial Machinery	5.9	Industrial Construction	8.0
			Exports	5.4
IO 63	Electrical Apparatus	4.3		
IO 60	Machine Shop	3.4		

The input structure is similar to the other industries in the heavy machinery group, with the addition of the electrical apparatus industry.

The industry is concentrated in both the Midwest and Middle Atlantic states. Three states in the Midwest produced over 40 percent of the output in 1965:

Ohio (15.9 percent), Michigan (12.4 percent), and Illinois (12.2 percent). Three Middle Atlantic states produced over 28 percent: Pennsylvania (10.5 percent), New Jersey (9.4 percent), and New York (8.5 percent). California produced 7.1 percent.

The regression equation (6.56) yielded excellent results. The R^2 for the change in output was .7906, while the R^2 for the level of output was .9937.

$$(6.56) \quad \Delta QD_{56} = 789.1194 - 114.1305 TI_{45} - .0861 VL$$
$$(870.3374) \quad (88.5964) \quad (.0458)$$

$$+ .1275 Q_{56} + .6059 EQ_{37} + .0172 Q_{63}$$
$$(.0208) \quad (.3408) \quad (.0076)$$

Only one transportation variable TI_{45}, showing the importance of iron and steel, was retained in the equation. The four not retained (TQ_{56}, TI_{59}, TI_{63}, and TI_{60}) were multicollinear. VL, Q_{56}, EQ_{37}, and Q_{63} were significant indicating the industry is cost-oriented. The positive sign on output reflects economies of scale in the industry.

Five additional variables were not retained because of multicollinearity: DEN, EQ_{55}, CN_4, Q_{59} and Q_{60}. The other variables were either insignificant or forces previously entered variables to insignificance.

IO 57 Metal-working Machinery and Equipment

The industry is composed of 5 four-digit SIC sectors. The table below shows that while SIC 3544 is the largest sector in terms of 1967 output, one product does not dominate the industry.[73]

SIC	Product	Percent of Output
3541	Machine Tools, Metal Cutting Types	28.3
3542	Machine Tools, Metal Forming Types	9.5
3544	Special Dies, Tools, Jigs, Fixtures	29.3
3545	Machine Tools Accessories	17.4
3548	Metalworking Machinery, NEC	15.4

The largest market of the industry is the equipment sectors, primarily the iron and steel, and nonferrous metals. The 1966 summary interindustry table also shows that the transportation equipment industries are good customers of the industry on current account.

	Suppliers	Percent		Buyers	Percent
IO 45	Iron and Steel	8.0		Equipment Sectors	41.5
IO 59	General Industrial	3.9	IO 69	Motor Vehicles	7.8
IO 63	Electrical Apparatus	3.0	IO 70	Aircraft and Parts	7.5

The major inputs are iron and steel and products of the heavy equipment group.

The industry is concentrated in the Midwest and Northeast. Four states in the Midwest accounted for over half of production in 1965: Michigan (20.8 percent), Ohio (17.3 percent), Illinois (11.1 percent), and Indiana (3.7 percent). Three Northeastern states produced over one-fifth: New York (8.8 percent), Pennsylvania (7.7 percent), and Massachusetts (5.1 percent). Colorado (5.4 percent) was the only other state with a high output level.

The regression equation (6.57) produced good results, given the diversity of the output of the industry. The R^2 for the change in output was .4454, and it was .9911 for the level of output.

$$(6.57) \quad \Delta QD_{57} = 3672.8464 - 345.7907TI_{45} + .0675DEN$$
$$(1278.5424) \quad (157.5030) \quad (.0746)$$

$$+ .1276EQ_{29} + .9716EQ_{30} + .0054Q_{69}$$
$$(.0603) \quad (.1544) \quad (.0007)$$

The second transportation variable entered, TI_{45}, was significant; however, the other three (TQ_{57}, TI_{59}, and TI_{63}) were not retained because of multicollinearity. This industry along with others in the basic metals group is associated with iron and steel. The changes in output appear to be market-oriented as indicated by the significance EQ_{29} (iron and steel), EQ_{30} (nonferrous metals), Q_{69}, and Q_{70}. DEN was accepted with t ratio of less than one to allow the other variables to enter.

Value of land was not retained because of multicollinearity. The other variables were either insignificant or forced previously entered variables to insignificance.

IO 58 Special Industrial Machinery

This industry produces machinery for the food processing, lumber, furniture, paper, and printing industries as the following table illustrates.[74]

SIC	Product	Percent of Output
3551	Food Products Machinery	16.6
3552	Textile Machinery	14.3
3553	Wood-working Machinery	6.3
3554	Paper Industries Machinery	11.0
3555	Printing Trades Machinery	15.1
3559	Special Industrial Machinery, NEC	36.7

The largest sector is special industrial machines, not elsewhere classified, and includes machinery used by glass, mineral processing, leather, paint, and tobacco industries.

The industry's major market is equipment as the summary 1966 interindustry table reveals.

	Suppliers	Percent	Buyers	Percent
IO 45	Iron and Steel	9.0	Equipment sectors	70.4
IO 59	General Industrial Machinery	5.5	Export	16.0
IO 63	Electric Apparatus Machinery	3.8		
IO 57	Metal-working Machinery	2.5		

Its major inputs are iron and steel and products of the other industries in the heavy machinery group. The major equipment purchasing sectors are the paper industry and the printing and publishing industry.

The industry is concentrated in the Northeast and the Midwest. Four Northeastern states accounted for over 37 percent of the industry's output in 1965: New York (11.9 percent), Massachusetts (19.0 percent), Pennsylvania (8.5 percent), and New Jersey (6.6 percent). Three Midwestern states accounted for one-fourth of production: Ohio (9.6 percent), Illinois (9.5 percent), and Wisconsin (5.9 percent).

The regression equation (6.58) produced moderate results, which could be expected given the diversity of the output of the industry. The R^2 for the change in output was .3101, and for the level of output .9912.

$$(6.58) \qquad \Delta QD_{58} = 1662.2357 - 56.8099 TI_{45} + .5139 EQ_{39}$$
$$(537.3128) \quad (53.1684) \qquad (.3816)$$

$$+ .0939 DEN + .0643 EQ_{16} + .1818 EQ_{18}$$
$$(.0312) \qquad (.0411) \qquad (.0630)$$

Only one transportation variable was retained, TI_{45}, showing the industry's affinity for iron and steel. The other four (TQ_{58}, TI_{59}, TI_{63}, and TI_{57}) were multicollinear. The other significant cost variables were EQ_{39} and Q_{59}. The changes in output show some degree of market orientation as revealed by the positive sign and significance of DEN and EQ_{16} (paper) and EQ_{18} (printing and publishing). DEN is a proxy for the other markets of the industry that are located in urban areas.

Wages were rejected because of an incorrect sign, while VL was multicollinear. The other variables were either insignificant or forced previously entered variables to insignificance.

IO 59 General Industrial Machinery

While IO 58, special industry machinery produces equipment designed for unique industrial processes, the general industrial machinery sector produces commodities sold to most manufacturing industries. A list of these items appears in the following table.[75]

SIC	Product	Percent of Output
3516	Pumps and Compressors	31.9
3562	Ball and Roller Bearings	19.2
3564	Blowers and Fans	7.6
3565	Industrial Patterns	2.9
3566	Mechanical Power Transmission Equipment	18.3
3567	Industrial Furnaces and Ovens	7.2
3569	General Industrial Machines, NEC	13.0

The most important products are pumps and compressors, followed by ball and roller bearings and mechanical power transmission equipment. The primary market of the industry is the equipment purchasing sectors as the 1966 summary interindustry table indicates.

	Suppliers	Percent		Buyers	Percent
IO 45	Iron and Steel	12.2		Equipment sectors	32.8
IO 63	Electric Apparatus	2.5		Export	8.9
IO 52	Hardware, Plating	2.2	IO 54	Farm Machinery	5.5
IO 57	Metal-working Machinery	2.2			

The principal inputs are iron and steel and products of the heavy machinery group. The major equipment purchasing sector is the basic chemical group.

The industry is concentrated in the Midwest and the Middle Atlantic states. Five Midwestern states produced 43 percent of the industries output in 1965: Ohio (13.8 percent), Illinois (9.1 percent), Michigan (7.4 percent), Indiana (7.0 percent), and Wisconsin (6.0 percent). The Middle Atlantic states' share was over one-fourth: New York (11.7 percent), Pennsylvania (8.3 percent), and New Jersey (6.6 percent). The only other state with an appreciable output level was California (7.4 percent).

The regression equation (6.59) produced good results given the diversity of the output of the industry. The R^2 for the change in output was .4963, and it was .9898 for the level of output.

$$(6.59) \qquad \Delta QD_{59} = 4898.3300 - 684.7245 TI_{52} + .0941 Q_{59}$$
$$(3642.3389) \quad (468.3477) \qquad (.0095)$$

$$+ .1052 EQ_{19} + .0383 EX_{59} + .0165 Q_{54}$$
$$(.0679) \qquad (.0353) \qquad (.0095)$$

Only one of the five transportation variables (TQ_{59}, TI_{45}, TI_{63}, TI_{57}, and TI_{52}) was retained. The others were multicollinear. Economies of scale are important to the industry as confirmed by the significance of Q_{59}. There is some market orientation in the industry's change in output as the significance of EX_{59} and Q_{54} reveal.

Two other variables were not retained because of multicollinearity: DEN and Q_{52}. The other variables were either insignificant or forced previously entered variables to insignificance.

IO 60 Machine Shop and Misc. Machinery

This industry consists of one four-digit SIC 3599 product group, producing nonelectrical machinery. The products of the industry range from amusement park equipment, pistons and piston rings, flexible metallic hose, and valves to weather vanes. Unlike the other industries in the heavy machinery group, its major market is not the equipment purchasing sectors, but other industries on current account. The 1966 summary interindustry table shows that aircraft and parts is the industry's major buyer.

	Suppliers	Percent		Buyers	Percent
IO 45	Iron and Steel	8.4	IO 70	Aircraft and Parts	29.3
IO 57	Metal-working Machinery	3.2	IO 69	Motor Vehicles	13.5
IO 47	Aluminum	2.1	IO 45	Iron and Steel	9.1
IO 52	Hardware and Plating	1.7			

The major inputs are from the basic metal group and metal-working machinery. The iron and steel industry is both a major supplier and buyer.

The state with the largest share of output in 1965 was California with 12.4 percent. The location in California is presumably market oriented, since California leads the nation in the production of aircraft and parts. Five states in the Midwest accounted for over one-third of the industry's output: Michigan (10.8 percent), Illinois (9.8 percent), Ohio (7.8 percent), Indiana (4.5 percent), and Missouri (4.1 percent). Other states with appreciable output levels were New York (10.4 percent), Illinois (9.8 percent), and Ohio (7.8 percent).

The regression equation (6.60) produced excellent results considering the diversity of output in the industry. The R^2 for the change in output was .7153 and .9930 for the level of output.

$$(6.60) \quad \Delta QD_{60} = 28.8761 - .0169VL + .1472Q_{60} + .0003Q_{69}$$
$$(119.3743) \quad (.0154) \quad (.0065) \quad (.0002)$$

None of the transportation variables (TQ_{60}, TI_{45}, TI_{57}, TI_{47}, and TI_{52}) were retained. The cost variable VL was marginally significant. Output was highly significant with a positive sign indicating the importance of economies of scale to the industry. The retention of Q_{69} implies a degree of market orientation.

Three variables were not retained because of multicollinearity: EQ_{41}, *DEN*, and Q_{52}. Q_{45} and Q_{57} had incorrect signs. The other rejected variables were either insignificant or forced previously entered variables to insignificance.

IO 69 Motor Vehicles

The motor vehicle industry is the largest nonservice industry in the study with output of $50 billion in 1965. The industry is also one of the most rapidly growing in the nation. It grew faster than population in the decade from 1958 to 1968. This growth has been attributed to a rising standard of living that has changed American life styles and made automobiles a necessity rather than a luxury.[76] This growth has not appreciably modified the regional concentration of the industry. In 1965 Michigan accounted for 43.3 percent of total output. The Midwest contained four other states with appreciable output levels: Ohio (13.1 percent), Missouri (7.0 percent), Wisconsin (4.6 percent), and Indiana (4.6 percent). Other states with high output levels were California (6.9 percent) and New York (4.9 percent).

The motor vehicle industry is composed of four sectors.[77]

SIC	Product	Percent of Output
3711	Motor Vehicles	67.7
3713	Truck and Bus Bodies	1.8
3714	Motor Vehicle Parts and Accessories	28.8
3715	Truck Trailers	1.8

Motor vehicles dominated the industry in 1967. The sectoral definitions insure a large intraindustry flow of 32.5 percent of its output in 1966. The 1966 interindustry table reveals the simple market structure of the industry. The major buyer is *PCE*. Motor vehicles are also sold to the motor vehicle and trade equipment purchasing sectors.

	Suppliers	Percent		Buyers	Percent
IO 45	Iron and Steel	8.8		PCE	43.3
IO 51	Stamping, Screw	3.2		Equipment	18.3
IO 52	Hardware, Plating	3.0		Export	5.3
IO 40	Rubber and Plastics	2.6			

Iron and steel is the major input.

The regression equation (6.69) for the change in output produced good results. The R^2 was .4065 for the change in output, and it was .9986 for the level of output.

$$(6.69) \qquad \Delta QD_{69} = 9448.1775 - 1153.8984 TI_{45} - .0298 Q_{69}$$
$$(3730.9404) \qquad (418.1631) \qquad (.0023)$$

Only one of the five transportation variables (TQ_{69}, TI_{45}, TI_{51}, TI_{52}, and TI_{40}) was retained. The remainder were multicollinear. The retention of TI_{45} shows the dependence of the auto industry on iron and steel. The significance of TQ_{69} reflects economies of scale and the location stability of the industry.

EQ_{50} was not retained because of multicollinearity. Six variables had incorrect signs: EQ_{59}, EX_{59}, Q_{45}, Q_{51}, Q_{52}, and Q_{40}. The other variables were either insignificant or forced previously entered variables to insignificance.

IO 70 Aircraft and Parts

This industry, while only a fourth the size of motor vehicles in terms of output in 1965, had an employment level three-quarters that of motor vehicles. Aircraft manufacturing requires many types of employees. Metalworkers build the frames of aircraft, and skilled mechanics and electricians are needed to install the great variety of equipment necessary. Research and development personnel are also an integral part of aircraft companies' operations, and they present a special problem. They are offered such high salaries from all sides that salary is frequently not the deciding factor in choosing a company for which to work; working conditions, schools, and other public facilities, climate, and similar considerations become important. Thus, the company must locate its research facilities with these people in mind. California, an area with extremely pleasant climate, is thus a major production center.

Aircraft manufacture, like shipbuilding, has much in common with construction, since materials and parts are brought together at one plant for assembly. Assembly lines are housed in mile-long hangars; each station along the line performs a rather lengthy set of operations. Where climate is favorable, much of the manufacture can be done outdoors. Engines are produced in the Northeastern manufacturing belt, where the skills and materials available for the production of aircraft engines can be turned to other types of heavy engine manufacture when orders fall off in this highly cyclical industry.

The importance of exotic metals from IO 48 as an input is illustrated by the 1966 summary interindustry table.

	Suppliers	Percent		Buyers	Percent
IO 60	Machine Shop and Machinery	5.9		Defense	52.0
				Export	9.8
IO 66	Communication Equipment	4.0		Equipment Sectors	5.7
IO 57	Metal-working Machines	2.9		IO 13 Ordnance	4.3
IO 48	Other nonferrous	2.8			

The largest market of the industry is defense. Exports are also very important to the industry. The major equipment purchasing sector is the transportation industry. There is a large amount of intraindustry transfers, 16.1 percent of total output, primarily because of the structure of the industry as the following table illustrates.[78]

SIC	Product	Percent of Output
3721	Complete Aircraft	52.6
3722	Aircraft Engines and Engines Parts	25.1
3729	Aircraft Equipment	22.3

The locational orientation of engine manufacture is different from that of aircraft manufacture; and the location of small craft manufacture is different from that of airliner and military jet manufacture. The state with the largest share of output in 1965 was California with 28.3 percent. Other states with high output levels were Missouri (10.6 percent), Washington (7.7 percent) Colorado (7.6 percent), Ohio (5.4 percent), Georgia (5.4 percent), New York (5.2 percent), Texas (4.7 percent), and Kansas (4.2 percent).

The regression equation (6.70) produced excellent results. The R^2 for the change in output was .9888, and it was .9990 for the level of output.

$$(6.70) \quad \Delta QD_{70} = 6228.8604 - 5080.5855 TI_{66} - .6804 VL + .3000 Q_{70}$$
$$\quad\quad\quad (4315.3273) \quad (3192.9851) \quad\quad (.2771) \quad\quad (.0025)$$

Since defense expenditures are excluded from the dependent variable, the equation is an analysis of less than half of the output in the industry. Only one of the five transportation variables (TQ_{70}, TI_{60}, TI_{66}, TI_{57}, and TI_{48}) was retained. TI_{57} was multicollinear, while the others were insignificant. The importance of capital equipment and the size of the plant are revealed in the significance of VL and Q_{70}.

Three other variables were not retained because of multicollinearity: DEN, DEF_{70}, and Q_{13}. Five variables had incorrect signs: EQ_{51}, EX_{70}, Q_{66}, Q_{57}, and Q_{48}. The other variables were rejected either because of insignificance or because they forced previously entered variables to insignificance.

IO 71 Ships, Trains, Trailers and Cycles

The output of this industry is highly dissimilar as the following table indicates:[79]

SIC	Product	Percent of Output
373	Ship and Boat Building, Repairing	53.6
374	Railroad Equipment	24.8
375	Motorcycles, Bicycles, and Parts	4.3
379	Misc. Transportation Equipment	17.3

The three major markets of the industry are *PCE*, defense, and the equipment sectors (mainly the transportation industry) as the 1966 interindustry table indicates.

	Suppliers	Percent	Buyers	Percent
IO 45	Iron and Steel	12.8	Equipment sectors	34.7
IO 59	General Industry	4.4	*PCE*	25.4
IO 50	Heating and Plumbing	4.4	Defense	18.1
IO 28	Lumber and Products	3.7	Federal Government	4.4

The major input is iron and steel.

A major concentration of the industry occurs in the Midwest where four states accounted for over one-quarter of the industry's output in 1965: Illinois (8.9 percent), Indiana (6.9 percent), Michigan (5.5 percent), and Ohio (4.3 percent). Other states with appreciable output levels were Pennsylvania (9.6 percent), Virginia (7.9 percent), Colorado (7.6 percent), and California (6.7 percent).

The regression equation (6.71) yielded moderate results, probably because of the diversity of the products in the industry. The R^2 for the change in output was .2500, and it was .9962 for the level of output.

$$(6.71) \quad \Delta QD_{71} = \quad 594.1846 \ - \ 651.5906 TQ_{71} \ - \ 255.4289 TI_{28}$$
$$(1581.6642) \quad (548.6429) \quad\quad (154.6653)$$

$$+ \ .0235 Q_{71} \ + \ .1038 DEN \ + \ .0028 Q_{45}$$
$$(.0055) \quad\quad (.0711) \quad\quad (.0014)$$

Two of the five transportation variables (TQ_{71}, TI_{45}, TI_{59}, TI_{50}, and TI_{28}) were retained. The others were multicollinear. While the significance of TQ_{71} and *DEN* indicates the importance of market orientation, the other significant variables, TI_{28}, Q_{71}, and Q_{45}, reveal the importance of cost considerations.

VL and EQ_{56} were not retained because of multicollinearity. The other variables were either insignificant or forced previously entered variables to insignificance.

Group 11: Electric and Electric Products

The eight industries in this group produce the electrical equipment to provide service and communication for the American economy. A number of the industries produce commodities that have been familiar to generations of Americans: electrical apparatus and motors, household appliances, batteries, communications equipment, etc. Other products were nonexistent a few decades ago: computers, television, electronic components, etc.

There is a high degree of interdependency between the industries of the group. Electronic components are purchased by most of the other industries including IO 63 electrical apparatus and motors. The output of IO 63 is then sold to the industries in the group producing commodities at higher stages of fabrication: service industry machines, household appliances, and communication equipment.

The technology of the industries has improved during the last 20 years. Items which were formally produced in labor-intensive job shops can now be produced using automated assembly lines.[80] These changes in production techniques coupled with the increasing drive toward minimization has considerably reduced skilled labor requirements. In order to cut costs, the industries in the group are moving to cheap labor areas, which generally implies foreign countries. The rising tide of foreign competition could have unforeseen effects on the industry.

Table 6-12 shows that the industries in the groups are of moderate size. Four had output valued greater than $7 billion in 1965. The industries are spatially concentrated. The coefficients of localization range from .562 to .710 for personal income, and .444 to .703 for total demand. The shift ratios ranging from .1453 to .2450 indicate that the industries in the group are spatially mobile.

Table 6-12
Summary Statistics, Group 11: Electric and Electronic Products

Industry	Output 1966 Prices (000,000)		Employment (000)		Coefficient of Localization 1966 Output with		Output Shift Ratio 1965-1966
	1965	1966	1965	1966	Personal Income	Industry Demand	
61 Office and Computing Machines	5,765	7,915	178	216	.655	.444	.2450
62 Service Industry Machines	3,640	4,245	128	138	.606	.595	.1820
63 Electric Apparatus and Motors	7,006	7,890	337	378	.562	.527	.1643
64 Household Appliances	4,416	4,674	167	180	.710	.703	.1684
65 Electric Light and Wiring Equipment	3,136	3,347	156	172	.580	.624	.1453
66 Communications Equipment	10,276	13,118	558	621	.629	.652	.1849
67 Electronic Components	6,015	8,045	305	382	.582	.448	.2144
68 Batteries and Engine Electrical Equipment	2,055	2,467	91	108	.648	.624	.2298

IO 61 Office and Computing Machines

This is an old industry, whose major product, the electronic computer, is only two decades old. The other products of the industry are listed below.[81]

SIC	Product	Percent of Output
3572	Typewriter	10.4
3573	Electronic Computing Equipment	65.8
3574	Calculating and Accounting Machines	12.4
3576	Scales and Balances	2.4
3579	Office Machines, NEC	9.0

As shown in the 1966 summary interindustry table the market of the industry has three major segments: equipment, exports, and defense.

Suppliers		Percent	Buyers	Percent
IO 67	Electronic Components	7.6	Equipment sects	50.2
IO 47	Aluminum	1.9	Export	11.1
IO 85	Business Services	1.9	Defense	8.5
IO 40	Rubber and Plastics	1.9		
IO 51	Stamping, Screw	1.5		

Electronic components is the major input of the industry.

The state of New York, the home of IBM, had the largest share of output in 1965 with 33.6 percent. Other states with appreciable output levels were Ohio (12.6 percent), Minnesota (9.1 percent), California (9.0 percent), Michigan (6.5 percent), Massachusetts (5.9 percent), and Illinois (4.1 percent).

$$(6.61) \quad \Delta QD_{61} = 52597.9218 - 9159.1746TI_{67} + .1522EQ_{42}$$
$$(16440.5349) \quad (3112.1087) \quad (.0193)$$

$$+ .1003EX_{61}$$
$$(.0836)$$

Only one transportation variable, TI_{67}, reflecting the importance of electronic components, was retained. TQ_{61}, TI_{47}, TI_{40}, TI_{51} were insignificant. EQ_{42} was also highly significant. The retention of EX_{61} reveals the importance of overseas markets to the industry.

Four variables were not retained because of multicollinearity: VL, EQ_{42}, EQ_{60} and Q_{85}. WR_{61} had an incorrect sign. The other variables were either insignificant or forced previously entered variables to insignificance.

IO 62 Service Industry Machines

The output of this industry is utilized primarily in prepared food retailing, self-service retailing, dry cleaning, personal consumption, gasoline stations, restaurants, and household service industries as the following table illustrates.[82]

SIC	Product	Percent of Output
3581	Automatic Merchandising Machines	5.8
3582	Commercial Laundry Equipment	4.3
3585	Refrigeration Machinery	72.0
3586	Measuring and Dispensing Pumps	4.1
3589	Service Industry Machines, NEC	14.9

The industry is dominated by refrigeration equipment, which includes air conditioning and commercial and industrial refrigeration machinery. The equipment purchasing sectors (mainly the trade and service industries) are the major markets of the industry as the 1966 summary interindustry table indicates.

	Suppliers	Percent	Buyers	Percent
IO 63	Electric Apparatus	10.2	Equipment sectors	38.8
IO 45	Iron and Steel	7.1	PCE	13.8
IO 52	Hardware, Plating	4.5	Export	6.6
IO 51	Stamping, Screw	3.8		

The sales to the personal consumption expenditures sector include air conditioners. The major inputs are electrical apparatus and products of the basic metals group.

The industry is concentrated in the Midwest. Seven states in the region produced about half of the output of the industry in 1965: Ohio (9.4 percent), Illinois (9.4 percent), Michigan (8.1 percent), Missouri (6.0 percent), Indiana (5.5 percent), Wisconsin (5.2 percent), and Minnesota (4.6 percent). Other states with high output levels were New York (12.7 percent), Pennsylvania (7.1 percent), and Texas (5.1 percent).

The regression equation (6.62) produced good results. The R^2 for the change in output was .6505, and it was .9881 for the level of output.

$$(6.62) \quad \Delta QD_{62} = 529.6402 - 1281.9450 TI_{63} + .1447 Q_{62} + 2.1655 EQ_{43}$$
$$\quad\quad\quad (680.1920) \quad (1041.2890) \quad\quad (.0142) \quad\quad\quad (.8504)$$

Only one of the five transportation variables (TQ_{62}, TI_{63}, TI_{45}, TI_{52}, and TI_{51}) was retained. The significance of TI_{63} confirms the relationship of service industry machines with electrical apparatus and motors. Economies of scale are important in the industry as the positive sign on Q_{62} and the significance of EQ_{43} reveal.

Two variables were not retained because of multicollinearity: TQ_{62} and TI_{45}. TI_{52}, TI_{51}, Q_{45}, and Q_{51} were rejected because of incorrect signs. The other variables were insignificant or forced previously entered variables to insignificance.

IO 63 Electric Apparatus and Motors

The products of this industry are used to transform electrical power into mechanical and chemical thermal energy and to generate electric power. The commodities of the industry are listed in the table below.[83]

SIC	Product	Percent of Output
361	Electric Test, Distributing Equipment	46.8
3621	Motors and Generators	27.7
3622	Industrial Controls	12.7
3623	Welding Apparatus	5.7
3624	Carbon and Graphite Products	3.4
3629	Electrical Industrial Apparatus, NEC	3.8

SIC 361, which includes electric measuring instruments, transformers, and switchgear, dominates this industry. The equipment sectors (mainly the communication and utility industries) are the major markets of the industry as the 1966 summary interindustry table indicates.

	Suppliers	Percent	Buyers	Percent
IO 45	Iron and Steel	5.5	Equipment Sectors	32.2
IO 48	Other Nonferrous	4.3	Defense	6.2
IO 52	Hardware, Plating	2.2	Export	6.0
IO 67	Electronic Components	2.1		

The industry is concentrated in the Midwest and Middle Atlantic states. Five Midwestern states accounted for more than a third of the output in 1965; Ohio (12.3 percent), Illinois (8.0 percent), Wisconsin (7.6 percent), Indiana (4.9 percent), and Michigan (3.5 percent). Over one-fourth of the output was produced in the Middle Atlantic states: Pennsylvania (14.1 percent), New York (10.4 percent), and New Jersey (4.3 percent). California produced 7.5 percent.

The regression equation (6.63) produced good results. The R^2 for the change in output was .6322, and it was .9934 for the level of output.

$$(6.63) \qquad \Delta QD_{63} = -1565.5771 - 2681.6180 TQ_{63} + .1126 Q_{63}$$
$$(696.4089) \quad (1283.9747) \qquad (.0072)$$

Only one of the five transportation variables (TQ_{63}, TI_{45}, TI_{48}, TI_{52}, and TI_{67}) was retained. The significance of TQ_{63} shows that the change in output is market-oriented. The positive sign on output shows the importance of economies of scale in the industry.

Two variables were not retained because of multicollinearity: TI_{45} and TI_{52}.

Three variables had incorrect signs: DEF_{63}, Q_{45}, and Q_{48}. The other variables were either insignificant or forced previously entered variables to insignificance.

IO 64 Household Appliances

This industry produces the electrical equipment that has done so much to liberate the American housewife from her drudgery since the turn of the century. The products of the industry are listed below.[84]

SIC	Product	Percent of Output
3631	Household Cooking Equipment	1.8
3632	Household Refrigerators and Freezers	33.5
3633	Household Laundry Equipment	18.4
3634	Electric Housewares and Fans	2.1
3635	Household Vacuum Cleaners	5.5
3636	Service Machines	2.3
3639	Household Appliances	9.0

Refrigerators and laundry equipment dominate the industry. The major market is naturally the personal consumer expenditures sector as recorded in the 1966 summary interindustry table below.

	Suppliers	Percent		Buyers	Percent
IO 45	Iron and Steel	8.4		PCE	79.3
IO 40	Rubber and Plastics	7.1	IO 84	Hotel and Personal Services	4.7
IO 85	Business Services	6.6			
IO 63	Electric Apparatus	4.7			
IO 52	Hardware, Plating	4.6			

The industry is spatially concentrated in the Midwest. Six states in this region produced over 60 percent of the industry's output in 1965: Ohio (26.1 percent), Illinois (13.6 percent), Indiana (8.4 percent), Michigan (7.4 percent), Iowa (3.9 percent), and Wisconsin (3.7 percent). Other states with high output levels were Kentucky (9.0 percent), California (4.6 percent), and Colorado (4.6 percent).

The regression equation (6.64) produced good results. The R^2 for the change in output was .6063, while the R^2 for the level of output was .9957.

$$(6.64) \quad \Delta QD_{64} = 3684.4582 - 4198.3674TI_{63} - 361.9689WR_{64}$$
$$(1913.2429) \quad (2421.8760) \quad (219.9935)$$

$$- .2482VL - .0278Q_{64} + .6347EQ_{45} + .3194PCE_{64}$$
$$(.0445) \quad (.0101) \quad (.4552) \quad (.0286)$$

The changes in output are both cost- and market-oriented. Only one of the five transportation variables (TQ_{64}, TI_{45}, TI_{40}, TI_{63}, TI_{52}) was retained. The significance of TI_{63} confirms the importance of electrical apparatus and motors to the industry. All the other cost variables were significant. The high significance of PCE implies that the industry is located in proximity of its primary market.

Six variables were rejected because of multicollinearity: TQ_{64}, TI_{45}, DEN, Q_{84}, Q_{40}, and Q_{85}. Q_{45} had an incorrect sign. The other variables were either insignificant or forced previously entered variables to insignificance.

IO 65 Electric Light and Wiring Equipment

The output of this industry consists of the four basic products listed below.[85]

SIC	Product	Percent of Output
3641	Electric Lamps	20.3
3642	Lighting Fixtures	41.4
3643	Current-carrying Wiring Devices	21.7
3644	Noncurrent-carrying Wiring Devices	16.6

While the personal consumption expenditures sector is the major market of the industry, it does not dominate sales as the 1966 summary interindustry table reveals.

	Suppliers	Percent		Buyers	Percent
IO 45	Iron and Steel	5.3	PCE		14.9
IO 48	Other Nonferrous	4.0	IO 12	Maintenance Construction	7.0
IO 40	Rubber and Plastics	3.5			
IO 51	Stamping, Screw	3.3		Residential Construction	6.2
			IO 69	Motor Vehicles	5.5

Sales to other construction sectors were 34.3 percent. The products of the basic metals groups are heavily utilized as inputs in the industry.

The industry is spatially concentrated in the Northeast and Midwest. Four Northeastern states produced over one-third of the industry's output in 1965: New York (12.0 percent), Pennsylvania (10.8 percent), New Jersey (8.4 percent), and Massachusetts (4.1 percent). Over one-quarter of the output was produced in three Midwestern states: Ohio (12.5 percent), Illinois (10.6 percent), and Indiana (5.5 percent). Two other states with appreciable output levels were California (7.6 percent) and Colorado (6.0 percent).

The regression equation (6.65) produced good results. The R^2 for the change in output was .4215, and it was .9969 for the level of output.

$$(6.65) \quad \triangle QD_{65} = 628.8881 - 223.4520TI_{48} - .0796VL$$
$$(488.0151) \quad (155.4782) \quad (.0196)$$

$$+ .0202Q_{65} + .6338EQ_{46} + .2501PCE_{65}$$
$$(.0093) \quad (.2023) \quad (.1317)$$

Only one of the five transportation variables (TQ_{65}, TI_{45}, TI_{48}, TI_{40}, and TI_{51}) was retained. The industry appears to be cost-oriented as indicated by the significance of TI_{48}, VL, Q_{65}, and EQ_{46}. Market factors do play a role in the growth of the industry as the retention of PCE indicates.

Seven variables were rejected because of multicollinearity: TI_{51}, DEN, Q_{12}, CN_1, TI_{45}, TI_{40}, and Q_{40}. Q_{45}, Q_{48}, and Q_{51} had incorrect signs. The other variables were insignificant.

IO 66 Communications Equipment

This industry consists of the four sectors presented in the table below.[86]

SIC	Product	Percent of Output
3651	Radio and TV Receiving Sets	25.2
3652	Phonograph Records	1.8
3661	Telephone and Telegraph Apparatus	17.0
3662	Radio and TV Communications Equipment	56.0

Radio and TV communication equipment which dominates the industry includes a large number of products such as air traffic control systems, atom smashers, laser systems, missile control systems, etc., as well as radio and TV broadcasting equipment. The definition of SIC 3662 explains how defense expenditures could be the major market of the industry, as listed in the 1966 summary interindustry table.

	Suppliers	Percent		Buyers	Percent
IO 67	Electronic Components	20.5		Defense	32.0
IO 85	Business Services	3.0		PCE	27.6
IO 30	Household Furniture	2.0		Equipment Sectors	15.4
IO 51	Stampings, Screw	1.8			
IO 63	Electric Apparatus	1.6			

The major input of the industry is electronic components. The principal equipment purchasing sector consists of the communication and radio and TV industries.

The industry is concentrated in three spatially separate states: Illinois, California, and New York. Their share in the industry's output in 1965 was 16.0, 15.8, and 13.0 percent, respectively. Other states with high output levels were New Jersey (9.1 percent), Indiana (7.8 percent), and Massachusetts (7.2 percent).

The regression equation (6.66) produced exceedingly good results. The R^2 for the change in output was .9037, and it was .9920 for the level of output.

(6.66) $\Delta QD_{66} = 19696.8169 - 87870.2607TI_{30} - 1497.1761WR_{66}$
$\phantom{(6.66) \Delta QD_{66} = }(5214.2513) \quad (20650.6260) \quad\quad (551.9078)$

$ - .6295VL + .2996Q_{66} + .4380EQ_{57}$
$(.1894) \quad\quad (.0210) \quad\quad (.1344)$

Only one of the five transportation variables (TQ_{66}, TI_{67}, TI_{30}, TI_{51}, and TI_{63}) was retained. The importance of cabinets produced in the household furniture industry is revealed by the significance of TI_{30}. WR_{66} and VL were highly significant, but are not as statistically important as output. The retention of Q_{66} and EQ_{57} indicates that economies of scale are important in the industry.

Six variables were not retained because of multicollinearity: TI_{63}, DEN, PCE, Q_{67}, Q_{85}, and Q_{30}. TI_{67} and TI_{51} had incorrect signs. The other variables were either insignificant or forced previously entered variables to insignificance.

IO 67 Electronic Components

The output of this industry is a basic input of the other industries in the electric group. It is highly diversified ranging from cathode ray tubes, to transistors, to coils and stereo components. The 1966 summary interindustry table illustrates the intragroup dependences. The major market is communications equipment.

	Suppliers	Percent		Buyers	Percent
IO 51	Stamping, Screw	4.4	IO 66	Communication Equipment	42.1
IO 43	Glass and Glass Products	3.7		Defense	8.0
IO 40	Rubber and Plastics	3.4	IO 84	Hotels and Personal Services	7.8
IO 48	Other Nonferrous	2.7			
IO 85	Business Services	2.6	IO 13	Ordnance	6.8

The industry is spatially concentrated in the Northeast. Four states of this region produced almost 40 percent of the industry's output in 1965: New York (12.7 percent), Massachusetts (7.3 percent), and New Jersey (6.4 percent).

Other states with high output levels were California (15.0 percent), Illinois (8.1 percent), and Texas (5.0 percent).

The regression equation (6.67) produced very good results, even with the variation in the products in the industry. The R^2 for the change in output was .8881, and it was .9932 for the level of output.

$$(6.67) \qquad \Delta QD_{67} = - \ 95.2123 + .2176Q_{67} + 1.0581EQ_{48}$$
$$(485.9931) \quad (.0150) \qquad (.2648)$$

$$+ .0134Q_{84} + .0183Q_{13}$$
$$(.0058) \qquad (.0044)$$

None of the five transportation variables (TQ_{67}, TI_{51}, TI_{43}, TI_{40}, and TI_{48}) were retained. The importance of the industry size is revealed by the positive sign of Q_{67} and the significance of EQ_{48}. The significance of Q_{84} and Q_{13} indicates that the changes in output are somewhat market-oriented.

Three variables were not retained because of multicollinearity: Q_{66}, Q_{51}, and Q_{85}. Three variables had incorrect signs: VL, DEF_{67}, and Q_{40}. The other variables were insignificant.

IO 68 Batteries and Engine Electrical Equipment

The output of this industry can be classified into five sectors.[87]

SIC	Product	Percent of Output
3691	Storage Batteries	20.8
2692	Primary Batteries, Dry and Wet	11.1
3693	X-ray Apparatus and Tubes	8.4
3694	Engine Electrical Equipment	49.2
3699	Electrical Equipment, NEC	10.5

Engine electrical equipment is produced for use in internal combustion engines. Thus it is not surprising that motor vehicles and automotive repair are two of the major markets of the industry as indicated in the 1966 summary interindustry table.

	Suppliers	Percent		Buyers	Percent
IO 48	Other Nonferrous	11.9	PCE		18.9
IO 40	Rubber and Plastic	4.0	IO 69	Motor Vehicles	13.3
IO 45	Iron and Steel	2.8	IO 86	Automobile	
IO 35	Basic Chemical	2.5		Repair	10.3

The most important input is other nonferrous metals.

The industry is spatially concentrated in the Midwest. Five states in this region produced almost 60 percent of the industry's output in 1965: Indiana (24.8 percent), Michigan (11.6 percent), Ohio (10.9 percent), Illinois (7.3 percent), and Wisconsin (4.1 percent). Other states with high output levels were Pennsylvania (5.7 percent), New York (5.3 percent), and New Jersey (4.2 percent).

The regression equation (6.68) produced good results. The R^2 for the change in output was .7408, and it was .9906 for the level of output.

$$(6.68) \quad \Delta QD_{68} = 126.2384 - 1614.8325 TQ_{68} - 107.5711 WR_{68}$$
$$(817.9053) \quad (1143.7901) \quad (91.5482)$$

$$+ .1495 Q_{68} + 1.1533 EQ_{49} + .0028 Q_{45}$$
$$(.0130) \quad (.3357) \quad (.0011)$$

Only one of the five transportation variables (TQ_{68}, TI_{48}, TI_{40}, TI_{45}, and TI_{35}) was retained. The significance of TQ_{68} reveals proximity to the market is important for development of the industry. The other significant variables (WR_{68}, Q_{68}, EQ_{49}, and Q_{45}), however, imply that cost considerations are also important.

Two variables were multicollinear: TI_{40} and TI_{45}. The other variables were either insignificant or forced previously entered variables to insignificance.

Group 12: Precision Manufacturing

The output of this group is crucial to the development of technology, improved health standards and expanded recreational opportunities in our nation. The industries require highly trained workers in the production of their high value and scientifically sensitive output. Most of the products produced by the group have enjoyed rapid growth, spurred by the demand for automated technology, since World War II.

The national statistics of the industry are presented in Table 6-13. The industries are spatially stable, with shift ratios below .11. While the products of the group are diversified, the coefficients of localization are high, ranging from .446 to .689 for personal income and .423 to .694 for total demand.

IO 72 Instruments and Clocks

The output of this industry is extremely diverse. The product division listed below understates the complexity of the industry.[88]

Table 6-13
Summary Statistics, Group 12: Precision Manufacturing

Industry	Output 1966 Prices (000,000)	
	1965	1966
72 Instruments and Clocks	5,754	4,761
73 Optical and Photographic Equipment	2,986	3,711
74 Miscellaneous Manufactured Products	6,853	7,228

Industry	Employment (000)		Coefficient of Localization 1966 Output with		Output Shift Ratio 1965-1966
	1965	1966	Personal Income	Total Demand	
72	191	211	.599	.609	.1050
73	151	172	.689	.694	.1077
74	436	458	.446	.423	.0677

SIC	Product	Percent of Output
381	Engineering, Laboratory and Scientific Instruments	18.3
382	Measuring Control Devices Indicating Physical Characteristics	41.3
384	Medical Instruments and Supplies	28.7
387	Watches, Clocks, and Watchcases	11.7

The output of the industry is sold in appreciable quantities to a number of different sectors as the 1966 summary table indicates.

Suppliers		Percent	Buyers		Percent
IO 85	Business Service	5.1	Equipment Sectors		17.6
IO 45	Iron and Steel	2.7	PCE		11.0
IO 40	Rubber and Plastics	2.6	Export		10.3
IO 51	Stamping, Screws	2.1	IO 70	Aircraft and Parts	9.1

The technical superiority of American science is evidenced by the large percentage of the industry's output that is exported. The major equipment purchases service consists of the service industries.

The industry is locationally concentrated, tending to locate in the large industrial states. This location pattern indicates that the industry is market-oriented. New York and Illinois had the largest share of output in 1965 with 12.8 and 12.4 percent, respectively. Other states with high output levels were Pennsylvania (11.2 percent), Massachusetts (10.4 percent), Michigan (8.4 percent), California (7.4 percent), and Colorado (5.0 percent).

The regression equation (6.72) produced excellent results, considering the diversity of the output of the industry. The R^2 for the change in output was .8788, and it was .9921 for the level of output.

(6.72) $\quad \Delta QD_{72} = -1248.9830 - 5339.4827 TQ_{72} - .1969Q + .0196Q_{40}$
$\qquad\qquad\quad (1017.7879) \quad (5105.9899) \qquad\quad (.0103) \quad (.0090)$

The significance of TQ_{72} indicates that the industry's changes in output are somewhat market-oriented. The other three transportation variables (TI_{45}, TI_{40}, and TI_{51}) were not retained because of multicollinearity. The significance of Q_{72} and Q_{40} indicates input costs are important in location.

Q_{51} was not retained because of an incorrect sign. The other variables either were insignificant or forced previously entered variables to insignificance.

IO 73 Optical and Photographic Equipment

The output of this industry is well defined by use. The products of the industry are designed to record, utilize, or modify light waves. The industry has grown rapidly in the last two decades under the stimulation of governmental spending in the defense and space areas and consumer spending for recreation, health, and family remembrances.[89] Photographic equipment and supplies, including cameras and film, dominate the industry as the following table indicates.[90]

SIC	Product	Percent of Output
383	Optical Instruments and Lenses	27.0
385	Ophthalmic Goods	27.3
386	Photographic Equipment and Supplies	45.7

Ophthalmic goods include spectacles, contact lenses, and sunglasses. The industry's largest market is the personal consumption expenditures sector as the 1966 summary interindustry table reveals.

	Suppliers	Percent		Buyers	Percent
IO 35	Basic Chemicals	7.8	PCE		27.3
IO 85	Business Services	3.5	Equipment Sectors		19.8
IO 32	Paper and Products Exc. Containers	3.0	Export		7.6
IO 48	Other Nonferrous Metals	2.6	IO 85	Business Services	6.8
IO 40	Rubber and Plastics	2.1			

The major equipment purchasing sector consists of the service industries. Exports are also important to the industry. Basic chemicals is the major input. The business service industry is both a major buyer and supplier.

The industry is highly concentrated, principally in New York, which accounted for 49.7 percent of output in 1965. This occurs primarily because of the location of Kodak, Xerox, and Bausch and Lomb in Rochester, New York. Other states with significant output levels were Illinois (10.0 percent), Massachusetts (7.1 percent), New Jersey (6.4 percent), California (5.9 percent), and New York (5.0 percent).

The regression equation (6.73) produced excellent results. The R^2 for the change in output was .9943, and it was .9998 for the level of output.

$$(6.73) \quad \Delta QD_{73} = 1023.4077 - 1247.2034 TI_{32} + .2247 Q_{73} + .0081 Q_{35}$$
$$(1082.4364) \quad (844.3855) \quad (.0020) \quad (.0031)$$

Only one of the five transportation variables (TQ_{73}, TI_{35}, TI_{32}, TI_{48}, and TI_{40}) was significant. The industry is cost-oriented as the retention of TI_{32}, Q_{73}, and Q_{35} indicates. The high significance of Q_{73} shows the importance of economies of scale in the industry.

EQ_{54} was not retained because of multicollinearity. Four variables had incorrect signs: WR_{73}, EQ_{61}, Q_{85}, and Q_{40}. The other variables either were insignificant or forced previously entered variables to insignificance.

IO 74 Miscellaneous Manufactured Products

As could be expected the products of this industry are unrelated as the following table shows.[91]

SIC	Product	Percent of Output
391	Jewelry, Silverware, Plated Ware	15.6
393	Musical Instruments and Parts	5.2
394	Toys and Sporting Goods	26.6
395	Pens, Pencils, Office, Art Goods	8.7
396	Costume Jewelry and Notions	11.2
399	Misc. Manufacturers	32.7

The largest sector, SIC 399, includes products such as brooms and brushes, signs, morticians' goods, linoleum, etc. The primary market of the industry is *PCE* as the 1966 summary interindustry table reveals.

	Suppliers	Percent		Buyers	Percent
IO 40	Rubber and Plastics	4.8		*PCE*	50.8
IO 85	Business Services	3.8	IO 26	Apparel	4.9
IO 45	Iron and Steel	3.4	State and Local Government		2.3
IO 48	Other Nonferrous	2.7			
IO 36	Plastics and Synthetics	2.6	IO 85	Business Services	2.0

The industry is concentrated in the Northeast. Five states in this region produced almost half of the industry's output in 1965: New York (23.9 percent), Pennsylvania (7.3 percent), New Jersey (6.4 percent), Massachusetts (5.6 percent), and Rhode Island (4.0 percent). Other states with high output levels were Illinois (9.3 percent), California (7.1 percent), Colorado (5.2 percent), and Ohio (4.5 percent).

The results of the regression equation (6.74) were good given the diversity of the output of the industry. The R^2 for the change in output was .5604, and it was .9984 for the level of output.

$$(6.74) \quad \Delta QD_{74} = -\ 112.0406 - 1595.0599TQ_{74} - 102.4078WR_{74}$$
$$(425.4683) \quad (881.2377) \quad (78.3023)$$

$$-\ .2106VL + .0328Q_{74} + 1.3055EQ_{55}$$
$$(.0301) \quad (.0046) \quad (.2834)$$

$$+\ .0123Q_{36} + .0074Q_{40} + .0077Q_{48}$$
$$(.0048) \quad (.0019) \quad (.0043)$$

It is not surprising that with the wide range of products in the industry, both market and cost factors were significant in (6.74). Only one of the five transportation variables (TQ_{74}, TI_{40}, TI_{45}, TI_{48}, and TI_{36}) was retained. TI_{36} had an incorrect sign while the others were multicollinear. The significance of TQ_{74} reveals a degree of market orientation in the industry. The other significant variables WR_{74}, VL, Q_{74}, EQ_{55}, Q_{36}, Q_{40}, and Q_{48} reflect cost factors.

Three other variables were not retained because of multicollinearity: DEN, GOV_9, and Q_{85}. Q_{45} had an incorrect sign. The other variables either were insignificant or forced previously entered variables to insignificance.

Group 13: Regulated Utilities

The industries in this group are primarily service industries having the common bond that crucial parts of their operations are regulated by federal, state, and local governments. The exception is the coal industry, which was included because its major market is the electric utility industry. Strip mining regulations, mine safety legislation, and pollution controls of mine waste do account, however, for a substantial amount of governmental control of the coal industry.

The industries in the group are highly stable, except for radio and TV broadcasting which has a shift ratio of .2343. The shift ratios for the other industries in the group range from .0656 to .1254, as Table 6-14 indicates. The high equipment and construction expenditures required in these industries plus

Table 6-14
Summary Statistics, Group 13: Regulated Utilities

Industry	Output 1966 Prices (000,000) 1965	1966	Employment (000) 1965	1966	Coefficient of Localization 1966 Output with Personal Income	Industry Demand	Output Shift Ratio 1965-1966
7 Coal Mining	2,402	2,489	154	155	.904	.751	.1141
76 Communications	14,588	16,267	770	798	.195	.111	.0656
77 Radio, TV Broadcasting	2,601	2,754	111	120	.424	.334	.2343
78 Electric Utility	16,470	17,576	426	431	.229	.127	.0835
79 Gas Utility	6,734	7,556	153	152	.419	.103	.1220
80 Water Utility	2,346	2,380	35	37	.532	.171	.1254

their market orientation to *PCE* (except for coal) are the causes of the stability. Their market orientation is the primary reason for the diffuse levels of spatial concentration in the group as Table 6-17 indicates. Coal is resource-orientated and its coefficients of localization are substantially above the norm.

All the industries in the group are and will continue to grow at moderate rates. The increasing demands for power are expected to continue. Natural gas shortages and rationing occurred in New York in 1971. The growth of the information industries, communications, and radio and TV broadcasting is fostered by increased technology and rising consumer incomes. The growth of the water utility industry, which also includes sewer, refuse and sanitary systems, is ensured by population growth and the federal government's water and solid waste antipollution campaign. Four of these industries sell directly to consumers (IO 76, IO 78, IO 79, and IO 80), but estimates of *PCE* were directly related to output. Therefore personal income (*PI*) is substituted for *PCE* as a major buyer in the equations for these industries.

IO 7 Coal Mining

The coal mining industry is extremely localized and is ridden with problems. It is smaller than crude petroleum and gas and more dependent on its use as a power source than is petroleum. This is a resource industry, and thus its location is limited to areas where the resource is available. Analysis of shifts in the location of employment and output must account for variable rates of growth in these areas—or, in the case of coal over the past two decades, variable rates of decline. Coal is presently used chiefly to generate electrical power, rather than being consumed directly by energy users. The iron and steel industry is its next most important user. The input-output relations of the coal industry are summarized below:

Suppliers		Percent		Buyers	Percent
IO 55	Construction and Mining Machines	3.9	IO 78	Electric Utility	29.7
IO 45	Iron and Steel	1.6	IO 45	Iron and Steel	19.0
IO 53	Engines and Turbines	1.6	Exports		9.5
IO 35	Basic Chemicals	1.4			

As with other resource industries, the coal industry is heavily dependent on capital goods and even buys inputs from capital-producing industries on current account.

Two principle products come out of the coal industry—bituminous coal and anthracite. Anthracite (hard coal) is used principally for personal consumption and is a declining sector in relation to total output. Bituminous (soft coal) is used by electricity—generating plants and factories.

The data below illustrate the importance of the bituminous sector in relation to the anthracite sector.[92]

SIC	Product	Percent of Output
11	Anthracite Mining	5.0
12	Bituminous Coal and Mining	95.0

Improvement in transportation service and the location of elective generating plant at mine mouths have been partially responsible for increased labor productivity in coal mining and hence reduced costs in the coal industry. The development of the unit train in 1960 and its spread throughout the industry has made the shipments of coal less expensive than the shipment of oil by pipeline. The use of long distance electric power transmission lines has stimulated the construction of mine-mouth utility plants. This trend not only reduces transportation costs, but it has the beneficial external effect of reducing air pollution in urban areas. The National Power Survey (1963) predicts that 25 percent of all new power generating capacity will be mine-mouth by 1980.[j]

The location of output in coal mining in 1965 shows that it is strictly an Eastern industry, although vast coal deposits exist in the West. Coal fueled the industrial revolution in the United States and was particularly important in developing the iron and steel industry in this country. The location of coal had a good deal to do with the location of industrial activity until the most recent quarter century. The industry is concentrated in a few states, with the first six states accounting for almost 85 percent of output in 1965. These states are West Virginia (28.9 percent), Pennsylvania (22.9 percent), Kentucky (12.1 percent), Illinois (8.6 percent), Ohio (6.3 percent), and Virginia (5.9 percent).

The regression equation (6.7) yielded moderate results with an R^2 of .2568 for the change in output and .9340 for the level of output.

---

[j]*Technological Trends of Major American Industries*, pp. 20-25, contains a discussion of the future structure of the industry.

(6.7) $\Delta QD_7 = -424.1714 - 66.9190 WR_7 - .1750 VL + .0452 Q_7$
              $(680.4455) \quad (66.4235) \qquad (.0909) \qquad (.0270)$

              $+ .1810 EQ_2 + .0239 Q_{78} + .0767 Q_{55}$
              $(.1412) \qquad (.0146) \qquad (.0253)$

The industry is primarily cost-oriented, although Q_{78}, the output of the electric utility industry, reflects market factors. All the transportation variables (TQ_7, TI_{55}, TI_{53}, TI_{45}, TI_{35}) were insignificant. The other cost variables, however, were significant, with value of land being important. However, the variable with the highest t ratio was the agglomeration variable Q_{55} (construction and mining machines), verifying the importance of capital equipment in the future development of the industry.

   DEN was not retained because of multicollinearity. The other variables were rejected either because of statistical insignificance or because they forced previously entered variables to insignificance.

IO 76 Communications

This industry encompasses all communications, except radio and television. there are three sectors in the industry: SIC 481 telephone communication; SIC 482 telegraph communications; SIC 489 communication services, NEC. The last sector includes cablevision, radar station operations, and telephoto services. Telephone communications dominate the industry. Their revenues were almost 50 times as large as telegraph in 1966.[93] PCE is the major market of this industry as the 1966 summary interindustry table reveals.

	Suppliers	Percent		Buyers	Percent
IO 12	Maintenance Construction	3.0	PCE		43.1
IO 83	Real Estate and Rental	1.9	IO 82	Finance and Insurance	6.9
IO 85	Business Services	1.8	IO 81	Wholesale Trade	5.4
IO 66	Communication Equip.	1.3			
IO 39	Petroleum Refining	.7			

No one commodity dominates the input structure of the industry, since most of the input is in the form of value added.

   New York with 11.4 percent and California with 10.4 percent lead the nation in output in 1965. Other states with appreciable output levels were New Jersey (6.6 percent), Texas (6.3 percent), Pennsylvania (5.3 percent), Illinois (4.8 percent), Ohio (4.7 percent), and Michigan (4.6 percent).

The regression equation (6.76) yielded good results. The R^2 for the change in output was .7308 and .9962 for the level of output.

(6.76) ΔQD_{76} = 19.9277 + .1044Q_{76} + .1906DEN + .0029Q_{66}
               (42.3914) (.0025)   (.0435)   (.0013)

Neither of the transportation variables (TI_{66}, TI_{39}) was retained. TI_{66} was insignificant, while TI_{39} had an incorrect sign. The positive sign and high significance of Q_{76} are caused by the high capital intensity of the industry. *DEN* reflects market factors, while Q_{66} is a cost variable.

Six variables were not retained because of multicollinearity: EQ_{57}, VL_{76}, *PI*, Q_{81}, and Q_{85}. Q_{39} had an incorrect sign, while the other variables were insignificant.

IO 77 Radio and TV Broadcasting

This industry is dominated by SIC 4833 TV broadcasting, which accrued 2½ times as much revenue as SIC 4832 radio broadcasting in 1967.[94] The sales of the industry are made almost exclusively to business services, which purchases time for advertising, as the 1966 summary interindustry table reveals.

	Suppliers	Percent		Buyers	Percent
IO 76	Communication	4.5	IO 85	Business Services	97.5
IO 85	Business Services	4.1			
IO 83	Real Estate and Rental	2.2			
IO 66	Communication Equipment	.3			

The major inputs are purchased from communications and business services.

In 1965 the industry was concentrated in New York, which accounted for 21.5 percent of revenues. Other states with significant levels of revenue were California (13.6 percent), Illinois (4.8 percent), Ohio (4.6 percent), Pennsylvania (4.4 percent), and Texas (4.1 percent).

The regression equation (6.77) yielded good results. The R^2 for the change in output was .8103, and .9077 for the level of output.

(6.77) ΔQD_{77} = $-$ 158.9734 $-$ .9022Q_{77} + .7199DEN + .0411Q_{85}
               (171.3748) (.0209)   (.0791)   (.0007)

The only transportation variable, TI_{66}, was insignificant. The other variables retained in the equation show that there is a strong degree of market orientation in the industry. While business services is the recorded major buyer, the broadcasting services are ultimately consumed by the viewers and listeners. Thus areas of dense populations are usually growth areas for the industry. The negative sign on output presumably is caused by physical and FCC constraints limiting an increase in broadcasting in already developed areas.

Three variables were not retained because of multicollinearity: VL, EQ_{57}, and Q_{66}. The other variables were either insignificant or forced previously entered variables to insignificance.

IO 78 Electric Utility

The electric utility industry is indispensible in running our factories and in maintaining our high standard of living. Its major market is *PCE* as indicated in the 1966 summary interindustry table.

	Suppliers	Percent	Buyers	Percent
IO 7	Coal Mining	5.0	*PCE*	39.2
IO 79	Gas Utility	3.4	Retail trade sectors	7.5
IO 85	Business Services	2.1	State and Local	
IO 39	Petroleum Refining	1.2	Government	7.4

Its major inputs reflect the power sources, excluding hydro, of the industry: coal, petroleum, gas. Atomic power was insignificant at this time.

The industry is located in the heavily populated states. New York and California produced 9.2 and 8.9 percent of the industry's output in 1965. Other states with high output levels were Texas (7.5 percent), Ohio (5.9 percent), Pennsylvania (5.7 percent), Illinois (5.4 percent), Michigan (4.2 percent), and Massachusetts (3.8 percent).

The regression equation (6.78) yielded good results. The R^2 for the change in output was .6199, and it was .9943 for the level of output.

$$(6.78) \qquad \Delta QD_{78} = -174.3373 - .1074VL + .0729Q_{78}$$
$$(63.8483) \quad (.0238) \qquad (.0042)$$

$$+ .0066Q_{39} + .0452Q_{79}$$
$$(.0009) \qquad (.0055)$$

Neither of the transportation variables (TI_7 and TI_{39}) was significant. The retention of VL and Q_{78} reflects the high cost and the economics of scale in modern power plants. The other significant variables, Q_{39} and Q_{79}, express agglomeration factors important in controlling costs.

Five variables were not retained because of multicollinearity: EQ_{58}, *DEN*, *PI*, GOV_9, and Q_{85}. TI_{39} had an incorrect sign, while the other variables were insignificant.

IO 79 Gas Utility

This industry consists of four interdependent sectors: SIC 4922 natural gas transmission; SIC 4923 natural gas transmission and distribution; SIC 2924 natural gas distribution; and SIC 4925 mixed, manufactured, or LP gas production and/or destination. The sale of gas between sectors is very high; the industry purchased 38 percent of its own output in 1966. The major market of the industry is *PCE* as indicated in the 1966 summary interindustry table.

	Suppliers	Percent		Buyers	Percent
IO 8	Petroleum Mining	17.2	*PCE*		32.4
IO 12	Maintenance C Construction	2.0	IO 78	Electric Utility	4.6
IO 75	Transportation	1.6			
IO 85	Business Services	1.6			

The major input is natural gas purchased from the petroleum mining industry.

The industry is located in conjunction with population although not to the extent of the electric utility industry. California with 11.7 percent had the largest share of output in 1965. Other states with high output levels were Ohio (8.3 percent), New York (7.6 percent), Illinois (7.4 percent), Pennsylvania (6.7 percent), Texas (6.5 percent), and Michigan (5.8 percent).

The regression equation (6.79) produced very good results. The R^2 for the change in output was .7785, and it was .9949 for the level of output.

$$(6.79) \qquad \Delta QD_{79} = -\ 204.1123 + \ .1538Q_{79}$$
$$(78.0138) \quad (.0030)$$

The only transportation variable entered, TI_8, was insignificant. The positive sign of Q_{79}, the only significant variable, reflects the importance of capital infrastructure in the industry.

EQ_{58} was not retained because of multicollinearity, while Q_{78} and Q_8 had incorrect signs. The other variables were insignificant.

IO 80 Water Utility

This industry is composed of the four dissimilar sectors presented below.[95]

SIC	Service	Percent of 1967 Employment
494	Water supply	45.8
495	Sanitary Services	44.4
496	Steam Companies and Systems	3.9
497	Irrigation	5.9

Sanitary systems include solid waste disposal as well as sewerage systems. The major market is *PCE* as recorded in the 1966 summary interindustry table.

	Suppliers	Percent		Buyers	Percent
IO 12	Maintenance Construction	12.7		*PCE*	50.1
IO 35	Basic Chemicals	2.0	IO 88	Medical and Educational Institutes	6.5
IO 39	Petroleum Refining	1.8			
			IO 99	Retail Trade Sectors	5.3

The major input is maintenance construction.

California, a state with severe water shortage problems, had 26.8 percent of the revenues in 1965. Other states with appreciable revenues were Pennsylvania (9.8 percent), Illinois (6.8 percent), New Jersey (6.7 percent), and New York (4.9 percent).

The regression equation (6.80) produced good results considering the diversity of output in the industry. The R^2 for the change in output was .5319, and it was .9975 for the level of output.

$$(6.80) \qquad \Delta QD_{80} = -19.7177 - .0698Q_{80} - .0989VL$$
$$(95.2003) \quad (.0053) \qquad (.0150)$$

$$+ .0005PI + .0033Q_{35}$$
$$(.0001) \quad (.0025)$$

The industry is primarily cost-oriented. Neither of the two transportation variables, TI_{35}, and TI_{39}, was significant. The variables reflecting cost considerations that were significant include VL, Q_{80}, and Q_{35}. The positive sign on Q_{80} reflects economies of scale. The significance of PI implies a degree of market orientation in the industry.

Three variables were excluded because of multicollinearity: EQ_{58}, DEN, and Q_{78}. The other variables either were insignificant or forced previously entered variables to insignificance.

Group 14: Services

The service industries are generally not encumbered in their locational orientation by the heavy investment in fixed capital and equipment that keeps manufacturing industries in their places. They arise as the need for them comes into being in a region, although there are some special regions where these functions cluster for particular reasons. Generally speaking, these industries fit the definition of "central place functions," along with transportation and warehousing, trade, and government. These services are affected with a hierarchy of sorts, in which larger cities have disproportionately larger employment in them. For example, a small city is not likely to have a major league ball park, one of the largest items in the amusement industry. Nor will any but the largest cities have important stock exchanges. Banks in large cities perform many services for banks in small places, employing people that no one smaller bank could use. In general, these industries cannot afford the luxury of locating with the lowest cost labor inputs or even in the low land-cost areas. It is necessary that these services be performed in places where people live or work, as the coefficients of localization in Table 6-15 show. Business Services is the only industry in the group that appears not to be located in almost perfect relation to total demand and personal income. This is understandable, since by definition, the sales of business services are made to other firms who are not necessarily spatially distributed in the same pattern as personal income or total demand.

While low fixed cost increases the potentiality of the service industries to relocate, they are among the most locationally stable industries, as measured by the shift statistics in the study. The average shift ratio is .0480 for the group.

The relative sizes, measured by levels of output and employment, are given in Table 6-15. Included in this group are the very largest industries in the study: finance and insurance, real estate, business services, and medical and educational institutions. The high labor-intensive characteristics of service industries and rising wages could affect their future growth. Consumers may substitute their own labor for those of firms providing services in a manner similar to the "do it yourself" fad of the 1950s that resulted in a substitution of household for professional labor of the carpentering, painting, and general household maintenance tasks.

Table 6-15
Summary Statistics, Group 14: Services

	Output 1966 Prices (000,000)		Employment (000)		Coefficient of Localization 1966 Output with		Output Shift Ratio
Industry	1965	1966	1965	1966	Personal Income	Industry Demand	1965-1966
82 Finance and Insurance	41,323	43,265	2629	2688	.267	.063	.0183
83 Real Estate and Rental	99,044	105,176	762	787	.288	.092	.0437
84 Hotels, Personal, and Repair Services	18,264	19,056	2475	2659	.175	.185	.0385
85 Business Services	60,426	66,176	2164	2187	.358	.286	.0437
86 Automobile Repair Services	14,821	15,587	468	476	.178	.115	.0583
87 Amusements and Recreation	8,856	8,849	640	659	.282	.050	.0601
88 Medical and Educational Institutions	43,528	46,647	4046	4367	.207	.032	.0650

All these industries sell directly to consumers, but *PCE* data estimates in all but IO 84 were directly related to output; therefore, personal income (*PI*) is substituted for *PCE* in the equations except IO 84.

IO 82 Finance and Insurance

This is the second largest of the industries in the study in terms of employment and also one of the easiest to locate. It is located with people and income, particularly in urban and retirement areas. The following table shows the 1965 employment size distribution of the major service subgroups within this industry:

SIC	Sectors	Percent of Employment
60	Banking	33
61	Other Credit Agencies	13
62	Securities Handling and Exchange	5
63	Insurance Carriers	38
64	Insurance Agents	10

The industry is locationally diffused, except for New York, which as the financial capital of the nation has special reasons for retaining a substantial share of the activity. Other regions have been growing more rapidly than New York, but in 1965, that state alone accounted for 17.7 percent of the industry's total output. Aside from New York, four states account for 5 percent or more of the industry's total. These are California (11.4 percent), which is almost as large as New York and is growing more rapidly, Illinois (6.7 percent), Texas (5.0 percent), and Pennsylvania (5.3 percent).

The input-output structure of the industry is summarized in the following table:

	Suppliers	Percent		Buyers	Percent
IO 85	Business Services	7.9	PCE		54.8
IO 83	Real Estate and Rental	4.8	IO 83	Real Estate	
IO 76	Communication	2.7		and Rental	4.9
IO 34	Printing and Publishing	1.0			
IO 32	Paper Products	.6			

The regression equation (6.82) produced excellent results with an R^2 of .8032 for the change in output and .9993 for the level of output.

$$(6.82) \quad \Delta QD_{82} = 743.5662 - 712.3968TI_{34} - 586.4663TI_{32} + .0565Q_{82}$$
$$(305.2897) \quad (474.8608) \qquad (321.1663) \qquad (.0006)$$

Both of the transportation variables (TI_{34} and TI_{32}) were significant. The industry is dependent on paper products and the printing industry for its many paper forms as the significance of the transportation variables indicate. The output variable has a high t ratio, and the significance of this variable is a function of the stability and agglomeration economics of the industry.

Six variables were not retained in the equation because of multicollinearity: EQ_{60}, PI, Q_{83}, Q_{34}, Q_{85}, and Q_{76}. Q_{32} had an incorrect sign. The other variables either were insignificant or forced a previously entered variable to insignificance.

IO 83 Real Estate

This industry is the largest in terms of output in the study. The major output of this industry consists of the property rent and the imputed rent of owner occupied homes as evidence by the large percent of sales to the personal consumption sector. The level of employment is not high in relation to output since there is no imputed labor to correspond to the imputed rent.

The SIC sectors of the real estate industry are presented below. The last two subsectors engage in activities that create new real estate, while the first two deal with the management and sale of existing real estate. Since the addition to the stock of real estate is small in percentage terms in any given year, it is understandable why (as the following table shows) the last two sectors had small employment percentages of the total in 1965.[96]

SIC	Sectors	Percent of Employment
651	Real Estate Operators	66
653	Agents, Brokers and Managers	15
655	Subdividers and Developers	10
656	Operative Builders	8

New York State accounted for 22.8 percent of the industry's output, principally because of the New York City, Westchester, and Long Island region, which alone accounted for 92 percent of the state total. Other states accounting for more than 4 percent were California (12.5 percent), Florida (4.4 percent), Illinois (7.8 percent), Ohio (4.5 percent), and Pennsylvania (4.3 percent). The output generated in SMSA are 90.7 percent of the total, revealing the heavy orientation of the real estate industry toward urban areas.

The input-output structure of the industry is summarized in the following table:

	Suppliers	Percent		Buyers	Percent
IO 12	Maintenance Construction	8.7	PCE		66.0
IO 82	Finance and Insurance	2.1	IO 88	Medical and Education	3.7

Suppliers	Percent		Buyers	Percent
		IO 82	Finance and Insurance	2.0
		IO 85	Business Services	1.7

The regression equation (6.83) produced good results with an R^2 of .4097 for the change in output and .9992 for the level of output.

(6.83) $\quad \Delta QD_{83} = 2024.7130 - .9868VL + .0294Q_{83}$
$$\qquad\qquad (349.6044) \quad (.1547) \qquad (.0011)$$

Transportation variables were not entered in the equation, since the industry purchases transportable commodities in only minor quantities. Land value was a very significant variable. The slowly changing capital structure in the industry resulted in the high significance of Q_{83}.

Multicollinearity was a pervasive problem in this equation. Variables that were rejected because of multicollinearity were EQ_{61}, DEN, PI, Q_{85}, Q_{88}, and Q_{82}. The only other variable entered in the equation, WR_{83}, was rejected because of an incorrect sign.

IO 84 Hotels, Personal, and Repair Services

The personal service industry is probably the most diverse of the service industries, defined as it is in terms of its output market, rather than in terms of the type of operation performed. Capital inputs are important to this industry; they consist of machinery and equipment for the most part, but also include construction and furniture. The table below shows the percentages of the industry's employment contributed by the most important service groups.[97]

SIC	Sector	Percent of Employment
70	Hotels and Lodgings	38
72	Personal Service	59
721	Laundries	(32)
723	Beauty Shops	(14)
724	Barber Shops	(5)
76ex 7694,7699	Electrical and Other Repair Services	3

Differences among the relative rates of growth of these subsectors will have less effect on the location of employment growth in the industry than it would in the case of a manufacturing industry, because most of the subsectors are located in response to similar factors. Even in areas specializing in recreation, where resort hotels are located, other personal services must be provided.

New York, with 13.9 percent, had the largest share of the industry's output in 1965. Only six other states produced more than 4 percent. Together, these states accounted for more than half (53.3 percent) of the total output: California (11.9 percent), Illinois (6.8 percent), Florida (5.9 percent), Pennsylvania (5.5 percent), Texas (4.8 percent), and Ohio (4.5 percent).

The input-output structure of the industry is summarized in the following table:

	Suppliers	Percent	Buyers	Percent
IO 83	Real Estate and		PCE	79.4
	Rental	5.7		
IO 67	Electronic Compo-			
	nents	2.9		
IO 85	Business Services	2.8		
IO 74	Misc. Manufactured			
	Products	1.9		
IO 37	Drugs, Cleaning, and			
	Toilet Items	1.7		

The regression equation (6.84) produced moderate results, which is understandable given the diversity of the industry; the R^2 was .3632 for the change in output and .9987 for the level of output.

$$(6.84) \quad \Delta QD_{84} = 2637.1312 - 427.2949 TI_{67} - 690.1571 TI_{74}$$
$$(750.9287) \quad (134.4186) \quad (304.6869)$$

$$- .2650 VL + .0179 Q_{84} + .0180 Q_{67}$$
$$(.0172) \quad (.0017) \quad (.0030)$$

$$+ .0111 Q_{37}$$
$$(.0015)$$

Two of the transportation variables that were entered were highly significant. The third transportation variable, TI_{37}, was not retained because of multicollinearity. The significance of TI_{67} reflects the electrical and other repair sectors of the industry. The high t ratio for the value of land reflects the cost of land in vacation areas for the hotel sector as well as the cost of urban land for the other sectors. The low shift ratio helps explain the high level of significance of output. The two other significant variables, Q_{67} and Q_{37}, reflect supplier agglomeration economies.

Excluding TI_{37} there were five other variables rejected because of multicollinearity: EQ_{61}, DEN, PCE_{84}, Q_{85}, and Q_{74}. The other variable, WR_{84}, was rejected because of insignificance.

IO 85 Business Services

Business and professional services are performed for a greater variety of customers and are difficult to describe. The SIC major groups involved in this industry are 654 title abstract companies, 73 miscellaneous business services excluding 736 private employment agencies; 81 legal services; and 89 miscellaneous services excluding 892 nonprofit research agencies. SIC 73 includes advertising; credit reporting, adjusting and collection agencies; duplicating, addressing, mailing, and similar services; such services to buildings as window cleaning, disinfecting, and exterminating; new syndicates; private employment agencies, research, development, and testing laboratories; consulting services for businesses. SIC 81 is simply legal services, for which no further detail is provided. SIC 89 includes engineering and architectural services; accounting, auditing, and bookkeeping services; and a variety of others. The important sales and purchases of this industry for 1966 are summarized in the following table:

	Suppliers	Percent		Buyers	Percent
IO 34	Printing and Publishing	13.1	PCE		8.8
IO 77	Radio and TV Broadcasting	5.2	IO 81	Wholesale Trade	7.9
			IO 82	Finance and Insurance	7.7
IO 83	Real Estate and Rental	3.9		Retail Trade	7.6
IO 73	Optical and Photographic Equipment	.6		Defense	4.6

Federal government purchases are largely in the form of consulting and research services. Real estate uses the services of engineers and architects; so does finance and insurance, although legal services are probably the important elements in their purchases. The trade industries probably purchase the most advertising.

There were important concentrations of the industry in 1965 in New York (20.7 percent) and California (16.3 percent), but the only other state with 5 percent or more of industry's output was Illinois (7.6 percent). Other states with substantial output were New Jersey (3.7 percent), Ohio (4.0 percent), Pennsylvania (4.6 percent), and Texas (3.7 percent). New York's dominance is related to its concentrations of communications (advertising) and financial activities. California is an important center for research and development, as well as a communications node.

The regression equation (6.85) produced excellent results given the diverse output of the industry. The R^2 was .9721 with the change in output and .9995 with the level of output.

$$(6.85) \quad \Delta QD_{85} = 459.7303 - 4433.1010TI_{34} - .1425Q_{85} + .2225DEN$$
$$(530.3898) \quad (1262.2669) \quad (.0011) \quad (.1207)$$

Two transportation variables, TI_{34} and TI_{73}, were entered into the equation. TI_{34} was significant, but TI_{73} was not retained because of multicollinearity. The level of output is an extremely important factor in the growth of this industry as indicated by the level of significance of Q_{85}. The other significant variable, DEN, shows the importance of large urban areas.

Seven other variables were rejected because of multicollinearity: VL, EQ_{61}, PI, Q_{81}, Q_{82}, DEF_{85}, and Q_{34}. The wage rate was insignificant, and Q_{77} and Q_{73} had the wrong sign.

IO 86 Automobile Repair Service

The location of the automobile repair service industry depends upon the location of population, but varies according to the driving habits of the people of the region. The following table shows the distribution of employees for three-digit level industries.[98]

SIC	Sector	Percent of Employment
751	Automobile Rentals, Without Driver	11.9
752	Automobile Parking	11.2
753	Automobile Repair Shops	58.2
754	Automobile Services, Except Repair	18.7

A breakdown of the automobile repair shops category is not very rewarding, since most of them are general repair shops and repair shops not elsewhere classified. Automobile services, except repair, is largely composed of what the Census calls automobile laundries. The interindustry relations of the industry are as follows:

Suppliers		Percent	Buyers		Percent
IO 69	Motor Vehicles	8.3	PCE		61.7
IO 81	Wholesale Trade	8.1	IO 81	Wholesale Trade	7.5
IO 83	Real Estate and Rental	2.8	IO 75	Transportation	5.4
IO 40	Rubber and Plastic Products	2.4	IO 69	Motor Vehicles	3.3
IO 68	Batteries and Engine Electrical Equipment	2.1			
IO 60	Machine Shop and Misc. Machinery	1.4			
IO 39	Petroleum Refining	1.1			

As of 1965, the industry was extremely diffused, with only five states producing as much as 5 percent of the total. These are California (12.2 percent), New York (9.9 percent), Pennsylvania (7.0 percent), Ohio (5.0 percent), and Illinois (6.3 percent).

The regression equation (6.86) yielded good results with an R^2 of .5108 for the change in output and .9976 for the level of output.

$$(6.86) \qquad \Delta QD_{86} = 27.1743 - .2177VL + .0566Q_{86} + .0138Q_{68}$$
$$\qquad\qquad (61.1911) \quad (.0173) \qquad (.0019) \qquad (.0108)$$

All four transportation variables (TI_{69}, TI_{40}, TI_{68} and TI_{60}) were insignificant. Value of land continued to be a significant variable for the industries in the service group as was the level of output. The suppliers agglomeration variable, Q_{68}, was retained.

Six variables were rejected because of multicollinearity: EQ_{61}, DEN, PI, Q_{81}, Q_{75}, and Q_{60}. The other variables were not retained because of insignificance or because they forced previously entered variables to insignificance.

IO 87 Amusements and Recreation

Outside of motion picture and theatrical production employment, which is concentrated in California and New York, the amusements industry is quite diffused as to location. The other elements of the industry are, in fact, much more local-service type industries than the services provided by Hollywood and Broadway. The distribution of 1965 employment for the industry is given below.[99]

SIC	Sector	Percent of Employment
781	Motion Picture Production and Distribution	9.8
782		
783	Motion Picture Theaters	21.3
791	Dance Halls, Studios, and Schools	2.6
792	Theatrical Producers, Entertainers	10.0
793	Bowling Alleys, Billiard Parlors	19.4
794	Other Amusement and Recreation Services	36.8

The industry's sales are not related so uniformly to personal consumption as might be imagined, as the summary table of its interindustry relations shows:

	Suppliers	Percent		Buyers	Percent
IO 83	Real Estate and Rental	9.8		PCE	69.2
IO 85	Business Services	4.6	IO 77	Radio and TV Broadcasting	8.0
IO 73	Optical and Photographic Equipment	1.5			
IO 35	Basic Chemicals	1.0			

The industry purchases 17.8 percent of its own output, which indicates the high degree of dependence of the sectors of the industry on each other. Presumably, the relation of amusements to radio and TV has become stronger since 1966, although it is unlikely that even in the distant future all entertainment will be broadcast or otherwise provided by nonlocal employees.

Entertainment and amusement are mainly functions of central places, but there is also some employment associated with resort areas, which may not have important population concentrations during the "off season." Nationally, the amusements industry has been declining, perhaps because of the greater coverage of mass media (whose output is classified in the radio and TV industry, IO 77) and also because of the mechanization of bowling and other recreations. California had the largest output in the industry with 18.3 percent of the output in 1965, and is followed by New York, which produced 16.9 percent. Other states with 4 percent or more were Illinois (5.2 percent), Pennsylvania (4.7 percent), Ohio (4.8 percent), and Florida (4.3 percent).

The regression equation (6.87) produced good results with an R^2 of .4942 for the change in output and .9986 for the level of output.

$$(6.87) \qquad \Delta QD_{87} = -56.0622 - .4190VL + .0231Q_{87} + .0773Q_{77}$$
$$\qquad\qquad\qquad (55.1693) \quad (.0165) \qquad (.0020) \qquad (.0073)$$

Both transportation variables enterd in the equation (TI_{73} and TI_{35}) were insignificant. Value of land is a very important variable as ascertained by the high t ratio. The influence of "talent pools" is revealed in the high significance of the agglomeration variable Q_{87}. The importance of the purchases of radio and TV broadcasting to the amusements and recreation industry is substantiated by the significance of Q_{77}.

Four variables were not retained because of multicollinearity: EQ_{61}, DEN, PI, and Q_{85}. The other variables not included were insignificant.

IO 88 Medical and Educational Institutions

In addition to medical and educational services, this industry includes museums of all types and nonprofit membership organizations. Medical and other health services (SIC 80) include offices of physicians, surgeons, dentists, dental surgeons, osteopathic physicians, and chiropractors; hospitals; medical and dental laboratories, sanatoria, convalescent and rest homes; and other health services. Educational services (SIC 82) include elementary and secondary schools; colleges, universities, professional schools, junior colleges, and normal schools; libraries; correspondence schools and vocational schools; and schools and educational services of various minor types such as music schools, child guidance clinics, language schools, and short-term examination preparatory schools. Museums, art galleries, and botanical and zoological gardens (SIC 84) need not be broken down further. Nonprofit organizations (SIC 86) can be identified as business associations, professional membership organizations, labor unions, civic, social, and fraternal associations, political organizations, religious organizations, and charitable organizations, plus the inevitable nonclassifiable remainder. The industry also includes private employment agencies (SIC 736) and nonprofit research agencies (SIC 892). Of these, the medical and educational services and nonprofit membership organizations employ by far the largest number as the percentages presented below indicate.[100]

SIC	Industry Sector	Percent
736	Private Employment Agencies	.6
80	Medical and Other Health Services	56.7
82	Educational Services	18.3
84	Museums, etc.	.4
86	Nonprofit Membership Organizations	21.9
892	Nonprofit Research Agencies	2.1

The medical and educational industry had the greatest number of employees—4,046,000 in 1965—of any industry in the study. However, its 1965 output of $43.5 billion was surpassed by IO 69 motor vehicles, IO 75 transportation, IO 81 wholesale trade, IO 83 real estate, and IO 85 business services, indicating the labor intensity of the industry.

The interindustry relations of this industry are among the simplest in the study. The distribution of the major inputs and sales for 1966 is shown in the following table:

	Suppliers	Percent		Buyers	Percent
IO 83	Real Estate and Rental	8.1	PCE		88.0
IO 85	Business Services	2.0			
IO 12	Maintenance Construction	2.0			
IO 37	Drugs, Cleaning, and Toilet Items	1.8			
IO 34	Printing and Publishing	1.3			

Capital inputs are of importance in the industry's structure as well; these consist mainly of inputs from construction but also include inputs from the electrical machinery and miscellaneous industries.

The industry is locationally diffused although New York accounted for 15.6 percent and California 10.7 percent of the output of the industry in 1965. The only other states with more than 4 percent of the total are Pennsylvania (7.0 percent), Illinois (6.8 percent), Massachusetts (5.5 percent), and Ohio (5.2 percent).

The regression equation (6.88) yielded poor results; the R^2 was only .1594 for the change in output, but a high .9994 for the level of output.

$$(6.88) \quad \Delta QD_{88} = 223.9908 - 9.5490 WR_{88} + .0084 Q_{88} + .1399 DEN$$
$$(100.1946) \quad (9.4867) \quad\quad (.0008) \quad\quad (.0378)$$

Both of the transportation variables (TI_{37} and TI_{34}) had incorrect signs. WR_{88} was marginally significant, but Q_{88} reflecting agglomeration economies of skilled professionals, was the most important variable. The significance of DEN implies that the industry is oriented to large urban areas.

Five variables were not retained because of multicollinearity: VL, EQ_{61}, PI, Q_{85}, and Q_{34}. The other variables either were insignificant or forced previously entered variables toward insignificance.

Notes

Notes

Chapter 1
Introduction

1. Johann H. Von Thunen, *Von Thunen's Isolated State* (translated by Carala M. Wartenburg), Pergamon Press, Oxford, 1966.

2. Alfred Weber, *Theory of the Location of Industries*, (translated by C. Friedrich), University of Chicago Press, Chicago, 1929.

3. Walter Isard, "Some Locational Factors in the Iron and Steel Industry Since the Early Nineteenth Century," *Journal of Political Economy*, vol. 56, 1948.

4. John Cumberland and Walter Isard, "New England as a Possible Location for an Integrated Iron and Steel Works," *Economic Geography*, vol. 50, 1950.

5. Walter Isard and Robert E. Kuenne, "The Impact of Steel Upon the Greater New York-Philadelphia Industrial Region: A Study in Agglomeration Projection," *Review of Economics and Statistics*, vol. 35, Nov. 1953.

6. Edgar Hoover, *Location Theory and the Shoe and Leather Industries*, Harvard University Press, Cambridge, Mass., 1937.

7. August Losch, *The Economics of Location*, Yale University Press, New Haven, 1954.

8. Walter Isard, *Location and Space Economy*, The M.I.T. Press, Cambridge, Mass., 1956.

9. Ibid., p. 79.

10. Leon Cooper, "Solutions of Generalized Locational Equilibrium Models," *Journal of Regional Science*, vol. 7, Summer 1967.

11. Gerald J. Karaska and David Bramhall, eds., *Locational Analysis for Manufacturing*, The M.I.T. Press, Cambridge, Mass., 1969.

12. William Alonso, "A Reformulation of Classical Location Theory and Its Relation to Rent Theory," *Papers, The Regional Science Association*, vol. 19, 1967.

13. Clopper Almon, Jr., *The American Economy to 1975*, Harper and Row, New York, 1966, presents the basic model of this project.

Chapter 2
The Location Model

1. James Henderson and Richard Quandt, *Microeconomic Theory*, McGraw-Hill Book Company, New York, 1958, pp. 72-75.

2. Edgar M. Hoover, *The Location of Economic Activity*, McGraw-Hill Book Company, New York, 1948.

3. Isard, *Location and Space Economy*, pp. 172-188.

4. Von Thunen, *Von Thunen's Isolated State.*

5. Losch, *The Economies of Location.*

6. Edgar S. Dunn, Jr., *The Location of Agriculture Production*, University of Florida Press, Gainesville, Fla., 1954.

7. Lowdon Wingo, *Transportation and Urban Land*, Johns Hopkins Press for Resources for the Future, Baltimore, 1961.

8. William Alonso, *Location and Land Use*, Harvard University Press, Cambridge, Mass., 1964.

9. Alfred Weber, *Theory of the Location of Industry.*

10. Edgar M. Hoover, *Location Theory and the Shoe and Leather Industries; The Location of Economic Activity.*

11. Losch, *The Economics of Location.*

12. Isard, *Location and Space Economy.*

13. Melvin Greenhut, *Plant Location in Theory and in Practice*, University of North Carolina Press, Chapel Hill, N.C., 1956.

14. Leon Cooper, "Solutions of Generalized Locational Equilibrium Models."

15. Ibid.

16. Hoover, *The Location of Economic Activity*, pp. 145-165.

Chapter 3
The Transportation Variables

1. See Don Patinkin, *Money, Interest and Prices*, Row, Peterson and Company, Evanston, Ill., 1956.

Chapter 4
Data Requirements

1. Charles F. Phillips, Jr., *The Economics of Regulation: Theory and Practice in the Transportation and Public Utility Industries*, Richard D. Irwin, Inc., Homewood, Ill., 1966, pp. 441-482, reviews the historical development of transportation rate regulation in the United States.

2. Glenn Brokke, *Nationwide Highway Travel* (mimeograph), Bureau of Public Roads, U.S. Department of Commerce, June 9, 1966.

3. John B. Lansing, *Transportation and Economic Policy*, The Free Press, New York, 1966, pp. 333-336.

4. Edgar M. Hoover, *The Location of Economic Activity*, pp. 19-21.

5. Merrill J. Roberts, "Transport Costs, Pricing, and Regulation," in *Transportation Economics*. Compiled papers of a conference of the Universities National Bureau Committee for Economic Research, New York, 1965, pp. 3-42.

6. Ibid.

7. *Distribution of Rail Revenue Contribution by Commodity Groups, 1960*, (Statement No. 2-62), 1962, Bureau of Accounts, Interstate Commerce Commission.

Chapter 5
The Location Equations

1. Obtained from U.S. Department of Commerce, Bureau of Census, *1964 Census of Agriculture* with comparable additional estimates in urban counties not covered in the census.

2. Henri Theil, *Principles of Econometrics*, John Wiley & Sons, Inc., New York, 1961, pp. 603-607.

3. Ibid., p. 604.

4. Ibid.

5. Donald E. Farrar and Robert R. Glauber, "Multicollinearity in Regression Analysis: The Problem Revisited," *The Review of Economics and Statistics*, vol. 49, no. 1, (February 1967), pp. 92-107.

6. Carl F. Christ, *Econometric Models and Methods*, John Wiley & Sons, Inc., New York, 1966, pp. 532-534.

Chapter 6
Locational Analysis by Industry

1. Victor R. Fuchs, *Changes in the Location of Manufacturing in the United States since 1929*, Yale University Press, New Haven, 1962, pp. 39-43, discusses this and related measures.

2. Walter Isard, *Methods of Regional Analysis: An Introduction to Regional Science*, The Technology Press of M.I.T. and John Wiley & Sons, Inc., New York, 1960, p. 252.

3. *Input-Output Structure of the U.S. Economy*, 1963, vol. I, Office of Business Economics, U.S. Department of Commerce, 1969.

4. *U.S. Statistical Abstract, 1968*, Bureau of Census, U.S. Department of Commerce.

5. Marion Clawson and Charles L. Steward, *Land Use Information*, The Johns Hopkins Press, Baltimore, 1965, p. 83. This figure includes improved pasture.

6. Ibid. This percentage excludes improved pasture.

7. M. Clawson, R. Held, C. Stoddard, *Land for the Future*, Johns Hopkins Press, Baltimore, 1960, pp. 236-237.

8. *Employment and Wages, Fourth Quarter 1965 and Annual Summary*, U.S. Department of Labor, p. 20.

9. *Pulp and Paper*, C-M Business Publications, New York (April 4, 1966).

10. *1967 Census of Manufactures*, Bureau of Census, Department of Commerce, January 1971, vol. 1, p. 28.

11. *Growth Pace Setters in American Industry 1958-1968*, U.S. Department of Commerce, U.S. Government Printing Office, Washington, D.C. (October 1968), pp. 71-73.

12. *1967 Census of Manufactures*, vol. 1, p. 28.

13. Ibid.

14. Ibid.

15. Ibid.

16. Ibid.

17. Ibid.

18. Ibid.

19. Ibid.

20. Ibid., p. 30.

21. *Textile World*, McGraw-Hill Publications, New York, June 1965 and April 1966.

22. *Technological Trends in Major American Industries*, Bulletin No. 1474, U.S. Department of Labor, February 1968. U.S. Government Printing Office, Washington, D.C. (1968) pp. 148-153.

23. S.M. Stelzer, "The Cotton Textile Industry," in *The Structure of American Industry*, 3rd edition, ed. by Walter Adams, The Macmillan Company, New York, 1961, pp. 57-60.

24. *1967 Census of Manufactures*, vol. 1, p. 30.

25. Ibid.

26. *Technological Trends in Major American Industries*, pp. 155-160.

27. *1967 Census of Manufactures*, vol. 1, p. 30.

28. *Growth Pace Setters in American Industry, 1958-1968*, pp. 62-64.

29. *1967 Census of Manufactures*, vol. I, p. 32.

30. Ibid.

31. *Pulp and Paper*, August 30, 1965.

32. *1967 Census of Manufactures*, vol. I, p. 32.

33. Ibid.

34. Ibid.

35. Ibid.

36. Ibid.

37. Ibid.

38. *Growth Pace Setters in American Industry, 1958-1968*, pp. 87-90.

39. Alfred E. Kahn, "The Combined Effects of Prorationing, the Depletion Allowance, and Import Quotas on the Cost of Producing Crude Oil in the United States," *Natural Resources Journal* January, 1970, pp. 53-61.

40. *1967 Census of Mineral Industries*, vol. 1, p. 16.

41. Ibid.

42. *1967 Census of Manufactures*, vol. 1, p. 34.

43. Alfred E. Kahn, "The Chemical Industry," in *The Structure of American Industry*, p. 249.

44. *1967 Census of Manufactures*, vol. 1, p. 34.

45. Ibid.

46. *Growth Pace Setters in American Industry, 1958-1968*, pp. 103-105.

47. *Technological Trends in Major American Industries*, pp. 179-183.

48. Joel B. Dirlam, "The Petroleum Industry," in *The Structure of American Industry*, pp. 288-290.

49. *1967 Census of Manufactures*, vol. 1, p. 34.

50. Ibid.

51. *Growth Pace Setters in American Industry, 1958-1968*, pp. 114-115.

52. *Technological Trends in Major American Industries*, pp. 188-189.

53. *1967 Census of Manufactures*, vol. 1, p. 34.

54. Ibid.

55. *1967 Census of Mineral Industries*, vol. 1, Bureau of Census, U.S. Department of Commerce, p. 16-18.

56. *1967 Census of Manufactures*, vol. 1, p. 34.

57. Ibid.

58. *1967 Census of Mineral Industries*, vol. 1, p. 16.

59. Ibid.

60. *1967 Census of Manufactures*, vol. 1, p. 36.

61. Ibid.

62. *The Iron Age*, Chilton Co., New York, January 20, 1966.

63. *1967 Census of Manufactures*, vol. 1, p. 36.

64. Ibid.

65. Ibid.

66. Ibid.

67. Ibid.

68. Ibid., p. 42.

69. Ibid., p. 30.

70. *Growth Pace Setters in American Industry, 1958-1968*, pp. 43-45.

71. *1967 Census of Manufactures*, vol. 1, p. 38.

72. Ibid.

73. Ibid.

74. Ibid.

75. Ibid.

76. *Growth Pace Setters in American Industry 1958-1968*, pp. 80-81.

77. *1967 Census of Manufactures*, vol. 1, p. 40.

78. Ibid.

79. Ibid.

80. *Technological Trends in Major American Industries*, pp. 91-96.

81. *1967 Census of Manufactures*, vol. 1, p. 38.

82. Ibid.

83. Ibid.

84. Ibid.

85. Ibid.

86. Ibid., pp. 38,40.

87. Ibid., p. 40.

88. Ibid.

89. *Growth Pace Setters in American Industry, 1958-1968*, pp. 91-92, 107-108.

90. *1967 Census of Manufactures*, vol. 1, p. 40.

91. Ibid., pp. 40, 42.

92. *1967 Census of Mineral Industries*, vol. 1, p. 19.

93. *U.S. Statistical Abstract*, 1969, p. 496.

94. Ibid., p. 499.

95. *1967 County Business Patterns*, U.S. Summary, Bureau of Census, U.S. Department of Commerce, p. 15.

96. *1965 County Business Patterns*, U.S. Summary, pp. 1-17.

97. Ibid., pp. 1-18.

98. Ibid.

99. Ibid., pp. 1-19.

100. Ibid.

Appendixes

Employment

The location model requires county output data by industry sector, but in order to make good output estimates it was necessary to obtain county employment data. The principal source of the employment data is County Business Patterns (CBP), published by the Bureau of the Census, which has been available annually for four-digit SIC industry sectors since 1965. Since the data come from social security reports filed by employers, in March of each year, they do not account for 100 percent of the total employment. The data report the number of jobs, not the number of persons holding jobs; therefore, individuals holding more than one job are counted twice. Estimates of employment not covered by CBP will be explained first, followed by a discussion of the problem in using the CBP data files.

The sectors not covered in the CBP are the self-employed and workers in government, agriculture, railroads, and households. Table A-1 shows the March 1965 and 1966 employment balance for the United States, including unemployment and labor force. Similar tables could be constructed for each state and county, and the employment from CBP can be broken down further by industry sector. Note in Table A-1 that there is a row for net commuting. There is no entry in the U.S. table, but there will be in the state and county tables; the CBP data are by place of work, and the unemployment and the labor force data are by place of residence.

The employment balances for states and counties are not given, but the sources of the state and county estimates are given in Tables A-2 and A-3, respectively. In no case was there a regional data series that matched the national data exactly. The state data as given in the sources were used to allocate the national data to states, and the county data as given in the sources were used to allocate the state estimates to counties.

Adjustments in County Business Patterns
County Data

Data in CBP are available on computer tapes, but if a consistent set of county data by industry for all counties in the United States is required, it is necessary to make estimates of missing data and to adjust some of the existing numbers. The types of problems encountered are:

233

Table A-1

National Employment and Unemployment, 1965-1966 (Numbers in Thousands)

Job Sector	March 1965	March 1966
Employees under Social Security[a]	47,743	50,734
Agriculture[b]	3,989	3,780
Household service[c]	2,345	2,415
Railroads[d]	729	711
Federal civilian government[e]	2,326	2,460
State and local civilian government[e]	7,555	8,207
Nonagricultural self-employed[c]	6,845	6,612
Military[f]	(1,616)	(1,793)
Total civilian jobs	71,532	74,919
Multi-job holders[g]	1,363	2,896
Net workers commuting	–	–
Total civilians employed[h]	70,169	72,023
Civilian unemployment[h]	3,740	3,037
Civilian labor force[h]	73,909	75,060

[a]U.S. Department of Commerce, U.S. Bureau of Census, *County Business Patterns*, U.S. Summary 1965 and 1966.

[b]U.S. Department of Labor, Bureau of Labor Statistics, *Employment and Earnings*, Table A-1, June 1965 and 1966.

[c]U.S. Department of Labor, Bureau of Labor Statistics, *Employment and Earnings*, Table A-16, May 1965 and 1966.

[d]U.S. Department of Labor, Bureau of Labor Statistics, *Employment and Earnings*, Table B-2, May 1965 and 1966.

[e]U.S. Department of Labor, Bureau of Labor Statistics, *Employment and Earnings*, Table B-1, June 1965 and 1966.

[f]Military stationed in U.S. only, as of June 30, 1965 and 1966. Obtained from Directorate for Statistical Services, Office of Secretary of Defense, U.S. Department of Defense.

[g]Residual: Total civilian jobs less total civilians employed. This represents multi-job holders of employees under Social Security since the other categories report persons employed. The numbers appear to underestimate the actual multi-job holders, probably because of under reporting in *County Business Patterns*.

[h]U.S. Department of Labor, Bureau of Labor Statistics, *Employment and Earnings*, Table A-1, May 1965 and 1966.

1. Data in the published volumes contain errors.
2. Data on tapes do not agree with data in published volumes.
3. Data are missing because of the Census disclosure rules.
4. Data are missing because there are fewer than 100 employees or 10 firms in a county for a particular industry.
5. The industry classifications include "administration and auxiliary" and "unclassified" categories that do not have Standard Industrial Classifications (SIC) numbers.

6. Some of the data are not classified by county but put into a "state-wide" category.

Table A-2
Sources of State Employment and Unemployment, 1965 and 1966

Employees under Social Security
U.S. Department of Commerce, Bureau of the Census, *County Business Patterns*, March 1965 and 1966. Adjustments to numbers are described in the text.

Agriculture
"Total Workers on Farms, Revised Estimates" in U.S. Statistical Reporting Service, *Farm Labor*, March 1966 and 1967. Numbers for Hawaii are set at the 1964 level as reported in Table 7 and Table 8, U.S. Department of Commerce, *1964 Census of Agriculture*, vol. i, part 50. The 1965 and 1966 state numbers are adjusted proportionately to sum to the national totals for agriculture as given in Table A-1.

Household Service
State per capita employment in private households from 1960 Population Census multiplied by 1965 and 1966 population and adjusted proportionately to sum to the national totals in Table A-1.

Railroads
"State Distribution of the Average Number of Employees Covered by Railroad Retirement and Railroad Insurance Acts 1962-1966," U.S. Railroad Retirement Board, Office of Actuary and Research. The distribution by state is estimated from data compiled by Bureau of Railway Economics, Association of American Railroads, on the number of employees of class 1 railroads and switching and terminal companies, classified by states, as of the payroll periods which included March 12 of 1963, 1965 and 1967. The 1965 and 1966 state numbers are adjusted proportionately to sum to the national totals as given in Table A-1.

Federal Civilian Government
"Federal Civilian Employment in the United States by Geographic Area (December 31, 1966)," U.S. Civil Service Commission, Statistics Section, May 1968. The equivalent 1965 figures were taken from *County and City Data Book, 1967*, U.S. Department of Commerce, Bureau of the Census. Employment in the Central Intelligence Agency and the National Security Agency are excluded. The state numbers are adjusted proportionately to sum to the national 1965 and 1966 totals as given in Table A-1.

State and Local Government
"Employees on Government Payrolls (in thousands) by State, 1939-1967" in U.S. Department of Labor, Bureau of Labor Statistics, *Employment and Earnings for States and Areas*. Maryland, D.C., and Virginia figures are revised since data are given for the Washington, D.C., metropolitan area, for the rest of Maryland and for the rest of Virginia. The 1965 and 1966 state numbers are adjusted proportionately to sum to the national totals as given in Table A-1.

Nonagricultural Self-employed
"Workers with Taxable Earnings, Estimated Number by State," Table 44 in U.S. Department of Health, Education and Welfare, *Social Security Bulletin, Annual Statistical Supplement* 1965 and 1966. The 1965 and 1966 state numbers are adjusted proportionately to sum to the national totals as given in Table A-1.

Military
Military stationed in U.S. only, as of June 30, 1965 and 1966. Obtained from Directorate for Statistical Services, Office of the Secretary of Defense, U.S. Department of Defense.

Table A-2 (cont.)

Multi-job Holders
State multi-job holders are estimated by applying the national ratio of multi-job holders to employees under social security to the state figures for employees under Social Security.

Net Workers Commuting
The net number of workers commuting were estimated for counties, as described in Table A-3, and summed to the state level.

Total Civilians Employed
This is equal to the total number of jobs minus multi-job holders and net commuters.

Civilian Unemployment
U.S. Department of Labor, Bureau of Employment Security, *Area Trends in Employment and Unemployment*, July 1968. The 1965 and 1966 state numbers are adjusted proportionately to sum to the national totals as given in Table A-1.

Civilian Labor Force
Sum of total civilians employed and civilian unemployment.

The procedures used to overcome these problems will be explained in detail, but first it is useful to describe what we refer to as matrix balancing.

A matrix is considered balanced if the sum of each row equals its control total and the sum of each column equals its control total. In the hypothetical matrix below rows represent regions and columns represent industries.

		Industry			Region Controls
Region	1	10	20	5	40
	2	5	5	10	20
	3	20	5	20	40
Industry Controls		30	40	30	100

The above matrix is not balanced; not all the rows and columns sum to their controls. The balance is achieved by first adjusting each row proportionately to force them to add to the region controls; then, since this is no assurance that the entries in the column will sum to their controls, proportional adjustments are made by column. There is still no assurance at this point that the matrix is balanced. If not, the process is repeated until an acceptable balance is achieved. In our application the process was stopped when the maximum discrepancy between any one column or row sum and its respective control was less than 0.7. The illustrative matrix when balanced and rounded off to the nearest unit is as follows:

Table A-3
Sources of County Employment and Unemployment, 1965 and 1966

Employees Under Social Security
U.S. Department of Commerce, Bureau of Census, *County Business Patterns*, March 1965 and 1966. Adjustments to numbers are described in the text.

Agriculture
U.S. Department of Commerce, Bureau of Census, *1964 Census of Agriculture*. County data are for number of farms which is equivalent to number of operators. The county numbers are adjusted proportionately to sum to 1965 and 1966 state totals.

Household Service
U.S. Department of Commerce, Bureau of Census, *Population Census, 1960*. The 1960 numbers are multiplied by the ratio of 1966 county population to 1960 county population. Then they are adjusted proportionately to sum to 1965 and 1966 state totals.

Railroads
U.S. Department of Commerce, Bureau of the Census, *Population Census, 1960*. The 1960 county numbers are adjusted proportionately to sum to the 1965 and 1966 state totals.

Federal Civilian Government
"Federal Civilian Employment in the United States by Geographic Area," (December 31, 1966), U.S. Civil Service Commission, Statistics Section, May 1968. The equivalent 1965 figures were taken from *County and City Data Book, 1967*, U.S. Department of Commerce, Bureau of Census. Figures exclude employment in the Central Intelligence Agency and National Security Agency. The county numbers are adjusted proportionately to sum to 1965 and 1966 state totals.

State and Local Government
"Local Government Employees," October, 1962, U.S. Department of Commerce, Bureau of Census, *County and City Data Book, 1967*. The figures are multiplied by the ratio of 1966 county population to 1960 county population and adjusted proportionately to sum to both the 1965 and 1966 state totals for state and local government employment.

Nonagricultural Self-Employed
County figures for total nonagricultural self-employed are the sum of the number of self-employed estimated by input-output sector. The procedure for obtaining self-employed by input-output sector is described in the text.

Military
The number of military is allocated to counties within each state for 1965 and 1966 using fiscal year 1968 military active duty pay obtained from "Federal Outlays by Geographic Location," Bureau of the Budget.

Multi-job Holders
County multi-job holders are estimated by applying the appropriate state ratio of multi-job holders to employees under social security to the county figures for employees under Social Security.

Net Workers Commuting
Net commuting rates for most counties were derived from the Journey to Work Data, *Census of Population 1960*, U.S. Department of Commerce, Bureau of Census. The net commuting rate (C) is defined as:

Table A-3 (cont.)

$$C = \frac{E_W - E_L}{E_L}$$

where E_W is workers working in the county and E_L is workers living in the county. Some county data could not be obtained because of problems with reading the computer tape containing E_W. Using the good data, a regression equation was fitted explaining E_W, then the predicted values of E_W for the missing counties were used to estimate the commuting rates.

The 1960 commuting rates are applied to the 1965 and 1966 number of workers working a county (number of jobs less number of multi-job holders) to obtain the net number of commuters.

Total Civilians Employed
This is equal to the total number of jobs minus multi-job holders and net commuters.

Civilian Unemployment
Local unemployment estimates for 1965 and 1966 are from three sources: (1) data for 150 Major Labor Areas from U.S. Department of Labor, Bureau of Employment Security, *Area Trends in Employment and Unemployment*, July 1968, (2) data made available by the Economic Development Administration for approximately 1540 counties that have ever qualified under Title I, Section 102 and Title IV, Section 401 (a) of the Public Works and Economic Development Act of 1965, and (3) data estimated by some states under employment security programs.

The 1965 and 1966 unemployment estimates for counties for which there were no data were made by first applying the population growth rate between 1960 and 1966 to the 1960 level of unemployment as reported in the *Population Census 1960* and then adjusting the county numbers to sum to higher appropriate Major Labor Area numbers or appropriate state numbers. Of the 150 labor areas, 138 were conterminous with SMSAs, which are defined as counties or groups of counties. Actual county data was subtracted from labor area data for those counties within the labor area, then the first approximations of unemployment based on population growth are adjusted proportionately to sum to the adjusted labor area totals. The same procedure using state totals is followed for estimating unemployment in counties not in labor areas.

Civilian Labor Force
Sum of total civilians employed and civilian unemployment.

		Industry	
Region	1	2	3
1	9	27	4
2	4	7	9
3	17	6	17

The industry data, by SIC codes, are available for four levels—industry divisions, two-digit, three-digit, and four-digit. The sum of two-digit numbers within an industry division should be equal to the industry division total; the three-digits should sum to the appropriate two-digit; and the four-digits to the appropriate three-digit. CBP data were obtained for the nation and states separately because of the missing data on the county level; i.e., the sum of the county data within each state was less than the respective state totals. The state matrices for each of the SIC groups are first balanced to the national totals; then the county matrices within each state are balanced to state totals.

On the first balance the state industry divisions are balanced to the national totals.

States	Industry Divisions				State Totals
	1	2	$\cdots$	N	
1					
2					
$\cdot$					
$\cdot$					
$\cdot$					
51					
National Control Totals					

The data for this first balance were adjusted by hand as far as possible. That is, errors that could be found in the published volumes, as well as errors on the tape, were corrected before the arbitrary balancing procedure was allowed to operate. Beyond this point, except in a few cases, no hand corrections were made. In all, some 42 errors were hand-corrected in the 1965 employment and 8 in 1966. Some examples of the errors found are:

1. The 1966 tapes recorded construction in West Virginia at 2,002,168, whereas it should have been 21,680.
2. In 1966 the industry division totals for New York on the tape do not agree with those published. However, it was determined that the numbers on the tape were correct since they sum to a state total of 5,666,621 which is the correct number to be used in summing the state totals to the total national figure. In one table of the published volume the New York total was 5,666,621, whereas in other tables it was 5,659,424, the sum of the supposedly incorrect industry division totals. The same problem occurred with Ohio.

The next set of adjustments balance the two-digit SIC industries to the appropriate industry divisions. The first of this set is seen in the following table.

Following the two-digit balances, each of the three-digit industries was then adjusted to the appropriate two-digit industry; finally, four-digit industries were balanced to the three-digit industries.

		07	SIC 08	09	State Industry Division No. 1 Total
States	1				
	2				
	.				
	.				
	.				
	51				
National Control Totals					

In the above balances the "unclassified" industry sector was treated as an industry division and the "administration and auxiliary" sectors—there is one corresponding to each industry division except for the division called Agricultural Services, Forestry, and Fisheries—were treated as two-digit industry sectors. After the balances these sectors were distributed proportionately to the appropriate SIC industry sectors—the "unclassified" sector was distributed to the identifiable SIC divisions and the "administrative and auxiliary" sectors are distributed to the identifiable SIC two-digit industries within each industry division.

Also during the matrix-balancing procedure the "statewide" categories were treated as additional counties within each state; then after the matrices were balanced, the rest-of-the state figures by industry were allocated proportionately to the counties within each state.

Estimates for the Missing Data

As indicated above, state and county data are available from the CBP files only when the disclosure rules are not violated and when there are at least 10 firms or 100 employees in an industry. When employment is missing because of the disclosure rules, however, the number of reporting units by employment class size is given. The first approximation to the undisclosed employment data is obtained by multiplying the number of reporting units in each class by an assumed average number of employees and summing over all classes. The employment-size classes and the assumed averages are:

	Employment-size Class							
	1 to 3	4 to 7	8 to 19	20 to 49	50 to 99	100 to 249	250 to 499	500 or more
Assumed Average No. of Employees	2	6	14	30	75	175	375	1,000

The figure of 1,000 employees for the "500 or more" employment-size class was selected because it appeared to be representative based on a national breakdown of the number of firms in larger size classes.

The first approximations of the undisclosed data plus the actual data in each cell of the matrix to be balanced were subtracted from both the row and the column totals of the matrix. If the difference was positive for any row or column, it was assumed that some of the zero cells in those rows or columns should have actually contained data. Estimates of these missing data were made using the following formula:

$$M_{ij} = \frac{CC_j \cdot RC_i}{SR_i}$$

where

$$SR_i = \sum_{k=1}^{m} CC_k \qquad (\text{if } k \in J_i)$$

M_{ij} is the estimate of missing data for region i, industry j; CC_j is the difference between the national (or state) control total for industry j and the sum of the data in the jth column of the matrix that includes actual data and estimates of undisclosed data; RC_i is the difference between the ith state (or county) overall control total and the sum of the data in the ith row of the matrix that includes actual data and estimates of the undisclosed data; and SR_i is the sum of the CC's for those industries that have missing data in state (or county) i. Thus J_i is a set of industries for which no data were reported in state (or county) i.

At this stage we have the first approximations to the missing data; the next step is to balance these to control totals. The actual data are subtracted out of the data matrix, including the row and column control totals; then the matrix, which includes only estimates of missing and undisclosed data, is balanced. Next the actual data are re-entered into the matrix and the matrix is balanced again. This last balance is necessary because even when actual data are given for all cells in a particular row or column, there is no guarantee that the sum of the row or column is equal to its control total.

Conversion to Input-Output Sectors

As the final step in the adjustment of the CBP data, the SIC industry data were aggregated into the input-output industry sectors. There are separate input-output sectors for new construction and maintenance construction, but the employment data represent both sectors. Construction employment is divided between the two sectors by first applying the national output/employment ratios of the two sectors to the county outputs which are available separately for new and maintenance construction; then these estimates are adjusted proportionately to sum to the county construction employment.

The final step in obtaining county employment estimates is to assign the non-CBP data (see Table A-1) to employment sectors. Agricultural employment is assigned to input-output sectors 1 and 2, livestock and crops. It is divided between the two sectors by first applying the national output/employment ratios for livestock and crops to the county livestock and crop outputs, and then adjusting these estimates of livestock and crops employments proportionately so that they sum to the county employment for agriculture. Railroad employment is added to input-output sector No. 75—transportation. Other transportation employment for this sector is reported in CBP.

In addition to the 99 input-output industry sectors used in this study, there are four extra employment sectors. These are the households, state and local government, federal civilian government, and military sectors.

The nonagriculture self-employed are allocated to the input-output sectors by first applying national self-employed/employee ratios by industry to the county employment figures. Next the county sums are derived and adjusted proportionately to sum to the appropriate state totals. Then the county self-employed by industry are adjusted proportionately to sum to the county totals.

The employment by industry sectors described above when summed over industries for each county represents the number of jobs at the place of work. In order to compare employment with unemployment, it is necessary to make two adjustments—one for multiple holders and the other for commuting. The procedures for making these adjustments are explained in Tables A-2 and A-3.

Payrolls

This section describes how 1965 and 1966 county payrolls are estimated for those input-output industry sectors reported in County Business Patterns (CBP). These payroll estimates are used in obtaining output. The procedure begins with the fully balanced employment series.

Since the employment estimates are different from those published in CBP because of our adjustment and balancing procedures, it is also necessary to revise the published payroll numbers. The procedure for estimating payrolls is to assign a payroll/employment ratio to each SIC industry for each state and county, multiply by the appropriate state and county balanced employment, and then balance these first payroll estimates to state and national controls.

The payroll/employment ratios are obtained from the unbalanced CBP employment and payrolls. If an estimate of missing employment has been made on the state level, then the national payroll/employment ratio is used; and in cases of missing county data, state ratios are used. The payroll balancing follows the same procedure described for employment. State data are balanced to the national controls within each SIC industry group, and county data are balanced to the state controls within each SIC industry group. Two levels of balancing were performed within each geographic grouping. The first level balanced just those state (county) payrolls that were estimated with national (state) payroll/employment ratios when payroll data were missing. The next level balanced all the payroll estimates—those for which data were given in CBP and the approximation to the missing data.

It was also necessary to hand correct some of the payroll figures as given on the CBP tapes. An example of where both the number on the tape and the published number were wrong was the 1966 U.S. figure for SIC industry 174. The number was 1,084,292; but by checking the addition it was determined that this number should have been 284,292.

Output

In order to estimate 1965 and 1966 county output for the 99 input-output (IO) sectors, it is necessary to have the employment and payroll estimates described in previous sections. The output estimating procedures are described by broad industry classifications since the procedures themselves vary by industry. All the county output estimates by industry sector sum to the 1956 and 1966 national output estimates developed by Almon's Interindustry Forecasting Project.[a] The 1965 output is expressed in 1966 dollars.

Agriculture (IO 1-2)

Agriculture is divided into two sectors: livestock and crops. State figures were estimated by distributing the national controls to states using cash receipts for farm marketings as published by the U.S. Department of Agriculture, Economic Research Service, *The Farm Income Situation*. This source did not include data for Alaska and Hawaii; therefore their cash receipts for 1965 and 1966 were estimated by allowing their 1964 cash receipts, obtained from the 1964 Census of Agriculture, to grow at the national rates.

The state figures were then distributed to counties using the 1964 county values of livestock and livestock products and crops sold obtained from the 1964 Census of Agriculture.

Forestry and Fisheries (IO 3)

There is only one national control total for both forestry and fisheries, but regional data are available separately; therefore the national control was divided into forestry and fisheries in proportion to the national payrolls data.

---

[a]For a description of earlier years, see Clopper Almon, Jr., *The American Economy to 1975*, Harper and Row, New York, 1966.

State data on the value of fish landed and the number of fishermen are available from the U.S. Department of the Interior, U.S. Fish and Wildlife Service, Bureau of Commercial Fisheries, *Fishing Statistics of the United States*, 1965 and 1966. The state output/employment ratios computed from the fishing statistics were assigned to the counties within each state, and the first approximation to county fisheries output was made by applying the county employment to the ratios. In deriving the employment estimates by input-output sector from the *County Business Patterns*, described previously, fishery and forestry employments were saved separately and combined after output estimates were made. The final estimates of county fishery output were made by adjusting the first approximation proportionately to sum to the national controls.

County forestry output was estimated by distributing the national output to counties using the county payroll data. The forestry output was then added to the fisheries output to obtain the output for input-output sector 3.

Mining (IO 5-10)

The first step in obtaining 1965 and 1966 county output in the mining sector was to multiply the county 1963 output/payroll ratio obtained from the *1963 Census of Mineral Industries*, Vol. II, by the 1965 and 1966 payrolls obtained from *County Business Patterns*. This was done at the SIC industry detail and then aggregated to the input-output sectors. These figures were then adjusted proportionately to sum to the national controls for each sector in each year.

Construction (IO 11-12)

In input-output analysis, new construction is classified as a final demand sector. There is one final demand sector for each type of construction, and entries in the matrix show sales from the input-output industries to the various types of construction. Therefore the "sales" from the new construction industry to final demand would be value added by the new construction industry.

By definition of construction activities value is added at the site of the demand, except in cases where the contractor preassembles some of the material components elsewhere. Thus the output (supply) of the construction industry is found simply by setting it equal to demand. The procedure for estimating demand is described in Appendix B.

Similarly, maintenance construction output (supply) is determined by setting it equal to demand.

Manufacturing (IO 13-74)

Output-payroll ratios for states were obtained from the *Annual Survey of Manufactures, 1965 and 1966,* and multiplied by county payroll figures to get a first approximation to county output by industry sector. These figures were then adjusted proportionately to sum to the national controls. The data from the annual surveys are not always complete; that is, data may be missing in states with small amounts of output for particular industries. In these cases the output/payroll ratios were obtained from data reported for the nine census regions, or, if necessary, for the nation.

The output/payroll ratios were applied to the county payrolls at the maximum SIC industry detail available and then aggregated to the input-output industry sectors. The *County Business Patterns* payroll data are available at the four-digit level, and output was derived before the payroll data were aggregated.

Transportation (IO 75)

Because of the lack of regional data the national output (markup margins) in the transportation industry was distributed to counties using county payroll data in the transportation industry.

Communications (IO 76-77)

Input-ouput industry 76 is the telephone and telegraph services while 77 is radio and television boradcasting. Regional output data were not available for radio and TV therefore the national output was distributed to counties using the county payrolls data from *County Business Patterns.*

We did obtain some state data on telephone activity from the Interstate Commerce Commission, *Statistics of Communications Common Carriers, 1965 and 1966.* At the state level this source includes the number of local calls and the number of toll calls, and at the national level the dollar revenues received from local and toll calls. The first step was to obtain an approximation to state output by distributing the national revenues from local and toll calls to states, using the state number local and toll calls, respectively, and then summing the two sources of revenues. Next, state output/employment ratios were computed using the state employment data from *County Business Patterns,* and the county output figures were approximated by multiplying the county employment by the appropriate state output/employment ratios. These approximations were then adjusted proportionately to sum to the national control totals.

Utilities (IO 78-80)

There are three input-output sectors for utilities. We obtained some state output data for the electric and gas utilities (79 and 80) but none for the water utilities (78). The county output for water utilities was estimated by distributing the national output using the county payrolls in water utilities.

Estimates of 1965 and 1966 state electric utility output were made from 1964 data. Operating revenues were available from the Federal Power Commission, *Statistics of Electric Utilities in the United States, 1964.* [b] The revenues are reported by states for privately owned and publicly owned utilities, but revenues from federal projects were listed by project only. In cases where a federal project included more than one state as determined by maps, the revenues were divided equally among the affected states. A ratio of 1964 state output to number of kilowatt-hours was computed and applied to the number of kilowatt-hours for 1965 and 1966 available by states from the *Statistical Abstract of the United States.* These computed state outputs were then adjusted proportionately to sum to the total U.S. output. The next step was to compute state output/employment ratios and apply these to the appropriate county employment figures. The estimated county output figures were then adjusted proportionately to sum to the national control totals.

State revenue figures for 1965 and 1966 for gas utilities were directly available from *Statistical Abstract of the United States.* Output/employment ratios were computed and applied to the county employment figures. These estimated county output figures were then adjusted proportionately to sum to the national control totals.

Trade (IO 81, 89-99)

Although output of the trade sectors in input-output analysis is a measure of the markup margins, sales are used to distribute the national margins to counties. The first step for the wholesale trade estimates was to obtain county sales (output)/employment ratios from the *1963 Census of Business* and apply them to the county employment figures for 1965 and 1966 obtained from *County Business Patterns.* These estimated county output figures were then adjusted proportionately to sum to the national control totals for 1965 and 1966. The national controls as derived from Almon's Interindustry Forecasting Project contained one total for all the trade sectors. This number was divided among wholesale trade and the 11 retail trade sectors in proportion to the payrolls in each sector. The national output for each of the 11 retail sectors was distributed to counties using county estimates of their sales. The sales estimates are described in Appendix B.

---

[b]Since these estimates were undertaken, statistics for 1965 and 1966 have become available.

Services (IO 4, 82-88)

County sales data are available for selected services from the *1963 Census of Business*. Output/employment ratios for 1963 were derived at the maximum SIC detail available and were applied to 1965 and 1966 employment from *County Business Patterns*. Next, the county outputs were aggregated into the input-output sectors. Three of the IO industries were judged to be sufficiently covered by the *Census of Business* data, namely, hotels 84, car repairs 86, and amusements 87. Then output estimates for these three industries were adjusted proportionately to sum to the national controls for 1965 and 1966. The county output for the other service sectors was estimated by distributing the national totals to counties using payroll data. The national control for Business Services 85 was defined to include output of the dummy industries: business travel, entertainment and gifts, and office supplies.

Imports

The derivation of a county distribution of imports begins with the national control totals at the four-digit SIC level, obtained from the U.S. Bureau of Census, *U.S. Commodity Exports and Imports as Related to Output*, 1965 and 1966. Data contained in *Report FT 350, U.S. General Imports by Commodity, Country and Method of Transportation*, published by the U.S. Bureau of Census, provide the means to allocate each control total among four subtotals: (1) by vessel, (2) overland from Canada, (3) overland from Mexico, and (4) by air. An example of the data from this publication for plywood and veneers is shown below; this particular commodity category is Schedule A code 631.2, which is equivalent to SIC 2432.

Value (thousands of dollars)

Country of Origin	All Methods of Transportation	Vessel	Air
Total	$150,339	$142,661	$1,810
Canada	7,061	49	1
Mexico	278	–	–

For each product group, the proportions imported by air and vessel are readily obtained. The proportion imported by land From Canada is found by subtracting from total Canadian imports the amounts imported by vessel and air. The process is repeated for Mexico.

The vessel control total for each SIC is allocated to counties using data from Department of the Army, Corps of Engineers, *Waterborne Commerce of the*

United States. These are annual port data, in tons, of waterborne imports of commodities classified by a coding system specific to this data. The initial step in generating a county distribution of the value of imports by vessel is to allocate the port quantity data to counties. For each port contained entirely within a county, the quantities of imports are assigned to that county. For ports covering two or more counties, the quantity data is allocated to the counties involved on the basis of each county's share of employment in waterborne transportation activities (SIC 44) as reported in *County Business Patterns*.

To each element of the vector of four-digit SIC codes representing the vessel control totals is assigned one or more Waterborne Commerce code(s). The correspondence between the two coding systems is established on the basis of given product category descriptions. Generally, the Waterborne Commerce categories are less detailed than the SIC product groups. Each four-digit vessel control total is then distributed to counties in proportion to each county's share of the quantity of imports associated with the corresponding Waterborne Commerce product group(s).

Canadian and Mexican land import control totals are allocated separately to the northern and southern border counties in the following manner. Bureau of Census data on imports by Customs Districts, published in *Highlights of U.S. Export and Import Trade*, Report FT990, December, 1967, is used to allocate the Canadian land control totals to the three Districts on the U.S.-Canadian border. The Mexican land control totals are divided evenly between the two Districts on the Mexican border, rather than allocating the control totals to these districts on the basis of their actual shares; the shares include water transport and would give too much weight to the district containing Californian ports. This problem is not serious with respect to the Canadian border. The Bureau of Customs provided a listing of all border locations for the transfer of commodities from Canada and Mexico to the United States. The counties in which these locations exist were identified and assigned to their respective customs districts. The customs district control totals were then allocated to the border counties on the basis of each country's share, within its respective customs district, of employment in land transportation activities (SIC 42), as reported in *County Business Patterns*.

The control totals for air imports are allocated to counties having international airports in proportion to each county's share to total imports of manufactured goods by air. The U.S. Bureau of Census also supplies these data in *Highlights*. In the case of New York, where the city contains several counties (boroughs), air imports are further allocated to counties on the basis of their shares of employment in air transport activities—employment category—4500 of *County Business Patterns*.

The resulting regional distribution of imports by four-digit SIC involves 209 counties. Each SIC import total, after the county allocation, is subdivided among three consumption categories: (1) competitive imports, (2) noncompetitive, (3) and noncompetitive personal consumption imports. These categories correspond to those used in the national input-output tables published by the Office of Business Economics. A large majority of the SIC controls fall in one of the three categories, although some imports controls are allocated among all three. At the county level, the import values allocated to consumption categories (2) and (3) are aggregated across SICs and stored in two "artificial" commodity categories. Finally, each county's competitive imports are aggregated to the input-output sectors.

Appendix B:
Procedures for Estimating
County Demand

Consumer Expenditures

This section describes how estimates of county consumer expenditure were made for the years 1965 and 1966. The first part of the report describes how total 1963 county sales for 11 major types of retail outlets are estimated. The next part reports on obtaining the 1963 sales by Merchandise Line Code (MLC) and their conversion to input-output sectors. The third part relates how the 1963 sales are updated to 1965 and 1966. The last part ties some loose ends together.

Total County Sales by 11 Major Types of
Retail Outlets

Total county sales by 11 types of retail outlets are reported in Vol. 2, Retail Trade Area Statistics, of the 1963 *Census of Business*. The SIC number for the 11 outlets are shown in Table B-1.

As with other Census county data, there are data omissions caused by disclosure rules; therefore, a procedure was developed to estimate the missing data. The first step of the procedure makes a preliminary estimate of the undisclosed data of outlet *i* by assigning it a value obtained by multiplying the

Table B-1
Standard Industrial Codes for Eleven Major Types of Retail Outlets

	SIC
1. Lumber, Building Materials, Hardware, Farm Equipment Dealers	52
2. General Merchandise Stores	53 exc. 532
3. Food Stores	54
4. Automotive Dealers	55 exc. 554
5. Gasoline Service Stations	554
6. Apparel, Accessory Stores	56
7. Furniture, Home Furnishings, Equipment Stores	57
8. Eating, Drinking Places	58
9. Drug and Proprietary Stores	591
10. Other Retail Stores	59 exc. 591
11. Nonstore Retailers	532

total sales of the county by the ratio of the state sales of the outlet i to the total sales in the state.

If the sales data for these counties were aggregated over the 11 outlets after these estimates have been made, the figure would probably differ from the reported county total. A similar discrepancy probably would occur if the county sales for each of the 11 outlets were added and compared with the state totals for that outlet. Therefore, the second step was to adjust these preliminary estimates so that their sums would add to the published totals. This involved setting up a matrix of the preliminary estimates of the omitted data for each state with one column for each of the 11 outlets and one row for each county in the state. The control totals for each column are the state sales by type of outlet minus the actual county data, and the control totals for each row are the total county sales minus the actual county data. The matrix was then balanced so that the sum of each row was equal to its control total and the sum of each column was equal to its control total.

County Sales by Merchandise Line Code

The *1963 Census of Business* also has sales data classified by Merchandise Line Code (MLC), which is a classification of sales by type of goods sold. This information is available by each of 11 major types of outlets and by suboutlets within each major outlet for Standard Metropolitan Statistical Areas (SMSAs) and for rest-of-the-state areas. As an example, the first two pages of data available for the Baltimore SMSA are reproduced from the *Census of Business* as Table B-2. We refer to aggregates of MLC as Broad Merchandise Line Codes (BMLC—these are the three-digit codes that have zero as their last digit). Each major type of outlet has suboutlets; for example, SIC 52, one of the major outlets, has seven suboutlets—SICs 521 in two parts, 522, 523, 524, 5251, and 5252. A further breakdown of the BMLC into MLCs is available for some suboutlets. For example, BMLC 340 in suboutlet 521 has 14 detailed MCLs, 341 to 355. Altogether, there are 186 MLCs.

Our objective is to adjust the data so that we have a detailed list of the MLCs for each of the major outlets for each SMSA and rest-of-the-state area. The first step in the adjustment procedure makes proportional adjustments to the detailed MLCs for each BMLC within each suboutlet, forcing the MLCs to sum to the total of BMLCs as reported for each suboutlet. Where the figures were not given because of the disclosure rules or because of their small size, they are assumed to be zero. Next, the total of each detailed MLC was derived by summing the MLCs from each suboutlet. Then, each of the MLCs was summed into its respective BMLC, and percentage distributions expressing each MLC as a percent of its BMLC were derived. Finally, these percentage distributions were applied to the BMLC totals given for each of the major outlets.

Data for the detailed MLCs were given only if the sales were large. For example, the breakdown of BMLC 340, lumber and building materials, is given only for four of the seven suboutlets within SIC 52.

Table B-2

Sample Pages of Data Available on Merchandise Line Codes from 1963 Census of Business; Maryland—Standard Metropolitan Statistical Areas: 1963, Baltimore SMSA (Includes only Establishments with payroll.)

Retail Trade—Merchandise Line Sales   South Atlantic—Md. 7F-281

Merchandise Line Code	Kind of Business and Merchandise Line	Establishments (Number)	Sales ($1,000)	Percent of Sales Accounted for by the Specified Merchandise Line
	Retail trade, total	10,133	2,189,485	(X)
	Reptg sales by broad mdse lines	7,555	1,929,167	100.0
020	Groceries-Other foods	2,167	415,812	21.6
040	Meals-snacks	2,246	119,797	6.2
060	Alcoholic drinks	1,340	57,756	3.0
080	Packaged alcoholic beverages	1,287	60,344	3.1
100	Cigars-cigarettes-tobacco	1,711	40,523	2.1
120	Cosmetics-drugs-health needs-cleaners	1,213	79,136	4.1
140	Men's-boys' clothing, exc. footwear	566	68,323	3.5
160	Women's-Girls' Clothing, exc. footwear	740	146,530	7.6
180	All footwear	474	37,857	2.0
200	Curtains-draperies-dry goods	408	39,248	2.0
220	Major appl.-radio-TV- musical Instr.	539	56,293	2.9
240	Furniture-sleep equip. floor coverings	362	63,565	3.3
260	Kitchenware-home furnishings	531	25,781	1.3
280	Jewelry-optical goods	450	17,241	0.9
300	Sporting-recreation equipment	300	16,376	0.8
320	Hardware	422	22,292	1.2
340	Lumber-building materials	344	46,458	2.4
380	Automobiles-trucks	246	289,501	15.0
400	Auto fuels-lubricants	1,029	93,588	4.9
420	Tires-batteries-accessories	1,012	52,757	2.7
440	Farm equipment, machinery	33	4,913	0.3
460	Hay-grain-feed-farm supplies	62	7,615	0.4
480	Household fuels-ice	144	28,000	1.5
500	All other merchandise	1,556	78,721	4.1
520	Nonmerchandise receipts	2,249	60,584	3.1
	Lumber, bldg. matls., hardware, farm equip. dealers (SIC 52)			
	Total	328	63,638	(X)

Table B-2 (cont.)

Merchandise Line Code	Kind of Business and Merchandise Line	Estab-lishments (Number)	Sales ($1,000)	Percent of Sales Accounted for by the Specified Merchandise Line
	Reptg sales by broad mdse lines	252	50,643	100.0
020	Groceries-other foods	1	(D)	(D)
100	Cigars-cigarettes-tobacco	1	(D)	(D)
120	Cosmetics-drugs-health needs-cleaners	3	(Z)	(Z)
140	Men's-boys' clothing, exc. footwear	1	(D)	(D)
200	Curtains-draperies-dry goods	7	(Z)	(Z)
220	Major appl.-radio-TV-musical instr.	4	102	0.2
240	Furniture-sleep equip. floor coverings	12	(D)	(D)
260	Kitchenware-home furnishings	45	521	1.0
280	Jewelry-optical goods	3	(Z)	(Z)
300	Sporting-recreation equipment	29	205	0.4
320	Hardware	173	9,896	19.5
340	Lumber-building materials	219	33,610	66.4
380	Automobiles-trucks	3	(D)	(D)
400	Auto fuels-lubricants	4	(D)	(D)
420	Tires-batteries-accessories	6	214	0.4
440	Farm equipment, machinery	17	4,096	8.1
460	Hay-grain-feed-farm supplies	12	(D)	(D)
480	Household fuels-ice	10	484	1.0
500	All other merchandise	8	125	0.2
520	Nonmerchandise receipts	81	666	1.3
	Lumber yards (SIC 521 Part)			
	Total	51	26,289	(X)
	Reptg sales by broad mdse lines	39	20,634	100.0
240	Furniture-sleep equip.-floor coverings	3	(D)	(D)
240	Reptg addl detail for line 240	3	(D)	100.0
240	Furniture-sleep equip.-floor coverings	3	(D)	(D)
241	Floor coverings	3	(D)	(D)
320	Hardware	21	675	3.3
340	Lumber-building materials	39	19,602	95.0
340	Reptg addl detail for line 340	38	20,332	100.0
340	Lumber-building materials	38	19,375	95.3
341	Lumber	37	9,893	48.7

Table B-2 (cont.)

Merchandise Line Code	Kind of Business and Merchandise Line	Estab-lishments (Number)	Sales ($1,000)	Percent of Sales Accounted for by the Specified Merchandise Line
342	Plywood	35	2,282	11.2
343	Windows, doors, and frames-metal	21	449	2.2
344	Kitchen cabinets	8	88	0.4
345	All other millwork	32	2,620	12.9
346	Wallboard	33	1,274	6.3
347	Asphalt and asbestos products	32	723	3.6
348	Paint-glass-wallpaper	27	547	2.7
349	Heating and plumbing equipment	5	43	0.2
351	Metal roofing and siding	10	84	0.4
352	Masonry supplies	28	625	3.1
353	Insulation	27	340	1.7
354	Prefabricated buildings and parts	4	80	0.4
355	All other building materials	17	394	1.9
460	Hay-grain-feed-farm supplies	1	(D)	(D)
480	Household fuels-ice	3	43	0.2
500	All other merchandise	1	(D)	(D)
520	Nonmerchandise receipts	22	293	1.4
	Building Materials Dealers (SIC 521 Part)			
	Total	46	11,946	(X)
	Reptg Sales by Broad Mdse Lines	31	9,624	100.0
020	Groceries-other foods	1	(D)	(D)
100	Cigars-cigarettes-tobacco	1	(D)	(D)
120	Cosmetics-drugs-health needs-cleaners	1	(D)	(D)
240	Furniture-sleep equip. -floor coverings	1	(D)	(D)
240	Reptg addl detail for line 240	1	(D)	100.0
240	Furniture-sleep equip.-floor coverings	1	(D)	(D)
241	Floor coverings	1	(D)	(D)
260	Kitchenware-home furnishings	2	(D)	(D)
320	Hardware	6	468	4.9
340	Lumber-building materials	31	8,608	89.4
340	Reptg addl detail for line 340	19	7,978	100.0
340	Lumber-building materials	19	7,247	90.8
341	Lumber	5	302	3.8

Table B-2 (cont.)

Merchandise Line Code	Kind of Business and Merchandise Line	Estab-lishments (Number)	Sales ($1,000)	Percent of Sales Accounted for by the Specified Merchandise Line
342	Plywood	4	86	1.1
343	Windows, doors, and frames-metal	8	758	9.5
344	Kitchen cabinets	2	(D)	(D)
345	All other millwork	2	(D)	(D)
346	Wallboard	8	1,048	13.1
347	Asphalt and asbestos products	7	190	2.4
348	Paint-glass-wallpaper	6	337	4.2
349	Heating and plumbing equipment	1	(D)	(D)
351	Metal roofing and siding	1	(D)	(D)
352	Masonry supplies	7	1,006	12.6
353	Insulation	5	69	0.9
354	Prefabricated buildings and parts	4	1,745	21.9
355	All other building materials	10	1,629	20.4
460	Hay-grain-feed-farm supplies	3	(D)	(D)
480	Household fuels-ice	3	(D)	(D)
500	All other merchandise	2	(D)	(D)
520	Nonmerchandise receipts	9	71	0.7
	Heating, Plumbing Equip. Dealers (SIC 522)			
	Total	5	(D)	(X)
	Paint, Glass, Wallpaper Stores (SIC 523)			
	Total	38	2,105	(X)
	Reptg Sales by Broad Mdse Lines	32	1,840	100.0
260	Kitchenware-home furnishings	1	(D)	(D)
300	Sporting-recreation equipment	1	(D)	(D)
320	Hardware	7	(D)	(D)
340	Lumber-building materials	32	1,728	93.9
340	Reptg addl detail for line 340	29	1,698	100.0
340	Lumber-building materials	29	1,627	95.8
356	Other lumber-building materials	14	(D)	(D)
357	Paint-varnish, etc.	27	1,196	70.4
358	Paint sundries	20	103	6.1
359	Wallpaper-other wall coverings	19	210	12.4
361	Glass	4	(D)	(D)
520	Nonmerchandise receipts	12	18	1.0
	Electrical supply stores (SIC 524)			
	Total	2	(D)	(X)
	Hardware Stores (SIC 5251)			
	Total	164	16,566	(X)

Table B-2 (cont.)

Merchandise Line Code	Kind of Business and Merchandise Line	Estab-lishments (Number)	Sales ($1,000)	Percent of Sales Accounted for by the Specified Merchandise Line
	Reptg sales by broad mdse lines	132	13,580	100.0
120	Cosmetics-drugs-health needs-cleaners	2	(D)	(D)
140	Men's-boys. clothing, exc. footwear	1	(D)	(D)
200	Curtains-draperies-dry goods	7	10	0.1
220	Major appl.-radio-TV Musical instr.	3	(D)	(D)
240	Furniture-sleep equip. -floor coverings	8	92	0.7
260	Kitchenware-home furnishings	42	515	3.8
280	Jewelry-optical goods	3	(Z)	(Z)
300	Sporting-recreation equipment	28	(D)	(D)
320	Hardware	132	8,573	63.1
320	Reptg addl detail for line 320	117	11,086	100.0
320	Hardware	117	6,961	62.8
322	Gardening equipment—supplies	92	801	7.2
323	Plumbing-electrical supplies	99	1,191	10.7
324	Other hardware-tools	115	4,950	44.7
340	Lumber-building materials	114	3,357	24.7
340	Reptg addl detail for line 340	103	9,809	100.0
340	Lumber-building materials	103	2,932	29.9
348	Paint-glass-wallpaper	102	2,283	23.3
356	Other lumber-building materials	37	646	6.6
420	Tire-batteries-accessories	1	(D)	(D)
440	Farm equipment, machinery	1	(D)	(D)
460	Hay-grain-feed-farm supplies	6	71	0.5
480	Household fuels-ice	4	(D)	(D)
500	All other merchandise	4	(D)	(D)
520	Nonmerchandise receipts	32	172	1.3
	Farm equip. dealers (SIC 5252)			
	Total	22	6,020	(X)
	Reptg sales by broad mdse lines	16	(D)	100.0
	General Merchandise Group Stores (SIC 53 Part**)			
	Total	336	367,419	(X)

Table B-2 (cont.)

Merchandise Line Code	Kind of Business and Merchandise Line	Estab- lishments (Number)	Sales ($1,000)	Percent of Sales Accounted for by the Specified Merchandise Line
	Reptg sales by broad mdse lines	249	354,828	100.0
020	Groceries-other foods	120	14,911	4.2
040	Meals-snacks	76	6,721	1.9
060	Alcoholic drinks	4	(D)	(D)
080	Packaged alcoholic beverages	9	(D)	(D)
100	Cigars-cigarettes-tobacco	31	1,273	0.4
120	Cosmetics-drugs-health needs-cleaners	137	11,195	3.2
140	Men's-boys' clothing, exc. footwear	186	32,605	9.2
160	Women's-girls' clothing, exc. footwear	187	92,756	26.1
180	All footwear	153	12,962	3.7
200	Curtains-draperies-drygoods	185	29,499	8.3
220	Major appl.-radio-TV-musical instr.	119	23,295	6.6
240	Furniture-sleep equip.-floor coverings	112	22,571	6.4
260	Kitchenware-home furnishings	171	17,853	5.0
280	Jewelry-optical goods	134	6,730	1.9
300	Sporting-recreation equipment	102	6,051	1.7
320	Hardware	146	9,424	2.7
340	Lumber-building materials	45	8,253	2.3
400	Auto fuels-lubricants	15	(D)	(D)
420	Tires-batteries-accessories	38	8,776	2.5
440	Farm equipment, machinery	7	(D)	(D)
460	Hay-grain-feed-farm supplies	7	(D)	(D)
480	Household fuels-ice	1	(D)	(D)
500	All other merchandise	162	25,464	7.2
520	Nonmerchandise receipts	144	20,921	5.9
	Department Stores (SIC 531)			
	Total	40	290,575	(X)
	Reptg Sales by Broad Mdse Lines	40	290,575	100.0
020	Groceries-other foods	27	10,994	3.8
040	Meals-snacks	27	4,766	1.6
080	Packaged alcoholic beverages	2	(D)	(D)
100	Cigars-cigarettes-tobacco	12	850	0.3
120	Cosmetics-drugs-health needs-cleaners	31	8,615	3.0

Table B-2 (cont.)

Merchandise Line Code	Kind of Business and Merchandise Line	Estab-lishments (Number)	Sales ($1,000)	Percent of Sales Accounted for by the Specified Merchandise Line
140	Men's-boys' clothing, exc. footwear	40	28,171	9.7
140	Reptg addl detail for line 140	36	286,601	100.0
140	Men's-boys' clothing, exc. footwear	36	27,917	9.7
141	Men's clothing	36	20,416	7.1
142	Boys' clothing	36	7,496	2.6
160	Women's-girls' clothing, exc. footwear	40	82,383	28.4
160	Reptg addl detail for line 160	33	282,500	100.0
160	Women's-girls' clothing, exc. footwear	33	80,127	28.4
161	Children's-infants wear	32	7,385	2.6
162	Handbags-accessories	31	6,354	2.2
163	Millinery	32	2,076	0.7
164	Hosiery	32	3,298	1.2
165	Lingerie	32	11,098	3.9
166	Women's coats-suits-furs-rainwear	32	10,272	3.6
167	Women's dresses	33	17,321	6.1
168	Women's sportswear	33	14,422	5.1
169	Girls'-subteen-teen wear	33	6,603	2.3
171	Other women's-girls' clothing-access.	5	204	0.1
180	All footwear	40	11,278	3.9
200	Curtains-draperies-dry goods	40	21,767	7.5
200	Reptg addl detail for line 200	33	282,500	100.0
200	Curtains-draperies-dry goods	33	20,734	7.3
201	Piece goods-notions	29	6,886	2.4
202	Curtains-draperies	33	13,926	4.9
203	All other domestics	4	193	0.1
220	Major appl.-radio-TV-musical instr.	35	19,966	6.9
220	Reptg addl detail for line 220	30	267,536	100.0
220	Major appl.-radio-TV-musical instr.	30	19,205	7.2
221	Major household appliances	22	11,161	4.2
222	Radios-TV's-Musical instruments	29	(D)	(D)
223	All other appliances	1	(D)	(D)

Table B-2 (cont.)

Merchandise Line Code	Kind of Business and Merchandise Line	Estab-lishments (Number)	Sales ($1,000)	Percent of Sales Accounted for by the Specified Merchandise Line
240	Furniture-sleep equip.-floor coverings	34	20,079	6.9
240	Reptg addl detail for line 240	27	249,190	100.0
240	Furniture-sleep equip.-floor coverings	27	18,277	7.3
241	Floor coverings	26	6,498	2.6
242	Furniture-sleep equipment	27	12,331	4.9
260	Kitchenware-home furnishings	38	14,186	4.9
260	Reptg addl detail for line 260	31	279,938	100.0
260	Kitchenware-home furnishings	31	13,711	4.9
261	China-glassware	31	(D)	(D)
262	Kitchenware-housewares	30	8,963	3.2
263	Other kitchenware-home furnishings	5	(D)	(D)
280	Jewelry-optical goods	39	5,902	2.0
300	Sporting-recreation equipment	29	4,711	1.6

Standard Notes: — Represents zero. (D) Withheld to avoid disclosure. (NA) Not available. (X) Not applicable. (Z) Less than 0.05%.

Another problem encountered was that not as much detailed information was available for some BMLC groups in small SMSAs as was available for large SMSAs. In these cases, estimates of detailed information by BMLCs in small SMSAs were made by assuming that the SMSAs detailed distributions were the same as the detailed distributions for the nation.

Once the MLC data was adjusted so that we had consistent estimates for each area, then the data were reclassified into input-output sectors. This task was facilitated by the fact that the MLC classifications are very similar to the consumer expenditure classifications used by the Office of Business Economics, and OBE has a table that converts their consumer data type to the input-output sectors. Table B-3 shows how the MLCs are converted to input-output industry sectors.

Once the data by IO category was estimated for each SMSA and each rest-of-the-state area; then the percentage distributions of these data were applied to the appropriate county total sales by each of the major outlets. Thus it was assumed that counties within an SMSA and counties within rest-of-the-state areas had the same input-output sector distribution as the SMSA and rest-of-the-state area, respectively.

Updating the Retail Sales to Recent Years

In order to make estimates for 1965 and 1966, estimates for 1964 were made first. The procedure for making estimates of county sales by input-output sector

Table B-3

Conversion of Consumer Expenditures by Merchandise Line Codes to Input-Output Sectors (Percent of Total Merchandise Line Sales)

Input-Output Sector	MLC	%	MLC	%	MLC	%
1. Livestock	20	(2.544)	40	(.614)	60	(.614)
	80	(2.544)				
2. Crops	20	(2.606)	40	(.901)	60	(.901)
	80	(2.606)				
3. Forestry and Fishery Products	20	(.354)	40	(.346)	60	(.346)
	80	(.354)	501	(.700)		
4. Agricultural Services	No sales to consumers					
5. Iron Ore Mining	No sales to consumers					
6. Nonferrous Ore Mining	No sales to consumers					
7. Coal Mining	480	(3.000)				
8. Petroleum Mining	No sales to consumers					
9. Minerals Mining	123	(.150)				
10. Chemical Mining	No sales to consumers					
11. New Construction	No sales to consumers					
12. Maintenance Construction	No sales to consumers					
13. Ordnance	300	(3.200)	501	(4.300)	503	(3.200)
	504	(3.200)	505	(3.200)	506	(3.200)
	516	(3.200)				
14. Meat Packing	20	(16.979)	40	(12.157)	60	(12.157)
	80	(16.979)				
15. Dairy Products	20	(9.412)	40	(6.739)	60	(6.739)
	80	(9.412)	123	(1.115)		
16. Canned and Frozen Foods	20	(6.140)	40	(4.396)	60	(4.396)
	80	(6.140)				
17. Grain Mill Products	20	(7.033)	40	(5.035)	60	(5.035)
	80	(7.033)				
18. Bakery Products	20	(5.846)	40	(4.186)	60	(4.186)
	80	(5.846)				
19. Sugar	20	(1.597)	40	(1.143)	60	(1.143)
	80	(1.597)				
20. Candy	20	(1.838)	40	(1.316)	60	(1.316)
	80	(1.838)				
21. Beverages	20	(9.164)	40	(6.562)	60	(6.562)
	80	(9.164)				
22. Misc. Food Products	20	(7.157)	40	(5.124)	60	(5.124)
	80	(7.157)				
23. Tobacco	100	(61.400)				

Table B-3 (cont.)

Input-Output Sector	MLC	%	MLC	%	MLC	%
24. Fabrics and Yarn	140	(2.590)	160	(.060)	200	(7.913)
25. Rugs, Tire Cord, Misc. Textiles	140	(.100)	200	(.323)	241	(41.721)
	245	(41.721)	246	(41.721)	501	(.400)
26. Apparel	140	(59.778)	160	(57.750)	200	(.269)
27. Household Textiles and Upholstery	123	(.056)	140	(.310)	160	(.040)
	200	(21.318)	300	(1.600)	420	(2.078)
	503	(1.600)	504	(1.600)	505	(1.600)
	506	(1.600)	516	(1.600)		
28. Lumber and Products, excluding Containers	200	(1.763)	262	(.301)	265	(.916)
	341	(62.319)	342	(62.319)	345	(62.319)
	354	(62.319)	362	(62.319)	363	(62.319)
	480	(1.400)				
29. Wooden Containers	No sales to consumers					
30. Household Furniture	221	(.400)	223	(.400)	224	(.400)
	242	(54.300)	243	(54.300)	244	(54.300)
	247	(54.300)	262	(.316)	264	(.400)
	344	(54.300)				
31. Office Furniture	200	(2.354)	242	(.300)	243	(.300)
	244	(.300)	247	(.300)	248	(54.900)
	344	(.300)				
32. Paper and Products, excluding Containers	121	(3.500)	122	(3.500)	140	(.240)
	346	(66.434)	359	(66.434)	501	(.200)
	502	(5.701)	508	(43.666)	512	(13.300)
33. Paper Containers	508	(2.616)				
34. Printing and Publishing	200	(.108)	234	(71.000)	501	(1.300)
	502	(44.334)	508	(8.264)	512	(31.700)
	513	(67.713)				
35. Basic Chemicals	20	(.036)	80	(.036)	123	(1.797)
	420	(2.513)	480	(.200)	501	(.500)
36. Plastics and Synthetics	200	(.215)				
37. Drugs, Cleaning, and Toilet Items	121	(42.800)	122	(42.800)	123	(42.649)
	420	(1.063)				
38. Paint and Allied Products	123	(.248)	357	(48.649)	358	(5.000)
39. Petroleum Refining	400	(47.700)	480	(31.250)		
40. Rubber and Plastic Products	121	(1.400)	122	(1.400)	123	(.056)
	140	(.070)	160	(.010)	180	(5.500)
	200	(.162)	241	(1.054)	245	(1.054)
	246	(1.054)	262	(3.140)	265	(9.571)
	300	(.700)	420	(38.714)	501	(1.000)
	502	(.257)	503	(.700)	504	(.700)
	505	(.700)	506	(.700)	508	(.153)
	512	(.600)	516	(.700)		
41. Leather Tanning	No sales to consumers					
42. Shoes and Other Leather Products	140	(2.250)	160	(2.260)	180	(50.100)
	200	(.415)	225	(.120)	226	(.120)

Table B-3 (cont.)

Input-Output Sector	MLC	%	MLC	%	MLC	%
	232	(.120)	233	(.120)	281	(1.800)
	283	(1.800)	284	(1.800)	285	(1.800)
	300	(1.000)	503	(1.000)	504	(1.000)
	505	(1.000)	506	(1.000)	516	(1.000)
43. Glass and Glass Products	200	(.706)	261	(25.360)	265	(9.222)
	361	(47.292)				
44. Stone and Clay Products	123	(.443)	200	(.706)	261	(26.210)
	265	(9.531)	352	(50.758)	353	(50.758)
45. Iron and Steel	200	(.108)	480	(.200)	502	(.129)
	508	(.076)	512	(.300)		
46. Copper	No sales to consumers					
47. Aluminum	221	(.055)	223	(.055)	224	(.055)
	262	(.119)	264	(.055)	265	(.229)
48. Other Nonferrous Metals	221	(.045)	223	(.045)	224	(.045)
	262	(.098)	264	(.045)	265	(.191)
49. Metal Containers	No sales to consumers					
50. Heating, Plumbing Structural Metal Products	221	(1.500)	223	(1.500)	224	(1.500)
	262	(1.187)	264	(1.500)	324	(31.982)
	343	(47.980)	349	(47.980)	351	(47.980)
51. Stampings, Screw Machine Products	200	(.323)	262	(5.750)		
52. Hardware, Plating, Valves, Wire Products	123	(.810)	200	(2.742)	262	(1.814)
	300	(.700)	323	(53.200)	420	(.580)
	503	(.700)	504	(.700)	505	(.700)
	506	(.700)	516	(.700)		
53. Engines and Turbines	300	(6.300)	503	(6.300)	504	(6.300)
	505	(6.300)	506	(6.300)	516	(6.300)
54. Farm Machinery and Equipment	200	(.166)	322	(50.000)		
55. Construction and Mining Machinery	No sales to consumers					
56. Material Handling Equipment	No sales to consumers					
57. Metal-working Machinery and Equipment	200	(.600)	324	(15.977)		
58. Special Industrial Machinery	200	(.388)				
59. General Industrial Machinery	No sales to consumers					
60. Machine Shops and Misc. Machinery	No sales to consumers					
61. Office and Computing Machines	200	(.182)	502	(4.116)	509	(51.327)
	511	(51.327)				
62. Service Industry Machinery	200	(.043)	221	(4.500)	223	(4.500)
	224	(4.500)	262	(3.561)	264	(4.500)
	420	(.773)				

Table B-3 (cont.)

Input-Output Sector	MLC	%	MLC	%	MLC	%
63. Electric Motors and Apparatus	123	(.089)	200	(.166)	501	(.070)
64. Household Appliances	121	(.060)	122	(.060)	200	(1.159)
	221	(52.000)	223	(52.000)	224	(52.000)
	262	(41.144)	264	(52.000)		
65. Electric Lighting and Wiring Equipment	123	(1.965)	200	(2.645)	420	(.725)
	501	(2.100)				
66. Communication Equipment	225	(46.970)	226	(46.970)	232	(46.970)
67. Electronic Components	225	(5.140)	226	(5.140)	232	(5.140)
	233	(5.140)				
68. Batteries, X-ray and Engine Electrical Equipment	123	(.496)	225	(.627)	226	(.627)
	232	(.627)	233	(.627)	286	(.300)
	420	(7.876)	501	(.310)		
69. Motor Vehicles	121	(.180)	122	(.180)	380	(69.800)
	420	(3.915)				
70. Aircraft and Parts	300	(.800)	503	(.800)	504	(.800)
	505	(.800)	506	(.800)	516	(.800)
71. Ships, Trains, Trailers and Cycles	200	(.097)	300	(16.400)	380	(3.000)
	503	(16.400)	504	(16.400)	505	(16.400)
	506	(16.400)	516	(16.400)		
72. Instruments and Clocks	121	(2.300)	122	(2.300)	200	(1.413)
	281	(8.420)	283	(8.420)	284	(8.420)
	285	(8.420)	286	(9.150)		
73. Optical and Photographic Equipment	200	(.060)	286	(24.390)	300	(9.600)
	501	(6.500)	503	(9.600)	504	(9.600)
	505	(9.600)	506	(9.600)	516	(9.600)
74. Misc. Manufactured Products	123	(2.197)	200	(1.884)	228	(57.390)
	229	(57.390)	231	(57.390)	241	(8.475)
	245	(8.475)	246	(8.475)	281	(42.400)
	282	(51.230)	283	(42.400)	284	(42.400)
	285	(42.400)	300	(13.700)	358	(2.703)
	501	(33.500)	502	(2.315)	503	(13.700)
	504	(13.700)	505	(13.700)	506	(13.700)
	508	(1.376)	512	(5.400)	514	(59.310)
	516	(13.700)				
75. Transportation	20	(4.005)	40	(2.089)	60	(2.089)
	80	(4.005)	100	(1.300)	121	(2.000)
	122	(2.000)	123	(2.000)	140	(1.620)
	160	(1.790)	180	(1.400)	200	(1.569)
	221	(1.900)	223	(1.900)	224	(1.900)
	225	(1.110)	226	(1.110)	228	(1.800)
	229	(1.800)	231	(1.800)	232	(1.110)
	233	(1.110)	234	(4.100)	241	(1.510)
	242	(1.900)	243	(1.900)	244	(1.900)
	245	(1.510)	246	(1.510)	247	(1.900)
	248	(1.900)	261	(2.580)	262	(1.936)

Table B-3 (cont.)

Input-Output Sector	MLC	%	MLC	%	MLC	%
	264	(1.900)	265	(2.255)	281	(1.600)
	282	(1.610)	283	(1.600)	284	(1.600)
	285	(1.600)	286	(1.100)	300	(1.200)
	323	(1.600)	324	(2.041)	341	(6.522)
	342	(6.522)	343	(2.020)	344	(1.900)
	345	(6.522)	346	(4.662)	349	(2.020)
	351	(2.020)	352	(3.789)	353	(3.789)
	354	(6.522)	357	(2.703)	359	(4.662)
	361	(3.659)	380	(1.800)	400	(3.400)
	420	(1.837)	480	(7.900)	501	(1.600)
	502	(3.147)	503	(1.200)	504	(1.200)
	505	(1.200)	506	(1.200)	508	(3.693)
	509	(1.770)	511	(1.770)	512	(3.000)
	513	(3.865)	514	(8.146)	516	(1.200)
76. Communication			Not reported			
77. Radio, TV Broadcasting			No sales to consumers			
78. Electric Utility			Not reported			
79. Gas Utility			Not reported			
80. Water Utility			Not reported			
81. Wholesale and Retail Trade	20	(25.271)	40	(49.370)	60	(49.370)
	80	(25.271)	100	(37.300)	121	(47.800)
	122	(47.800)	123	(43.706)	140	(39.140)
	160	(38.090)	180	(43.000)	200	(43.800)
	221	(38.900)	223	(38.900)	224	(38.900)
	225	(45.720)	226	(45.720)	228	(40.810)
	229	(40.810)	231	(40.810)	232	(45.720)
	233	(45.720)	234	(24.900)	241	(47.240)
	242	(43.100)	243	(43.100)	244	(43.100)
	245	(47.240)	246	(47.240)	247	(43.100)
	248	(43.100)	261	(44.850)	262	(40.005)
	264	(38.900)	265	(44.430)	281	(45.200)
	282	(47.160)	283	(45.200)	284	(45.200)
	285	(45.200)	286	(65.000)	300	(44.200)
	322	(50.000)	323	(45.200)	324	(50.000)
	341	(31.159)	342	(31.159)	343	(50.000)
	344	(43.100)	345	(31.159)	346	(28.904)
	349	(50.000)	351	(50.000)	352	(45.455)
	353	(45.455)	354	(31.159)	357	(48.649)
	358	(50.000)	359	(28.904)	361	(47.561)
	380	(25.100)	400	(48.900)	420	(39.633)
	480	(55.750)	501	(46.800)	502	(39.337)
	503	(44.200)	504	(44.200)	505	(44.200)
	506	(44.200)	508	(39.748)	509	(47.788)
	511	(47.788)	512	(44.100)	513	(28.382)
	514	(38.844)	516	(44.200)	526	(40.000)
	531	(100.000)	533	(100.000)		
82. Finance and Insurance			Not reported			
83. Real Estate and Rental			Not reported			
84. Hotels, Personal, and Repair Services	300	(.400)	503	(.400)	504	(.400)
	505	(.400)	506	(.400)	516	(.400)
	521	(100.000)	522	(100.000)	526	(60.000)
	527	(100.000)	529	(100.000)		

Table B-3 (cont.)

Input-Output Sector	MLC	%	MLC	%	MLC	%
85. Business Services			Not reported			
86. Automobile Repair Services			Not reported			
87. Amusements and Recreation			Not reported			
88. Medical and Educational Institutions			Not reported			
89. Federal Government Enterprises			Not reported			
90. State and Local Government Enterprises			Not reported			

for 1964 was to treat the 1963 data as preliminary estimates and adjust them to 1964 control totals. A matrix of the 1963 sales data was set up as preliminary estimates for 1964 with one column for each input-output sector and one row for each of the 11 outlets in each county. Since there are 3,112 counties and 11 outlets, there were 34,232 rows in this matrix. The control totals for the columns were 1964 national sales to consumers by IO sector. The control totals for the rows were derived by multiplying the county 1964 payrolls as reported in *County Business Patterns* for each of the 11 outlets by a 1963 sales/payroll ratio derived from the appropriate state. The 1963 payroll data by type of outlet was available only at the state level and not the county level. The matrix was then balanced so that the sum of each row was equal to its control total and the sum of each column was equal to its control total. The matrix-balancing procedure makes proportional adjustments to each cell, making them sum to the column controls; then they are forced to add to the row controls. This process is reiterated until the matrix is balanced.

The 1965 and 1966 estimates were made with the same methodology using 1964 and 1965 data as preliminary estimates, respectively.

Other Considerations

Not all the industry sectors sell directly to consumers, and some that do sell services that are not reported as merchandise. Sales to consumers of services that do not go through retail outlets, e.g., medical services, were estimated by assuming that the county ratio of consumption to output for each sector was the same as the national ratio.

Table B-3 shows wholesale and retail trade as one sector (81), but on our study this sector is broken down into 11 retail sectors and a separate wholesale sector. In order to make the county estimates of "sales" (markup margins) of the trade sectors to the consumer expenditure sector, it was assumed that each county's ratios of consumer expenditure margins to total margins (output) was the same as the national ratios.

Two of the 186 types of merchandise lines were farm equipment and hay-grain-feed-farm supplies. These sales were subtracted from total retail sales of the first major retail outlet since they are not sales to consumers in the input-output accounting framework. Farm equipment is classified as a sale of investment goods, and farm supplies are treated as intermediate goods.

Investment Expenditures

This section describes methods that were used to estimate county investment expenditures by input-output sector for the years 1965 and 1966. The construction and equipment investment components were estimated separately. The first step in estimating both components was to estimate investment by purchasing sector; then, the next basic step was to convert these statistics into investment by input-output producing sector using national capital coefficient matrices. The construction purchasing sectors are listed in Table B-4, and the capital investment purchasing sectors are listed in Table B-5.

Construction

Data from the F.W. Dodge Division, McGraw-Hill Information Systems Company, obtained through the Economic Development Administration, were used as the basic construction data. The Dodge county data were furnished by type of structure, and each structure was classified according to ownership—private and four types of public ownership. It was also classified by whether or not it was new, an addition, or an alteration. The types of structures used by the Dodge Corporation are listed in Table B-6. The numbers in this table correspond to the numbers in Tables B-4 and B-5, which show how the Dodge data were aggregated into the input-output purchasing sectors.

Construction by Purchasing Sector. The Maryland Interindustry Forecasting Project uses 28 construction purchasing sectors in the national input-output model. With the Dodge data we were able to estimate figures for 20 of these sectors. There were two sectors for which no Dodge data were reported—11 farm and 12 oil and gas well drilling and exploration. Some Dodge data were available for the other six sectors, but the regional coverage was too incomplete to allow them to be used. Table B-7 shows how county data were estimated for each of the eight sectors for which Dodge data could not be used.

Table B-4
Correspondence between Types of Construction as Reported by F.W. Dodge Division and Construction by Purchasing Sector as used by the Maryland Interindustry Forecasting Project

MIFP Code	Construction Purchasing Sector	Dodge Codes[a]
Private Construction		
1	Residential Housekeeping	70, 71, 75-78
2	Residential Alterations and Additions	70, 71, 75-78
3	Nonhousekeeping Residential	58, 69, 72-74, 79, 104
4	Industrial	9-40
5	Offices	3, 5-7, 103, 10, 110, 122-126, 134-136, 203
6	Stores, Restaurants, and Garages	1, 2, 4, 8, 101, 108
7	Religious	53-55, 102, 116, 253, 303
8	Educational, Private	41-49, 56, 57, 62, 140-143
9	Hospital and Institutional, Private	93-95
10	Misc. Nonresidential Buildings, Private	59-61, 63-65, 67, 68, 105, 118, 256, 257, 262
11	Farm	Not Available
12	Oil and Gas Well Drilling and Exploration	Not Available
13	Railroad	66, 92, 121, 127, 133, 154, 184
14	Telephone	145
15	Electric Light and Power	87, 106, 151, 160, 164, 166, 171, 187, 191, 287
16	Gas and Petroleum Pipelines	90, 91, 120, 163, 190, 197
17	All Other Private Construction	80-82, 84-86, 88, 89, 107, 111, 112, 113, 115, 117, 119, 128, 129, 132, 146, 147, 152, 153, 155, 156, 161, 162, 165, 170, 172-174, 180, 185, 186, 188, 189, 192-196, 204, 210, 211
Public Construction		
18	Highway	80, 81, 115, 128, 150, 180
19	Military	83, 105, 113
20	Conservation and Development	84, 86, 112, 117, 152-154
21	Sewer Systems	107, 111, 192
22	Water Systems	88, 119, 152, 193-195
23	Public Residential	69-79, 104
24	Public Industrial	9-40
25	Public Educational	41-49, 56, 57, 62, 82, 140-143

Table B-4 (cont.)

MIFP Code	Construction Purchasing Sector	Dodge Codes[a]
26	Public Hospital	93-95
27	Other Public Buildings	5-7, 50-52, 100, 109, 210, 211
28	Misc. Public Construction	1-4, 8, 53-55, 58-61, 63-68, 85, 87, 89-92, 101-103, 106, 108, 110, 114, 116, 118, 120-127, 129, 132-136, 145-147, 151, 184-191, 196, 197, 203, 253, 256, 257, 262, 287, 303

[a]See Table B-6.

Table B-5

Correspondence between Types of Construction as Reported by the F.W. Dodge Division and Equipment Purchasing Sector as Used by the Maryland Interindustry Forecasting Project

MIFP Code	Equipment Purchasing Sector	Dodge Codes[a]
1	Farm	Not Available
2	Mining	Not Available
3	Oil and Gas Wells	Not Available
4	Construction	Not Available
5	Ordnance	926, 826, 726, 026
6	Meat	910, 810, 710, 010, 017
7	Tobacco	919, 819, 719, 019
8	Fabrics and Yarn	
9	Rugs, Tire Cord	
10	Apparel	916, 816, 716, 016
11	Household Textiles and Upholstery	
12	Lumber and Lumber Products, excluding Containers	925, 825, 725, 025
13	Wooden Boxes	
14	Household Furniture	928, 828, 728, 028
15	Office Furniture	
16	Paper, excluding Containers	911, 811, 711, 011
17	Paper Containers	
18	Printing and Publishing	913, 813, 713, 013
19	Basic Chemicals	
20	Plastics and Synthetics	

Table B-5 (cont.)

MIFP Code	Equipment Purchasing Sector	Dodge Codes[a]
21	Drugs, Cleaning, and Toilet Items	009, 039, 709, 809, 909
22	Paint and Allied Products	
23	Petroleum Refining	912, 812, 712, 012, 927, 827, 727, 027
24	Rubber and Plastic Products	915, 815, 715, 015, 938, 838, 738, 038
25	Leather Tanning	918, 818, 718, 018
26	Shoes and Other Leather Products	
27	Glass and Glass Products	914, 814, 714, 014
28	Stone and Clay Products	
29	Iron and Steel	920, 820, 720, 020
30	Nonferrous Metals	921, 821, 721, 021
31	Metal Containers	
32	Heating, Plumbing, Structural Metal Products	
33	Stampings, Screw Machine Products	922, 822, 722, 022
34	Hardware, Plating, Valves, Wire Products	
35	Engines and Turbines	
36	Farm Machinery and Equipment	
37	Construction and Met. Handling Equipment	
38	Metal-working Machinery	923, 823, 723, 023
39	Special Industry Machinery	
40	General Industry Machinery	
41	Machine Shops and Misc.	
42	Office and Computing Machines	
43	Service Industry Machinery	933, 833, 733, 033
44	Electric Apparatus and Motors	
45	Household Appliances	
46	Electric Lighting and Wiring	
47	Communications Equipment	924, 824, 724, 024
48	Electronic Components	
49	Batteries, X-ray, and Engine Electric Equipment	
50	Motor Vehicles	929, 829, 729, 029
51	Aircraft and Parts	930, 830, 730, 030
52	Ship, Trains, and Cycles	931, 831, 731, 031, 932, 832, 732, 032, 937, 837, 737, 037

Table B-5 (cont.)

MIFP Code	Equipment Purchasing Sector	Dodge Codes[a]
53	Instruments and Clocks	934, 834, 734, 034
54	Optical and Photographic Equipment	
55	Misc. Manufacturing	935, 835, 735, 035, 940, 840, 740, 040, 036
56	Transportation	089, 129, 196, 165, 091, 092, 184, 154, 127, 133, 134, 135, 136, 186, 121, 122, 123, 124, 125, 203, 303, 003, 103, 066, 067, 068
57	Communication	145, 146
58	Utility	193, 194, 195, 119, 162, 166, 187, 087, 287, 106, 171, 151, 191, 160, 164, 090, 190, 120, 197, 163, 082, 192, 153, 161, 111, 107, 088, 170, 152
59	Trade	001, 101, 002, 004, 008, 126, 110, 116
60	Finance and Insurance	005, 006, 007
61	Service	041-049, 093, 094, 095, 141, 140, 057, 257, 062, 262, 064, 164, 061, 069, 072, 073, 055, 065, 104, 064, 140, 105, 108, 085, 185, 115, 074, 053, 253, 102, 054, 056, 256, 058, 059, 060, 143, 063, 142
62	Dairy	
63	Canned Food	
64	Grain	
65	Bakeries	910, 810, 710, 010, 017
66	Sugar	
67	Confectioneries	
68	Beverages	
69	Misc. Food	

[a]See Table B-6.

Table B-6
F.W. Dodge Division's Construction Codes by Type of Structure

Code	Type of Structure
Nonresidential Buildings	
001	Store buildings
101	Shopping centers
002	Eating and drinking places
005	Office buildings
006	Bank buildings
041	Schools—elementary
042	Schools—junior high
043	Schools—senior high
044	Schools—Combination (elementary and high)
045	Schools—industrial, vocational and trade
046	Schools—junior college
047	Schools—university and college
048	Schools—unclassified classroom buildings
093	Hospitals
094	Health treatment buildings, other than hospitals
100	Government administration buildings
050	Penal and correctional buildings
051	Post office buildings
052	Police and fire stations
109	Misc. government service buildings
053	Houses of worship
253	Auxiliary church buildings
102	Religious training buildings
054	Misc. religious buildings
056	Auditoriums and community buildings (school/college owned)
256	Auditoriums and community bldgs. (other ownership)
058	Club and lodge buildings (excluding fraternity and sorority houses)
059	Theatres, concert halls, and opera houses
060	Studio buildings (radio, TV, movie, music, art, etc.)
143	Museums, art galleries, archives bldgs., etc.
063	Exhibition and fair bldgs. (excluding museums, art galleries, etc.)
142	Libraries
141	Observatories, planetariums, etc.
140	Laboratories—not manufacturer-owned
057	Coliseums (sports)—enclosed (school/college owned)
257	Coliseums (sports)—enclosed (other ownership)

Table B-6 (cont.)

Code	Type of Structure
062	Gymnasiums and field houses (school/college owned)
262	Gymnasiums and field houses (other ownership)
061	Bowling alleys
104	YMCA, YWCA, YMHAs, etc.
064	Misc. amusement, recreational and assembly bldgs.
066	Passenger terminal buildings–railroad
067	Passenger terminal buildings–bus
068	Passenger terminal buildings–air
105	Armories
108	Parking garages
008	Commercial garages (other) and auto service stations
133	Equipment service and equipment storage buildings–railroad
134	Equipment service and equipment storage buildings–bus
135	Equipment service and equipment storage buildings–truck
136	Equipment service and equipment storage buildings–air (excluding hangars)
186	Hangars
121	Freight terminal buildings (including warehouses)–railroad
122	Freight terminal buildings (including warehouses)–truck
123	Freight terminal buildings (including warehouses)–air
124	Freight terminal buildings (including warehouses)–maritime
125	Freight terminal buildings (including warehouses)–combinations
203	Warehouses (refrigerated)–commercial
303	Warehouses (refrigerated)–not manufacturer-owned and NEC
003	Warehouses (not refrigerated)–commercial
103	Warehouses (not refrigerated)–not manufacturer-owned and NEC
166	Power & heating plants, noncommercial (not manufacturer-owned)
126	Grain elevators
083	Military buildings, NEC
188	Nonresidential buildings, NEC (not miliary)

Residential Building

073	Hotels and motels (1, 2, or 3 stories)
072	Hotels and motels (4 s tories or more)
069	Hotels and motels (number of stories unknown)
074	Dormitories
075	Apartment buildings–3 or 4 housing units
070	Apartment buildings–5 units or more (1, 2, or 3 stories)
071	Apartment buildings–5 units or more (4 stories or more)
078	Apartment buildings–5 units or more (number of stories unknown)
076	One-family houses
077	Two-family houses
079	Other shelter

Table B-6 (cont.)

Code	Type of Structure
Western States Only	
004	Store and other mercantile buildings
007	Office and bank buildings
036	Manufacturing plants, warehouses, labs, heating, and power plants
049	Educational and science buildings
095	Hospitals and other health treatment buildings
055	Religious buildings
065	Amusement, recreational, and assembly buildings
118	Misc. nonresidential buildings

Code				Industry Classification
Manufacturing Facilities				*(Plants, Warehouses, Laboratories, Power Plants)*
926	826	726	026	Ordnance and accessories
910	810	710	010	Food and kindred products (excluding frozen food plants)
910	810	710	017	Refrigerated plants and warehouses (including frozen food plants)
919	819	719	019	Tobacco products
916	816	716	016	Textile mill products (including apparel and other finished fabric specialties)
911	811	711	011	Paper and allied products
913	813	713	013	Printing, publishing, and allied products
909	809	709	009	Chemical and allied products (enclosed plants)
909	809	709	039	Chemical and allied products (outdoor plants)
912	812	712	012	Petroleum refineries
927	827	727	027	Petroleum and coal products
915	815	715	015	Rubber products
938	838	738	038	Plastic products (model and fabricated finished products)
918	818	718	018	Leather and leather products
914	814	714	014	Stone, clay, and glass products
920	820	720	020	Primary ferrous metals industries
921	821	721	021	Primary nonferrous metals industries
922	822	722	022	Fabricated metal products, excluding ordnance, machinery, and transportation equipment
925	825	725	025	Lumber and wood products, excluding furniture
928	828	728	028	Furniture and fixtures
923	823	723	023	Machinery, excluding electrical
924	824	724	024	Electrical machinery, equipment, and supplies
929	829	729	029	Motor vehicles and equipment
930	830	730	030	Aircraft and parts
931	831	731	031	Ship and boat building, and repairing
932	832	732	032	Railroad equipment
937	837	737	037	Other transportation equipment, NEC

Table B-6 (cont.)

Code				Industry Classification
934	834	734	034	Precision goods
933	833	733	033	Industrial service plants
935	835	735	035	Miscellaneous manufacturing industries
940	840	740	040	Manufacturing plants: industry classification unknown

Code	Type of Structure

Electric Power and Heating Plants—Not Manufacturer-owned

187	Electric generating plants—hydroelectric
087	Electric generating plants—not hydroelectric (including nuclear)
287	Electric generating plants—outdoor
106	Electric substations
171	Dams and reservoirs—hydroelectric
151	Tunnels—hydroelectric
191	Electric transmission and distribution systems (overhead and underground)
160	Combinations: power plants, lines, etc.
164	Combinations: heating plants, lines, etc. (including steam and air conditioning)

Gas (Natural and Manufactured)

090	Plants
190	Gas transmission pipelines
120	Gas storage tanks
197	Gas distribution lines
163	Combinations: plants, lines, etc.

Sewerage and Waste Disposal

082	Sewage treatment plants
192	Sewage collection and disposal lines
153	Sewage tunnels
161	Combinations: plants, lines, etc.
111	Dry waste disposal (including incinerators)
107	Industrial waste treatment plants

Water Supply

088	Water treatment plants
170	Dams and reservoirs—water supply
152	Tunnels—water supply
193	Water transmission pipelines
194	Water distribution lines
195	Water lines—not classified
119	Water towers, tanks, and standpipes
162	Combinations: plants, lines, etc.

Table B-6 (cont.)

Code	Type of Structure

Irrigation

172	Dams—irrigation
155	Tunnels—irrigation
117	Canals, ditches, conduits, etc.—irrigation

River, Harbor, and Waterfront Development

112	Docks, piers, and wharves
084	Dredging and drainage
086	Levees, seawalls, jetties, etc.
173	Dams—flood control

Streets and Highways

080	Roadways (contracts include paving)
180	Roadways (contracts not including paving, or indefinite)
081	Bridges—vehicular and pedestrian (including elevated highways)
150	Tunnels—vehicular and pedestrian
128	Lighting—roadway, street, bridge, and tunnel

Railroad (Excluding Buildings)

092	Railroad bed and tracks
184	Bridges—railroad
154	Tunnels—railroad
127	Railroad operating and safety signal systems

Airport (Excluding Buildings)

089	Airport runways, taxiways, and aircraft parking areas
129	Lighting—airport
196	Airport service systems (including fuel, water, sewerage and drainage)
165	Combinations: runways, lighting, service systems, etc.

Electronic Communications

145	Telephone and telegraph lines, poles, towers, etc.
146	Radio and TV transmission and control towers (including air traffic control)
147	Guidance, detection, and tracking systems (excluding air traffic)

Missile and Space Facilities

| 210 | Launching complexes (above or underground) |
| 211 | Research and testing facilities |

Other Nonbuilding Structures

091	Petroleum transmission pipelines
085	Parks, playgrounds, etc.
185	Stadiums, arenas, etc.—outdoors

Table B-6 (cont.)

Code	Type of Structure
116	Storage tanks, excluding water supply (above, on, or underground)
110	Storage structures (excluding tanks, grain elevators, and whses.)
115	Sidewalks, driveways, and outdoor auto parking areas
132	Lighting-outdoor (excluding roadway, street, etc., and airport)
174	Dams and reservoirs, NEC (including multipurpose structures)
189	Bridges, NEC
156	Tunnels, NEC
113	Military nonbuilding structures, NEC
114	Other nonbuilding structures, NEC (not military)

Source: F.W. Dodge Division, McGraw-Hill Information Systems Company, proprietory data provided by special permission.

Table B-7

Procedures for Estimating County Construction for Eight Types of Construction, 1965 and 1966

Type of Construction	County Allocator[a]
2 Residential Alterations and Additions	Residential Construction
11 Farm	Farm Equipment Purchases
12 Oil and Gas Well Drilling	Output in Petroleum Mining Industry
13 Railroad	Output in Transportation Industry
14 Telephone	Output in Telephone and Telegraph Industry
15 Electric Light Power	Output in Electric Utilities
24 Public Industrial	Misc. Public Construction

[a]The county series listed in this column was used to distribute the national construction of the type listed in the first column to counties.

The county construction estimates by purchasing sectors were adjusted proportionally, forcing them to sum to the national control totals provided by the Maryland Interindustry Forecasting Project.

Construction by Producing Sector. The county construction statistics by purchasing sector were multiplied by a national construction coefficient matrix in order to derive producers' sales by input-output sector to the construction industry. The original form of the construction coefficient matrix, which was published in the May, 1965 issue of the *Survey of Current Business*, had only 21 construction sectors using 1958 national data. The Maryland Interindustry Forecasting Project, with access to unpublished OBE data, expanded the 1958 matrix to the full 28 sectors. The 1958 matrix was then updated to make the coefficients consistent with national annual data for the 28 construction purchasing sectors and the 55 input-output sectors that sell to construction. The adjustment procedure minimizes the summation of the percentage changes in the 1958 coefficients.

Equipment Investment

The calculation of equipment investment was more complicated than construction because of the lack of a single consistent data series for all input-output sectors. Our estimates were obtained using a variety of governmental sources: *1963 Census of Business*, the *Annual Survey of Manufactures*, annual *County Business Patterns* employment and payroll series, the Dodge construction data.

Equipment Investment by Purchasing Sector. Because of the multiple data sources, four different methods were used to obtain estimates of investment by purchasing sector. These were agriculture, construction, manufacturing, and all others.

Agriculture (Equipment Purchasing Sector 1). The equipment purchases made by the agricultural sector were estimated from data in the *1963 Census of Business*, where farm equipment sales were reported as a merchandise line of retail outlets. The procedure for adjusting sales made through retail outlets is explained in the previous section on Consumer Expenditures. We classify the farm equipment sales in the investment sector instead of the consumer expenditures sector. The county figures were then adjusted proportionally to sum to the national control totals in each year.

Construction (Equipment Purchasing Sector 4). Equipment bought by the construction sector in each county was estimated by assuming that each county's ratio of equipment purchases to total construction was the same as the national ratio.

Manufacturing (Equipment Purchasing Sectors 5-55, 62-69). The procedure used to calculate equipment purchases in the manufacturing sectors consisted of two basic steps—one for obtaining state estimates and the other for county estimates.

State equipment purchases by manufacturing sector were estimated by distributing national equipment to states according to the distribution of total investment by sector. State total investment estimates were obtained by SIC group from the *Annual Survey of Manufactures, 1965 and 1966.* In cases where total investment was not reported because of its small size, estimates were made based on regional or national investment/payroll ratios from the *Survey* and state payrolls aggregated from *County Business Patterns*. Once these estimates of total investment were made for the SIC groups; then they were aggregated into our input-output sectors.

The next basic step was to distribute the state equipment estimates to counties. This was done by first grouping construction into the equipment purchasing sector classification and then assuming that each county's ratio of equipment purchases to construction by sector was the same as the appropriate state ratio. The F.W. Dodge construction data were aggregated into the equipment sectors according to the correspondence shown in Table B-5. As can be seen from this table, there are 59 manufacturing equipment sectors, but only 25 separate combinations of the 59 for which the Dodge codes could be matched. The Dodge data were aggregated into the 25 groups, then disaggregated proportionally, based on the county relationship of total investment purchases between the 59- and 25-order sectors. County total investment for the 59 sectors was estimated by applying the state investment/payroll ratios by SIC group estimated from the *Annual Survey of Manufactures* to county payrolls by SIC group estimated from *County Business Patterns*. The SIC groups were then aggregated into the input-output sectors.

Other Equipment Purchasing Sectors (2, 3, 56-61). The method used to obtain investment for other equipment purchasing sectors, including mining transportation, communication, utilities, trade and services, was the least satisfactory estimating procedure. For each purchasing sector, a county's proportion of the national equipment purchases was assumed to be equivalent to the ratio of the county output to the national output. There was an attempt to use investment data from the *1963 Census of Mineral Industries*, but the data were too incomplete and had to be dropped.

Investment by Producing Sector. The equipment investment by purchasing sector was multiplied by a national capital coefficient matrix in order to obtain equipment investment by producing sector. It was assumed that each county has the same capital coefficient matrix as the nation. The original capital coefficient matrix was published by the U.S. Department of Labor, *Flow Matrix 1958*. The Maryland Interindustry Forecasting Project updates this matrix annually using the same procedures that were used to update the construction coefficient matrix.

Government Expenditures

The demand for goods by the federal government is estimated by four broad functional groups—defense, National Air and Space Administration (NASA), federal enterprises, and general government. The national data from the

Maryland Interindustry Forecasting Project contain the sales of goods, other than construction, from the producing sectors to each of the four government groups. County data on federal outlays by program were obtained for the U.S. Office of Management and Budget for fiscal year 1968. The national totals for both 1965 and 1966 were allocated to counties using data from the FY 1968 file since the government data were not available for earlier years.

The national defense expenditures were distributed to counties using county data on prime defense contracts. Since the input requirements for these contracts vary by the type of contract, such as for aircraft, ordnance, and military uniforms, it was decided not to use the national coefficients to find which producing sectors supplied inputs in each county. Instead a large industry-by-county matrix was set with the county defense figures as column control totals and the national figures by industry producing sector as row totals. The initial in the cells in the matrix were made by assuming that the producing industry distribution of each county's defense expenditures was the same as the distribution of total output of the producing industries. At this point the matrix was balanced so that each row and column summed to its control total. A check was made to see that the sales to defense of each industry in each county did not exceed the county's output of that industry. This method of obtaining county demand for defense goods assumes that the location of the demand is situated in the county of the prime contractor.

NASA expenditures were allocated to counties using county outlays by NASA. Since these outlays include salaries and construction expenditures, it is assumed that each county's relation between purchases of goods, salaries, and construction is the same as the nation's. The county demand by producing sector was derived by applying national coefficients to the county NASA total.

The national figures on federal government enterprises were allocated to counties using county outlays of post offices since the post office function is the principal government enterprise. These outlays include salaries and construction expenditures, but by FY 1968 most of the new post offices were being constructed by the private sector and rented to the government. The county demand by producing sector was derived using national coefficients.

In the national vector showing sales from producing sectors to general government there may be negative entries. These represent "sales" of government to the industry sectors: They are industry functions or services performed by the government such as meat inspection, forest management, and the selling of government-owned inventories. Four sectors that may contain negative entries were handled separately; they are livestock, crops, forestry and fisheries, and lumber products. The allocation of national "sales" of livestock and crops to government was performed using county federal outlays data on programs set up to control production of farm products. The forestry and fisheries and lumber products totals were allocated to counties using county data on the functional category of forest resources. The county estimates in these four categories were added to the county's supply, instead of allowing them to remain as components of demand. Had they been classified as demand, some counties would show a total negative demand for the goods of these industry sectors.

With the above four items removed from general government the national figure was allocated to counties using county data on the sum of other government programs that were not used for allocation of other items. Also excluded from the general government outlays were loans, grants, and items that were identified as construction. The allocating figures still included salaries and some construction. County sales of producing industries to general government were estimated using national coefficients.

The regular state and local government sector in final demand and the state and local enterprises were lumped together into one demand sector. The figures do not include construction or wages and salaries. County data were estimated from the *Census of Governments 1962* published by U.S. Bureau of Census. The 1962 county per capita outlays, excluding capital outlays, were applied to the 1965 and 1966 county populations in order to obtain a first approximation to the 1965 and 1966 state and local outlays. These first county figures were then adjusted proportionally to sum to the national control. The county demand by industry producing sector was derived using national coefficients.

Exports

Control totals for U.S. national exports were obtained from the U.S. Bureau of Census, *U.S. Commodity Exports and Imports as Related to Output*, 1965 and 1966 at the four-digit SIC level. These values are in domestic port prices.

Each control total is subdivided into four categories: (1) vessel exports, (2) exports to Canada overland, (3) exports to Mexico overland, and (4) exports by air. Data contained in *Report 750, U.S. Exports—Commodity, Country and Method of Transportation* published by U.S. Bureau of Census provide the means to allocate the control totals among these categories in the same manner that the import control totals are allocated.

The vessel export control totals are allocated to counties using data from the Department of Army, Corps of Engineers, *Waterborne Commerce* of the United States. These are quantities of exports, by port, in tons. For each port contained in a single county, the quantities are allocated to that county. For ports covering more than one county, the quantities are allocated to the counties according to each county's share of employment in water transport activities—employment categories 4200 and 4400 of *County Business Patterns.*

To each element of the vector of four-digit SIC codes representing the vessel control totals is assigned one or more *Waterborne Commerce* code(s). The correspondence between the two coding systems is established on the basis of given product category descriptions. Each four-digit vessel control total is distributed to counties according to each county's share of the quantity of exports associated with the corresponding Waterborne Commerce product group(s).

Canadian and Mexican land control totals for exports are allocated to northern and southern border counties in two steps. First, border trans-shipment points for commodities, identified by the Bureau of Customs, are assigned to their respective counties. The counties are grouped into customs districts—three districts on the northern border and two on the southern. The land control totals for Mexican and Canadian exports are allocated first to the customs districts on the basis of their shares of the respective land control totals; the data are found in *Highlights U.S. Export and Import Trade*, Report FT900, December 1967, published by U.S. Bureau of Census. This process produces customs district control totals for land exports which are then allocated among the counties in each district on the basis of each county's share, with respect to its appropriate customs district, of employment in land transport activities—employment category 4200 of *County Business Patterns*.

The control totals for air exports are allocated to counties having international airports in proportion to each county's share of total exports by air of manufactured goods. The U.S. Bureau of Census also supplies these data in *Highlights*. In the case of New York, where the city contains several counties (boroughs), air exports are further allocated to counties on the basis of their shares of employment in air transport activities—employment category 4500 of *County Business Patterns*.

The resulting regional distribution of exports by four-digit SIC groups involves 209 counties. Each county's exports are aggregated into the input-output sectors as a final step in the process.

Appendix C:
Procedures for Estimating the Coefficients of the Objective Function of the Transportation Problem by Input-Output Sector

Introduction

This appendix describes in detail the procedure used to calculate each commodity's intercounty transportation costs that are used as coefficients in the objective functions of the linear programming transportation problems. These techniques are illustrated in the text for a shipment unit of IO 33 (Paperboard Containers). Four sets of data are required to calculate the coefficients: distance, cost to the carriers, markup ratios, and the unit shipment bundle.

The rate-estimating procedure for the two modes of transportation considered[a]—rail and trucks—is expressed as

(C.1) $$\qquad {}_kC_{ij}^w = {}_kTer_i^w + {}_kLh_{ij}^w + {}_kTer_j^w$$

where k = mode of transport, 1 for rail, 2 for truck,

$\quad\quad\; i$ = region originating shipment,

$\quad\quad\; j$ = region of destination,

$\quad\quad\; w$ = weight class of shipment,

$\quad\quad\; Ter$ = terminal cost,

$\quad\quad\; Lh$ = line-haul cost,

$\quad\quad\; {}_kC_{ij}^w$ = total cost to carriers of a w pound class shipment between counties i and j by mode of transport k ;

and

(C.2) $$\qquad t_{ij} = \sum_{w=1}^{n} a^w \left[\underset{k}{Min} \left({}_kC_{ij}^w \, Mup_k \right) \right]$$

where Mup_k = markup ratio of the kth mode

$\quad\quad\; a^w$ = number of shipments in the unit shipment bundle of the wth weight class,

$\quad\quad\; n$ = number of weight classifications,

$\quad\quad\; t_{ij}$ = transportation cost of shipping a total unit shipment bundle be-the ith and jth counties.

---

[a]See Chapter 4, pp. 58-60, for the rationalization of why other modes were neglected.

283

Equation (C.1) is the general form for calculating the cost incurred by the kth carrier for shipping a commodity between the ith and jth counties. Equation (C.2) specifies the formulation used to calculate the coefficients of the objective functions. It aggregates over all weight classes the minimum of either rail or truck transportation cost for each weight class, times the number of shipments in each weight class. The distance measurements required to calculate line-haul cost were obtained from the Bureau of Public Roads, while the cost and markup statistics were derived from ICC publications.

The unit shipment bundle reflects the national distribution of shipments by weight for each commodity. Since trucking has lower terminal cost and higher line-haul cost than rail, small shipments will normally be shipped by truck and large shipments by rail. The coefficients thus reflect not only the influence of distance between counties but also the weight of shipment and competition between carriers for the shipment of commodities.

Distance Measurements

The first step, that of obtaining distances between counties, consisted of utilizing distance measurements obtained from the Bureau of Public Roads.[b] These measurements are particularly useful for the model since they are not straight airline distances, but approximate actual land transportation routes.

The Bureau of Public Roads used two basic operations to obtain these measurements. The first was to create a network listing hypothetical transportation paths among all counties. The network was constructed by using population centers (1950 Census of Population) of the counties as nodes or intersections of transportation routes. Once the nodes were determined, the procedure consisted of extending a network from each county node to the nodes of up to eight of the adjacent counties until the nation-wide network was completed. In some cases, the network could not be connected through the central nodes of each county (e.g., when there were more than eight adjacent counties), and therefore dummy nodes (a total of 211) were created.[c] A graphical representation of the network is presented in Figure C-1. Once the network was obtained, the distance measurements were calculated by determining the minimum distance along the network from each county to all other counties. An example of these calculations is illustrated in Figure C-2 for Tuscaloosa, Alabama.

Unit Shipment Levels

The *1963 Census of Transportation* lists shipments by commodity, weight bracket, and mode of transportation. The industrial classification scheme used in

---

[b]Glenn E. Brokke, *Nationwide Highway Travel* (mimeograph), Bureau of Public Roads, U.S. Department of Commerce, June 9, 1966, is the source used for the descriptive comments about the distance measurements.

[c]Brokke, op. cit., p. 3.

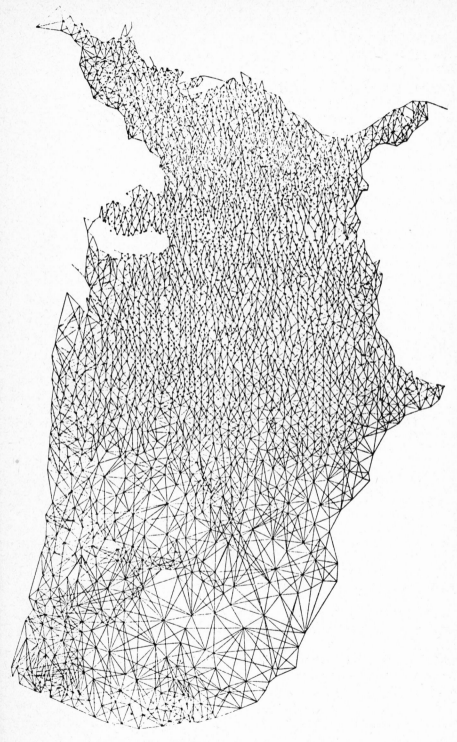

Figure C-1. United States Spiderweb Network as of February 25, 1965.

Figure C–2. Minimum Path (Tree) from Tuscaloosa, Alabama. Source: Brokke, p. 6.

the *Census of Transportation* (TCC) differs from the SIC codes. Table C-1 shows the TCC codes for our input-output (IO) sectors.

Table C-2 illustrates the format used in the *1963 Census of Transportation* to report shipments by weight class and means of transport. The unit shipment level used in the transportation problem, as derived from Table C-2, consists of a shipment bundle reflecting the weight distribution of shipments presented in the table. The tons-of-shipment column of Table C-2 was multiplied by the percent of shipments for the first three modes (rail, motor common carrier, and private truck), and these figures summed to obtain weights of shipments for each weight class. The average weight for the "over" classification was assumed to be one-third more than the minimum limit of the weight listed for that class. The largest weight figure was then used as the foundation for determining the shipment bundle. Each shipment bundle contained one shipment of the largest weight class and the number of shipments of the other weight classes as determined by their tonnage relative to that of the largest shipment class. This was accomplished, as illustrated in Table C-3, by dividing the average weight of each weight class (column 1) into the total weight shipped in each class (column 2 times 2,000 lb) to obtain an estimate of the number of shipments in each class (column 3). These figures were then divided by the total number of shipments of the largest weight class (column 4), and these results rounded off to obtain a vector of the number of shipments of each weight class relative to that of the largest class (column 5). The number of shipments in a unit bundle is then multiplied by the average weight of each weight class (column 1 X column 5) to obtain the amount shipped in the unit bundle by weight class (column 6). The sum of column 6, (157,700 lb) is the total weight in a unit bundle.

Rail Cost Calculation

The method used to calculate rail transport cost was derived from a paper entitled, "Transport Cost, Pricing, and Regulation" by Merrill J. Roberts,[d] who applies a markup ratio classified by commodity type to out-of-pocket costs to approximate rail rates. *Procedures for Developing Rail Revenue Contribution by Commodity and Territory*, issued yearly, while not providing the ratios, does provide the statistics and outlines the method used to calculate these ratios. The TCC commodity classification scheme was used in this publication and their correspondence to IO categories is presented in Table C-1. Table C-4 illustrates the 1965 markup ratios and related statistics for IO 33 paper containers. The data was listed regionally by shipments within and between three major regions: Official (New England, Middle Atlantic, Eastern, and Mid-West), South (east of the Mississippi River), and West.

---

[d]Merrill J. Roberts, "Transport Costs, Pricing, and Regulation," in *Transportation Economics* compiled papers of a conference of the Universities-National Bureau Committee for Economic Research (New York, 1965), pp. 3-42.

Table C-1

Census of Transportation Codes (TCC) Used in Deriving Unit Shipments and Rail Mark-Up Ratios by Input-Output Sector

IO	Rail Markup TCC	Unit Shipment TCC
1	014	a
2	011,012,013	a
3	084	a
5	101	a
6	102,103,105,106,109	a
7	111,112	a
8	131	a
9	141,142,145,149	a
10	147	a
14	201	201,202,2094
15	202	201,202,2094
16	203	203
17	204	204
18	205	207
19	206	206,209,(−2094)
20	207	207
21	208	208
22	209	206,209,(−2094)
23	211	211,212,213,214
24	227,229	221,222,223,224,225,227, 228,229,311,312,313,314, 315,316,319,231,233,235, 237,238,239
25	227,229	221,222,223,224,225,227, 228,229,311,312,313,314, 315,316,319,231,233,235, 237,238,239
26	227,229	221,222,223,224,225,227, 228,229,311,312,313,314, 315,316,319,231,233,235, 237,238,239
27	227,229	221,222,223,224,225,227, 228,229,311,312,313,314, 315,316,319,231,233,235, 237,238,239
28	241,242,243	242,243,249
29	244,249	244
30	250	251
31	250	251
32	261,262,264,266	262,264
33	265	265
34	272	261,262,263,264,266

Table C-1 (cont.)

IO	Rail Markup TCC	Unit Shipment TCC
35	281,286,289	281
36	282	282
37	284	284
38	285	285
39	291,295,299	291
40	301,306,307	301,302,303,306,307
41	227,229	221,222,223,224,225,227, 228,229,311,312,313,314, 315,316,319,231,233,235, 237,238,239
42	227,229	221,222,223,224,225,227, 228,229,311,312,313,314, 315,316,319,231,233,235, 237,238,239
43	321,322	322
44	325,327,329	329
45	331,332	331,332,339
46	333,335,339	333,335,336
47	333,335,339	333,335,336
48	333,335,339	333,335,336
49	344	341,348,349
50	343	343,344
51	346	345,346
52	349,348	342
53	352	351,352,357,358
54	352	351,352,357,358
55	353	353
56	353	353
57	354	354
58	356	355,356
59	356	355,356
60	359	359
61	358	351,352,357,358
62	358	351,352,357,358
63	356	355,356
64	363	363
65	364	364
66	365	365,366
67	365	365,366
68	356	355,356
69	371	371
70	374	372,373,374,375,379

Table C-1 (cont.)

IO	Rail Markup TCC	Unit Shipment TCC
71	374	372,373,374,375,379
72	394	381,382,383,384,385, 386,387
73	394	381,382,383,384,385, 386,387
74	394	381,382,383,384,385, 386,387
13	359	359

aMedian LBS shipped obtained from: *Freight commodity statistics class I railroads in the United States for year ended December 31, 1965.* Bureau of Transport Economics and statistics, Interstate Commerce Commission, Table 3.

Table 1 of the ICC publication provided estimates of the out-of-pocket costs of operation incurred by the railroad companies in shipping commodities by type of rail car. Table C-5 lists this out-of-pocket cost data for general service box cars. The transportation costs used in Equation (C.1) were calculated assuming that all shipments were made on the rail car type carrying the largest proportion of tonnage within and between each region.

The rail out-of-pocket cost for a shipment of 20,000 pounds of paper containers, 120 miles, in the Official Region, is calculated in Table C-6 using the cost data on the first line of Table C-5 plus an allowance for loss and damage. The shipment would cost the railroads $117.72. The transportation charges to the commodity owners are calculated by applying the markup ratio of 1.12844 presented in Table C-4 to the costs; it would be $132.14 for the 120 mile shipment. If the shipment went a greater distance, the costs would be the same except for the line-haul through train cost. The way-train cost remains the same in each region regardless of distance. Had the distance been 1,060 miles, the out-of-pocket cost would have been $334.24 and the charge to the customer would have been $377.17.

Highway Cost Calculation

The procedure used for calculating common carrier trucking cost was derived from *Cost of Transporting Freight by Class I and Class II Motor Carriers of General Commodities for 1965*, compiled by the Interstate Commerce Commission. The costs of operation of the motor carrier plus a markup adequate to ensure a reasonable return on invested capital as specified by the ICC was used as the rate the common carrier would charge its customers and as the cost of using unregulated and manufacturer-owned trucking. Tables 5 and 7 in the ICC publication, illustrated here as Table C-7 and C-8 for the Middle Atlantic region, were used to calculate highway costs. Table C-7 lists the terminal cost of

Table C-2

Shipments by Weight and Mode of Transport: Paper Containers (IO 33)

Weight of Shipment	Tons of Shipments[a] (Thousands)	All Means of Transport	Rail	Motor Carrier	Private Truck (Percents)	Air	Water	Other	Unknown
United States, total[a]	6,559	100.0	16.2	57.6	25.5	–	0.2	0.4	0.1
Under 1,000 pounds	340	100.0	1.9	81.4	10.9	0.2	1.0	4.5	.1
Under 200 pounds	41	100.0	2.5	81.4	3.9	.4	–	11.0	.8
200 to 499 pounds	120	100.0	1.3	85.7	6.0	.2	1.3	5.5	–
500 to 999 pounds	179	100.0	2.2	78.5	15.8	.1	1.0	2.4	–
1,000 to 9,999 pounds	2,080	100.0	1.1	61.6	36.5	–	.3	.4	.1
1,000 to 1,999 pounds	340	100.0	2.1	65.0	30.7	–	1.0	1.0	.2
2,000 to 2,999 pounds	274	100.0	.5	60.3	39.0	–	–	.2	.2
3,000 to 4,999 pounds	495	100.0	.7	59.5	39.7	–	–	.1	.1
5,000 to 9,999 pounds	971	100.0	1.3	61.9	36.2	–	.2	.3	.1
10,000 to 29,999 pounds	2,514	100.0	12.9	59.1	28.0	–	–	–	–
30,000 pounds and over	1,665	100.0	43.0	45.6	10.9	–	.1	.2	.2

Source: *1963 Census of Transportation*, Vol. III, Parts 3 and 4, p. 242.

[a]Includes only shipments represented by bills of lading and invoices. Summary records which did not show individual weights of shipments are not included.

Table C-3

Calculation of the Unit Shipment Bundle: Paper Containers (IO 33)

(1) Average Weight of Each Class (Pounds)	(2) Tons (1,000)	(3) Total No. of Shipments	(4) Relative Shipment	(5) Number of Shipments in Unit Bundle	(6) Amount Shipped in Unit Bundle (Pounds)
100	36.0	720.0	8.69	9	900
350	111.6	637.7	7.70	8	2,800
750	172.7	460.6	5.56	6	4,500
1,500	332.5	443.4	5.35	5	7,500
2,500	273.5	218.8	2.64	3	7,500
4,000	495.5	247.3	2.99	3	12,000
7,500	965.2	257.4	3.11	3	22,500
20,000	2,514.0	251.4	3.04	3	60,000
40,000	1,656.7	82.8	1	1	40,000
Total					157,700

Table C-4

Box Car Revenue to Out-of-Pocket Cost Ratios by Region, 1965: Paper Containers (IO 33)

Region	Revenue (Dollars)	Out-of-Pocket Cost Dollars	Ratio of Revenue to Out-of-Pocket Cost
Official	97,434.	86,343.	1.12844
Off to Sou	26,042.	20,531.	1.26836
Off to Wes	30,553.	23,173.	1.31844
Sou to Off	6,926.	5,548.	1.24836
Sou to Sou	18,233.	11,936.	1.52747
Sou to Wes	3,720.	3,192.	1.16506
Wes to Off	9,050.	7,558.	1.19729
Wes to Sou	3,496.	2,097.	1.66650
Wes to Wes	74,276.	57,561.	1.29036

Source: Interstate Commerce Commission, *Procedures for Developing Rail Revenue Contribution by Commodity and Territory*, year 1965, Table 8.

transportation divided into three classifications: pickup and delivery, platform handling, billing and collection. The table is divided into two major parts, one for terminal costs of shipments under 300 pounds and the other for those over 300 pounds. The three terminal costs of transportation are broken down into weight brackets. The major difference between the over and under 300-pound weight shipment is that the terminal cost for the higher weights are listed in cents per hundredweight, while the lower weights are listed by total terminal cost by weight class. Table C-8 lists the line-haul costs in terms of cents per hundredweight mile, by mileage bracket and weight classification.

Table C-5

Box Car Carload Out-of-Pocket Unit Costs in Cents per Service Unit Based on 1965 Operations

	Terminal		Line Haul			
			Way Train		Through Train	
Region	Per Carload	Per Ton	Per Car-Mile	Per Ton-Mile	Per Car-Mile	Per Ton-Mile
Official	8,508.818	3.84953	28.93028	.44754	21.07229	.22973
South	4,701.157	3.34812	20.59375	.31134	16.48554	.20496
West	7,730.155	9.57808	24.38405	.41767	16.78269	.21953
Off to Sou						
Sou to Off	6,604.988	3.59882	24.76202	.37944	18.77892	.21734
Off to Wes						
Wes to Off	8,199.486	6.71380	26.65716	.43260	18.92749	.22463
Sou to Wes						
Wes to Sou	6,215.656	6.46310	22.48890	.36450	16.63412	.21224

Source: Interstate Commerce Commission, *Procedures for Developing Rail Revenue Contribution by Commodity and Territory*, year 1965, Table 1.

Table C-6

Calculation of Rail Out-of-Pocket Costs for Shipping 20,000 Pounds of Paper Containers by Box Car 120 Miles within the Official Region in 1965

	Unit	Cost Per Unit	Number of Units	Out-of-Pocket Costs
Terminal Cost	Car	$85.088	1	$85.09
	Ton	.039	10	.39
Line Haul				
Way-Train (32 miles)[a]	Car-Mile	.289	32	9.25
	Ton-Mile	.004	320	1.28
Through train (88 miles)	Car-Mile	.211	88	18.57
	Ton-Mile	.002	880	1.76
Loss and Damage	Ton	.076[b]	10	.76
Total				$117.10

Source: This method of competing out-of-pocket costs is given by the Interstate Commerce Commission, *Procedures for Developing Rail Revenue Contribution by Commodity and Territory*, year 1965, illustration 2.

[a]The average shipment went 32 miles by way-train in the Official Region in 1965.

[b]Rate varies by commodity.

The lower mileage listed in each mileage bracket is referred to as the rate-making mileage, and the line-haul costs in Table C-8 are for those rate-making miles. Most shipments, however, involve distances that exceed their rate-making mileage. The number of miles a shipment exceeds the

Table C-7

Motor Common Carrier Out-of-Pocket Terminal Cost (Middle Atlantic Region), 1965

Line No.	(1) Weight Bracket (Pounds per Shipment)	(2) Pickup or Delivery Service[a]	(3) Platform Handling[a]	(4) Billing and Collecting
	Costs in Cents per Shipment			
1	50	117.5	12.1	62.4
2	100	131.3	24.1	62.4
3	200	155.5	48.2	62.4
4	300	178.5	72.3	62.4
	Costs in Cents per Hundredweight			
5	300-499	51.0	24.1	16.1
6	500-999	37.4	23.7	9.0
7	1,000-1,999	28.0	22.3	4.7
8	2,000-4,999	20.8	19.0	2.2
9	12,000-19,999	10.9	3.7	.4
10	20,000-29,999	8.2	.9	.2
11	30,000-39,999	6.1	.6	.2
12	40,000 and over	4.7	.6	.1
13	0-299	103.5	24.1	46.4
14	0-999	63.8	24.0	23.9
15	0-1,999	53.3	23.4	18.2
16	0-4,999	42.1	21.9	12.7
17	0-5,999	41.0	21.4	12.2
18	0-9,999	37.0	19.9	10.4
19	1,000-4,999	23.4	20.2	3.1
20	2,000-5,999	20.3	18.0	2.1
21	5,000-9,999	15.5	11.3	.9
22	6,000-11,999	14.3	8.7	.7
23	10,000-19,999	11.7	3.7	.5

Source: Interstate Commerce Commission, *Cost of Transporting Freight by Class I and Class II Motor Carriers of General Commodities for 1965.*

[a]The pickup and delivery costs and platform handling costs represent the average cost at the origin or the destination but not both.

rate-making mileage expressed on a percentage basis is called circuitry. The line-haul cost must be adjusted for circuitry, and the ICC bulletin recommends that the cost for the rate-making miles be increased by a percentage equal to the circuitry involved.[e] Since there are economies of distance in line-haul cost,

[e]*Cost of Transporting Freight by Class I and Class II Motor Carriers of General Commodities for 1965*, Interstate Commerce Commission, U.S. Government Printing Office, Washington, D.C., 1966, p. 6.

Table C-8

Motor Common Carrier Out-of-Pocket Line-Haul Costs per Hundredweight-Mile (Middle Atlantic Region)

Line No.	(1) Distance Bracket (Actual Miles)	(2) 0- 9,999 (Pounds)	(3) 10,000- 19,999 (Pounds)	(4) 20,000- 29,999 (Pounds)	(5) 30,000 and Over (Pounds)
			Line-haul Intercity Trip Costs in Cents per Hundredweight-Mile		
1	0-9	.46680	.38587	.30788	.23820
2	10-19	.46304	.37831	.30464	.23722
3	20-29	.45577	.36868	.29990	.23626
4	30-39	.44526	.35951	.29382	.23340
5	40-49	.42877	.35081	.28655	.22969
6	50-74	.30116	.25913	.21224	.17275
7	75-99	.26218	.24355	.20353	.16818
8	100-124	.23037	.21843	.18653	.15615
9	125-149	.22073	.20974	.18251	.15331
10	150-199	.20883	.19975	.17521	.14768
11	200-299	.19912	.19083	.16962	.14312
12	300-399	.19605	.18714	.16601	.13956
13	400-499	.19605	.18714	.16534	.13908
14	500-599	.19605	.18714	.16534	.13908
15	600-699	.19520	.18633	.16463	.13849
16	700-799	.19350	.18471	.16319	.13729
17	800-899	.18926	.18065	.15961	.13427
18	900-999	.18926	.18065	.15961	.13427
19	1,000 and over	.18926	.18065	.15961	.13427

Source: Interstate Commerce Commission, *Cost of Transporting Freight by Class I and Class II Motor Carriers of General Commodities for 1965*, p. 59.

this procedure has the undesirable property that line-haul cost, in special circumstances, can cease to be a monotonic function of distance. For example, shipping 20,000 pounds of paper containers 74 and 75 miles, the line-haul cost using the ICC procedure would be \$13.41 and \$30.53, respectively. The alternate procedure that we used is given in

$$\text{(C.3)} \qquad CA - CR = \left(\frac{MA - MR}{MR_{+1} - MR} \right) \left(CR_{+1} - CR \right)$$

where MA = actual mileage,

MR = rate-making mileage (lower limit in the distance bracket determined by the actual mileage),

MR_{+1} = rate-making mileage of the next highest distance bracket,

CA = computed cost per hundredweight mile,

CR = cost per hundredweight mile of rate-making mileage,

CR_{+1} = cost per hundredweight mile of rate-making mileage in the next highest distance bracket.

The right-hand term of (C.3) is the cost adjustment made for circuitry. When this adjustment is added to the rate-making mileage cost, the resulting cost per hundred figure is multiplied by the hundredweight miles and added to terminal cost.

The cost of shipping 20,000 pounds of paper containers 120 miles by the motor carrier in the Middle Atlantic region is $80.64 as illustrated in Table C-9. By applying the markup ratio of 1.179 for the Middle Atlantic states presented in Table 4-6 to the cost data calculated in Table C-9, we can determine that the transportation charge to the customers would be $95.16. Had the mileage been 1,060, the out-of-pocket cost and charge would have been $375.18 and $440.47, respectively.

Table C-9
Calculation of Motor Common Carrier Out-of-Pocket Cost for Shipping 20,000 Pounds of Paper Containers 120 Miles in the Middle Atlantic Region

	Unit	Cost per Unit	Number of Units	Cost
Terminal Cost				
Pickup and delivery	Cwt	$.08200	400	$32.80
Platform handling	Cwt	.00900	400	3.60
Billing and collecting	Cwt	.00200	200	.40
Line-haul Cost				
Rate-making miles (100)	Cwt-mile	.00187	20,000	37.40
Adjustment for circuitry (20 miles)[a]	Cwt-mile	.00161	4,000	6.44
Total				$80.64

[a]Using equation (C.3).

Conclusion

The rail and highway charges are estimated for each weight-size shipment in the unit shipment bundle, and the lower of the two charges is then multiplied by the number of shipments of the weight class. Thus for the example that has been presented in the chapter for a shipment of 20,000 pounds of paper containers, the relative cost of highway compared to rail would dictate that for the 120-mile case, motor carrier should be used ($95.16 versus $132.14); while in 1,060-mile example, rail would become the lower cost mode ($440.47 versus $377.17). These figures are then aggregated over all weight classes to provide a weighted average figure reflecting the distribution of shipments by the least cost mode of transportation by weight. These final statistics are used as the coefficients of the objective function and are calculated for each county source to county destination pair.

Index

agglomeration: and dairy production, 110; economies, 4; effect, 23, 65, 97; factors, 20; in I/O classification scheme, 95; variables, 14, 15, 18, 19, 82, 114; variables and coal mining, 207; variables and diversity, 119

agriculture, 243; equipment purchase, 278; influence, 92; services, 95; services definition, 105

aircraft, 188, 189

air transport, 58

Alabama: fabrics and yarn, 124, 125; ordnance, 178

Almon, C.: Maryland Interindustry Forecasting Project, 8, 243–246

Alonso, W.: urban land use, 19

aluminum: structure, 167, 168

American Can Co.: antitrust case, 171

amusement, 89, 219, 220

Annual Survey of Manufacturing, 1965, 1966, 56

apparel: structure, 126

Arizona: copper, 166; nonferrous ore, 163

automation: computers, 166; electric products, 191; heating, plumbing, structural metal, 173, 174; metal containers, 171, 172; shoes, 154; tobacco, 120

automotive repair services, 88, 218

bakery products, 113

basic chemicals, 88; influence, 92; oligopolistic structure, 144

batteries, 199

beverages, 92, 93; input-output structure, 116

biotic raw materials, 95–99

Bureau of Census, 8, 89

Bureau of Public Roads, 58, 284

business services, 89, 217, 218

buyers, 19

California: agricultural services, 106; airplanes, 189; amusement, 220; bakery products, 114; beverages, 117; business services, 217; candy, 116; canned and frozen food, 111; chemical minerals, 143; crops, 103; electric utility, 209; fisheries, 105; livestock, 102; machine shop machinery, 186; meat packing, 109; metal containers, 172; miscellaneous food products, 118; minerals mining, 156; ordnance, 178; paint, 148; petroleum, 149; sugar, 115; wooden containers, 132

Canada: entry, 52; land control, 248

candy: input-output structure, 116; spatial mobility, 115

canned and frozen foods: input-output table, 111

capital, 17; costs, 89; stock and measures of, 93

CBP (County Business Pattern), 45, 48–51, 84; and conversion to I/O sectors, 241; data series, 39; payrolls, 243

Census of Business, 1963, 55–58

Census of Transportation, 1903, 284

chemical mining, 142, 143

chemicals and petroleum, 96, 140, 141

coal mining: input-output relations, 205, 206

Colorado: iron ore, 161; sugar, 116

commodity: flow patterns of, 37; producing sectors, 97

Common Market, 104

communications, 207, 208, 245; equipment, 197, 198

competitive trade model, 34

constant cost curve, 29

construction, 8, 180; cost, 93; equipment purchasing sector, 278; final demand sector, 244; purchasing sector, 267–277

consumer: expenditures, 251; sales and input-output sector, 261–266

Cooper, L.: model, 21; location and business decision, 20

copper, 92, 96, 166, 167

Corfram, 153

Corps of Engineers: Waterborne Commerce, 52

cost: function, 9; marginal in 1965 and 1966; minimization approach in Weber and Hoover, 20; out-of-pocket, 61; variable, 82

county: data estimates, 240; demand, 251; as geographic unit, 24; and input/output, 53, 66; problems, 233–236; rationale of use, 45; sales, 251–260; supply, 233; variation in the change in output of industry, 66

crops, 95, 102

cross-hauls, 24, 45

Cumberland, J. and Isard, W.: New England iron and steel, 26

dairy products, 102; interindustry structure, 109

defense: airplanes, 189; expenditures, 56, 69

299

About the Authors

Curtis C. Harris, Jr. is Associate Professor of Economics at the Bureau of Business and Economic Research and at the Economics Department of the University of Maryland. He has been with the U.S. Department of Commerce and the University of California, Davis. Professor Harris received the B.S. in economics from the University of Florida in 1956, and the M.A. and Ph.D. from Harvard.

Professor Harris has published numerous articles in professional journals and has served as a consultant to the federal government and private industry. He has specialized in regional and urban economics at the University of Maryland.

Frank E. Hopkins, Assistant Professor at the School of Management at the State University of New York at Binghamton, received the undergraduate degree in economics from Hofstra University in 1964, and the Ph.D. at the University of Maryland in 1971. He has published articles in professional journals, has served as a consultant to private industry, and has actively participated in Regional Science Association meetings. He was Secretary-Treasurer of the Middle Atlantic States section of the Regional Science Association in 1971.